HISTORY OF THE TENTH TEXAS CAVALRY
(DISMOUNTED) REGIMENT
1861—1865

HISTORY OF

THE TENTH TEXAS CAVALRY (DISMOUNTED) REGIMENT 1861—1865

*"If we ever got whipped,
I don't recollect it"*

by

Chuck Carlock

with

V. M. Owens

Smithfield Press

An imprint of D. & F. Scott Publishing, Inc.

P.O. Box 821653

N. Richland Hills, TX 76182

817 788-2280

info@dfscott.com

www.dfscott.com

05 04 03 02 01 5 4 3 2 1

Library of Congress Cataloging-in-Publication Data

Carlock, Chuck, 1945-
    History of the Tenth Texas Cavalry (Dismounted) Regiment, 1861-1865 :
"if we ever got whipped, I don't recollect it" / by Chuck Carlock, with V. M. Owens.
        p. cm.
Includes bibliographical references.
    ISBN 1-930566-06-9 (trade paper : alk. paper)
    1. Confederate States of America. Army. Texas Cavalry Regiment, 10th. 2. United
States—History—Civil War, 1861-1865—Regimental histories. 3. Texas—History—
Civil War, 1861-1865—Regimental histories. 4. United States—History—Civil War,
1861-1865—Campaigns. I. Owens, V. M. (Vicki Morris), 1951- II. Title.
    E580.6 10th .C37 2001
    973.7'464—dc21

                        2001003402

Page design and layout by KC Scott

The cover picture shows Lt. M.W. Armstrong, Tenth Texas Cavalry (Dismounted), capturing the Union flag at Allatoona Pass, Georgia. The Union officer with the chair was Colonel Redfield, who was killed in the battle. The chair was brought to him after he was wounded in the leg.

The painting was prepared by Jeanne Glenn from a charcoal drawing done prior to 1902. The drawing appeared in General French's book, *Two Wars: An Autobiography*. There is some confusion as to whether the drawing portrays a Missouri soldier. French was clear that Armstrong took the Union flag, and the other flag captured was the colors of the Ninety-Third Illinois. The Union officer with the chair was with the unit that lost the Union flag.

*The Texans displayed "magnificent courage"
as they overran a Union Regiment
armed with 15-shot Henry rifles.*

Staff Officer of Federal General Corse,
Commander, Allatoona Pass, Georgia

*Hood's army on the retreat from Tennessee
was a "bunch of disorganized rabble.
The rear guard, however, was undaunted and firm,
and did its work bravely to the last."*

Federal Gen. "Rock of Chickamauga" Thomas

*When the Texans
charged at Chickamauga it
"excited my admiration."*

Confederate Gen. Nathan Bedford Forrest

*"Wild Texas Boys,
they are good in a fight but are wild
and reckless and troublesome,
hard to manage."*

Mississippi soldier, 1864

TABLE OF CONTENTS

Page

PREFACE ix

ACKNOWLEDGMENTS x

INTRODUCTION xi

CHAPTER 1.　*"Spiling' for a fight"*
　　　　　　　Organization of the
　　　　　　　Tenth Texas Cavalry (Dismounted) Regiment 1

CHAPTER 2.　*"Glorious retreat"*
　　　　　　　Action Around Corinth, Mississippi 9

CHAPTER 3.　*Hippo over no horses*
　　　　　　　Camp Life 21

CHAPTER 4.　*"Ain't you a Texican?"*
　　　　　　　Operations in Kentucky— Battle of Richmond, Kentucky . . 25

CHAPTER 5.　*"Fiendish propensities of the infuriated clan"*
　　　　　　　Retreat out of Kentucky and Preparations
　　　　　　　Around Murfreesboro 41

CHAPTER 6.　*"Killed still holding firmly to his pot of coffee"*
　　　　　　　Battle of Murfreesboro 46

CHAPTER 7.　*He ain't heavy, he is my son*
　　　　　　　Events after the Battle of Murfreesboro 69

CHAPTER 8.　*"Gander pullin' and Greyback cracking"*
　　　　　　　Camp life — Early 1863 73

CHAPTER 9.　*"Strain out the wiggletails"*
　　　　　　　Operations to Relieve Vicksburg
　　　　　　　and Battle of Jackson, Mississippi 79

CHAPTER 10.　*"Eyes stuck out far enough to hang a hat on"*
　　　　　　　Battle of Chickamauga 93

CHAPTER 11.　*"Wearing their hog-killing suits"*
　　　　　　　Events Concerning Men Captured at Chickamauga 113

CHAPTER 12.　*"Almost makes me weep to think of your situation"*
　　　　　　　Winter of 1863-64 — Camplife and Military Operations . . 117

CHAPTER 13.　*Can't sleep with artillery shells shining*
　　　　　　　"through his closed eyelids"
　　　　　　　Atlanta Campaign Under General Johnston 129

CHAPTER 14. *"All the bravest men have been killed"*
Atlanta Campaign after General Hood Takes Over 155

CHAPTER 15. *"Magnificent courage" —*
all the brave boys aren't dead
Battle of Allatoona Pass, Georgia 167

CHAPTER 16. *"Corn hauled up and issued out*
to us like we were horses"
March to Tennessee 183

CHAPTER 17. *"The path to glory leads but to the grave"*
Battle of Franklin, Tennessee. 189

CHAPTER 18. *"Lord, direct these bullets!"*
Battle of Nashville, Tennessee 195

CHAPTER 19. *"Ragged, barefooted invincibles*
sprang forward like hungry tigers"
Fighting Rear Guard on the Retreat from Nashville 207

CHAPTER 20. *"Many others will bite the dust"*
Siege at Spanish Fort 225

CHAPTER 21. *"They shucked their part of the corn"*
Conclusion. 243

APPENDIX A List of Engagements, Battles, Sieges, and Skirmishes
of the Tenth Texas Cavalry Dismounted 246

APPENDIX B Schedule of Personnel 247

APPENDIX C Schedule of Soldiers Listed Under "Other" Category 248

APPENDIX D Commanders of Tenth Texas Cavalry Dismounted 250

APPENDIX E Commanders of Ector's Brigade
(called Ector's Texas Brigade) 251

APPENDIX F Tenth Texas — Roll of Honor — Bravest of the Brave 252

APPENDIX G Men Who Surrendered with the Unit at Citronelle,
Alabama, May 4, 1865 254

APPENDIX H Regimental Statistics by Company 256

APPENDIX I Personnel of the 10th Texas Cavalry Dismounted 257

BIBLIOGRAPHY 293

NOTES 295

ABOUT THE AUTHORS 300

PREFACE

After General Hood's disaster at the Battle of Nashville, his defeated army retreated in the snow, sleet, and ice. Hood knew that his last hope for escape was reliance on a powerful rear guard of his best infantry. The Tenth Texas Cavalry (Dismounted), having entered the war with 1,200 soldiers and now having less than sixty available for service, volunteered for the mission. General Forrest, commander of the rear guard, inspected his 1,621 volunteer troops and found that almost three hundred of the beleaguered men were shoeless. They improvised with old pieces of carpet and animal skins to protect their freezing feet from the dismal conditions. Forrest was forced to empty provisions from his available wagons in order to provide some form of transportation for his foot-weary soldiers as they rested part of the time and exited to fight when necessary. (By this time, the infantry referred to themselves as "Hood's Cavalry" because they were eating the same rations as Hood's remaining cavalry horses.) General Forrest described the rear guard fighting as "largely hand-to-hand."

The men were cold, hungry, and exhausted; yet they still received grudging respect from their enemy, Union Gen. George H. Thomas:

> With the exception of this rear guard his army had become a disheartened and disorganized rabble of half-armed and barefooted men, who sought every opportunity to fall out by the wayside and desert their cause, to put an end to their sufferings. The rear-guard, however, was undaunted and firm and did its work bravely to the last."

As an East Texan said, these boys "would fight them till Hell would freeze over and then finish on the ice!

ACKNOWLEDGMENTS

I undertook the writing of this book to document the actions of a dedicated, brave group of men that I felt history had ignored.

Thanks are due to many people for the successful completion of this book. I acknowledge with grateful thanks:

Ms. Peggy Fox with the Harold B. Simpson History Complex, Hillsboro, Texas, for her friendly, helpful attitude and assistance to the writing of this book.

Jim Dale, a dedicated Civil War historian and part-time tour guide at Kennesaw Mountain Battlefield, for the information and assistance he provided. It's possible he had a distant relative in the Tenth Texas who was killed at the Battle of Allatoona.

Ector County Library History and Genealogy Department.

Mr. Jon Harrison, McAllen, Texas, Civil War expert, who had a great-granddad in Company C.

Mr. Mark Reid, Jr., Wood County Genealogical Society.

Ms. Faye Harris, Van Zandt County Genealogy Society.

Randy Farrar, Irving, Texas, for his help in researching information for this book.

Bob Parsons, Nashville, Tennessee, a dedicated Civil War historian and a fellow Firebird helicopter gunship pilot in Vietnam. Bob passed away prior to the completion of the book.

Ms. Vonnie Zullo for her research in the National Archives.

Ms. Virginia Knapp, Rusk County Historical Foundation.

Mr. John A. Templeton, Cherokee County Historical Commission.

Mr. Randy Gilbert, Smith County Historical Society.

Ms. Leila LaGrone, Panola County Historical and Genealogical Association.

I also want to thank all the people who donated material to the Harold B. Simpson History Complex, Hillsboro, Texas, for I used a lot of it in the book. For that reason, all proceeds from this book go to the Harold B. Simpson History Complex.

Finally, to my dear wife goes my thanks and love for her unfailing support.

INTRODUCTION

Many years ago I started researching my great-grandfather's Civil War military unit, the Tenth Texas Cavalry Regiment. Finding no definitive works on the Tenth Texas, I remarked to one of my daughters that it was a shame none of the soldiers bothered to write about their experiences. She immediately commented that I had not written about my helicopter unit in Vietnam. I postponed research on my great-granddad's unit and wrote *Firebirds*, about my adventures in Vietnam. I have now returned my focus to the Civil War and the Tenth Texas Cavalry, Dismounted.

Several family stories about the Civil War had peaked my curiosity during my youth. One story explained my grandmother's terrible mistrust and dislike for Irish Catholics. During the conflict, Reb soldiers were told that the Yanks had imported shiploads of Irish immigrants to fight for the North. The feelings brought on by this information had transcended the years; so, when I decided to marry my Irish Catholic sweetheart a hundred years later in the 1960s, my mom had to do some fast talking to calm my Southern grandmother. Another story dealt with my great-granddad being shot in the leg. His personal circumstances are covered in this book.

I was determined not to write in the manner typical of many Regimental histories that cover extreme details, such as every road marched down and the names of most officers on the battlefield. I certainly did not want to write a history of the Civil War. I wanted to use as much actual narrative as possible from ordinary soldiers in the unit and related units. The words of the actual soldiers project images of dramatic action, which a third-hand writer could never duplicate. I concentrated on the "lowly privates" when possible because these were the guys on the receiving end of the shock, pain, and humor. They were the men who fought, suffered, lived, and survived the terrifying events described. Also, my great-granddad started as a private and ended as a private.

The main problem encountered in writing this book was the limited sources that were left behind by the men of the Tenth Texas. These were items such as letters, documents, diaries, or other written accounts. Many of these farm boys were not well educated and certainly were not in the habit of corresponding regularly with anyone. After the fall of Vicksburg, it was nearly impossible to get letters home. Most of the time, the men sent messages home by other soldiers heading back to Texas. Besides, mailing a letter was an expense many could not afford.

I also wanted to cover the motivation for these men to fight as fiercely as they did. How does one feed men the same as horses, leave them barefoot in the winter, and still get them to fight to the death? I hope this account will shed some light on their thoughts and circumstances.

I discovered many interesting facts while working on the history of the Tenth Texas. One item was that these dismounted cavalry men drew higher pay than regular foot soldiers. Whether this had anything to do with their location on various battlefields is unclear, but in most battles, they were located on the army's flanks close to the always present mounted cavalry. They were left flank at Richmond, left flank at Murfreesboro, right flank at Chickamauga (first day), left flank at Peachtree Creek, left flank at Ezra Church, left flank at Nashville, left flank at Spanish Fort. Another fact touched on was how the combat soldiers viewed the noncombat men. In Vietnam, they were referred to as "Chairborn Rangers." In the Civil War, these men were sometimes referred to as "Fireside Rangers" or "Featherbed Generals." Also included are some absorbing accounts that occurred during various battles and during camp life. There is an old saying that an army moves on its stomach, and these hungry guys had numerous stories about food. I found one about a soldier making coffee from ears of corn fascinating.

One particular point became clear as I did my research on this unit. When the commanders ordered the Tenth Texas to charge, no "file closers" were needed behind them. File closers were armed soldiers that shot or arrested stragglers. As a matter of fact, it could be said that the men from Texas muddled up things at Murfreesboro and Chickamauga. Once given the order to charge, their commanders had a difficult time stopping them or even directing the angle of attack.

The fundamentals of war never change. Intentions may vary and participants may differ, but key elements remain the same. Throughout the ages, the basic precepts of war are constant; there are strategies, casualties, victories, and defeats. Some factors are decided by men and others by fate. The outcome can be determined by overwhelming force or a slight shift in circumstance. I found this repeatedly borne out during my research on two wars that were a century apart in time but not in essence. As I read the accounts of the soldiers from the past, I came to realize just how much I did have in common with my great-grandfather. We answered a call to duty, did the best job we could, and were able to come home and share our experiences.

CHAPTER 1

"Spiling' for a fight"

ORGANIZATION OF THE TENTH TEXAS
CAVALRY (DISMOUNTED) REGIMENT

TO MANY EAST TEXANS, the election of Abraham Lincoln in November 1860 spelled doom for the United States. Prior to his election, the citizens of East Texas were on guard for abolitionist spies. They even attempted to suppress all music deemed to be dangerous or subversive to the Constitutional rights and liberties of the South. The name of Lincoln was uttered like a curse. One newspaper reported that slaves in Texas were dancing to the sound of the snapping necks of abolitionists as they were hung. Another newspaper wrote about several fires across the state that had to be the work of abolition emissaries.[1] Tensions were extremely high, with suspicion of anything "Yankee" on everyone's mind.

On December 20, 1860, the state of South Carolina voted to secede from the United States. Other Southern states soon followed. Texas passed an ordinance of secession on February 1, 1861.

At the special convention to vote on secession, out of 174 delegates, only eight men voted to stay in the Union. The first man to stand and vote to stay in the Union was James Throckmorton from Collin County. When a great hiss came from the crowd, the Civil War nearly started then and there. Mr. Throckmorton responded, "Mr. President, when the rabble hiss, well may patriots tremble!"

It is safe to say that the vast majority of Texans had no comprehension that the South had only one-third the population of the North, nor did they comprehend that the South had only 8 percent of the production capacity of the North.[2] In 1861, Texas had a population of 602,432. Of that figure, there were 421,411 whites, 399 free blacks, and 180,682 slaves. By July 1862, Texas furnished forty-eight regiments or forty-five thousand men out of a voting population of forty-four thousand. The excess number was made up by young men under the voting age. In November 1863, the numbers showed that only fifty-five hundred men between the ages of sixteen and sixty were not in military service.[3]

On February 8, delegates from the seceding states met in Montgomery, Alabama, and formed the Confederate States of America. Jefferson Davis of

Mississippi was elected president and P.G.T. Beauregard, provisional commander of the Southern forces. This all took place before the newly elected United States president, Abraham Lincoln, was inaugurated on March 4, 1861. On April 11, General Beauregard demanded the surrender of Fort Sumter in the harbor of Charleston, South Carolina. The Union officer in command of the fort refused. At 4:00 a.m. on April 12, 1861, bombardment of the fort commenced. The Civil War had begun. President Lincoln quickly issued a call for seventy-five thousand volunteers from the various states to help put down the rebellion, and both sides began preparation for a full-scale war.

By the beginning of August 1861, the conflict was well underway. During the same month, the Tenth Texas Cavalry Regiment was organized at Goose Lake, Texas, in Van Zandt County. M. F. Locke was elected colonel; J. M. Barton, lieutenant colonel; and W. Q. Craig, major. The unit was initially called the Texas Mounted Volunteers while it was under state control.

Col. Matthew F. Locke organized the unit. Prior to this, he was twice elected speaker of the Texas House of Representatives. He presided over the Secession Convention; and, it can certainly be said he did his part to get Texas into the Civil War. Shortly before his election as colonel, Locke wrote to the adjutant general of the State of Texas. He confidently stated, "I believe that there will be little difficulty getting a Regiment if I can promise them a prospect of fighting soon."[4] Later in the war, Colonel Locke had to resign from the military because of bad health. The Tenth Texas surgeon, A.B. Flint, said he suffered from "affection of the spine, asitis and chronic hepatitis." All

Col. Matthew F. Locke, who formed the
Tenth Texas Cavalry Regiment and led
them at the Battle of Murfreesboro.

Gen. P. G. T. Beauregard

these ailments stopped him from fighting and finally led to his death at the ripe old age of eighty-seven![5]

Per Confederate regulations, a regiment had ten companies, the regimental officers, which were a colonel, lieutenant colonel, and a major, a group of musicians, a quartermaster, an adjutant, a surgeon, and a chaplain. Each company was to also have one captain, three lieutenants, four sergeants, four corporals, two musicians, and from sixty-four to one hundred privates. The Tenth Texas was formed out of East Texas with ten companies comprising the regiment:

Company Commanders

A	Capt. C. D. McKnight	Men from Quitman, Wood County
B	Capt. J. Wilson	Men from Quitman (called "Wood County Rebels")
C	Capt. J. Rucker	Men from Upsher County
D	Capt. A. Earp	Men from Starrville, Upsher County
E	Capt. R. Redwine	Men from Rusk County (called "Bully Rocks")
F	Capt. W. Craig	Men from Panola County
G	Capt. J. Barton (promoted to Lt. Col.)	Men from Rusk County (called "Texas Troopers")
H	Capt. A. Whetstone	Men from Van Zandt County (called "Warriors")
I	Capt. R. Martin	Men from Cherokee County (called "Cherokee Cavalry")
K	Capt. J. Todd	Men from Tyler, Smith County

In the compiled service records, nearly all members of the Tenth Texas who listed their occupations were farmers. The Tenth Texas did include at least three merchants, one carpenter, two mechanics, two school teachers, two physicians, two lawyers, one druggist, one blacksmith, one surgeon-dentist, and one politician.

As Colonel Locke began the organization of the Tenth Texas at Goose Lake, he noted in a letter to the adjutant general that the initial company commanders were personal friends. The colonel was writing to try to obtain state funds and support. The state responded that the only materials they could supply, at the time, were abridged copies of military manuals. Colonel Locke wrote back and restated his need for help. He felt the least they could do would be to send one copy of the unabridged manual. He also pleaded for 125 guns for the number of men he had who had no weapons. He additionally appealed to the state for some much needed blankets by stating in his letter that "the wives have deprived themselves in many instances of blankets" so their men could use them. Colonel Locke advised the state officials that the soldiers of the Tenth Texas "could not afford to leave home just to leave home . . . we want active service."[6] To come up with guns for its military units, the state of Texas implemented total gun control on the state population. Each county was responsible for registering each rifle and pistol and even each Bowie knife. Apparently pen knives were free from registration.[7]

Shortly after this correspondence, the Tenth Texas received orders to leave East Texas and travel to an area just north of Dallas. There, they were to join up with another regiment and be officially sworn into the Confederate Army. However, when they arrived at the assigned area, the other cavalry unit had already departed for Galveston, Texas. Obviously, Colonel Locke, who found himself caught up in the world of bureaucratic limbo, was somewhat frustrated. He fired off another letter to state officials and said that he was at "a very great loss to know what to do." Locke made a decision on action by himself. Because of the inadequate supply of both blankets and tents, and with the threat of winter approaching, Locke and his men headed for the port at Galveston. While they were en route, the exasperated governor of Texas wrote to the leading Confederate official in Texas and stated the Tenth Texas "was beyond my control. Can you subject them to your orders?" Confederate officials finally caught up with the Tenth Texas in Navarro County. There they were officially mustered into the army and promptly ignored once again. They received no orders, so Colonel Locke led them back to East Texas. One consequence of the confusion about supplies and orders was that two companies left the unit before the Tenth Texas ever left the state. Captain Griffin's unit, the Company of Rockwall, and Captain Wharton's Company of Cedar Grove, from Kaufman County, both abandoned the Tenth Texas.[8]

On October 31, 1861, the unit was mustered into the Confederate Army at Taos, Texas. The unit was enlisted for twelve months or sooner discharged. Major Chilton wrote the following:

> I certify on honor that I have carefully examined the officers whose names are borne upon this role their horses and equipments. I have accepted them into the Confederate state service for 12 months, from the 31st of October, 1861. George W. Chilton, Major C.S.A.

(Chilton was the Texas leader of a secret society called Knights of the Golden Circle, a militant pro-slavery group that persuaded influential Texans to side with the Southern slave states in the war.)

After the Tenth Texas arrived back in East Texas, there was much grumbling and complaints about the expense of moving around the state. One soldier told the Marshall, Texas *Republican* newspaper, in its January 4, 1862, issue, that the East Texans complaining about the cost were "fireside heroes and featherbed generals." All the disorganization was probably the reason the rosters of the Tenth Texas show ninety-nine men signing up for duty and never leaving the state with the unit. These were the "fireside heroes" the soldier mentioned. Another reason the "featherbed generals" may have been complaining was that this was around the time Texas passed an income tax to pay for the war.

While these men were becoming Confederate soldiers, East Texas civilians were also making preparations to fight the Yanks. The young women of Eastern Texas Female College even organized their own military unit. One civilian stated, just like the Tenth Texas later did, "We would fight them till Hell would freeze over and then finish on the ice."[9] They had no intentions of being stepped on by the polluted tread of the abolitionist hordes.

The wife of Captain Redwine made the flag for the regiment. It was patterned after the Confederate Stars and Bars with a large white star for Texas surrounded by smaller white stars for the ten other seceded states. Four red stars represented the Choctaw, Creek, Cherokee, and Chickasaw Indian nations. The center stripe of the flag contained the words "Strike for your altars and your homes." Three men were shot down, with two of them killed, carrying this flag on December 31, 1862, at the battle of Murfreesboro, Tennessee. This same flag currently hangs in Austin, Texas. The only Yankee that grabbed this flag was shot dead on December 31, 1862, while in a hand-to-hand fight with the Texan flag bearer. Mrs. Redwine also made the flag for Company E, Tenth Texas, which currently hangs at Austin. It bears the company name, "Bully Rocks." The term "Bully Rocks" was synonymous with the word assassins.

A soldier from Tennessee gave us some understanding as to the symbolism of the flags:

> Flags made by the ladies were presented to companies, and to hear the young orators tell of how they would protect that flag, and that they would come back with the flag or come not at all, and if they fell they would fall with their backs to the field and their feet to the foe, would fairly make our hair stand on end with intense patriotism, and we wanted to march right off and whip twenty Yankees. But we soon found out that the glory of war was at home among the ladies and not upon the field of blood and carnage of death, where our comrades were mutilated and torn by shot and shell.[10]

In joining the cavalry unit, the records reflect the value of the soldiers' horses. The highest valued horse was owned by Lieutenant Colonel Barton and valued at $250. The average horse was valued at $150. Private B.Y. Ratcliff had a horse valued at $50. (They must have had to put red pepper on its rump to make sure it was alive!) These East Texas boys signed up to fight for twelve months on horseback, in Texas. They soon found out they would be fighting far from home, on foot, for the duration of the war. They did manage to briefly remount themselves with captured Yankees' horses towards the end of the war, but they received the short end of the stick again when the provost marshall took the horses away. General Polk had also promised to remount the Tenth Texas, but he messed around and was blown up by a cannonball before he actually ordered the remounting. W.V. Cogswell, Company F, who later died in a Yankee prisoner of war camp after being captured at Chickamauga, donated a wagon and four fine mules to the Confederacy when he joined the regiment.

Jacob Ziegler, who ultimately became the commander of the Tenth Texas at the end of the war, joined up with the "Wood County Rebels." The commander of the "Rebels" wrote a letter dated August 5, 1861, and said, "You please accept us and put us in service, just as quick as possible. We are 'spiling' for a fight."[11]

The reasons most often cited for the rush to join the military were adventure, a chance to travel to far-off places, and the perceived glory of battle. To all the East Texas farm boys who knew their life was preordained to be spent looking at the rear end of a plow mule, a glorious war was the chance of a lifetime. The opportunity to see and ride on a train, or travel by steam boat, must have excited the young men who lived very simple lives. While in Arkansas, J.W. Bird, Company F, Tenth Texas, referred to the first train many had ever seen: "The cars came a belching last night and the boys all broke for the road to see the cars."[12] The naive young men quickly found out that military life mostly consisted of one long, boring event interrupted by brief episodes of stark terror.

From August 1861 to February 1862, the unit spent time drilling and training. Private Templeton, Company I, Tenth Texas, portrayed the training:

> We drill twice each day. Two hours in the forenoon and two after. There is no drill this evening except the officers. They are drilling. The orders are very strict. No gambling, horse racing or horse swapping to be done. The latter can be done by getting permission from the Capt. We have to stand guard all the time. The roll is called three times a day and if there is any absent they have to make a good excuse or stand guard forty-eight hours.
>
> Col. Locke has issued orders for no grazing of horses, no going to town or washing of clothes without a commissioned officer at their head. Guards are kept out at night to mind horses and keep them from getting hurt with the rope. Over half the horses in our company are crippled with the rope. My horse has never hurt himself yet. He seems to know the rope by heart.[13]

The comment about the rope hurting the horses referred to the fact that cavalry horses had to be trained to be tied at night instead of grazing for food as they were accustomed. Private Templeton did have a problem with his horse. It had a "cruvious" back. He was told to put some whiskey on it, and he says, "So I did and it helped it some."

Templeton also described the rumors being told about the Tenth Texas:

> There are some very bad reports come into camps from a distance about our regiment. Sum about fighting with one another. There has never been a fight in the regiment that amounted to anything. There was a little shooting done between one of Capt. Redwine's men and one of Capt. Wilson's. One shot the other one four times with a pistol. The shot one is getting well and the other one run off. And has not been heard of.[14] (To these East Texas boys, shooting a guy four times was nothing that amounted to much.)

Later, in 1863, there was another shooting between members of the Tenth Texas and 3rd Cpl. Alex Mobley was killed.

Not to leave the impression that the East Texas boys were all a bunch of heathens, Templeton's Company I was the "civilest" company of the regiment:

Our Company gets the praise for being the civilest one in the regiment. We dismissed one fellow for not having sense. . . . Our company was at meeting last Sunday night & he was swearing before the ladies, & Capt Martin helped him off with about forty shot guns & told him if he was caught in three miles of here it would not be healthy for him.[15]

Company I (the Cherokee Cavalry) also had a band:

We have a singing band in our company & they have drawn the attention of the ladies of this country. There was five ladies took dinner with Capt Martin today. Some of the singers are talking of trading their shotguns off for [song] books.[16]

Some of the singers apparently decided singing for the ladies was preferable to using those shotguns on the Yanks.

In the summer of 1861, Frances R. Lubbock was elected governor by 124 votes. As an intelligent man, he realized the fate of the Confederacy depended upon quick and decisive military action before the North could bring its superior manpower and resources to bear. He decided that Texans must fight wherever needed if the South was to have any chance against the overwhelming resources of the North.[17] Many men assumed they would never fight anywhere else but Texas; they were wrong. On February 12, 1862, the Texans left for Arkansas to join the Army of the West. Following the Confederate defeat at Shiloh from April 6 to 8, 1862, General Beauregard with his Army of Mississippi withdrew to Corinth, Mississippi. There he began fortifying the town and issued a call for reinforcements. Among the reinforcements ordered to Corinth was the Army of the West. This, of course, included Colonel Locke's Tenth Texas Cavalry. The men were going to war because the war had not yet come to them.

When they left Texas, "they were in high spirits. Wives and sweethearts were waving their handkerchiefs, calling out their farewells and cheering them on. The men, marching proudly, were confident of an early victory and many promised to 'bring home a pet Yankee.'"[18]

The East Texas farm boys had a burning desire to smell the smoke of battle. Through all the training and preparation for "the glorious battles," they did not realize that the South, in the manufacturing of gunpowder, obtained some of their niter (potassium nitrate) from human urine.[19] The Tenth Texas was about to be literally and figuratively urinated on!

CHAPTER 2

"Glorious retreat"

ACTION AROUND CORINTH, MISSISSIPPI

THE TENTH TEXAS left the state with about eleven hundred men. They signed up about one hundred in route to Mississippi for a total of approximately twelve hundred. The numbers are uncertain because the records reflect men who signed up for duty, but apparently never left Texas.

Before the Tenth Texas ever fired a shot in anger, the dying began. As they rode into Arkansas, nearly the entire command came down with measles at the rate of about thirty per day. These rural boys were tough as nails but had no immunity to common diseases that even children of the towns and cities had. The number of deaths, 217 through July 14, 1862, seems high, but it has been said that overall the Rebs lost three dead to illness for every soldier killed in action.[1] These young men also did not have much money. Pvt. William Parker, of Company G, died with only $1.25 to his name. Pvt. L.G. Holcomb, of Company I, was worse off than that; he died with no assets.

Henry Watson, private, Company H, described the illness that swept through the Tenth Texas:

> Jacksonport Jackson Co. Arkansas, Feb. 1862
> Dear Father & Mother,
> I take my seat to write you a few lines to inform you that I am enjoying tolerable good health at present. I have not been well for the last three weeks. I have had the measles but I have got well. I had a very tight time of it. I taken them a day or two after we left Little Rock and it was four days before I knew what was the matter with me. I rode four days before the measles broke out on me before I got to Jacksonport and it had like to have killed me. There was no body that wanted to take a person in there houses with the measles after we got here there was eight of our Company that had them and we had to go to the hospital and I and James Forsyth stayed in there sixteen days that we never saw outside of the house. . . . We had nothing to eat but some soup made out of strong dried beef and a little cof-

fee and bread which was not fit for a sick person to eat. There is two things I can give Arkansas praise for and that is the ladies and the water. There is the kindest ladies and the best water that I ever saw in Arkansas . . . at one time there was about half of the regiment down with the measles. The regiment was ordered to Salem the other day and there was only about five hundred that was able to go.[2]

A letter from Private Littlejohn, Company G, described the illnesses that disabled most of the men of the Tenth Texas:

My Dear Wife,
We are fourteen miles from Jacksonport. . . . We arrived in camps last Friday about 11 o'clock. We were about ten days and a half in getting here. I was very much fatigued by riding so far and so long. It is about one hundred miles north of Little Rock. . . . We found the Regiment in very bad health. A great many have died, and they are still dying. The most prevalent disease is measles — some cases of fever. Some seven or eight were buried the day before we came into camps. One last night. A great many of the boys were sent off on the boats down White River to Little Rock, to the hospital. The boys from different companies were left all along road from Clarksville (Texas) to Jacksonport. Some have died and some have recovered. E.L.G.[3]

Private Templeton said, "It seemed like the stoutest men died first" from illness. Pvt. J.W. Bird, while in Arkansas, referred to the sick saying, "They are scattered from here to Texas."

Special Order No. 52, dated April 15, 1862, was received at the headquarters of the TransMississippi Department at Des Arc, Arkansas. It directed Colonel Locke's regiment to be dismounted and proceed at once to Memphis, Tennessee. Now the Tenth Texas Cavalry became the Tenth Texas Cavalry, Dismounted, and served under that designation throughout the remainder of the war. The order to take away the horses of the Tenth Texas Cavalry probably brought them close to open mutiny. Being in a cavalry unit was like owning a good life insurance policy compared to being in the infantry.

P.A. Blakey, whose brother, A.A. Blakey, served with the Tenth Texas and was killed at the Siege of Spanish Fort, related some of the circumstances surrounding the dismounting of the Tenth Texas Cavalry:

Joseph L. Hogg was appointed brigadier general by the Confederate War Department about February, 1862. When his commission came he was ordered to report for duty at Memphis, Tenn., where he would

10

be assigned to the command of a brigade of Texas Troops. . . . A number of Texas regiments were ordered to cross the Mississippi River among them the 3rd and the 10th Texas Cavalry. Company C, of the 3rd and Company (E) of the 10th were made up in Rusk, Texas. General Hogg's oldest son, Thomas E. Hogg was a private in Company C and these two regiments formed part of his brigade. General Hogg met the 3rd Texas at Duvall's Bluff, on White River where we (the 10th Texas) sent horses home and went by steamer to Memphis accompanied by General Hogg.[4]

Curiously, P.A. Blakey referred to "we" when he related information about the Tenth Texas Cavalry. I found no record that he ever served with the unit. He was with the Fourth Texas Cavalry.

When the Tenth Texas Cavalry was dismounted in Arkansas, Pvt. G.G. Pierce and Pvt. J.A. White were assigned to take the horses back to Texas. They never came back. Another private from Company F, J.W. Malor, apparently left the unit because he did not want to burn shoe leather. With only a limited number of men assigned to move all the horses back to Texas, they had to tie the horses together, tail to neck. Each man then led a train of horses.

Another soldier, Jim Watson from Company G, went back to Texas with the horses, and it only took him eleven months to make it back. Somehow, he was attached to Lane's Regiment, Texas Partisan Rangers, and fought two battles with them in Arkansas. He made it back to the Tenth Texas in March 1863. His brother Benton was with the Tenth Texas but died of disease.[5]

Henry Watson described the dismounting, his expectations, and the trip to Corinth, Mississippi:

> DesArk Ark., April the 17th, 1862
> We are now here in desArk, Arkansas and we have to dismount here and go the Memphis and there we will take the Rail Road at Memphis and go to Corinth; there will be the big Battle. They have been fighting for sometime and we have wiped them every time yet our Regiment was very much opposed to dismounting until we got here and the General said that it was impossible for us to get forage for our horses and we concluded rather than disband and go home that we would dismount and take it afoot. We will not be considered as Infantry and we will receive the same wages that we did when we was Cavalry. They could not have forced us to dismount but I thought rather than be disbanded and have to go home at this season of the year I would try it afoot although did not like to give up my horse much but our Country needs our assistance at the present

and I expect to serve my twelve months out. Some way if I live if I can't ride I will walk. . . . Henry Watson.

DesArc is located fifty miles from Little Rock on the White River.

At this time, Private Littlejohn expressed his shock at the morals of some of his fellow soldiers:

> There are so many temptations in a camp life. You have no idea what wickedness there is. There is four times as much vice now as I ever saw before. Those who left home pious and devout Christians, have now turned out to be the bitterest profanity, cursing, and vice of every crime. Instead of its decreasing it is increasing, among youths and old men.

The life of a combat soldier can lead to a certain reduction in moral standards. Even though there were major outbreaks of "religion" from time to time, neither side had a lock on morality or immorality. The Tenth Texas did not seem to be comprised of too many wicked men because only R. Felton and J. Sentill were thrown out of the unit for having "syphilis consecutiva." This J. Sentill must have been an evil, wicked man! It is bad enough that Pvt. Jim Watson wrote home and said Sentill killed a soldier at Enterprise, Mississippi, committing what he called a "bad murder." It is also bad when he said, "John Sentill is a thief." The worst thing Sentill did was apparent from the letter Jim Watson sent home referring to Sentill's wife: "She is said to be of a good family. There is no doubt that she is a fine woman. She is one ruined girl." The reader must remember the type of disease Mr. Sentill had![6] On May 13, 1862, Yank General Butler (the com-

Privates Howell P. Hale and James M. Watson (l. to r.). Hale was wounded at Atlanta and Watson at Chickamauga. Note their uniform tops.

mander at New Orleans) offended Southern men and women alike. He issued an order that any woman who insulted a Yank would be regarded and held liable to be treated as a woman of the town plying her avocation. The Rebs used this as propaganda for the entire war.

Private Littlejohn shared his observations concerning the war:

> We are constantly receiving news here, some of which is reliable and a great deal false, travelers coming in from Corinth bring bad news. They say that there is a great dissatisfaction among our troops. A great many are deserting, their time being expired they do not wish to be forced into the ranks by the Conscript Act that has been passed by Congress. A great many people are of the opinion that it will ruin the Southern Army, and cause a mutiny among the soldiers. Gloom and distress seem to hang over us, and we are just on the verge of destruction. Yesterday about thirty or forty soldiers came in from Corinth giving these statements. They also say that there is a great deal of sickness in the army; almost one-half of the regiments. Unless there is some decisive movement manifested in a short time I believe our cause will be beyond redemption. At least it seems so from the best information I can gather. It looks like our officials are managing badly. Ruin is brooding over us anyway. If we gain the victory at Corinth, then may we be more lucky hereafter; but if we are conquered, woe be the consequences. Both parties have very large forces there and I expect when a battle is fought there, it will be one of the most desperate on record. . . .

Upon reaching Corinth sometime between April 15 and 30, 1862, the Tenth Texas Cavalry, Dismounted, comprising about 1,052 men, the others being left behind either sick or dead, was assigned to the First Brigade commanded by Brigadier General Hogg. Blakey continued his account of the formation of Hogg's brigade:

> We were transported by rail in command of General Hogg to Corinth, or rather we were dumped off on the side of the railroad some two or three miles west of that town, and became a part of General Beauregard's Army, which had fallen back from Shiloh.

Corinth, a city in northeastern Mississippi, held the key to the railroad system in this part of the Confederacy. It had two railroads that intersected. One Texan said upon arriving at Corinth he was told it was easy to find the "Texians" because they were the dirtiest troops in the army.[7] Later the Tenth Texas had to send troops home to get more clothes. The old ones had either rotted off or worn out.

The Tenth Texas moved out to support a combat action at Farmington, Mississippi. Templeton complained they did not get to shoot at the Yanks, but they did capture one from Illinois. This was the first contact the Tenth Texas had with a real live Yankee from "Yankeedom" (a term used by Templeton in his letters). Farmington was eight miles east of Corinth. The action was on May 9 and just happened to be the day General Hogg died.

The Tenth Texas was able to bust a few caps on the Yanks in a skirmish at Boonesville. There the Rebs were trying to maneuver into position to defend a disabled ammo train. The Yanks got there first and the train made a big bang when it exploded. Six cars out of a ten car train were totally destroyed.[8] Henry Ransom, the adjutant of the Tenth Texas, was captured at Boonesville and never returned to duty after being paroled. This occurred on May 29, 1862. Also, Pvt. James Rose, Company K, Tenth Texas was severely wounded. This appeared to be the first combat casualty of the regiment. He was dropped from the roster apparently for medical reasons. May 29, 1862, was the same day the Rebels started their retreat from Corinth when the Yanks showed up in force.[9]

Littlejohn described the "Glorious retreat" from Corinth:

Shannon, Mississippi June 3rd, 1862
My Dear and Affectionate Sallie,
Soon we were rolling along to the scene of Battle, as we thought, but instead of that, it was the scene of retreat. We arrived at Corinth about 12 o'clock, which is ninety-four miles from Memphis. And here everything seemed to be in confusion and uproar. Soldiers marching to and fro, and everything else to inspire a feeling of suspense. We had to hunt for our regiment among a hundred thousand (as reported) men. We first went to the Provost Marshal's office and got a pass, and started about 2 p.m. We continued going until sundown before we found the regiment. When I found it, it was drawn up in line, all ready to march, but no one knew where. I found my company but I did not find many men in it. There were about twenty men from our company in ranks. I was surprised to see so small a number able for duty out of so large a company. As I was not able to march with them, the Capt. (Kilgore) sent me to the camps where all the sick were. I got there just at dark. The boys were eating supper. . . . I had just had time to eat a little supper when General Beauregard rode up in haste and ordered every man who was able to walk at all to leave immediately and those were not able would be put on the cars. So there we were, I was broken down in hunting for

14

the regt. . . . We went on till 11 o'clock in the night and then we got lost we lay down on the ground and slept till daylight. That night nearly the whole army passed along in its retreat. We walked on just as we could and when we felt like it. We had to buy our provisions and you may be sure they were hard to get where so large an army has passed. I can say now that I have had to beg bread. As I passed a house I went to the kitchen and asked an old negro woman for a piece of bread, which she gave to me. And it was a sweet morsel, too. Sallie, I have seen lots of men who had nothing to eat for three or four days. I never saw any suffering till I came here. The sick are thrown on the cars like dead hogs; and frequently four or five die before they leave the depot. They just dig a hole about a foot deep, and wrap their blankets around them, and throw them in. It is enough to melt a heart of adamant to see how the poor soldiers are treated. Far worse than the savage would treat them, it seems to me. I could write a dozen pages about this Glorious Retreat as it will be called in the papers, provided I had time. But perhaps I may have the chance to tell you verbally.

We walked on in the manner mentioned above for three days in a southern direction we had no orders where to go nor nothing. But we intended to keep as near the main army as possible. . . . The people of this country are very hospitable to the sick soldiers. You can't find a house but what there is three or four men, and sometimes more. We aim to stay here until our money gives out, which won't be long with me. Sallie, I never saw humanity suffering to such a degree in all my life. Of all the Civil wars, Ancient or Modern, that I ever read of, I never met with anything that surpasses this in cruel treatment of the sick. I have heard sick men lying in the cars begging and praying for water and no one to give it to them. What feelings of awe it brought over me, to witness such things. A great many died along the road trying to get away from Corinth. Men threw away their guns, blankets, coats, knapsacks of good clothing and everything that impeded their speed in any way. I threw away the coverlid that I got from Mrs. Wallace and a blanket which Reuben gave me at Little Rock. Thousand of dollars worth of clothing was thrown away along the road.

And at Corinth I wouldn't hesitate a moment in saying there was $200,000 worth of property burned. Everything that you can think of. All of our wearing clothes were sent off on the cars, but I never expect to see one rag of mine any more. I have just got the clothes that I wore from home, I made a shift to get them washed when I got here; they were black enough sure. I can't tell what we will do. You will see some account of this retreat in the papers as being a magnificent one, but you may take my word for is; it is anything else. . . .

There is a great deal of sickness in the army. Our regiment has not more than 200 men able for duty. Everybody has the diarrhea. I have had it myself in a mild form, but we can't get anything to stop it. There is no chance to get any medicine here. There is great dissatisfaction among the Texan boys. They think it is the water and the climate that is working upon them so. I would not be surprised if some of them did not come back to that side of the river.

I hope and pray to God that this war will soon end so we may all return to our homes. . . . I would give the world if I could but be with you. . . . your loving husband, E.G. Littlejohn.

The Captain Kilgore, mentioned by Littlejohn, later had the city of Kilgore, Texas, named after him.

Littlejohn apparently was concerned that the press would portray the miserable retreat as a glorious one. The Rebs used wooden cannons and had brass bands playing at night to make the Yanks think that reinforcements were arriving while all along they were retreating. Later in the war, when the Tenth Texas was retreating out of Kentucky, Littlejohn thought the Reb generals were very smart.

One reason the soldiers were getting so sick around the Corinth area was the water they had to drink. One soldier explained:

The rate at which our men fell sick was remarkable, as well as appalling, and distressing in the extreme. The water we had to drink was bad, very bad, and the rations none of the best. The former we procured by digging for it; the earth around Corinth being very light and porous, holding water like a sponge. When we first went there the ground was full of water and by digging a hole two feet deep we could dip up plenty of a mean milky-looking fluid but as the season advanced the water holes were from eight to twelve feet deep, still affording the same miserable water. My horse would not drink a drop of the water the men had to use, and if I failed to ride him to a small running branch some two miles away he would go without drinking.[10]

In May 1862, the Army of Mississippi was reorganized. Concurrently, the Tenth Texas elected new officers. Around this time the Confederacy began to test elected officers for competency. It is unclear if any of the Tenth Texas personnel were tested. In 1863, the Confederacy did away with election of officers. There is little question that an elected officer had trouble maintaining discipline. The officer ranks of the Tenth Texas were drastically changed in this election. Of the forty officers at the company level, four per company, twenty-six resigned, went absent without leave (AWOL), dropped out, left for sickness in the family, or died. William Moore was demoted and apparently not allowed to resign because he was a "paid substitute" for W.P. Davis. He was then arrested for an unknown reason, then managed to be assigned permanently to Company Q. Company Q was the term for sick call. He spent most of the remainder of the war in the hospital.

The new company commanders were:

A	J.J. Wright	F	A.J. Booty
B	J.W. Cannon	G	Buck Kilgore
C	W.G. McGee	H	T.W. Summers
D	R.W. Smith	I	J. F. Hall
E	R.A.S. Redwine	K	Q. Gibson

Prior to the Battle of Chickamauga, Redwine was promoted to the regimental staff and replaced by W.F. Young. Buck Kilgore was promoted to brigade staff and replaced by G.W. Trammell. T.W. Summers died and was replaced by R.S. Lyles. All the company commanders, after the above changes, were killed or wounded at the Battle of Chickamauga. Lyles was wounded, captured, and recaptured. (Maybe the author's great granddad wasn't so dumb remaining a private!)

General Bragg replaced General Beauregard. Being a believer in strong discipline, he instituted "organization, discipline, and instruction." His

Gen. Braxton Bragg

17

strict dealing with desertion reduced these offenses. His rigorous enforcement of discipline in the past had also caused some disgruntled troops. Col. David Urquhart, a member of General Bragg's staff, related an intriguing story of an incident the general experienced during the Mexican-American War. He stated that General Bragg talked about how, when he was asleep, some of the men of his battery placed a shell under his cot. The shell exploded, tore everything to pieces, but did not harm the general.[11] (In similar fashion, toward the end of the Vietnam War, officers that believed in discipline and instruction were subject to being "fragged" — having a fragmentation grenade rolled into their tent or bunker.)

Around this stage of the war, the Texans learned of, and saw implemented, the Confederate Conscription Law (official law for a mandatory draft), which Littlejohn mentioned in his letter. Because there was still good communication across the Mississippi River, the Tenth Texas heard how the Conscript law was being implemented in Texas. By 1862, an incredible number of Texas men had volunteered for service; but General Lee, in Virginia, was unable to raise a volunteer army. His influence was instrumental in securing the passage of a Confederate Conscription Law. The concept was no more popular in Texas than it was later in the North. The first law passed, in April 1862, applied to all white males between eighteen and thirty-five. Soon after, the limits were lowered to seventeen and raised to fifty. While this early draft was frequently praised as military realism, it definitely had a dubious effect.

Poorly drawn and executed, the draft was discriminatory and unevenly applied. Officeholders, even petty ones, were exempt as were men "considered indispensable." Exemptions in medicine and frontier defense made sense. Substitution was also permitted. As in the North, a wealthy man could hire a poor one to go in his place. Finally, in Texas, the law was interpreted to exempt almost any substantial man of property and affairs. It was regarded bitterly both by the civilian population and a large proportion of the soldiers, including those who had volunteered.[12]

Two men from the Tenth Texas, W.P. Davis and D.L. Neal, were able to furnish substitutes. The substitute for D.L. Neal, J.W. Valentine, was noted to have been drawing his pay. Valentine eventually disappeared from the records. In December 1863, the Confederate Congress stopped substitutions.

A soldier from another unit, who was present at the reorganization of the Army of Mississippi, had this view of the Conscript Law and General Bragg's discipline:

Men were shot by scores and no wonder the army had to be reorganized. Soldiers had enlisted for twelve months only and had faithfully complied with their volunteer obligations; the terms for which they had enlisted had expired and they naturally looked upon it that they had a right to go home. They had done their duty faithfully and well. They wanted to see their families, in fact, wanted to go home anyhow. War had become a reality they were tired of it. A law had been passed by the Confederate States Congress called the Conscript Act. A soldier had no right to volunteer and to choose the branch of service he preferred. He was conscripted.

From this point on until the end of the war, a soldier was simply a machine, a conscript. It was mighty rough on rebels. We cursed the war, we cursed Bragg, we cursed the Southern Confederacy. All our pride and valor had gone, and we were sick of war and the Southern Confederacy.

A law was made by the Confederate States Congress about this time allowing every person who owned twenty Negroes to go home. It gave us the blues; we wanted twenty Negroes. Negro property suddenly became very valuable and there was raised the howl of rich man's war — poor man's fight. The glory of the war, the glory of the South, the glory and the pride of our volunteers had no charms for the conscript.[13]

The Tenth Texas released nineteen men because of the Conscript Act. Most of these men were either too old or too young. Also, there were not many East Texans that owned twenty slaves, and there were none in the Tenth Texas. Cyon Pace, of Company C, was forty-seven years old when he was discharged. C.C. Wilson, of Company B, was released because he was only sixteen years old. John Templeton, of Company I, wrote home with the expectation of also being released since he was only sixteen. They kept him until he turned seventeen and became legal.

One of the men released for being too young was Monroe Fite on January 1, 1863. Apparently, he had been shot in the leg at the Battle of Murfreesboro the day before. He also had five brothers and a dad that fought for the Confederacy. His dad was in the Tenth Texas for several years, and after giving six sons to the Confederacy, and two years of his own life, the dad, N.O. Fite, decided he had done enough. He just left. Three of N.O. Fite's sons were in the Tenth Texas: Monroe was shot in the leg at Murfreesboro, S.L. was disabled with a wound at Chickamauga, and A.M. had an arm ruined at Atlanta.[14]

To increase the number of available soldiers, the officers of the Tenth Texas were always attempting to recruit replacements. In the practice of warfare, it has always been believed that the foot soldier didn't require the highest I.Q. Here it seemed that if a guy wasn't smart enough to fire his weapon, a bayonet could be attached to the end and he could at least stick the guy with the blue coat. However, when J.T. Berry signed up with the Tenth Texas on April 29, 1862, he apparently could not tell blue from gray. He only lasted about a month before they discharged him for "IDIOCY."

From the time the Tenth Texas got to Corinth, until the end of the war, they were able to recruit only ten additional soldiers. Seven were from Texas, one was from Shreveport, Louisiana, and two were from Mississippi. One of the men from Mississippi, W.F. McClanahan, of Company F, was signed up as a "tooter" (musician) instead of a "shooter." Seemingly, he was made into a shooter somewhere along the route, because he was wounded at Chickamauga. He was also ordered from the brigade band to his company prior to the Atlanta campaign. Many times during battles, musicians were used as stretcher bearers for the wounded.

General Hood had a statement written on the side of his tent: "An army that can obtain no recruits must eventually surrender."[15] This statement certainly proved to be true.

CHAPTER 3

Hippo over no horses

CAMP LIFE

Littlejohn sent home a letter describing camp conditions:

> Camp Priceville, Mississippi, June 27, 1862
>
> My dear Wife,
> There is a great deal of sickness in camps now, but not so much as there has been. A great many out of our regiment have died. We are entirely without news in camps, except camp rumors which is common. We have just got orders to be ready to move in the morning but we don't know where to. . . . It has commenced raining and I have no tent to get in nothing but a brush arbor, which is but a poor shelter for one that wants to write. Everybody is in an uproar about starting. It is the rumor that we are going to Chattanooga, but I don't believe it. No one knows where. . . .
>
> Sallie, I never knew anything about hard times before. We have very scarce rations indeed. We don't draw meat but two days in every seven (that is bacon). We have plenty of flour bread but we have not got anything to put in it, but salt and water and sometimes a little grease. We have some poor beef. Our bread is baked for us in a bakery. E.G.L.

The Tenth Texas did move to Chattanooga. Littlejohn sent home another letter from there:

> Chattanooga Ten., July 16, 1862
>
> My Dear Sallie
> This letter leaves me in tolerable good health, with the exception of the diarrhea which was brought on by eating too many apples. You will recollect we are in an apple country now. I am as fleshy now as ever before. I will be very thankful if I continue to keep my health. Garner came into camps a few days since, yet unwell. He had now got the yellow jaundice and looks badly. I think he has got the Hippo the worst of any man I every saw. He is grieving because he had to be dismounted. . . .

21

Well Sallie, we came very near having an exciting time here the other evening; occasioned by this circumstance. Some time since a private in one of the companies of our regt. disobeyed the orders of his captain in a small point. The Capt. reported him to headquarters, he was court marshaled and condemned to wear a ball and chain that weighs twenty pounds for sixty days and to have one half of his head shaved. This kind of treatment did not meet with the approbation of the regt. and resolved to take the chain off and they did take it off in a little time. It was then the business of the officers to find out who did it, but no one could be found. A part of the regt. was called out to arrest the other part. I began to think we would have a serious time of it. But the mutiny was quelled without any harm being done. There is about twenty thousand troops in that part of Tennessee. We are right in among the mountains. Three miles from Chattanooga. We have splendid water and plenty of it. We are living tolerable scanty at present. We draw beef, bacon, flour, and sugar. Everything else that we get we have to go out in the country and buy at very high prices. We get butter, irish potatoes, collards, beans, chickens and anything in the world that is fit to eat.

The health of our Regt. is improving considerable. But it is much less than when we were cavalry. We were then 1,200. We are now 410. That shows what ravages death has committed.

When Littlejohn referred to his friend having "Hippo" over having their horses taken away, he is referring to depression. One wonders how his friend, William Garner, felt when he found out he was about to go on a "stroll" that would eventually cover one thousand miles. They were about to walk north so they could drink from the Ohio River and see Cincinnati, Ohio.[1] A British military observer hit the nail on the head when he said you couldn't get infantry soldiers in Texas because "no Texan walks a yard if he can help it."[2] These Texans were going to learn how to burn up that shoe leather. Littlejohn's friend, William Garner, took a job as a teamster so he did not have to walk as much.

One reason the Confederacy lost the war, besides lack of the number of potential soldiers and the ability to manufacture military equipment, was its inability to move men, supplies, and equipment rapidly and efficiently to the various battlefields. The roads and railroads were limited and became even more unusable as the war progressed. To get from Tupelo, Mississippi, to Chattanooga, Tennessee, the Tenth Texas got a good tour of the Confederacy. Instead of going nearly due east to Chattanooga, they took the shortest train route south across Mississippi to the south end of Alabama (Mobile), then northeast to Atlanta, Georgia, then northwest to Chattanooga. On this trip, the troops were showered with fruit and flowers as they came into each train station. The Tenth Texas got their first, but not their last, views of Allatoona Pass, Kennesaw Mountain, and the Chickamauga River. As Private Templeton said, "I have got to see a good deal of the old States."

The Tenth Texas was moved to Chattanooga to get ready to invade Kentucky. This got them in position to "drive" the Yankees for the first time.

Littlejohn's previous letter mentioned the twelve hundred soldiers who were there before disease killed so many. His reference to 410 soldiers would have been the number fit for combat and not the ones present or on the unit's roster. Another thing that reduced the number of fighting soldiers was the various service jobs just like in any modern army. A brigade had cooks, cook wagon drivers, butchers, ordinance wagon drivers, ambulance drivers, guards, drivers for tool wagons (shovels, picks, and axes), farriers to care for the officers' horses, plus men on detail to the division staff for guards. Also, the division supplied bridge guards and railroad guards in the area where they were operating. The Tenth Texas had five men transferred to the Douglas Texas Battery (artillery), four men to the Fourteenth Texas Cavalry, three men to the Third Texas Cavalry, and four others to a general's body guard.

On July 20, the Texas regiments demanded a Texas Brigade commander instead of an interloper from Arkansas, Colonel McCray, who had replaced General Hogg after he died. The Texans selected M.D. Ector but the change was not approved until after the Kentucky campaign.[3]

Another soldier from the Tenth Texas, Private Templeton, recounted his harrowing experience in a "suck" (whirlpool):

In the year 1862 the 10th Texas Regiment was at Chattanooga, Tenn. Sometime in July Company I of that regiment was sent down the Tennessee River to a point opposite the "suck" in the river on picket duty. The writer and another member of the company, Thomas Stafford, found a small canoe or skiff hid under the boughs of trees, and, seeing a house on the opposite side of the river, rowed across to get some forage. There was a small paddle in the skiff, and on reaching out into the current the frail little craft began to go up and down on the water almost like a feather. Stafford became excited and said he could not use the paddle, and in handing it to the writer it came near falling into the river. However by good, hard strokes we finally made it across and found an old man at the house near the river bank. He expressed great surprise at seeing us, and on being informed that we had crossed nearly opposite his house he almost fainted, telling us that if we had been a few rods lower down we could have been swallowed up by the "suck," something of which we were entirely ignorant. The old man was very kind, and we took aboard all the Irish potatoes, chickens, and vegetables that our frail craft could carry; and being provided by this good man with two good paddles, and taking his advice to go up the river about half a mile to a certain tree before trying to cross, we returned safely, grateful that a kind Providence had again shielded us in time of danger. We had plenty of Confederate money; but our old friend declined taking it, saying he would take "railroad money" if we had any. We had several bills that had been issued by the railroads and that had the picture of the cars on them. With these he was fully satisfied.[4]

Tom Stafford, who was mentioned in the letter, made it to Atlanta in 1864 where his war ended with a gunshot wound. He survived to live until 1899.

From Templeton's letter concerning the refusal of the man to take Confederate money, it is clear that common people had started to doubt the ability of the Confederacy to survive. "Railroad" money was script issued by various railroads and was accepted as currency by most people in the areas adjacent to the railroads.

CHAPTER 4

"Ain't you a Texican?"

OPERATIONS IN KENTUCKY —
BATTLE OF RICHMOND, KENTUCKY

THE TENTH TEXAS CAVALRY, in August 1862, was commanded by Col. C.R. Earp, assigned to the First Brigade commanded by Colonel McCray. It is unclear, from reading the records, why Colonel Locke was not commanding the Tenth Texas. One soldier wrote years later about the journey into Kentucky:

In the month of August 1862 we entered the State at a little town called Barboursville, in the southeastern portion of the State. On the second day's tramp after leaving Barboursville, having extended our day's march into the night our pathway was lighted only by the jeweled stars of the firmament which from their empyrean heights shone in all their pristine glory and splendor. It must have been 9 p.m. and we were still trudging along footsore weary and hungry when I espied a strong masculine looking woman standing in the doorway of a little one-room cabin that stood several yards back from the road. She was shading her eyes with her hands from the light that came from some lightwood fagots which were burning in the broad deep fireplace of the cabin and as she peered out into the darkness attracted by the rumbling rustling noise made by the patter of the many feet, endeavoring to detect what it was, I could see her much more plainly than she could see me. As she stood directly between me and the burning lightwood knots, she did not see me until I was within a few steps of her. I made as stately a bow as I could and raising my greasy wool hat said: "Madam will you be so kind as to inform me how far ahead will it be before we find a stream of water?" Seeing my garb and judging from the time we had been in passing that we were the Southern army she doubtless the wife of one of those bushwhackers who had given us no little trouble ever since we reached the mountainous region of East Tennessee and Southern Kentucky and who was then in all probability lurking dangerously near seeking an opportunity to give us one of his murderous bullets, with a scornful, contemptuous look, answered me in a snappish petulant manner: "I guess you will find it in the Ohio River. . . ."

About ten o'clock that night we were turned into a large field where the bushes and briers were nearly as tall as one's head, growing along the banks of the creek. I have often wondered why it was that more of us were never snake or spider bitten but it was seldom that one ever heard of such a thing although we were turned into all kinds of thickets at all hours of the night the places where snakes, spiders, and other poisonous reptiles and insects naturally abound; and it was very rare that soldier ever made any kind of examination for being tired and sleepy he spread his blanket and threw his tired weary body down and in a very few moments was given over to "tired nature's sweet restorer."

The next morning before resuming our march a general order was issued requiring us to fill our canteens with water also stating that we were about to cross a small mountain known as Big Hill and the probabilities were that no more water could be had until we had crossed over, which would be after night. That was the only time during my war experience I was ever compelled to refuse a comrade a drink of water; but the hill, or portion where we traveled, was entirely destitute of water. It was eighteen well measured miles, a stream of water running at the base on each side and that alone was our dependence for water during that memorable day. Some of the men did not have water to last them longer than midday and there was a great deal of suffering. It was fully demonstrated that day that some men require or use a great deal more water than others. Taken all in all that was the most dreary, desolate, and fatiguing day's march I ever remember of making during my three years of soldier life. I do not remember seeing habitation or meeting a living soul outside of our command. The absence of animal life was very conspicuous — not a note from a bird or a chicken nor the deep mouthed welcome of the watchdog. They either did not inhabit that desolate lonesome territory or they had fled at our coming.

The hill divides the northern or blue-grass region of the State from the southern or mountainous portion. The former is rich and productive slightly undulating a lovely scenery to behold while the latter is generally barren wild and mountainous the contrast being most distinctive. It took us the whole of one long hot summer day hard and continuous walking to foot it across this Big Hill. We camped on the north side of Big Hill that night and it must have been about one o'clock in the midst of the deepest slumber when we were partially aroused by some great noise. Soon in our half-awakened state we distinguished the cry: "Horses stampeding! Look out for yourselves." I remember well that when I was aroused and knew well what I was doing I found myself halfway up a tree which I had climbed in my semi-conscious state. Others were running around and around in a sleepy condition calling for help. For twenty minutes it was a general uproar and everything was in a state of confusion and disorder. After awhile the horses were recaptured and securely fastened and we returned to our well-earned slumbers. . . .

When we started out on our next day's tramp, we found that we were walking on a macadamized roadway called a turnpike, with very slight elevations, or declivities. No more effort was required than would be to walk the paved streets of a city; quite a contrast to Big Hill and the roads south of it. Then the beautiful and luxuriant blue-grass meadows which extended on each side as far as the eye could reach, with here and there a fine grove of large forest trees, with no undergrowth, and occasionally we would pass one of those old ante-bellum Kentucky houses, a fine two-story mansion set back from the turnpike probably half a mile, with an avenue leading up from the pike, bordered on both sides with majestic forest trees, whose branches overlapped, obscuring the rays of the midday sun. In one of the beautiful meadows adjacent could be seen a herd of fine Jersey cattle; feeding just a little way off was a flock of Southdown sheep, whose broad backs indicated that they were full ready for market. Everything indicated peace and plenty, and it seemed a crime to invade such ideal happiness with war's rude alarms.[1]

The terms "bushwhackers" and "Jayhawkers" were used to describe Union sympathizers and bandits.

Pvt. John Wesley Davis, Company E, of the Tenth Texas described his experience in front of the army on the way to Richmond, Kentucky:

Most of our men were armed with shotguns and squirrel rifles. I had traded for a Mississippi rifle and when the Colonel called for two men from each company who were well armed John McNelson and I were sent from our company. We reported to headquarters and found about a hundred men. Col. Young of the 9th Texas was in command. We "put out" I didn't know where but when daylight came we were on a little stream called Stinking River and the bushwhackers were shooting at us from the cliffs above us. We picked up a negro who told us where ninety-six mules and twenty-four wagons were and we started up the river to get them. The wagons were loaded with all kinds of provisions and were guarded by 400 Yankees who were trying to get to Burnside at Cumberland Gap. We soon found the object of our pursuit and the battle opened. When the smoke had cleared away we had the ninety-six mules and twenty-four wagons and the boys said, 300 dead Yankees. I did not count them.[2]

The Battle of Richmond, Kentucky, was about to begin. The following is a brief summary of the battle:

On the morning of August 30, the armies met about nine miles south of Richmond. The Tenth Texas, in McCray's Brigade, came forward on the enemy's right flank, broke the enemy's lines, and drove them about two miles before the Yankees made another stand. McCray's Brigade then again hit their flank. Once more they broke the enemy's line and drove them to the outskirts of Richmond. All Rebel units then advanced, and the entire Yankee line collapsed. The Northern soldiers had somewhere between sixty-five hundred and sixteen thousand troops present. The Rebs captured ten thousand weapons. The Rebs had approximately eight thousand troops.

In the battle, the generals used massed Napoleonic tactics. The Napoleonic tactics utilized shock attacks as its key element for victory. The goal was to charge into and break the enemy's line and also charge with the defeated soldiers into the enemy's second line. This rapid charge hindered the second line from firing for fear of shooting the retreating soldiers from the front line. This is exactly how the Tenth Texas was able to overrun a fortified Union position with the Yanks firing fifteen-shot Henry repeating rifles. At Allatoona Pass, one of the Tenth Texas men apparently did not get mixed in with the retreating Yanks from the previous battle line because he had twenty-six holes bored in him and his clothes. The guy with the twenty-six holes must have decided he had seen all the Henry rifles he wanted to see because he captured a Yank horse and went home to Texas. Only after the loss of so many brave men did these tactics change. The Atlanta campaign saw the advent of trench warfare. The Battle of Richmond was the most complete victory the Tenth Texas participated in, more successful than Chickamauga because their losses were not as severe. The battle was also helpful to the Tenth Texas because it allowed the unit to arm itself with modern rifles captured from the Yankees.

The soldier continued his story about the trip and battle in Kentucky:

Just as we were opposite a brick store and doubtless a post office, as it was called Kingston, and nine miles from Richmond, in the midst of our observations and pleasant reasoning we were startled by the report of a cannon and then the unmistakable screech of a shell soon after we had left the pike and left-wheeled into one of the adjacent meadows. . . . We were soon moving by column across the beautiful blue-grass field, and upon reaching the top of the elevation and upon which our battery stood we could plainly see the Federals, who were in line ready to receive us. The order to charge being given, we made toward them in a double-quick. As we approached their line of battle the unmistakable "swish" of the Minie ball could be plainly heard, and every now and then a man of ours would go down. Moving either to the right or left, as the case might be, to close up the space occasioned by our men falling out, either by death or wounds, we thus kept our perfect alignment; and the nearer we approached them, the quicker and faster the shot and shell came. Our regular and steady approach under such a hot and continuous fusillade seemed to confuse the Federals, as they doubtless thought we should either stop or run from them. Remaining long enough to give us a volley or two, the Federals turned and fled; then it was that our battery that did good work. The country being nearly level, with nothing to obscure our vision, nearly every shot was effective.

The Federals, having relieved themselves of their blankets and extra luggage, left them all in a heap to one side, intending, it is supposed, to replace them as soon as they had driven us back; but as the result proved that we did the driving, and not stopping long enough to claim their baggage, it fell to us.

After driving the Federals some three or four miles they made another stand. When we came up to where they were, the order to charge was again given, they staying only long enough to give us a volley or two, when they precipitately and in great disorder retreated again. We killed, wounded, and captured a great many of them while they killed and wounded some of us. As fast as we could we followed them up. It was in the month of August and very hot. . . .

It must have been about three o'clock in the afternoon when the Federals made their third and last stand, the spot they had selected for that purpose being in the little cemetery just at the outskirts of the town of Richmond, Ky. They sheltered themselves behind the tombstones. We had to approach them through a field of corn which was very tall and in full ear and was enclosed by a high rail fence. Just beyond the cornfield and between the Federals and our troops was a beautiful grove with gentle declivity on each side. At the top of the other side was the cemetery, where the Federals were stationed. We moved in line of battle through the cornfield the sun shining in

29

full force and scaled the high fence about the grove where we found the trees very beneficial for shelter as we moved down the gentle slope. The Federals showed strong and stubborn resistance; but seeing that we steadily advanced toward them after giving us two or three rounds they broke into a deep run showing that they were in a wild and ungovernable panic. Then it was that we charged them with a double-quick killing, wounding, and capturing many of them. . . .

We pursued the flying Federals into and beyond the town of Richmond. . . . They had a great quantity of stores and munitions of war at this place, which seemed to have been a distributing bureau; and here I first saw how they were being fed — canned fruits of all kinds, condensed milk (the first I ever saw) cheese, and other edibles. They also had large quantities of clothing — shoes, hats, etc. all of which we put to good use. . . .

We were all nearly naked. The pants I wore (coat I had not) were made of some thin material and my canteen, haversack, and belt had worn holes on both sides and in a short time they would not have held together. I confiscated a pair of blue pants, a gray army shirt, a pair of excellent shoes, and hung my old ones out on a fence. In walking over the battlefield the next day I came across a wounded Federal who mistaking me for one of his comrades on account of my blue garb, asked me what command I belonged to and wished to confer with me in a confidential manner. This made me feel as if I were sailing under false colors, so when I returned to town I hung up my old breeches, which remained intact on the fence where I had left them. I felt much more comfortable both in body and mind, after I had made the last exchange and I laid the blue pants back where I had gotten them. A few weeks later my pants becoming so threadbare that it was not decent to wear them I had to apply to the quartermaster and from him purchased a pair of blue pants, the only kind he had and which were captured at Richmond. Thus was I forced to pay ten dollars for a pair of pants that I could have had three weeks before for nothing.

We remained in Richmond several days after the battle to bury the dead, see that the wounded were comfortable and properly cared for and gather together the captured supplies. We then moved on to Lexington some twenty miles distant. The day our army entered Lexington with Gen. Kirby Smith and staff riding at the head of the column, was truly a glorious jollification especially among those called Southern sympathizers and there was a considerable number of them in and around there. It reminded me very much of the description I have read of Washington's entry into Trenton, N.J. during the War of the Revolution as the ladies actually sprinkled flowers for General Smith to ride over.[3]

Major Redwine, Tenth Texas, was out front leading the charge riding on his $200 horse. After the battle, the government paid him the $200 the horse was worth since it was killed in action. Just prior to the opening of the battle, the company commanders of the Tenth Texas would have been giving the troops the standard instructions. Dress yourself (align) on the location of the flags, and most of all, they cautioned the men to not stop and render aid or assistance for their wounded comrades. Men were detailed to take care of the wounded and the best way to protect wounded friends was to drive the enemy from the field.

Pvt. James H. Harrison of Company C, Tenth Texas described an event that happened during the battle:

> I saw four or five men run behind a haystack and asked a comrade on my left if he saw them, and he said that he did, and that we would get them. We were running and at the same time loading our guns, stopping, and shooting. On reaching the haystack my comrade went around to the left and I to the right. I had discharged my gun just before reaching the stack and had reloaded but failed to put a cap on. A Yankee ran around on me and as I was not able to shoot, I caught the muzzle of my gun and let drive at him. He dodged and the gun struck the ground and broke off at the breech. When I struck at him and seeing my gun broken, I seized his with both hands. He could not shoot me, but we had it around and around until the other boys came up and captured him. He was a man who weighed 180 pounds, while I was a mere boy of eighteen years.[4]

J. M. Spinks of Company G, Tenth Texas related his action at Richmond:

> I cut my eyeteeth at Richmond, Ky., in 1862. The first time I shot I dropped on my knees to load, and my rear file rank man was shot through the heart. In our next engagement they shot in the muzzle of my gun. Caleb West, a citizen who was setting in a tree near by, told me that we fought forty-three minutes by his watch before we routed them. They were not more than seventy-five yards distant.[5]

One of the Texans, after driving the Yanks from their first position, leaned against a fence to rest before the second assault. A bullet hit the fence rail and ricocheted into the back of his neck. A buddy dug the bullet out, and it was back to the war. He said that on the second attack "there was a blue streak of dead and wounded men as far as you could see."[6]

J. W. Minick, Company B, Tenth Texas wrote a letter home describing the action at Richmond. The letter went on to tell his friend Bud he wanted to take him deer hunting when he returned. Apparently, after honing his skills shooting Yankees, he was ready to drop some deer:

> Nov. 26, 1862
>
> Bud, we have been up in Kentucky. There I saw the hardest times I ever saw in my life or ever want to see again. . . . The hardest days work ever went over my head was the 30th day of August. That was the day that we had the fight with the yanks. You ought to of seen them blue bellies bounce off of the ground. We found them twice that day and marched about 15 or 18 miles. Bud you ought to have been there to hear the bullets and cannon balls whistle over your head and under your feet on your left and on your right. We was in a ditch shooting when Tip got shot. I was right by his side when he got wounded. I had to go and leave him and never got to see him anymore. . . . But the first round or two I felt right bad, but after that I could take a good aim as ever I did at a deer and you know I have made some good shots. I don't know for certain whether I killed any one of them or not. There was so many shooting I could see them fall but I couldn't tell whether it was my bullet done the work for them or not.[7]

Minick went on to be wounded at Chickamauga and later was discharged for "turburcular deposit, right lung . . . debility and emaciation."

A Texan in the Eleventh Texas Cavalry Dismounted described the action. He referred to the brigade as Ector's. Ector was with the Fourteenth Texas and had not taken over yet. He said the Eleventh was the third regiment from the line. The Tenth Texas must have been the front regiment because, later, Littlejohn wrote that the Tenth suffered two-thirds of the casualties of the brigade:

> Late one evening we camped on a creek about twelve or fourteen miles from Richmond, and the next morning at sunrise we marched down the creek, crossing it, then, marching in column of fours we left the pike and marched through open woods at double quick. We were fired on by the Federal right wing, but our column never halted. We were ordered to "right oblique, double quick." The 11th

Texas was the third regiment from the front of Ector's Brigade, therefore we had to march rapidly to keep place with those in front. The Federals had formed their line of battle the evening before and had slept on their arms.

Our front engaged the enemy, first flanking their right wing, then broke their line and continued to press them and as our column continued to right oblique into line, the left of our regiment encountered the enemy first. They were continually flanked by our left reaching their rear and their entire line fell back rapidly. They could do nothing else; they had no time to reform their line, the confederates moved so rapidly.

The enemy in front of the 11th Texas then took position behind a stone fence. . . . The enemy could do nothing but retreat, being fired on enfilade and rear. They next took position in a fine country cemetery. Their reserves made a strong stand here being protected by the monuments and trees.

Our left, continuing to advance was soon in flank and rear of the cemetery and here the enemy lost all formality and a general rout ensued. It was no more a fight but a race between the Confederates and Federals and a good many would have gotten away, but Morgan's Cavalry closed in from the flanks and captured all the footmen. General Nelson was known by his people as "Bull" Nelson, because he had never before been whipped, he was a brave man and a good fighter. He was with his men trying to check our advance until all was lost. It was told at the time that his horse having been killed, he mounted a mule and escaped.[8]

Regulations defined a double quick march as 165 to 180 paces per minute.

Another soldier described how a good shot blocked the road used for the retreat:

So it went on until late in the evening, when our command moved to the rear of Richmond on the pike road toward Lexington and went into a cornfield and formed a line of battle. Every row went straight to the pike road and each man had a row to himself. Our company was on the left of the line. When we reached the fence the road was full of fleeing Yankee cavalry and one piece of artillery that had run the gauntlet. One of the boys on the extreme left of the company shot the lead horse through the neck and that blockaded the road so there was no more passing there. The driver on the lead horse was killed, mashed to death by the other horses. A brigade of infantry tried to escape but when they reached the ambush they threw down their arms and surrendered and were marched back to Richmond.[9]

Littlejohn gave his account of the action, his stomach problems, and his views:

Camp near Covington, Ky, September 14th, 1862
My Dear Wife and friend,
You doubtless will have heard of the fight at Richmond in which we were engaged. We left Louden, Tenn. 7th Aug. and started on an expedition we knew not whither. We marched day and night, all the way through Tenn. and crossed the Cumberland mountains. . . . We were bushwhacked by the citizens all the time; fortunately but one of our men got hurt. As we marched right through the southern part of Ky. We did not meet with many friends. But as we advanced farther into the state, the friends of secession became more numerous. But we began to hear of a Federal force ahead of us, and on the 30th Aug. early in the morning we came in hearing of heavy artillery firing. We quickened our pace, and soon we heard the small arms open. I knew then that the long expected moment was near at hand. We rushed on at double quick time, trying to flank them on the right. Gen. (Cleburne's) Brigade of Tenn. were pouring it to them on the left. They could not stand the fire and broke to run. Our brigade outflanked them and commenced firing on them as they run. They could not stand this and soon surrendered. Another part ran on farther and formed a line of battle behind a little hill. Our men advanced on them slowly until we came in sight of them. After the first engagement in the morning I took the diarrhea so that I could not keep up. We had to run so much and being unwell I gave out just before the second fight commenced. I was close behind when the firing began, and it was the most terrific I ever heard. The Feds fought bravely, but could not stand the charge of our boys, in which we took one battery. They ran then in every direction. The balls fell around me where I was sitting as thick as hail. In this engagement our company suffered severely, and in fact our whole regiment. . . . In the first charge in the morning our company lost one man killed and three wounded. In the second charge its loss was none killed and six wounded. Total ten lost in killed and wounded. I have since heard that Sam Spinks had died. He was wounded in the leg close to the body. He was not willing to have his leg taken off. I suppose it would have killed him anyhow. To show

how much our regiment suffered; out of seventy-five killed and wounded in our brigade, our regiment lost fifty-two. Two-thirds of the whole. Our whole loss is estimated at about 250 men. . . . After the fight we started to Covington which is on the opposite side of the river from Cincinnati. We passed through several towns of importance on our march, among which was Lexington. This is a fine place and the grandest display of secession feeling was made here I ever saw anywhere. The streets were thronged with men and women. We marched to within three miles of Covington, but owing to the superior numbers of the enemy we had to fall back a few miles. I think we will attack them in a few days as soon as our reinforcements come up. . . . The Kentuckians are volunteering rapidly.

Well Sallie, I can tell you that I have seen hard times now. I have lived eight days without tasting bread eating but roasting ears poor beef and apples and not half enough of that. But thanks to God I have stood it all very well. I have not been sick at all, only with the diarrhea which is very common in camp. . . . I remain your true and affectionate husband, E.G.L.

One of the wounded Texans had time to write a poem about the victory:

Early one morning in 1862
The gallant sons of Texas, with hearts brave and true,
Marched forth to meet the Yankees just at the break of day
On the green fields of Richmond in battle's dread array.

We marched along in silence until the sun arose;
We heard the boom of cannon alike of friends and foes;
We stopped awhile at Kingston, a village by the way,
To wait for further orders and listen to McCray.

Then we were ordered forward to turn the Yankees' right;
We marched through lane and cornfield until we came in sight;
We saw the broken columns — they had begun to flee
Away from our Southerners, the sons of Tennessee.

Then we were ordered to charge them, and they began to get
Away a little faster than we ever saw them yet.
They ran about two miles before they stopped to rest,
Then took a strong position, resolved to do their best.

There was no one to oppose them but our small brigade,
And yet we were undaunted, for no one was afraid,
Their Minie balls and bombshells incessantly did roar,
And many noble Texans there fell to rise no more.[10]

One factor that came into play during this battle was the relative distances between the battle lines and the Yanks firing a volley at the Rebs. It is estimated that on average it took twenty seconds to load, place a firing cap on a musket, and be ready to fire. With the battle lines at seventy-five yards or so, the Rebs could easily close to bayonet distance before the Yanks could reload. The only problem was that the men of the Tenth Texas carried mostly shotguns and squirrel guns. These were not equipped with bayonets. The Rebs had a saying that they did not need bayonets because they could not get a Yank to stand still while they stuck him. It wasn't manly to stick them in the back. The Rebs also did not like bayonets because, in the heat of battle while ramming home a charge in a rifle with a bayonet on it, the hand had a tendency to get stabbed by the bayonet while ramrodding the round into the barrel.

At the beginning of the war, most of the men of the Tenth Texas were additionally armed with large Bowie knives instead of bayonets. After walking hundreds of miles with the heavy knives, most of them were sold, traded, or thrown away.

Part of the twenty seconds it took to load a rifle (musket) was the process of tearing the twisted end of the cartridge off with the shooter's teeth. The cartridge was a tube of paper twisted on both ends with the powder and lead bullet inside. The soldier tore the paper with his teeth and, using the metal ramrod, drove the powder end first into the barrel. The powder inside the paper was ignited by the cap that was struck by the hammer of the gun. Some say that soldiers used to knock out their front teeth to get a transfer out of the infantry units. With no teeth, you could not tear the paper cartridge, so getting one's teeth knocked out was a good life insurance policy. The compiled personal records show numerous transfers from the Tenth Texas but none for lacking front teeth.

Artillery rounds used during the Civil War included two types of bursting shells: (1) fragmentation rounds that broke apart at the mouth of the barrel with multiple pieces flying out; and (2) shot that stayed intact and burst with a time fuse or a percussion fuse. The fragmentation round was called either a canister or grape. These were deadly up to two hundred yards. Early in the war, Rebel time fuses and artillery accuracy were defective because of poor grade powder. They also shot chains and nails at the Yanks.

Pvt. Henry Pool of Company K, Tenth Texas, shot in the hand in the battle, shared what happened when he walked into Richmond:

> Met a young man who said, "Ain't you a Texican?" I said, "Yes." And he said his mother and wife wanted to see a "Texican," and I went with him to the "Horse Block" in the front yard and the young man said, "Mother, here is a Texican." She commenced to undo my wounded hand, and told me that I must go home with her. I told her that I belonged to the doctor and then she had her son go with me to him and get permission for me to go. The old lady was eighty years old and had ridden six miles that day horseback. I liked the old lady because she was kind to me. I was a long way from my own mother. I stayed there six weeks and she made me a nice suit of clothes. I reported to the doctor once a week. I squirrel hunted and had a good time generally.[11]

Years after the battle some of the participants' comments are interesting. One Texan said, "We went in the Kentucky campaign with General Kirby Smith in which we met a Federal column commanded by General (Nelson) at Richmond, Ky. And gave them a genteel licking."[12]

Another Texan said in referring to General Smith: "With 6,000 men we whipped Bull Nelson at Richmond with 18,000 men. Out of thirty cannons we got twenty-nine of them, only leaving him one to salute his friends with when he got to Cincinnati, where we stopped running him."[13]

The Texans noted the Yankees had eighteen thousand men. The numbers are unclear. The Rebs captured ten thousand rifles. Nelson, in one report, says he had sixteen thousand men. Yankee General Manson contends the Feds only had sixty-five hundred men and they were "all new troops who had only been mustered into service for a few days."[14]

As listed in the casualty schedule that follows, the Tenth Texas suffered fifty-two casualties comprised of fourteen killed and thirty-eight wounded. Of the wounded, only eleven never returned to duty.

The following were the Tenth Texas casualties suffered at Richmond, Ky.:

Tenth Texas Cavalry
Killed at Richmond, Kentucky — 14 men

Company A	J.F. Yarbrough	
	J.W. Yarbrough	
	J. Bratcher	
Company B	J.C. Tritall	
	J. Belcher	
	W. Seltzler	
Company E	S. Berry	

Company F	B. Rowe	
	J. Reed	
Company G	J. Renfro	
Company H	W. Beaty	
	A. Belvin	
	C. Trammell	
Company K	T. Smith	

Tenth Texas Cavalry
Wounded at Richmond, Kentucky
Never Returned to Duty with Tenth Texas — 11 men

Company B	T.J. Moore	Shot through hips
Company C	J. Little	
	J. Montgomery	Shot in ankle
Company D	S. Burns	Very badly wounded
Company G	C. Reltig	Died 9/26/62
	S. Spinks	Died 9/5/62
	J. Tubbs	Right arm hit by rifle ball
Company H	B. Hardee	
Company I	M. Walker	Shot through thigh
Company K	J. Jarrett	Gunshot — fractured ulna
	J.H. Johnson	

Tenth Texas Cavalry
Prisoners of War
Captured in Kentucky or Left Sick — 27 Men
* Denotes never returned to duty with Tenth Texas — 15 men

Regimental Staff Surgeon	*C.C. Francis	
Company A	*J.R. Rowland	
	*W. Parker	Died 9/12/62, Covington, Ky.
Company B	J.S. Brown	
	*W.F. Hamilton	
	J. Johnson	
Company C	*S. Pierce	
Company D	*J. Bass	
	*S. Davis	Left sick at Cumberland Gap — died
	*M. Ellis	Left sick at Lexington, Ky. — died
	A. George	
	J. May	
	*J. Stellman	
Company E	*G. Berry	Left in Kentucky
	S. Buchanon	
	*J. Cunningham	Left in Kentucky
	J. Nelson	
	*R.F. Redwine	
Company G	*A. Martin	Left sick in Kentucky
Company H	H. Gibson	

	J. Gibson	
	J. Morris	
	*J. Wages	POW at Covington, Ky. — died
	J. Wise	
Company K	B. Dunn	
	J. Pool	
	*C. Lee	

While the Tenth Texas was fighting Yanks in Kentucky, back in Texas they were massacring the Yanks. Some unenlightened Texans formed the Texas Union Loyal League to protest the war. These Yank "wannabees" were promptly wiped out.

On October 7, General Bragg began to assemble troops at Perryville to fight the enemy troops. He had sixteen thousand troops to fight sixty thousand Yanks. At Versailles, Kentucky, the Tenth Texas was there with thirty-six thousand troops to fight twelve thousand Yanks. At 2:00 in the afternoon of October 8, Bragg attacked.

The Rebs broke the Yank line but Bragg decided that defeat was inevitable. The Rebs held the battlefield that night but later had to retreat. They realized how many enemy troops were involved. The Tenth Texas and the other Rebel troops missed the chance to thrash the twelve thousand Yanks at Versailles because Bragg ordered the retreat.

CHAPTER 5

"Fiendish propensities of the infuriated clan"

RETREAT OUT OF KENTUCKY
AND PREPARATIONS AROUND MURFREESBORO

T HE YANKEES, attempting to close the passes in the Cumberland
Mountains, forced the Confederates to rush their captured supplies and
troops to the mountains to get through before the closure of the passes. The
rapid march, after the movement across Tennessee and Kentucky, caused a
lot of men to physically fall out.[1] Many soldiers, sick and exhausted, were
captured. On the retreat out of Kentucky, fifteen thousand Rebels were
struck with typhoid, scurry, dysentery, and pneumonia. The Tenth Texas lost
twenty-seven more men in this manner. A few of them were later paroled and
rejoined the unit.

Littlejohn shared with his wife:

> Cumberland Gap, Ky., October 27th, 1862
> We came to the Gap about a week ago. . . . Our command has tra-
> versed the greater portion of middle Ky. We passed through the
> entire state from North to South, and visited all the principal towns
> and cities in that portion of the state. . . . After the battle of
> Perryville, it seems that a portion of Buell's forces were trying to get
> between us and the Gap; which would have been a fatal stroke to us,
> had it been accomplished, but our Generals were too smart for Mr.
> Buell; they defeated him at his own game, and we made a masterly
> retreat from the State. The reason why it would have been so detri-
> mental to us to have been cut off from the Gap is this: we had a very
> large train of wagons (about thirteen thousand five hundred) a great
> quantity of commissary stores, which we got in the state, and a vast
> amount of material for making clothes and some eight or ten thou-
> sand head of the finest beef cattle you ever saw in your life. I sup-
> pose, from what I have heard, that we got enough in the state to sup-
> port us through the winter. Now to have lost all this would have
> counted largely. We did not take all this from the enemy but bought
> them up at small prices.

In leaving the state, we left behind many noble and warm-hearted Kentuckians to suffer the malice and fiendish propensities of the infuriated clan that will follow us. I am firmly of the opinion that there are many zealous lovers of the Southern cause in Ky. who have been bowed down by oppression so long that they were almost afraid to make any demonstrations of joy. I saw some men and women so rejoiced that they even burst into tears and shouts. They felt like birds confined for a long time in a cage and then set free, by some friendly hand. They were the kindest people in the world to the soldiers. No matter what they had was not too good for the poor private. I ate several good dinners and breakfasts there, and got my canteen of milk nearly every time I would try. I recollect one Sabbath morning myself and Johnston (one of my mess) concluded to leave camps and see if we could not find some place where we could get dinner. We went about three miles from camps when we come to a common looking house. We went in and found a very old lady sitting alone reading her Bible. She was a true secessionist. She asked us to come in and sit awhile. We did so, and after sitting a few minutes, we inquired if we could get dinner with her; she said yes. After a while dinner was announced to be ready. We sat down to the table, and I can tell you, Sallie, I have not met with a better dinner, since I left home. It put me more in mind of eating with Aunt Caty than anything I have seen in a long time. The old lady after dinner gave us our canteens full of milk and as much butter as we could carry, and a handsome piece of lightbread. For all of this she would not have one cent. . . .

But on our retreat we saw hard times indeed. We marched day and night for two weeks, without scarcely anything to eat. . . . Well, after all our hard marching and fatigue we at last reached the noted and far-famed Cumberland Gap; we all looked for this place with great anxiety; for here we thought we would get something to eat and time to rest, as the wagons, once through the Gap was safe from the enemy. We have got to rest here about a week and plenty to eat part of the time. This Gap is a place of natural curiosity. It is a narrow pass in the mountains just wide enough for a wagon to pass, and about one-quarter of a mile in length. Along this pass on both sides are high points overlooking the surrounding country for some distance. Here five thousand men can guard this pass, against all the men that can come at them. Our division was fearful that it would be left here during the winter to guard the Gap, but we have heard this evening that we will go to Loudon. This would have been a desperate place to take up winter quarters. A snow fell here on the 25th about eight inches deep. One night when I went to sleep it was misting rain a little. I had no idea of such a thing taking place. But behold! When I awoke in the morning I was all covered up in snow. We had no tents and but mighty few blankets. It snowed the next day the hardest I ever saw. I tell you it seems mighty hard for men to have to suffer such things. We have to go about and pick up wood where we can. This is the deepest snow I have seen for several years. Sometimes I have a notion to leave them anyhow, and risk the consequences be what they may. But then again I think that won't do. It would be a stain upon my character forever. It seems very hard indeed for us not to have the privilege of returning home, when we only left home for six months. If they would let me come home only for a short time, so that I could make some arrangements about my little affairs, I would not think so hard of returning. A good many of our boys say they intend to come home anyhow. We have never drawn any money yet, but they keep us in spirits by telling us that we will draw in a few days. But we have been fooled so much and I don't believe anything they tell us. E.G.L.

On October 27, Pvt. Gilbert Leroy, of Company C, apparently decided all the traveling was too much for him. He was declared disabled. He was fifty-two years old. On November 3, the Tenth Texas had made it back to Loudon, Tennessee.

November 8 was payday! Littlejohn drew $191, which was six months wages, a fifty dollar bounty, and twenty-five dollars for clothes:

Today our company is drawing clothing. I don't think I shall draw any this time. When I went to Knoxville I bought me a shirt and vest. I think I can make out this winter if I can get a pair of pants. Clothing is extremely high. Coarse, kersey pants sell for $15.00, shirts from six to fifteen dollars. I got me a hickory shirt for six dollars, and a jeans vest for five. . . . I have got none of the clothing or anything else that I brought from home except my coat, woolen pants that you made, and old shirt, etc. I bought me a pair of splendid boots in Kentucky for six dollars. I think they will last me all the winter. Goods were cheaper in Ky. than they are here. We could buy soda for ten cents a lb. there, where we have to pay three dollars. So from this you may form some idea of the prices of goods. Benton had an overcoat which I will wear myself. So I think I can make out very well for this winter. Next spring if you should hear of anyone coming to us, you might send me a pair of cotton pants, shirt, drawers, etc. if I am alive. But the difficulty is you cannot get cards. If I had a chance of sending you a pair, I would do so. They can be bought for $15.00. This looks very high indeed. But it is better than to do without them entirely.

Sallie, I wish you and the girls were here to help us to eat apples. There is the greatest abundance of apples in this country. They are selling very high as well as everything else. Fifty cents a dozen is the price of them. Some are cheaper. On our march through Ky., I lived on apples nearly altogether. We had some of the finest you ever saw.

Some of the boys tried to buy a hog and they asked him eighteen cents a pound. Bacon, forty cents. Butter is worth one dollar and fifty cents a lb. in Knoxville. Does not this look like exorbitant prices? Soldiers are such blockheads that they will pay any price for anything they take a notion to.

I must begin to come to a close. I will send $20.00 by Lieut. Trammel for him to get you a pair of cards. . . . I remain your most affectionate husband, E. G. Littlejohn.

When the letter mentioned buying "cards," Littlejohn was referring to "cotton cards" used to comb cotton fiber. After the Federal blockade, the women of the South had to make all their cloth, and cotton cards were essential. Naturally, the prices went sky high. The state of Texas actually took over the rationing of cotton cards and sent so many to each county.[2]

On November 17, 1862, Colonel Earp and an officer from each company (Trammel) left for Texas to get clothing for the men. The Confederate-issue clothing was in bad condition.

Around this time, Col. Matthew D. Ector, the commander of the Fourteenth Texas Cavalry Dismounted, was promoted to command the Brigade.[3] Until the end of the war, the Brigade that included the Tenth Texas was always called Ector's Brigade, even after Ector lost his leg at Atlanta and was replaced as commander. It should be noted that Ector County, Texas (Odessa as county seat) was named for the general.

On November 20, 1862, the Army of Tennessee was organized. It was formed by combining Gen. Kirby Smith's Army of Kentucky with General Bragg's Army of Mississippi. General Bragg was in command. General Bragg then decided to attack into middle Tennessee and proceeded to move the Army to Murfreesboro. This was going to give the Tenth Texas another opportunity to run some Yanks.

On December 4, men from the Tenth Texas were rebuilding a railroad bridge on the Tennessee River. On December 6, the Tenth Texas was at Camp

Reederville, Tennessee, located about fifteen miles east of Murfreesboro. On December 23, 1862, while still at Camp Reederville, Tennessee, Littlejohn sent home a letter that contained the following:

> In the early part of the day, we had company and regimental drill. Gen. Ector drilled us awhile and also Maj. Gen. McCown. We are drilled about four or five hours each day, except Sunday. We are allowed one day out of every week to wash in. I am a poor hand to wash, but sometimes I have it to do. I washed yesterday two shirts and a pr. drawers. I would always prefer to hire my washing done if I could get out to do it; but they don't allow us to leave camps. They charge two bits a garment, that is mighty high. Two young men started home yesterday. They live close to Jimtown. Their names are Harden and Reynolds. I would have sent you a letter by them, but I was on picket guard Sunday and did not have time to write. . . .
>
> Enclosed you will find a plug that came out of one of my teeth. I send it home for you to take care of until I return, if ever I do. . . . E.G.L.

Littlejohn cited Harden and Reynolds as two young men leaving for home on December 22, 1862. The only Reynolds that served with the Tenth Texas was killed at Murfreesboro only nine days later. He was only nineteen. T.H. Harden was killed at Murfreesboro. He was just eighteen years old. Apparently, the two young men were stopped and sent back to fight the pending battle. Reynolds made the Confederate Roll of Honor for his actions on December 31, 1862.[4]

Brig. Gen. Matthew D. Ector.
The Tenth Texas served in Ector's Brigade
nearly the entire Civil War

CHAPTER 6

"Killed still holding firmly to his pot of coffee"

BATTLE OF MURFREESBORO

AS THE ARMY of Tennessee moved into position for the big battle at Murfreesboro, the privates observed the officers with interest:

It was Christmas. John Barleycorn was general-in-chief. Our generals, and colonels, and captains had kissed John a little too often. They couldn't see straight. It was said to be buckeye whiskey. They couldn't tell our own men from Yankees. The private could, but he was no general, you see. But here they were — the Yankees — a battle had to be fought.[1]

Another soldier contrasted the large party on Christmas Eve and the executions on Christmas day:

On Christmas Eve the officers gave a ball at the courthouse in Murfreesboro, which proved a magnificent affair. The beauty and the fashion of Middle Tennessee and many distinguished Confederate officers were present. The decorations were handsome. How well I remember them, although but a tiny lad, doing service in General Bragg's escort. . . . Among the decorations on the walls I noticed four large "B's" constructed of cedar and evergreens — Beauregard, Bragg, Buckner, and Breckinridge. . . . Conspicuous in the hall were numerous captured United States flags, with the union down, the starry field reversed — trophies belonging to Gen. John H. Morgan, and furnished for the occasion by his newly made bride, the beautiful Miss Mattie Ready.

In what strong contrast there comes the announcement of five military executions the next day — one by hanging and the rest by shooting! The first was a spy, a traitor, and a thief named Gray. The crime charged to the other four was desertion. Never will I forget the horrible execution of a young Kentucky soldier, whose officers the night before had given the ball in the Murfreesboro courthouse. His home was in Barren County, Ky., near Glasgow, and his family were noted for their wealth, culture, and high social standing. His mother, a widow in affluent circumstances, doted on this boy with all the inexpressible love and tenderness that fills a true mother's heart, and he was the idol of her life. During the famous raid made by General Bragg's army into Kentucky the young man, on furlough, went to his home and remained with his mother several weeks. When Bragg returned from the section, he rejoined his command, and was accounted by all his comrades a brave and dutiful soldier. Shortly after the Confederate army reached Murfreesboro he received intelligence that the enraged Federals had set fire to his mother's house, destroyed her beautiful homestead, and turned her out upon the cold charities of a pitiless world. He at once went to the colonel of his regiment and requested leave of absence to go to his mother and have her comfortably placed, promising to return in thirty days and rejoin his comrades. It being on the eve of battle, his colonel refused to recommend his application. Next he went to the brigade commander, then to the division general, and finally to General Bragg himself. His efforts were fruitless. Turning from General Bragg with flushed face and hot rebellion in his heart, he exclaimed through clinched teeth: "I will go, General Bragg, if you have me hanged for it."

This act of mutiny and insubordination greatly enraged the sternest disciplinarian of the Confederacy; and calling the guard, General Bragg at once ordered the young man's arrest and had him sent to the guardhouse, manacled with ball and chain. Two nights after the prisoner made his escape, and set out on foot for his Kentucky home. A squad of cavalry was sent in pursuit, and overtook him just as he had crossed the Tennessee boundary line near Scottsville. He was brought back, tried by court-martial, and condemned to be shot. Christmas day at 12 o'clock the order was carried into effect. The Kentucky brigade was marched to an open field and drawn up in line forming three sides of the hollow square. The day was dismal, and the very elements seemed to share in gloomy sympathy the sad hearts of the whole army of Confederates. As noon approached the clouds grew dark and heavy. The troops stood there in one of the heaviest rainstorms I ever remember until the prisoner was brought out into the center of the square, riding in a wagon seated on his coffin and followed by a hearse.

After bidding a few friends farewell, without kneeling or being blindfolded, the brave young fellow with firm step advanced and faced the executioners.

At 12 o'clock precisely the lieutenant's voice rang out clear and sharp with the awful command: "Ready, aim, fire!" The volley was deafening. The prisoner fell back dead, pierced by eleven balls. He had paid the penalty of military insubordination. His debt of love to his mother was washed away in the heart's blood of a hero.

General Breckinridge protested against the execution, and the whole army was in mutinous state. The Tennesseeans swearing vengeance if one of the 25th Tennessee was executed, and the Alabamians claimed exemption for one of their number. Bragg in despair, unable to quell the storm he had raised, applied to President Davis. By what means Mr. Davis did this is not known, but the Kentuckian and the Alabamian were executed, the Tennessee soldier was pardoned. General Bragg afterwards most rigidly enforced the death penalty for deserters; but never in the history of the Army of Tennessee was there a sadder scene than the death of young Lewis at Murfreesboro on Christmas day in 1862.[2]

While the Tenth Texas celebrated Christmas in Tennessee they learned of the early revelry back home. In October near Gainesville, Texas, a tree was decked out with many "ornaments." The "ornaments" happened to be thirty-two Peace Party members. Texans dispensed with peace protesters quickly.

General Bragg, in order to restore discipline, was a firm believer in execution for desertion. Executions made a lasting impression on the troops when they were forced to witness the event. The fear of being caught and executed made many men think twice before going AWOL.

During this turmoil, the armies were set for a full-scale encounter. The battle of Murfreesboro was a two-day battle that took place over three days. On December 30, 1862, the armies began their clash when artillery opened from each side. The Yanks made a limited attack the first day. At daybreak on December 31, the Tenth Texas smashed into the right flank of the Yank lines just as they had at Richmond, Ky. By the end of the second day, they had driven the Yanks over three miles. The Rebs remained stationary on January 1, 1863, assuming the battle was won. On the contrary, the enemy was not retreating as first thought and the Rebs attacked again on January 2. They were cut to pieces by the superior Yank artillery. On January 3, the situation was once again static; however, that night, Bragg was forced to retreat because of Federal reinforcements. This was the only time the Tenth Texas fought while in a total Texas Brigade that was commanded by a Texan.

The official report of Colonel Locke gave a good summary of the action. He wrote:

On Tuesday evening, [December] 30, [1862] while our battery and that of the enemy were firing directly across the right wing of my regiment, a ball from a rifle cannon of the enemy struck the cedar-rail barricade in front of the command, and timber from the fence bruised four of the privates and slightly wounded Lt. J.B. Griffin, of Company C, who was severely [wounded] the following day. Seeing that the situation of the Tenth Regiment was more exposed than that of any other in the brigade on that evening, owing to the facts that a gap of several hundred yards intervened between the right wing (this regiment being on the right of the brigade) and the next command, on our right, and that powerful efforts were being made by the enemy on that evening to gain a direct range of the line of the Texas Brigade with their artillery, and late in the day the enemy having shifted their position and placed their battery directly in front of this regiment, it was apparent that the fence which had obstructed the sight of the enemy would serve as an auxiliary in the enemy's hands if our position was discovered. Knowing this, although the weather was very inclement and disagreeable, I did not allow any fire, and the blankets having been left at camp, the men suffered very much; and but for the fact that they had been lying on their arms without sleep for two nights previous, sleep would have been impossible.

Having been kept in a silent, still position for two days and nights during disagreeable weather, on the morning of December 31, 1862, when orders came that the command would move forward, it was difficult to restrain the expression of joy and outburst of feeling manifested by the men at an opportunity being presented upon an open field (such as lay before us) of relieving ourselves from this unhappy condition, and of deciding the fate of the Confederacy to the extent that a little regiment was able to go. It will be remembered that, in the first charge made on the morning of the 31st, my orders required that I should keep close on General McNair's brigade, who had just moved into the gap alluded to on the right of my regiment, and that in doing so it threw the center of the Tenth Regiment directly in front of the enemy's battery, consisting of six brass pieces of superior quality, which opened upon our lines immediately after leaving the cedar fence barricade; and as there was no obstruction between this command and the enemy's lines in that direction, it must be that the houses, shade trees, and fencing on the left and the cedar timber and fencing on the right sheltered to some extent the brave troops on each side of us, causing the disparity in the number killed and wounded in the different regiments of the division and brigade. For some 400 yards before we drove the enemy from their position immediately in rear of the first battery and captured the same, my regiment marched in full view of the infantry and artillery, and before the sun rose we numbered of killed and wounded some 80 men.

At this point I will mention an incident in this bloody conflict: The enemy's lines having been formed immediately in our front, their standard-bearer, directly in front of mine, was waving his flag, casting it forward, and, by various motions, urging the Abolition column forward, when Sergt. A. Sims, flag-bearer of this regiment, discovered him and pressed forward with incredible speed directly toward the enemy's banner, and, on reaching within a pace or less of his adversary, he planted the Confederate flag firmly upon the ground with one hand and with a manly grasp reached the other after the flag-staff held by his enemy; but the other gave back, and in that moment they both fell in the agonies of death, waving their banners above their heads until their last expiring moments. My flag-bearer having fallen, and there being but one of my old color-guard left, Sergt. James T. McGee was only spared to advance a few paces toward his banner, when another of our noblest and bravest men fell to rise no more until aroused by the Trump of God to come to judgment. At this moment Private Manning, of Company H, gathered the flag-staff and rushed to the front with a spirit and nerve sufficient for any calling, and bore the same aloft throughout the day.

Two stands of colors are known to have been taken by this regiment, and, it is believed three; but as all were sent to the rear by the wounded and the infirmary corps, I have not had opportunity to look them up.

The loss sustained by this command will foot up as follows, to wit: The number of comm[issioned officers] engaged was 20, and of that number 11 were killed, wounded, or left in the enemy's lines. The total number in battle was about 350 men. Of that number 117 were either left in the enemy's lines, killed, or wounded.

As stated, we captured, it is confidently believed, three stand of the enemy's colors and at least six pieces of brass cannon (the colors of the Thirty-fourth Illinois were captured by this regiment).

All of which is most respectfully submitted, M.F. Locke.

General Ector, in his official report, stated that the Tenth Texas captured three stand of colors.

Pvt. P. R. Jones, of Company I, Tenth Texas, vividly described the action at Murfreesboro. He was careful to note that they did not drink whiskey to inspire courage:

About midnight of December 28, the entire command, consisting of one division at Readyville, was ordered out of their tents to march at once to Murfreesboro. Leaving a detail behind to look after camp equipage, we stuck the road, but on account of the continued cold rain falling, making the roads extremely muddy and almost impassable in places, we did not get there until about daylight. Here, in the suburbs near the railroad depot, we built fires and dried our clothing and guns as best we could. In the meanwhile the enemy was just beyond Stone's River in full force, attempting to cross. We could distinctly hear the rattle of musketry as well as cannon, which plainly foretold that we were up against a real battle. General Bragg had his lines well established. . . . The entire battle line was said to be about four miles in length. . . .

The two armies were now getting close to each other with their lines of infantry, the Federal, commanded by General Rosecrans, doing most of the advancing. On the 30th we maneuvered for position, and when nightfall came were in a line with rail fences on each side, about four hundred yards from the main line of this enemy. Orders were to speak only in a whisper, as the enemy's pickets were not more than one hundred yards in front, the plan of battle being to take them by surprise next morning.

We took down one of the lines of fence and spread the rails out over the ground next to the opposite string, which was left for breastworks. On the rails we passed the night without fires, most of the men sitting down watching the camp fires of the enemy some four hundred yards away, on an elevation. They were apparently ignorant of our being so close. We passed a most disagreeable night, having been on the battle field all of the night before and at times pelted with heavy showers during the 30th. I fortunately had a good wool blanket that I had brought from home, one of the old-fashioned kind, with a hole in the middle large enough for a man's head. I stuck my head through, pulled my hat down, took my loaded gun under the blanket, and thought of what would take place tomorrow.

Just before daybreak, General McNair brought his Arkansas brigade and placed it on our immediate right to fill up a gap, which appeared to complete all arrangements for the attack. At this juncture some whiskey was passed down the line, of which more than half of my company did not drink a drop, but others imbibed freely. It was not given to the soldiers to inspire courage, but to warm them up after their long exposure to the rain and cold weather.

Just about fairly good daylight, orders were given to move forward. The boys went over the rail fence and soon encountered the enemy's pickets, driving them back into their camps, which were well lit up with fires, around which they were cooking breakfast. Many were still in their "pup" tents asleep and were killed while lying there. The onslaught was so sudden and the slaughter so great that they retreated in great confusion, every fellow for himself and the devil take the hindmost. In going through their camps we noticed that they had abandoned everything in order to get away. I noticed one of their dead some two hundred yards to their rear who had been killed still holding firmly to his pot of coffee.

There was a battery or two some distance in the rear of their camp that turned loose on us about this time and killed a number of our men. It was here that our company had its first men killed. Joe Reynolds, whose widowed mother lived down about Pinetown, was the first to fall. . . . We had by this time become badly scattered, every fellow being his own general, keeping up a running fight for two and one-half miles to the cedar brake.

I fell in with Adjutant Sparks of my regiment soon after we became scattered, and, coming to a log pen in a cotton patch that appeared to have about sufficient seed cotton in it to make two bales, noticed that the top of the pile had been lately disturbed. Thinking there might be some Yankees hid there, Sparks picked up a stick (we had no matches) and remarked: "I will just strike a match and set this cotton on fire." With this he scratched his stick across the door, when lo and behold, eight Yankees jumped out of the cotton and raised their hands in token of surrender. By this time quite a number of our men overtook us and joined in the pursuit. We turned our prisoners over to some of our men, who carried them to the rear.

We continued in pursuit quite a distance from the cotton pen and ran up on a line of the enemy that looked like a brigade lying down on the crest of a ridge, doubtless expecting our men to run on them and be taken by surprise. But in this they were mistaken, for, while only their heads were visible, we took the drop on them by firing first, killing about half, the rest jumping up and running at full speed to their rear and disappearing in a dense cedar brake. We followed on through this cedar brake, which proved to be well known as the turning point of the battle. The cedars were very dense, making it difficult to keep an alignment while going through to open ground on the opposite side. Those who got

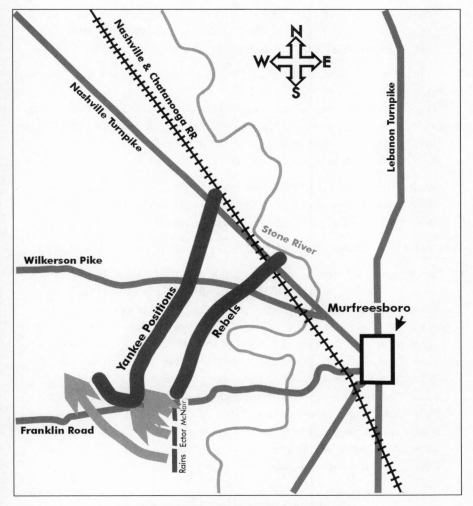

THE BATTLE OF MURFREESBORO
10th Texas was on right flank of Ector's Brigade.
Positions at start of the battle, Dec 30 to Jan 2, 1863.

through were met with such a volley of grape and canister from about forty cannon that had been hurriedly placed there by General Rosecrans that they beat a retreat back through the dense cedars as best they could, greatly demoralized. Ector's Brigade had several men captured among the cedars, among them two from my company. . . . Those of us who got back to an opening were greatly demoralized. The cannonading from so many cannon all at once appeared to completely demoralize the men. Littleton Fowler took refuge among these cedars behind some rocks and said that the cannonading was so terrific that he could have caught birds that were so benumbed they could not fly.[3]

The author of the above, Pinkney R. Jones, was wounded at Allatoona, Georgia, where his fighting days ended.

The Tenth Texas struck Kirk's Brigade first, and the Yanks had Willick's Brigade on its right but at a right angle, allowing the Rebs to charge down the flank of Willick's Brigade. Absolute panic ensued.[4]

Another Texan told of an incident prior to an attack:

At this time a rabbit jumped up, when Joe Russel of Collin County, Texas, saluted it as it ran off, and said: "Go it, cottontail! If I had no more at stake than you, I would be leaving too."[5]

Pvt. W. T. Coker, Company K, Tenth Texas, was also in the thick of things:

At the battle of Murfreesboro we made our first charge before sunrise; the man on my left and the man on my right were both killed. The charge surprised the enemy, and we captured twenty-four pieces of artillery and about 600 men. While following the retreating foe, my comrade in arms for the day and myself captured two artillerymen. The enemy made a stand near the creek, and were supported by sixty pieces of artillery, which mowed great gaps through our lines, causing us to retreat. When our command began the retreat, Sam Birdwell and I were so busy firing on the foe from behind a clay bank that we were left behind, and when we discovered the mistake we made the run of our lives, thinking that we would certainly be killed, but we escaped without a scratch.[6]

W.T. Coker's war ended at Chickamauga when he was taken prisoner. Sam Birdwell's war ended at Allatoona when he was wounded.

The Tenth Texas referred to the last charge of the day as the "Cedar Brake Charge." They refer to the Yanks' artillery as "masked," which meant the artillery was hidden across a clearing behind the cedar trees. Seemingly, the Yanks knew the trees would hinder the unit charge and only scattered groups clustered together would be able to make it through. This situation allowed the cannon, loaded with canister rounds, to blow away the small groups of men emerging from the trees.

To add to the problems, fire broke out in the cedar brake. Both the Yank and Reb wounded had to be moved during the midst of cannon fire. Chaos reigned, and one of the Yanks stated that the Tenth Texas drug the Yanks' flag through the mud. The Tenth Texas captured three flags, one being the flag of the Thirty-fourth Illinois.

A soldier from the Thirty-fourth Illinois wrote that they poured volley after volley into the Texans but nothing could stop them. A Yank artillery battery fired canister rounds into the melee. The Texans fired one volley into the artillery as the artillery men attempted to attach their horses to the guns, killing seventy-five horses. The Texans captured the artillery while the surviving Yanks ran for their lives. The soldier went on to write that the Thirty-fourth Illinois had five flag bearers shot down in quick succession with all the color guard killed or wounded. He witnessed the Tenth Texas capturing their flag and then dragging it through the mud.[7]

The Tenth Texas and the other units on the Confederate left by noon had driven the right side of the Yankee line back so that it was hook-shaped instead of a straight line. Bragg was on the verge of a great victory, but for reasons unknown, he was slow drawing troops from his right to help the Tenth Texas and related units. The Yanks easily moved soldiers around to reinforce the line and stop the push to collapse their entire line.

Littlejohn's letter portrayed his part in the battle:

Knoxville, Tenn., Jan. 12th, 1863

My Dear Wife and Friends,
This is Sunday morning and I feel like it was my duty to inform you all of my situation and condition, though I do not doubt that you will hear that I am wounded before this gets to you, as the other boys from the vicinity have been writing back to their friends. . . . We lay in sight of the Yankee camp fires. We soon came in sight of their skirmishers. The order to charge came down the lines with electric speed and onward we went dashing with a furious yell, against their well formed lines. They stood but a moment, and then they fled in disorder. But as they were running, they did not forget to shoot. I had shot my gun once, loaded again and was in a few steps of the spot where we took their flag, a minnie ball hit me on the right hip

bone, and I think scaled off a little piece of the bone. The ball passed out through the fleshy part of my thigh behind. It is not a serious wound, but I assure you it hurt very badly. But while I was laying on the ground, not being able to get away by myself, a canister shot from our own guns hit me on the top of the head. I thought then I was gone, yet I was perfectly conscious of everything that was transpiring. I still continued to lie on the ground until our boys had driven them out of hearing. By that time I tried to scramble off. One of our regt. who was not hurt, assisted me part of the way, and then I met a litter. On this they took me to a house close by. I staid here all night until the next evening. I was then carried to a hospital where I staid three days, and then moved to this place. I suffered a good deal while on the cars. We were two days and nights in coming from Murfreesboro to Chattanooga. I am at a very good hospital. . . . I have written to Pa the other day to come to see me and bring me some clothes. I lost all I had on the battlefield. If they will give me a furlough I am going home with Pa, if he comes. I think I will be able to hobble about on crutches in a week or two. . . . I remain your most affection Husband, E. G. Littlejohn

P.S. Jeff Rosson was shot in the arm but not badly. E.G.L.

Pvt. Henry Watson, relived the battle and informed loved ones of his health:

Jan. the 2nd. 1863
Camp near Shelbyville Tenn.

Dear Father and Mother,

I once more take my pen in hand to inform you that I am well at present and the health of the company is tolerable good at present. We had a little fight near Murfreesboro Tenn. on the 31st day of Dec. On the 30th it commenced about 10 o'clock in the morning and the pickets fought until night. We lay there behind a fence in the distance of about three hundred yards of the yankees until morning. About daylight next morning we was ordered to advance on them and we got over the fence and marched slowly along for about one hundred and fifty yards. And the yanks begun to fire on us, they were lying down when they began to fire on us. We was ordered to charge them and when we received the orders the boys raised the yell and started and when we got within about one hundred yards of them they rise a running about the time they started to run the minnie balls came apparently thick as ever I saw hail fall in my life, but we soon routed them and drove them back about two miles and they took another stand and they fought us there the balance of the day. Our brigade and one of the Arkansas Brigades charged some of their Artillery and did not succeed in taking it and, there was so strongly fortified that we had to fall back. . . . We killed two Brigadier Gens and one Maj. General. I have told you all that I know about the battle I came through the fight safe and sound without a scratch of a ball.

Thomas Sparkman is about to get a discharge he has had small pox but he is well now but he never will have the use of his hand any more, that was shot. The small pox is a getting very numerous in our hospitals but our Regiment has very near all been vaxinated. I have been vaxinated in both arms and it taken very well.

Col. Craig is a going to start home in a few days he was slightly wounded in the arm and he will get a furlow. I want to see you all very much but I do not see much probably of every getting to come home until the war ends. Henry Watson

A Texan from Ector's Brigade gave his insight about the action at Murfreesboro:

When we struck their skirmish line in the open field, we drove them back on their main line before they knew it. My regiment confronted a battery of six guns, I think, but they fired only two or three shots with artillery until we were among them. Many of the Yanks were either killed or retreated in their nightclothes. We pursued them with the Rebel yell. In advancing we found a caisson with the horses attached lodged against a tree and other evidences of their confusion. The Yanks tried to make a stand whenever they could find shelter of any kind. All along our route we captured prisoners who would take refuge behind houses, fences, logs, cedar bushes, and in ravines. We drove them helter-skelter for about three miles when we halted to re-form our lines and rest a few minutes.

After resting a few minutes we sent forward a line of skirmishes and then followed in line of battle. We encountered the enemy at the edge of the cedar brake. The ground was level, but overspread with large lime rocks with many lime sinks from a foot to two or three deep. The timber was principally cedar, interspersed with large white oaks and other trees. For some distance we drove them, as we had been doing; but about this time the artillery opened on us and cut the timber off over our heads and it seemed that the heavens and the earth were coming together. Our men sheltered themselves as best they could behind trees, ledges of rocks, etc. Their front of battle (for they had several lines) seemed to take fresh courage and began to advance upon us walking a few steps then firing and falling down to load.

In this critical situation we having only one line and the men badly scattered, I began to look around for a superior officer to advise with; but there was not one in sight. Very soon, however, I saw Colonel Andrews, of the 32nd Texas of our brigade, coming down the line from the right running from one large tree to another waving his hand to the rear which I knew meant retreat, which command was passed down the line. A retreat just then was as dangerous as an advance but was our only salvation from death or capture; so we retreated out of the cedars and across the open field, where we again re-formed our lines. We left several officers and many good men in that cedar brake, many of them killed and wounded and some captured. Other troops took our place in front of the cedar brake, and my brigade moved some distance to the right.

As it was now night, we bivouacked in line of battle after sending forward a strong skirmish line. The dead and wounded were thick all around us. It happened that there was a large lime sink four or five feet deep where my company was stationed. This afforded protection from the wind, which was very cold and we built little fires in there as they could not be seen by the enemy. Among the wounded we put in our resort was a Yank quite young and intelligent, shot centrally through the breast with a minnie ball. We divided water and rations with him, and next morning our young Yank, with assistance to rise could sit up awhile. We moved from that position and our skirmishers were constantly engaged; but we were not in any other general engagement till General Bragg retreated, my division going to Shelbyville.[8]

Another Texan in Ector's Brigade wrote not only of the battle, but also of his complaints about Confederate currency:

The command was given to go forward. Then you ought to seen the boys step off a quick time. Soon the bluebirds were seen then the order rang down the lines to charge. Then the most maddening shouts rang out from one end of the line to the other and away they went at breakneck speed. The terrified Yankees fled in the wildest confusion but not without giving us volley and volley. . . . Then they scattered every man for himself throwing their knapsacks guns and cartridge boxes to the four winds. Still they was closely pursued by our brave boys their maddening shouts making the morning ring with the most deafening peals until our brigade had captured sixteen pieces of artillery and a great many prisoners chasing the enemy some four or five miles. Then we was halted and flanked to the right. Some we came near to them or rather some more of them again. Still our columns moved on steadily driving their pickets before us until we came in sight of their lines. Then we charged again, but without the same success as before for it was masked batteries and masked columns of infantry that we were charging and they turned a most terrific fire upon us, and we had to retire in the face of their guns. Shot and shell as thick as hail fell around us but without causing us much loss of life. Thus ended the bloodiest part of the encounter.

I guess I have written all that could interest you much but as the state of feeling in this vicinity among citizens might please you, I will say a few things. I believe they are either pig or pup. When the Feds come along, they are good Union men, and when we come along, they are good Confederates, but there is things that proves conclusively to my mind that they do not place much confidence in the Confederate government, or in Confederate money, at least. For what you could buy for four bits in silver or the State Bank of Tennessee it takes about five dollars in Confederate money to buy. For instance, whiskey is worth $50 per gallon Confederate money, while you buy it from $3 to $4 in specie, and numbers boldly declare their attachment for the Union.[9]

A Yankee on the receiving end of the Rebel charges was told "to fight till Hell froze over." He also described the attitude of some Rebel prisoners:

By direction of Brig. Gen. John Beatty this writer fixed the line to receive and repel if possible the advancing Confederate line. Returning and reporting to General Beatty the brigade commander Major General Rousseau made the order to General Beatty, "Hold this position till h___ freezes over." And dashed off. . . . In his book of memoranda General Beatty wrote of this and said: "Concluding that hell had about frozen over, I about faced my brigade."

About ten o'clock on December 31, 1862, the Confederates uncovered from the cedar woods by three distinct lines visible for the charge. Never did troops move or drill more steadily than these men. Our artillery was supported well and amply by infantry, with cavalry on the right flank. When at close artillery range, the order to fire was given. The lanyards of thirty pieces struck and the deadly contents rained onto the Confederate ranks, almost entirely decimating or mowing down the advancing line. But another and yet another pressed forward until within short rifle range of our line. Under the smoke and underbrush forty or fifty Confederate privates throwing down their arms, crawled on hands and knees, surrendering as prisoners of war. By the line officer, to whom the surrender was made, they were turned over to this writer, whose duty as brigade inspector it was to turn them over to the provost marshal. A more forlorn, worn-out, and famished set of men would be hard to find. I said: "Boys, you are worn and hungry?" "Yes, on duty fighting or otherwise twenty-four hours, with little to eat." "Well, you must be fed," I replied. So marching to commissary headquarters, they were fed. Now comes a little fun I enjoyed greatly.

Provost headquarters lay in the direction of the front center, and there was fighting all along the line. Almost always in closely contested battles there are stragglers, full of pluck, out of range. Passing near a group, a voice rang out tantalizing: "Hello, Johnny Reb, where are you going?" "Down to the front, where you're afraid to go, d___ you," was the reply. "Just right, hit him again." I said, indulging a hearty laugh, in which all the "boys in gray" joined. "He who laughs last laughs best."[10]

Private Templeton told his father about the battle while he was assigned to the supporting artillery unit:

Camp Near Shelbyville, Bedford County, Tenn.
January 9, 1863

I am now with Capt. Good's old battery, commanded by Capt. Douglas, as a detail. I would not change for anything, as artillery service is much easier than infantry or cavalry. . . .

The battery was placed back in the reserve, and did nothing the first day, but about eight o'clock on the 31st we were ordered out, and were soon against a brigade of live Yankees. I thought we were going to be charged, as they were in less than one hundred yards of us, advancing and not a gun unlimbered. As soon as we got our guns ready they took to their heels, but our canister shot overtook a good many of them. We drove them away from a splendid battery of six or eight guns, which our brigade captured, but they got on our flank and recovered it. We were then placed on the extreme left wing. Our division came on them while they were preparing breakfast. The coffeepots and frying pans were on the fires steaming as we went through their camp. Our prisoners said that the First Ohio never ran before that morning.

Adjt. Jarvis and Lieut. Col. Craig were wounded slightly. Our men charged a cedar brake and failed, because the enemy had masked a battery.[11]

The First Ohio that Templeton referred to was the First Ohio Light Artillery, which the Tenth Texas overran, capturing its cannons. It is probable this unit's flag was one of the three captured by the Tenth Texas.

Being in an artillery unit at Murfreesboro was not the safest job around. This soldier clarified the hazards:

Instruction had been given the artillery not to open fire in response to any artillery shots directed against them, but to remain quiet as a masked battery and use the guns only in repelling an assault upon the position by an infantry charge. Occasionally some officer commanding a Federal battery, in line across the open fields between would take a notion to develop the state of things in the Confederate position there, and a sharp artillery fire would be opened on it. With orders to stand still and take the fire without replying, the artillerymen could only protect themselves as well as possible, the cannoneers getting behind the trees, and the drivers, who could not go away from their teams, lying down by the side of their horses. There had been rain the day and night before, and the ground was uncomfortably wet to lie down on. After one of the periodical shellings from across the way one of the veteran drivers on the wheel team of a piece was seen to prepare himself for more comfortable lying down. He had placed his own blanket, for more convenient carrying, on top of his saddle-blanket, and under his saddle, and this he proceeded to take out and spread on the ground where he had to lie down by the side of his horse. The First Lieutenant called the Captain's attention to it, and remarked, "Matthews is going to make himself as comfortable as possible, even under fire. He is a cool fellow; look at him now." The soldier referred to had just thrown himself down at full length on the blanket with a laugh, and remarked that he was tired of getting up and down, so he was fixed to stay during the performance. Soon after this the artillery opposite us commenced again a furious cannonade, which lasted several minutes and caused our men to "lay low" for protection. As soon as this was over the man Matthews sprang up, and shaking out his blanket, proceeded to put it back into its former position. Seeing this, the Lieutenant said to him, "What's the matter, Matthews, is your blanket getting too wet on the ground?" The soldier shook his head slowly and then, with a serio-comic expression on his face, answered, "Oh no, sir; I was not considering the good of the blanket, but of myself. When those things are flying over my head like that I want to be as close to the ground as possible, and just a minute ago that blanket seemed a foot and a half thick."[12]

It could also be dangerous to be an artillery soldier with no training:

The boys found a small cannon so determined to mount and load it and give the boys in blue a shot before they vacated. It was suggested that they lash the loaded gun on a big mule and after the shot take it along with them. All things were ready just about the time the blue-coats appeared in force on the west side of the river. The mule was led to the edge of the water and the new made gunner sounded out: "Match her off." The old mule stood quiet until the match was touched to the fuse that had been introduced into the touch hole, but when it began to sizz and the fire to fall upon his neck and withers his discomfort caused him to turn round and round. The boys except the one holding the mule's bridle instantly fell to the ground. The command, "Down boys!" attracted the captain from slumber in the old storm fort. Seeing the regiment in blue across the river and his men in a scattered condition on the ground, he commanded: "Up and into line, boys!" No one stirred. The command came again and again with deeper earnestness, when Sam Moore replied: "Up and thunder and lightning! We will stay down till that mule shoots." In another instant the gun fired, the mule tumbled down upon his knees and the shell stuck far from its mark on the hillside and exploded. The captain cried out: "Every man take care of himself; they are all around us." The laugh was on the captain, and all retreated in order with mule and gun.[13]

On December 31, the Rebels broke the Yank line and thought they had won the battle. Bragg telegraphed Richmond, Virginia: "The enemy has yielded his strong position and is falling back. We occupy the whole field and shall follow him, God has granted us a happy New Year."[14]

General Bragg had spoken too soon. On January 2, 1863, the Rebs made a fatal blunder and experienced the superior Yankee manufacturing capacity, i.e., the ability to make good cannons.

A soldier described the conclusion of the Battle of Murfreesboro when Bragg told Breckinridge to attack on January 2, 1863:

We listened for the signal gun. When it sounded, the line seemed to leap forward until it met the enemy in force in the woodland, through which I had three times ridden. Breckinridge's Division was sweeping forward with the Rebel yell. I was ordered to move our line forward faster, and at the command we took up the yell and in our rush captured a lieutenant colonel, and one hundred and seventy-five infantry. We seemed to have cleaned up all of their flanking force; for we moved at once to the top of the rise, and with two guns of Holtzclaw's Alabama Battery opened at almost point-blank range, enfilading the real line.

I wish I could adequately describe the splendid though awful sight on my left. Breckinridge's two lines were coming forward with an alignment that was almost perfect. His regiment seemed small at that end of his line. Their battle flags were thick, and the only breaks in the lines were made by men pitching heavily forward, while the lines swept on over them.

In battle scenes the artists have nearly always portrayed the generals in brilliant uniform, with brandishing swords, leading the way. I saw nothing of that kind, and no one could have lived a moment between those charging lines and that of the enemy's rain of bullets. The only men in front of our lines were those who now and then would run past and drop on their knees, taking better aim than when moving. . . .

Breckenridge's first line struck the enemy's first, and with a shock that was unmistakable drove them on their second. I had thought the firing was tremendous until then, but when the enemy's first line struck their second it seemed as if heaven and earth were coming together. Our first line moved more slowly until the second closed up, when briefly the dash was taken up again, but only for a short distance, for all at once both lines (indistinguishable by this time) seemed to falter and then literally to disintegrate. Retreating, more fell in every direction, while shell and shot did awful work among them. The charge was over and had failed.

I talked this over with General Breckinridge on our last march through South Carolina and into Georgia. (General Breckenridge) told me that in talking with Federal officers he had learned that they had ten thousand muskets and fifty-eight guns on that position. He said he had four thousand two hundred and fifty, and lost one thousand seven hundred and fifty in forty-five minutes. To me it didn't seem ten minutes.[15]

The records show that at the Battle of Murfreesboro, 350 men from the Tenth Texas were armed and ready to fight. Of this number, ten were killed, ninety-three were wounded, and fifteen were missing for a total casualty rate of 33.7 percent. Of the ninety-three wounded, fourteen later died from their wounds. Another forty of the wounded and captured never returned to active duty. One soldier who was finished fighting was Lt. John Griffin. His right foot was amputated at the ankle. He was assigned to the provost marshal and performed the task of gathering conscripts (draftees).

Some of the fifteen men missing became prisoners of war. One might ask how prisoners were lost when enemy lines were broken and driven for miles. In the Civil War, an attack up to the enemy lines had to be successful. Winning was paramount; retreat from face-to-face contact with an enemy battle line led to a bullet in the back. Situations like this led to the Rebs crawling into the Yankee lines in order to surrender and avoid the bullets passing over their heads. The Tenth Texas men were captured late in the day on December 31, 1862.

Many members of the Tenth Texas who were wounded during the war were sent to one of two hospitals: the Texas Hospital at Auburn, Alabama, and the Texas General Hospital at Quitman, Mississippi. The Tenth Texas had two men assigned to the Texas Hospital. One man assigned was A.G. Durkee, the Tenth Texas quartermaster. The other man that was assigned to hospital duty was J.F. Walker, who was listed as a hospital steward. He was given the cushy job (compared to walking and shooting) because he was "temperate and honest." The Confederacy practiced the policy of establishing hospitals by state for different state patients when possible. No records were found as to whether only Texas men were in these hospitals. The Texas legislature did appropriate money for medical care for its own. It is possible they were staffed only by Texans under the theory this was the best way to insure proper treatment for Texas' sick and wounded. The Texas General Hospital at Quitman had mineral water baths for the wounded, but General Sherman burned the hospital in 1864. It now has a cemetery there with more than 200 headstones.

At Murfreesboro, the Tenth Texas and other Texans were able to drive the Yanks more than three three miles but were not able to totally break their lines. One reason was that the Texans had to stop for resupply of ammunition, giving the Northerners time to move reinforcements to create a new battle line. Ector's men were supposed to carry forty rounds each. They had ammunition resupply at 10:00 a.m., 12:00 p.m., and 2:30 p.m. To overcome the problem of resupply and rest periods that were commonplace during the Civil War, the best solution came with the battle formations used by Reb General Longstreet at Chickamauga. He stacked his brigades five deep, giving him the drive to smash the enemy's lines. He also had a little luck when the Yanks moved a unit from his front just as he attacked. The succeeding unit took over the charge when the lead troops ran out of ammo and needed a rest. The stacking of assault units was a key to victory because outnumbering the opponent is not the key element. Being stronger at the critical point of engagement is the major component of a military victory. Stacking units was the classic Napoleonic tactic of exploiting the offensive through massed firepower and headlong assault. It should be mentioned that Cleburne's Division was intended to be stacked behind the Tenth Texas and related units. As the Tenth Texas attacked into the panicked Yank's units, General Ector, because of the terrain, could not stop his Texans and align them to the right where the undefeated Yanks were. They drove the enemy straight ahead when they should have turned on the Union troops to their right. Basically, the Tenth Texas chased the defeated Yanks from the battlefield and gave the others time to set up better defense lines. Cleburne's unit had to attack to the right of Ector's Brigade and, at the close of battle, wound up on the left of Ector's Brigade. This mix-up precluded a total route of the Federals because the stacking effect was lost.

The following is a list of the casualties suffered by the Tenth Texas at Murfreesboro:

Tenth Texas Cavalry
Killed in Action at Murfreesboro — 11 Men

Company A	A. Carter	
	A. Cooke	
	A. Moore, 1st Sergeant	
Company C	J.T. McGee, Sergeant	Killed carrying flag
	W. Davis	
Company D	A. Sims	Killed carrying flag fighting Yank flag carrier
Company F	A. Cauley	
	Sylvannaman T. Hillard (called Texas)	
Company I	J. Reynolds	"Shot through the head on the first charge and lived until late in the evening. He was indeed a fine young man." (Templeton letter)
Company K 2nd Sergeant	T. Murray,	
	R. Simmons	

Note. Other records show only 10 KIA.
The difference is probably A. Cooke or A. Simms who were initially listed as missing.

65

Tenth Texas Cavalry
Wounded, Missing, or POW at Murfreesboro
Never Returned to Active Duty with Tenth Texas — 56 men

Regimental Staff	J.J. Jarvis	Left arm
Company A	T. Alred	Knee joint in fixed position after wound
	S.L. Cook	Contraction of tendons after wound
	J. Dearborn	
	W. Maloney	Right arm — severe
	W.H. Turman	Died gunshot wound
Company B	S. Bailey	Gunshot to head
	B. Evans	Paralysis of left leg, shell wound
	B.F. Garrett	Lost at Murfreesboro
	J. Gunter	Severely in foot
	W. Harris	Died
	W. Lyles	Through both thighs
	J.H. Moseley	Foot — died
	W.L. Strickland	Wounded both thighs and right eye
Company C	J. Griffin	Foot amputated
	J. Andrews	Thigh
	W. Gillam	Left breast
	R. Ridley	Hand seriously — died
	W. Shepard	Arm — seriously
	A. Stiles	Arm — seriously
	N. Williamson	Knee — died
Company D	L. Hefner	Died gunshot wound
	W. Morris	Left arm — seriously
	S. Bailey	Shot in head
	G. Davis	
	W. Jones	Right arm slight, died of gunshot wound
	R. Ringo	Left arm — seriously
	W. Shelton	Head mortally
	J. Speare	Left arm — seriously
Company E	J. McCauley	Hip
	W. Quaid	Groin
	S. Wright	
Company F	J. Bell	Gunshot wound, lower extremity
	J. Loud	Left ankle
	J. Womack	Right knee
	S. Yates	
Company G	J. Furlow	Nurse at Murfreesboro — died
	J. Barham	Leg
	J.T. Furlow	Right arm — died
	C. Furlow	
	J. Hopson	Leg — mortally
	A. Irving	Thigh — severe

	J. Moore	Foot slightly, died 1/24/63
	W. Parker	Foot mortally, died 2/3/63
	T. Still	Thigh
	W.A. Robertson	Right thigh
Company H	J. Christman	Leg
	S. Hardee	Breast — died
	J.O. Manning	Died
	R. Hazelwood	Leg — died
Company I	T. Demitt	Thigh, bone fractured — died 2/17/63
	J. Francis	
	T. Holoway	Thigh
Company K	J. Jarman	Died from wound
	B. Dunn	Died
	B. Chambliss	Died
Note. After the Battle at Murfreesboro, some POWs were exchanged.		

In the February 12, 1864 *Austin Triweekly State Gazette,* the following members of the Tenth Texas were listed as being on the Confederate Roll of Honor for their courage and good conduct at the Battle of Murfreesboro. The list shows what happened then and later to these brave men:

Alex Cooke	Killed at Murfreesboro
F.M. Rogers	Killed at Chickamauga
J.T. McGee	Killed at Murfreesboro
A. Sims	Killed at Murfreesboro carrying the flag
James Terry	Captured at Chickamauga and became a Yank
W.W. Conly (Cauley)	Killed at Atlanta
Stokley Hutchins	Wounded at Murfreesboro and Chickamauga, home in Texas when the war ended
J.O. Manning	Died 2/14/63, apparently wounded at Murfreesboro
Joel Reynolds	Killed at Murfreesboro
S.L. Birdwell	Wounded at Allatoona, ended his soldiering

As one of the letters found later in this book states, "All the bravest men have been killed."

After the Battle of Murfreesboro, Maj. Wiley B. Ector of the Tenth Texas was assigned an unenviable task by his brother, General Ector, the brigade commander. He was serving as brigade quartermaster and had to go over the battlefield with a detail of men used to bury the dead. (General Ector, whose wife had died, also brought his fourteen-year-old son to the war with him. His son, Walton H. Ector, served with his dad through the entire Civil War.)

CHAPTER 7

He ain't heavy, he is my son

EVENTS AFTER THE BATTLE OF MURFREESBORO

AFTER THE BATTLE of Murfreesboro, Littlejohn corresponded home from South Carolina where his father took him to recover from his wound. His dad had to carry him on his back part of the way:

> Thickety, So. Ca. 1, Feby. 4th, 1863
>
> My ever dear and affectionate Sallie,
>
> Did you not get the letter I wrote you from Knoxville? I wrote you a letter from that place informing you of my situation. . . . After the Battle I was sent to Knoxville to the hospital, in which I stayed about two weeks. I then wrote word to Pa to come after me. It was some time before he got my letter. But as soon as he got my letter he started immediately after. I was might glad to see him, for I was fairing badly in the Hospital. I got a furlough for 30 days. Half of the time has already expired almost. But I have the privilege of staying at home until I get well, if ever I do. . . . I don't suppose there is any chance to cross the Miss. River now. If I were turned loose from the army I would try it anyhow. My anxiety is very great to be at Home for awhile at least, if not to stay all the time.
>
> I had a rough time going from Knoxville home. I was not able to help myself in the least. No one seemed to have any care for a wounded man. Pa had to pack me on his back some times because he could not find men who would help him to carry me. I had to sit up nearly all the way from Knoxville to Columbia. After I got there, I met up with one of my old schoolmates who got me a bed and put it in the car. I shall always recollect him for his kindness. . . . I remain your affectionate husband, E.G.L.

A Texan from Ector's Brigade recounted the retreat and the return to winter camp:

> On the night of the 3rd of January, Bragg retreated. We waded Stones River and the next morning at daylight we were on the march

covering thirty miles that day and camping on Duck River. The enemy did not follow and it being the dead of winter, we went into winter quarters.[1]

Another letter sent home by a Texan in Ector's Brigade described the weather on the retreat, his love for his girlfriend, and ended with a poem:

> The wind turn to the north and was very cold and we was al wet and muddy and only one blanket and they was wet and froze and our close soon was froze on our backs we was ordered back to camps in the morning and we got back to our camps a bout knight and we was pretty ner froze.
>
> A soldier life is a wery life hit causes a meny pore feler to loose his life there is sum talk of pease but I had rether see hit and to her tel of hit I think when old Abes (Lincoln) time is out we will have pease and pease will be ended with a meny pore feler before then. I don't make much calculations of evr getting hone my self all thoe I should live to see you onse more in life but best of friends has to part but hit all most brcks my hart to think of nevr seein you. So I am com pelled to bring my letr to a close give my respects to Miss cal and Jake and all the rest of the neighbours and shere a portion of your self (my pen is bad, my ink is pale, my love to you will never fail) so excuse my bad spellen so far well my friend I hop not for lif to Miss Loo.[2]

On January 21, 1863, the Eleventh Texas was remounted to regular cavalry and the Ninth Texas Infantry joined Ector's Brigade. Until the end of the war, the Ninth Texas Infantry, Tenth Texas Cavalry Dismounted, Fourteenth Texas Cavalry Dismounted, and the Thirty-second Texas Cavalry Dismounted all served in Ector's Brigade.

In February, after the large number of casualties suffered by the Tenth Texas at Murfreesboro, some of the men still had plenty of fight left in them. Buck Kilgore, Company G, poured out his feelings to the home folks: "We are fighting for our liberties, our homes, and everything that is dear to us. Can a brave and generous people determined to be free, be conquered? Never, Never, Never!"[3]

A soldier recalled his winter quarters:

> Our cabins were built of split logs, the cracks being "chinked" during the severest weather with red clay, thus making a very comfortable house indeed. An ample chimney was constructed of sticks "chinked" in the same manner as the house; and when the fireplace was piled up with wood and set going, we had as comfortable quar-

ters as to warmth as one could wish. Our bedsteads were four posts with end and side pieces nailed to them and boards were placed so as to give us room to fill in with straw and over this our quilts and blankets were spread.

Being a very large mess, our ration came in good-sized chunk, especially beef. Corn bread was our stand-by in that line. This was baked in a big old Dutch oven about fourteen inches in diameter two bakings of three pones each being required at each of our three meals per day. We used liberally of the little Mexican red peppers for seasoning which was a most healthy tonic for us. (Just here I shall digress to say that when we passed through Dalton in October, 1864, on our way into Tennessee the previous winter's camps could be located by the sea of pepper plants full of peppers that covered the country from the seed that had fallen on the ground). Occasionally bacon, with some kind of green vegetable varied our bill of fare. We ordered a five-gallon keg of Georgia cane syrup (it cost us only $300) which went splendidly with our corn bread for dessert.[4]

Another explained about the way the food was cooked:

I shall always remember the first time it was my duty to assist in preparing supper for our "mess" which consisted of three others besides myself. . . . The rations were ample and consisted of flour, corn meal, and bacon. To these afterwards were added rice, pickled beef, peas, sugar, coffee, sometimes vegetables, and always hard-tack. This was a kind of cracker prepared for the army sometime previous to the outbreak of the war and it was as hard as wood. No salt, shortening, soda, or other leaven whatever was used in its preparation, and it could be eaten only by those who had good sound teeth; but we found out later that it could be soaked with hot water and grease in an oven and be made quite palatable. In its original state, I suppose it would keep indefinitely in any climate. Each cracker was about six inches in diameter and about an inch thick. When broken with a hatchet or other instrument the edges of the fragments were shiny and showed its solid composition. Later in the war the Confederate government prepared a cracker that was far superior to this.

As soon as the messes were formed cooking utensils were issued to us. These consisted of one large sheet iron camp kettle, two iron pots, a frying pan, a "spider" or skillet, a small boiler, etc. Each man was given a tin plate, a tin cup, and knife and fork. A mess chest with an extension top that could be opened up to form a table was also given to each mess and we were all then ready to begin our domestic duties in camp. All things started off well but domestic trouble soon began and multiplied rapidly. Each member of the mess was expected to do the cooking for a day at a time and this was done in such a careless manner by some that numerous complaints went up to the captain. Fighting and quarrelling over the way in which the affairs of the messes were conducted were of daily occurrence. This state of things continued for some time when the captain grew tired of it and told our orderly sergeant to divide the men alphabetically into messes of six or seven each. In this rearrangement I lost two of my former friends and some came to us whose cooking nobody would like to eat. Though the youngest in the mess I took it on myself to do the cooking if the others would supply me with wood and water and relieve me of all other duty. The men unanimously agreed to this and I having had some experience in this line assumed the duty of chief cook and bottle washer. I drew the rations, cooked our meals, placed the food on the table, and afterwards cleaned up everything and kept things in order. While busy at this the other men sat around the fire telling jokes, singing songs, and smoking their long-stemmed pipes, criticizing my movements all the time.

As the war went on, our pots were now very few and were on double duty; but sometimes our wagons did not arrive, in which case we employed our steel ramrods. We wrapped the dough around them and held it over the coals, turning it all the time so as to bake every side of it thoroughly. And we broiled our meat in the same way, when we had any, or ate it raw.[5]

Around this period, the men of the Tenth Texas would have been hearing about the financial conditions back home. In January 1863, Panola County, where Company F was formed, was forced to sell the carpet out of the courthouse because of lack of funds. Panola County had 562 voters when the war started, with 550 of them serving in the war. No one was left to pay taxes. Of the 550 men that served the Confederacy, fewer than 50 percent returned alive.[6]

The Tenth Texas had a red star on their flag for their allies, the Cherokee Indians. In February 1862, the Cherokee Indians threw in the towel and became Yankees. They also freed all of their slaves. It is likely that sewing something over the Cherokee star on the flag was discussed around the campfires. The Tenth Texas men were certainly worried about their ex-allies raiding into East Texas. This would have had an impact on the number of desertions.

CHAPTER 8

"Gander pullin' and greyback cracking"

CAMP LIFE — EARLY 1863

FOR NEARLY FIVE MONTHS, the Tenth Texas was in winter quarters and engaged in no combat. The generals, after the bloodletting at Murfreesboro, could not muster up enough courage to go at it again in such a short period of time.

Camp life consisted of mundane routines and odd entertainment. A soldier commented on a little diversion in camp life that also led to winning a nice goose meal:

> The gander was tied to the limb of a tree, head down, neck greased, and some distance from the ground. The boys would stand off some distance then run and as they reached the bird, would make a jump to catch him by the neck. Some would miss, others would catch hold, but their hands would slip. The old gander would squall when this was done. This fun, or cruelty, went on for some time before the neck was pulled off. I believe the one doing this fell heir to the goose.[1]

Gander pulling was a common amusement in East Texas, though some of the ladies felt it was too cruel for them.[2]

Another soldier told of the lighter side of camp life:

> Our principal occupation was playing poker, chuck-a-luck and cracking graybacks (lice). Every soldier had a brigade of lice on him and I have seen fellows so busily engaged in cracking them that it reminded me of an old woman knitting. At first the boys would go off in the woods and hide to louse themselves, but that was unnecessary, the ground fairly crawled with lice. Pharaoh's people when they were resisting old Moses, never enjoyed the curse of the lice more than we did. The boys would frequently have a louse race. There was one fellow who was winning all the money; his lice would run quicker and crawl faster than anybody's lice. We could not understand it. If some fellow happened to catch a fierce-looking louse, he would call on Dornin for a race. Dornin would come and always win the stake. The

lice were placed in plates. This was the race course — and the first that crawled off was the winner. At last we found out D.'s trick: he always heated his plate.[3]

Some Rebs heated their shirts over fires and said the lice started popping just like popping corn. Another said he threw his shirt down at night and the next morning it was moving around as the lice started looking for a soldier to eat on.[4]

John Templeton sent home the following letter. Apparently Cousin Ham had been conscripted. He also mentioned Joel Reynolds, who made the Confederate Roll of Honor. Templeton made numerous references to not wanting to be a prisoner; ironically, he was later captured at Chickamauga. When he refers to not getting to go home, he should have been released under the Conscript Act because he was too young. They kept him until he was of legal age:

Camp Three Miles from Shelbyville
Bedford Co Tenn. Feb. 13th 1863

Dear Father

Yours of the 8th ult. came to hand yesterday. . . . I regret that I did not get off home as I expected but I am satisfied I am doing as well today as if I had got off. If I had went home I could not have stayed long and it is no pleasure to leave home to "go to the wars" I can tell you. We are doing well here, we have to fight the Yankees sometime but that is what we left home for. We get plenty to eat and now have plenty to wear and I don't see any reason to complain. For my part I am contented until peace is made. . . .

I am sorry Cousin Ham had to leave home for he was actually needed. I had rather went a dozen times myself than to see him leave. Cousin Ham will make a good soldier, one that will stand to his post. I am glad to hear of Capt. Thos Johnson's company participating in the late fight and escaping so well. The Yankees surely don't fight as well in Arks as they do here for even in the slightest skirmish they wound or kill some of our men. Somehow they are managing the affaires rather bad west of the River. We once heard that "old Kirby" Smith was ordered over there to take command. I was in hopes it was so for he would surely make a change. I am not surprised in hearing of so much sickness in our army about Little Rock for we tried that country once. There has not been a man died in our company since we left Mississippi. We have been in a healthy country since we left there. The "Grand Foraging Expedition" was decidedly an advantage to us. I allude to the trip into Kentucky. It hardened us to marching and we never saw a tent from the time we entered the state until we got back to Louden which was from the 7th August till the first of Nov.

The news of a "big fight" near Murfreesboro is true indeed. Our company lost three of its best members viz: James Murkns, John Goodson, & Joel Reynolds. The two former are missing. It is probable they were taken prisoners but it is the impression they were killed in the cedar brake. The latter was shot in the first charge through the head. He lived until late in the evening. He was a mess mate of mine and was indeed a fine young man. If the papers come any ways near telling the truth peace would be near at hand. They seem to be split up in the north. I am sorry to hear of Jno B. Long being taken prisoner for above all things deliver me from the hands of the enemy. I suppose they have quit exchanging prisoners. I am not surprised at there being many that are trying to get out of the service by some little office. It is the case everywhere. Extortion and speculation rules the day here. Every soldier has got to peddling. Eggs have sold in our camp at $6 pr. dozen. You may doubt this but it is so. Pork has sold at 50 cts. per pound. Common hats $20. Shoes are rarely met with. Pants from $12 to $15 common janes. Shirts are tolerable plenty. I have got just as many clothes as I would have. I have two pr pants thats plenty. Corn is very scarce. They have to go 20 miles for forage. I will close today and finish some other time. J.A.T.

On March 6, 1863, Pvt. Jim Watson wrote home and said that Company G of the Tenth Texas had never had a deserter. "Our company has all reenlisted for the war. We were the first Texans to reenlist in this department. Company G is the star company of Ector's Brigade and also the favorite company of all the officers."

Company G only had five men that went AWOL during the war. Only one was a possible AWOL prior to March 1863. The entry in J.A. Watkins' records says January-October 1863, "ordered back, but not returned." Possibly, Watson was correct.

On March 20, 1863, Col. Matthew Locke resigned from the command of the Tenth Texas and was replaced by Col. C.R. Earp.[5]

On April 11, 1863, 3d Cpl. Alex Mobley of Company C, Tenth Texas, was killed by Pvt. James Lowery of the same company. The records reflect Lowrey escaped by deserting. No further details were found as to what happened or why it happened.[6]

Private Templeton wrote the following letter from Shelbyville, Tenn., on April 22, 1863:

I again write you a few lines. I have given up all hope of ever receiving another letter from home. The mails being so uncertain is all that keeps me from accusing you of never writing to me. . . . I have no news that you have not heard. An important move must be in hand from present appearances, of things. We are ordered to send all our baggage to the rear, retaining only one tent fly to every sixteen men.

We are doing very well here now. We moved camp yesterday, and have the prettiest camp I ever saw. It has been a woods lot (before the fences around it were destroyed) with large beech, ash, and elm trees that afford good shade. I am afraid that some night when we get sound asleep orders will come for us to cook rations and be ready to march by daylight. This occurs when we get into some pleasant camp and begin to be comfortably situated. This time last year we had arrived at Memphis so it has been one year since we crossed the Mississippi River. I was in hopes that peace would be restored to our country by this time but can't see that it is any nearer at hand. I hope to "tell the tale" if the war lasts twenty years.[7]

Littlejohn sent another letter home outlining his thoughts about his wound and other matters. This letter referred to the son he had never seen:

I have been confined to my bed for five weeks, scarcely being able to turn over. The great cause of my getting worse was that a very large piece of bone secreted itself an inch or so below the wound which could not get out. It was very painful to me indeed. It was in there more than two months before it could be gotten out. The wound inflamed very much and caused me a great deal of uneasiness. It rotted and sloughed out until the sore became as large as the palm of your hand or larger. I was fearful it would rot out to the hollow as that is close by. I have not been able to walk a step even with my crutches in five weeks and in that length of time you may be assured I suffered immensely. Since I pulled the bone out it is getting better. I hope it will get well now if there are no more pieces of bone.

How often did I wish you were present with me. I know you could not alleviate the pain but your presence would have been a great consolation to me in my distress. I hope if nothing happens to me and I can get a discharge, I will try to come home in the course of three or four months. I don't think I will be able for duty soon. I do want to see you so much that I can scarcely content myself to stay until I get well enough to travel. I would have been glad had you known when Davis and his wife was coming so that you could have come with them. It would be a dangerous trip for you, I think. Davis says you have a fine big boy. I want to see him, too. . . . E.G.L.

Pvt. Charles Livingston of Company C was tired of all the walking and shooting. On May 11, 1863, he transferred to the Confederate Navy. The Tenth Texas was rested, reorganized, and ready for another rumble. First they would have to do a little walking.

CHAPTER 9

"Strain out the wiggletails"

OPERATIONS TO RELIEVE VICKSBURG
AND BATTLE OF JACKSON, MISSISSIPPI

IN MAY 1863, the Tenth Texas was ordered to Mississippi to aid in the relief of Vicksburg. On May 21, the Tenth Texas and fellow Texans arrived by train near Canton, Mississippi. The soldiers did not have artillery support, wagons, or ammunition resupply.[1]

A Texan from Ector's Brigade witnessed an internal rebellion:

> When the spring campaign opened, Ector's Brigade was sent to Mississippi to join Gen. Joseph E. Johnston in a movement to relieve Vicksburg. On this campaign, after much hard marching and counter-marching, the 14th Texas rebelled. We had been Dismounted and had often been promised that we should be remounted. One morning there was great confusion in camp. The boys commenced to stack their arms and cry: "Hell or horses." Then Captain Howze appeared in their midst. "Now boys, don't do that. I do not want a man of my company to lay down his gun. If the government does not see fit to give us our horses, let's serve our country in any capacity they want us to." Such was his influence that not a man disobeyed; but the other nine companies all stopped, their men swearing they would not fight until they were remounted. Later that day they saw a brigade of infantry with glistening bayonets and a battery of 12-pound Napoleon guns march down and halt in front of them, and being ordered to take up their arms, they were quick to obey. This act of discipline gave to Howze's company the title that the "Star Company" maintained. It was conceded that Howze had the best company in the brigade to the end of the war.[2]

One of two soldiers could be exaggerating. On March 6, Pvt. Jim Watson of the Tenth Texas stated that G Company of the Tenth Texas was the "Star Company" of Ector's Brigade. Now, a soldier from the Fourteenth Texas claimed Captain Howze's company was the "Star Company." It is possible, after the "Hell or Horses" rebellion, that the brigade officers felt they should reward a company in the Fourteenth Texas to restore morale and calm tempers. An age-old principle of getting men to fight is to instill in them a sense of unit pride.

At the Battle of Nashville, Captain Howze apparently was temporarily in charge of the Tenth Texas or at least a detachment of them.

The rebellious attitude of the Fourteenth Texas was a clear indication of the mind set of the other dismounted cavalry units, including the Tenth Texas. A Texan from Ector's Brigade related what General Walker thought about the brigade at this time:

> Ector's Brigade from Texas and McNair's from Arkansas were in the Army of Tennessee and fought side by side in many battles. Every man in these brigades remembers the time down on Big Black in Mississippi when Gen. Walker separated Ector's and McNair's Brigades. At this time he had a poor opinion of us. He said we had no discipline and ought to be discharged. Both Ector and McNair resented his remarks and called on him about it. After the two days' fight at Chickamauga, Gen. Walker apologized for what he said, and complimented both brigades very highly.[3]

Vicksburg fell to the Yankees on July 4, 1863. The Tenth Texas found out about it the next day. By cutting off the normal route across the Mississippi River, the defeat had a devastating effect on morale. Coupled with Vicksburg was news of the defeat of General Lee at Gettysburg. These setbacks, plus the endless walking, drove the Texas units close to open rebellion. The morale problem was personified by the desertion rate. In 1862, the Tenth Texas only had seventeen members that had gone AWOL. In the months of June, July, and August of 1863, the Tenth had fifty-six soldiers leave and never return. From the scant records, a total of eighty-six men deserted during the entire war. James Ray of Company A apparently had a change of heart. He deserted on August 26, 1863, but he came back six days later.

With the loss at Gettysburg and Vicksburg in the summer of 1863, Confederate desertions in Texas were reported as high as fifty or sixty a day.[4] In early 1863, Texas' Governor Lubbock referred to signs of a latent dissatisfaction, if not a positive disloyalty to the Confederacy.[5] It is possible that the reason why most of the Tenth Texas did not head for home was that it was very difficult to get across the Mississippi. Tom Hanson, Company B, Tenth Texas, was captured at the siege of Vicksburg with the Second Texas infantry. He apparently was dissatisfied with the Tenth Texas, went AWOL, and joined up with the Second Texas. He may have been trapped there trying to cross the Mississippi. The Tenth Texas, after the fall of Vicksburg, appeared to have had seven men captured attempting to cross the river while on furlough. One of these men, Capt. A.J. Booty, was himself being sent to Texas to round up absentees. Pvt. William W. Fannin had some bad luck. He was discharged for phthis pulmonalis and was apparently captured crossing the Mississippi. At least the Yanks allowed him to continue his journey home.

One reason for so many desertions from the Tenth Texas could have been the news they were receiving from East Texas. Back home, besides the economic problems brought on by the absence of most of the able bodied men, refugees were causing an additional problem. They were "running their slaves," moving them away from the Yankees in Louisiana and Arkansas. Most food supplies were being consumed, which caused an inflation of prices. With the husbands gone, many women and children suffered. It was impossible to remove men from an agrarian society and not cause unbearable strains on the economy. The state of Texas allocated some money to the poor, but mostly it fell to the county governments to help. Ninety Texas counties, not being able to help because of a shortage of money, printed their own currency. By 1863, the food shortage in Texas was being made worse by local Confederate units that were confiscating supplies. Groups of AWOL soldiers and conscript law dodgers ran and lived together. To obtain

Private J.T. Mings,
Company C.
He died April 27, 1863,
probably of measels.
Note his double
barrel shotgun.

Smith County Historical Society

food, some committed crimes. In 1863, it was estimated that three thousand deserters (bush soldiers) were living in the woods of East Texas. Naturally, this terrified many of the women left on their own. Van Zandt and Wood counties, where some of the Tenth Texans were from, were notorious for their deserters and the subsequent reign of terror. In early 1863, anti-war conventions were held in those counties urging Texas to rejoin the Union. Supposedly, deserters were very active in the anti-war crowds.

After being informed of the fall of Vicksburg, the Tenth Texas moved to Jackson, Mississippi, to await the attack from the conquerors of Vicksburg. Sherman and his Abolition Horde came after them. A soldier related the efforts to relieve Vicksburg and the details of the Battle of Jackson, Mississippi:

Among all my experiences of army life none impressed me more than the campaign under Gen. Joseph E. Johnston for the relief of Vicksburg in the spring and summer of 1863. As a result of that campaign I lay for weeks in a darkened room in a hospital with eyes inflamed until they were balls of blood; and though my sight was restored yet that experience left me a legacy of suffering from neuralgia of the eyes which continues with me to this day.

The campaign was a series of marches and countermarches of our small force, seeking some weak spot in the strongly fortified lines of General Grant's huge army where we might break through the cordon of besiegers and open a way for the escape of the beleaguered garrison.

Those marches were under blazing sun, along shadeless roads, over a country destitute of running streams, through blinding clouds of dust, sometimes in deep sand that made walking a labor, sometimes when the rain fell in torrents, through mud heavy and clinging. Yet it was all in vain. It was impossible for 25,000 at most to contend against 80,000, which could have been speedily reinforced to 130,000.

I note frequently in Northern statistics of the battles of this war a tendency to exaggerate the Confederate forces and to diminish the Federal forces engaged and in like manner to swell our losses while minimizing their own, all of it for the glory of the Federal troops and generals. Now a Confederate soldier is the last man to discount the courage and efficiency of the soldiers on the other side. The men commanded by Generals Grant and Sherman were mostly from the West and were our equals in fighting qualities and possibly superior in drill and discipline, certainly far superior in numbers and equipment. Yet whenever we met them as Bill Arp puts it, "we killed more of them than they did of us."

During the campaign it was frequently talked among the men that there was serious conflict of judgment between General Johnston and General Pemberton who commanded at Vicksburg. Such a disagreement cannot be concealed from the men of the army especially when like ours they are men of intelligence accustomed to discuss the meaning of all that concerned our war. The newspapers indulged in frequent criticisms of General Johnston's movements as slow and uncertain. It was generally known that there was considerable friction between President Davis and General Johnston and the apparently contradictory movement of our troops led to the belief that "someone had blundered." So I had opportunity to hear the expression of many opinions of both officers and privates. General Johnston had remarkable power of winning the confidence of his troops and as a general rule our men were his warm partisans.

. . . General Johnston's plan was to abandon Vicksburg and Port Hudson as no longer valuable to the Confederacy and to concentrate all of our forces in seeking to defeat General Grant. If that could be done we could destroy his army cut off as it would be from its base and then we could easily regain the abandoned posts. On the other hand if our army were divided and a large part of it shut up in those posts General Grant could easily defy the small force operating on the outside and ultimate surrender of the garrisons was certain.

Gen, Joseph E. Johnston

In a word, General Johnston's idea was to save the army if the post had to be given up. General Pemberton's idea was to save the post even at the risk of losing an army. It was often remarked by the men that even if we could defeat General Grant, Vicksburg would not be worth anything to us with a lot of gunboats and transports in possession of the river. And the stupidest soldier could see that General Johnston's army was utterly weak in comparison with Grant's army. It was a matter of surprise to me during the whole war to notice the remarkable shrewdness of the common soldier in penetrating the purpose of the various movements. Over and again we received by the grapevine line marvelous stories of big victories we had gained or of some advantage in position which would give us a victory that would end the war. But our men, after thinking over them, always discounted these stories.

The discomforts of the march on that campaign were aggravated by the dust and the heat and the lack of drinking water. Often the clouds of dust were so thick that one could not see twenty feet ahead. We were largely dependent for water to drink on ponds for the stock and sometimes the green scum was so thick on the surface of the pond that our horses would not drink it. We would fill our canteens from these ponds and strain out the wiggletails and young tadpoles. The water remaining in the tin cup was comparatively clear, though quite warm. I found a new use for a mustache. As mine was long, I drew it over my lips and made a strainer of it as I drank out of my canteen. In a number of places where there were cisterns we found the handles of the pumps taken away or the rope and windlass removed. This was not from any unkindness but was a necessity, for several thousand men and horses would soon have exhausted the cisterns of a neighborhood. . . .

Every day on the march, while General Johnston was maneuvering his army in the attempt to relieve the beleaguered at Vicksburg, men overcome by heat and dust and thirst fell out of the line. Some of them died by the roadside, some were taken in the ambulances and some after a rest of a couple of hours were able to go on and would rejoin us awhile after we went into camp. The orders against straggling were very strict, but in such cases they were not strictly enforced; and if a higher officer saw a man sitting by the road apparently tired out he generally understood the situation and rode on after an encouraging word to the weary soldier. . . .

With all our marching and countermarching we could find no

point in Federal lines of investment where we could make an attack with the least hope of success. On the 5th of July we began a rather rapid retreat toward Jackson. We soon learned that on the day before, on the 4th of July, General Pemberton had surrendered Vicksburg and his army of 30,000 men. Then General Grant with probably 75,000 men was free to follow our little army of say, 25,000.

We learned that the Federals had lost very heavily in assaults on our works, and that the garrison was literally starved into surrender; but the fact that the capitulation was on the 4th of July aroused suspicion against General Pemberton and the fact that he was a Northern man was quoted as confirmation of the suspicion. The only charges that really lie against him are incompetency and disobedience.

We reached Jackson in two or three days and very soon the Federals came up and began to plant batteries and shell the town. One of the ludicrous incidents of those days was a sudden "advance to the rear" of our regiment. It was on picket duty. During the night all our supports were withdrawn, the order of withdrawal having failed to reach us. When morning dawned we were confronted by a corps of the enemy and three batteries were placed to take our position front and on each side. The order was to get back inside the works the best way we could. Taking advantage of some ravines running from our lines, the men all got in safe. But one old fellow who had a stiff leg came stumping along, pursued by hissing bullets, and as he fell over the embankment with that stiff leg pointing skyward he prayed fervently: "O Lord, can't you make peace between these two nations?"

One of our boys who was very tall was writing home the next day to his mother, a very pious woman. He was describing our narrow escape and he put in some pious reflections albeit not very pious himself. He said that he was thankful that his life had been saved by the providence of God. He read the letter to his mess when one of them blurted out: "Providence of God! The devil! Them long legs of yours was what saved you." Undoubtedly, good legs formed the instrument that Providence used.

Shakespeare tells us, "there's such divinity doth hedge a king," but my experience is that it is nothing in comparison with the awful dignity assumed by some petty official "drest in a little brief authority." The greater the office, usually the easier the approach to the officer, for generally only great men attain to high office. Our dear "Old Joe" was more accessible than many a red-tape quartermaster.

The only times I ever was snubbed was by a provost marshal's clerk and by a young assistant surgeon just promoted from hospital steward. The latter incident occurred just as we were leaving Jackson. The morning before we evacuated the place I was told by the division surgeon that we would retreat that night and that we could leave our most seriously wounded in care of three or four young doctors and several nurses. This surgeon was Dr. Patton, of Missouri, of Cockrill's Brigade, a very kind-hearted, old-fashioned gentleman. He told me to visit the wounded of our brigade and find out if I could do anything for them. In my rounds I found a captain of the 30th Louisiana neglected by the nurses and in a dangerous condition from a very severe wound. The nurses, seeing that I had no mark of rank, paid no attention to my request for some wine for the captain. I then found a young lieutenant of Fenner's Battery whose arm had been broken by a fragment of a shell. It had swollen until the bandage had become so tight as to cause intense agony. All that was needed was to adjust the bandage. I went to get the doctor who had charge of that ward. It was only a few steps, and I found four young fellows in a big round tent. They were sitting around a table playing cards and had a bottle of whiskey on the table. They paid no attention to me until I was asked very impatiently what I wanted. When I told him and asked him to go with me and relieve my man, he said: "I have finished my rounds this morning, and I will see him at three o'clock." I said: "Why, it is only eleven o'clock now, and he is suffering terribly, and you certainly will not leave him until this afternoon."

He said he had regular times for making his rounds, and he didn't want to be disturbed. When I said that it was inhuman to neglect a wounded soldier in that way, he replied that he knew his business and I had better attend to my business, or he would make me do it. By that time I was indignant, and I told him I was attending to my business, and he couldn't make me do anything. He then asked: "Who the devil are you?"

I said, "Well, my rank is over yours, and I will see to it that you shall not stay here to neglect my men."

I went immediately to Dr. Patton. He went in a hurry first to relieve the sufferers, and then he went for that young doctor and the nurses who neglected the patients. He said that he would send them to the front to take part in the fighting. Whether he did or not, I don't know. He was very kind-hearted, and they may have begged off by fair promises.

That night we quietly left Jackson, but not until "Old Joe" had removed all that was worth moving.[6]

Another soldier described the action around Jackson:

On the evening of the 7th we reached Jackson, and the next day we were sent to a redoubt on the Raymond road in rather a sharp angle on the battle line and in a much-exposed position. Right on the Raymond road previous to our arrival there, a sixty-four pounder rifled piece was placed to command the road, and our two sections were put on the right and left of it. On the 10th the enemy moved up and drove in our pickets. Soon after several pieces of artillery came in sight and fired a few shots at our line, evidently to test the distance and locate our batteries. That night they began to fortify around the angle of our line which held the large gun and kept busy at the work the next day and night, though no guns could be seen, yet we knew they were there, because the embrasures revealed the fact. Thirty-six Parrott guns, to be run into position as soon as the works were completed, cast a gloom over our little band of heroes as they cast their eyes in that direction. The storm that was brewing became more ominous every minute, as the angle in the line would enable them to bring their guns to bear on our battery.

Sunday, July 12, was a beautiful day, and it seemed more like Sabbath indeed than any day I had seen in a long while. From the Northeast a gentle breeze was blowing, but save its whisperings, not a sound disturbed the stillness except an occasional picket shot reverberating among the hills. We were sitting on some seats which we had constructed along the parapet for our comfort when not engaged with the enemy, when suddenly we were aroused by a terrific fire from their artillery, which appeared to shake the very earth. For two hours the leaden storm raged around us. Cotton bales had been placed on the parapet to protect the men from the sharpshooters in buildings nearby, and these bales were knocked off by the enemy's shot, torn to pieces, and set on fire by the explosion of the shells. The tornado of shells, a ton coming every minute, put the air into cyclonic action, taking up the smoke of the burning cotton and whirling it around our little band of faithful men, cutting us off apparently from the sight of our enemies, their shells rising higher and higher as the minutes passed. As "heaven tempers the wind to the shorn lamb," did not kind Providence send the whirlwind to save our little band from utter annihilation? Just think of it, one hundred and twenty tons of metal thrown at us in those two hours! . . .

History nowhere records the concentration of so many pieces of artillery focused on a single object as that at Jackson. It is unprecedented in the annals of time. There are three incidents that occurred at Jackson which I wish to relate. The first is the keenness, accuracy, and the ability of the enemy's sharpshooters. Joe Willis, of the Maryland detachment, was detailed to cook and bring to the works my meals. One time he asked to be permitted to remain a few minutes longer than it was necessary for me to dispose of the food. I said: "No, Joe, go back to the wagon yard as quickly as you can, for the sharpshooters know you are here, and they are on the lookout for you." He persisted in remaining in a small crevice in the works beside a stake, placing his left hand on the top of it a few inches above the parapet in full view of the enemy. He was there but a few seconds before he returned to me with the blood running from his fingers. "Well, Joe, he caught you, and that is punishment in disobeying orders."

The second incident was one that we might say illustrated predestination. Henry Gordon, who succeeded Joe Willis in cooking my rations, brought my supper to the works that day and before returning asked to be promoted. I said: "Gordon, what do you mean by promotion?" "Why," he said, "I want to be made a cannoneer." I then pointed out to him the dangers on the firing line and the safety at the wagon yard. "If you persist in being made a cannoneer, get someone to take your team and report here tomorrow morning." He did so, and the next day he was killed.

The third incident was the frailty and unreliability of human courage. Two days after the avalanche of shells described in this article the major commanding our battalion of light artillery picked up courage in the lull of fighting to pay our battery a visit. A sharpshooter must have discovered the major's approach, particularly his bright uniform and the large gold star on his collar, and reported the same to the commander of the enemy's artillery. The major had scarcely reached our first gun when the ball opened. The occasion was one long to be remembered. The major's nerves gave way, he fell to the ground, then crawled beneath a large tarpaulin, and remained there till the engagement was over. Covered with dust, the major emerged from his hiding place and departed without even saying good-by.[7]

A member of Ector's Brigade related an event at Jackson shortly after the "Hell or Horses Revolt":

> While just in the rear of Vicksburg, we learned that the garrison had surrendered the day before and that a large force was trying to cut us off from Jackson. Then followed a hard march through heat and dust to Jackson, where we occupied breastworks already erected. Two days and nights of fighting followed. During the siege the pickets in front of Ector's Brigade were driven in, when General Johnston came riding down the line and called for a picked regiment to drive the enemy back and re-establish our picket line. General Ector called on the 14th Texas, the regiment that had stacked their arms but two weeks before. Now was their time. It was a perilous undertaking, it being five hundred yards across the old field, with the enemy in the timber. Our batteries on the right and left opened fire with grape and canister, and I don't think a rabbit could have escaped in that old field. When the batteries ceased the gallant 14th was ordered forward. Col. John L. Camp sprang over the works, ordered the colors forward, the regiment to double-quick, but not to fire a gun until we reached the timber. Then there was a deafening roar of musketry for a short time, the enemy fell back, and we re-established our picket line. The regiment was ordered back to take its place in the ditches; but to avoid exposure in the open field we returned by a zig-zag ravine, reaching our works with but little loss. A few nights later, along toward midnight, as our pickets were popping away in front, we were ordered out of the ditches. To press close to the man next in front was the only way to keep together in the dark. We were giving up Jackson. We fell back; and as the enemy did not follow, we rested for a while.[8]

J.M. Spinks, a member of Company G of the Tenth Texas, implies he was tired of capturing the same Yankees over and over:

> Were on our way to Vicksburg the day it surrendered, and turned to Jackson, and were besieged eight days. The federals charged our works and we killed so many of them that an armistice was declared for four hours for them to bury their dead.
>
> Our Company was on picket when the bugle sounded. During the armistice we met the Yankees half-way and talked. I talked to men there that I had captured three times.[9]

At Jackson, Mississippi, on July 10, the Yanks shot five artillery horses behind

89

the Tenth Texas defense lines. The Tenth Texas laid in the ditches for eight days and nights without shade in the open field. Pvt. Jim Watson wrote home:

> We had an armistice of four hours for the Feds to bury their dead. Our regiment was on picket that day. When firing ceased, we hailed to the Feds and told them to meet us half way, and they told us to lay down our guns and come on. We did so. We got along fine. We talked about them taking Vicksburg and things in general until some Fed officers came over and talked pretty sassy. The Feds are in fine spirits. They think they have us whipped. They boast of taking Vicksburg and Port Hudson. They say that they took thirty-two thousand prisoners at Vicksburg and six thousand at Port Hudson. The times look very gloomy. At this time some of our soldiers are badly whipped and deserting. The Mississippians are down in the mouth.

One thing Private Watson made very clear in his letter home was that "General Johnston is good on retreat. He knows all about retreating." Later, Johnston was relieved at Atlanta for being "too good" at retreating.

At Jackson, the Tenth Texas records reflected only two men wounded and one man, E. Farmer, as a prisoner of war. Farmer was listed as deserted several days before being listed as a prisoner of war. He died in prison.

On August 1, 1863, Jim Watson wrote home that prices were very high and chickens were going for two dollars apiece. There was not much going on, and he noted: "Howell and I made a chicken pie today and ate it by ourselves. I think it was as good as I ever saw in my life." On August 6, he wrote home from Morton Station and said, "We are camped here and have nothing to do at this time but to cook and eat and lay in the shade." He did go on to mention the problems when an army camps next to someone's property. He said, "They broke up every citizen that they camp near." He added that if the citizens did not have much property to lose, they would at least burn up their rail fences. On August 9, 1863, Jim Watson commented in a letter about two weddings back in East Texas: "They beat all weddings that I ever heard of in my life." Apparently, the widows of two men who died in the Tenth Texas married two other men discharged from the Tenth Texas. One of the men was discharged for a physical ailment called "varicolle." Some of the widows back home were not wasting time latching onto any available men. With the food shortages in East Texas, it was conceivable that the widowed women were remarrying for more than just love.

Also, in August, the Tenth Texas and Ector's Brigade were ordered to the area around Chickamauga to meet an advance by the Union army.

On the trip from Jackson, Mississippi, to Chickamauga, Pvt. R. Flourney of Company A was "killed by the company (railroad) cars at Meridian." Later in the war, Pvt. A.L. Birt, Company F, was injured in a railroad accident but returned to duty.

During the summer of 1863, the Confederacy formed a company of soldiers out of East Texas. Of the eighty-six men, all were from forty to fifty years old. Concurrently, the Yankees were releasing able bodied men that had served out their enlistment periods.[10]

On August 24, 1863, the Twenty-ninth North Carolina Infantry Regiment was assigned to Ector's Brigade. It joined the Ninth Texas, Tenth Texas, Fourteenth Texas, and Thirty-second Texas and remained with them until the end of the war.[11]

Pvt. George Birdwell, Company G, had two brothers, Charles and Benjamin, in the same company. George was elected chaplain in August 1863, and to ensure he did a good job, he went home to Texas and was ordained as a licensed minister. He then returned to the Tenth Texas.

CHAPTER 10

"Eyes stuck out far enough to hang a hat on"

BATTLE OF CHICKAMAUGA

ON AUGUST 30, 1863, the Tenth Texas arrived at Chickamauga Railroad Station.[1] Less than three weeks later, they fought in the Battle of Chickamauga, an area located in the northwestern corner of Georgia, just south of Chattanooga, Tennessee. It turned out to be the bloodiest two-day battle of the Civil War. The engagement began on September 19 with a flurry of attacks and counterattacks with chaotic fighting continuing all day and into the night.

The Battle of Chickamauga transpired over an area of about six miles by three miles in a mixture of dense woods and scattered open fields. The territory encompassed thickets of oak trees and cedar pine that were matted with underbrush. Confusion was rampant because higher ranking generals literally could not see their soldiers. The imposing landscape also hindered the use of artillery, which caused considerable combat at close range. Also, as units were changing positions, the muddled terrain caused inadvertent combat with the attacking lines at angles to one another. This was one of the few battles where the Confederates supposedly outnumbered the Yankees.

Here the Tenth Texas came under the command of the famous Gen. Nathan Bedford Forrest for part of the first day. He actually took Ector's Brigade without permission and sent them into the fight on Saturday, September 19. This was not the last time they served under General Forrest. He was known as one of the bravest and toughest soldiers in the Confederacy. His enemies referred to him as "that Devil Forrest." It is still widely accepted that, during the war, Forrest had thirty horses shot out from under him. The following story shows exactly how tough Forrest was. He had relieved a young lieutenant from his artillery support unit because of dissatisfaction over his conduct. Forrest told the lieutenant he was not going to change his mind. The young lieutenant pulled a gun and shot Forrest in the left hip. Forrest grabbed his assailant and slashed him with a pen knife. Forrest then walked to a doctor's office to get him to look at his wound. The doctor told him it was probably fatal:

At this Forrest rearranged his clothes, seized a pistol from a member of his staff who had followed him, and rushed out into the street, saying to those who tried to restrain him, "Get out of my way; he has mortally wounded me, and I intend to kill him before I die" Someone informed the wounded lieutenant that Forrest was coming after him, and he immediately ran out of the building and up the street until he fell from exhaustion. A crowd at once gathered around him, so that Forrest could not get close enough to shoot him. Someone said: "General, you need not trouble yourself to kill him, he is already dying." Forrest said: "All right, if you are sure of this I won't shoot him, but, damn him, he has killed me, and I am determined he shall die too." Being now convinced that the young lieutenant could not live, he directed some of his men to place his assailant on a stretcher, carry him to the hotel, and have him properly cared for. Forrest himself was by the time very weak from loss of blood, and had to be carried to the residence of a friend, where he rapidly recovered from his injury.

Two days later, when the young officer was rapidly sinking from septic peritonitis, which followed a perforation of the intestine, he sent word to General Forrest that, if it were possible, he desired to have him come to see him, as he wished to speak with him before he died. To this request Forrest acceded, and was carried into the lieutenant's room. An eyewitness to the interview informs me that the officer took the general by the hand and held it between both of his, saying, "General, I shall not be here long, and I was not willing to go away without seeing you in person and saying to you how thankful I

Gen. Nathan Bedford Forrest

am that I am the one who is to die and that you are spared to the country. What I did, I did in a moment of rashness, and I want your forgiveness." Forrest leaned over the bed upon which the young man was lying, told him he forgave him freely, and that his own heart was full of regret that the wound he had inflicted was fatal.[2]

A Confederate cavalry soldier under Forrest described how the units first made contact on September 19, 1863, at Chickamauga:

They filed off over the crest on the back track and had not been gone more than fifteen minutes when we were brought to our feet by the sound of a double volley not more than a quarter of a mile away, apparently. And this is what happened: The two battalions were riding along utterly oblivious of danger, chatting and joking as men will when on the march and confident that no danger impended. Croxton (a Yank unit) had been sent forward . . . and, marching rapidly through the woods in the direction of Reed's Bridge, no doubt saw first the two battalions riding along nonchalantly, and, waiting in the brush for them, poured two volleys into the unsuspecting troopers. The result of such a complete surprise may well be imagined. A wild flight back to the command, riderless horses, two on a horse, men afoot, some slightly wounded, some limping, some hatless, some without their guns — a wild rout. "Sauve qui peut." Who could blame them for "tearing out of the wilderness" to a point of community, if not of safety?

No sooner had we heard the volleys, which we instantly recognized as infantry fire, than we were on our feet and in the saddle even before the bugle could sound the "Mount." "Forward! Head of column left! Trot!" came from the Colonel, sharp, clear, and not to be mistaken. I was at the end of the column and had not much more than started when the head had crossed the crest. Just then the fugitives in a mass struck the head of the column, breaking and almost literally riding it down. For a moment greatest confusion prevailed. Colonel Hart shouted: "Stop them! Knock them off their horses if they don't stop!" Some rode through our ranks and disappeared in the rear, and I was too busy to note whether they came back or not. One big fellow passed me on the fly and would probably be running yet if his panic-stricken, blazed-faced sorrel could have held out. He was a picture I can never forget as he came flying down the slope. His sorrel had the bit. He had lost his hat and gun and was holding with both hands to the mane, or the pommel of his saddle, while his long yellow beard, neatly split, was flying back on each side and his blue eyes stuck out far enough to hang a hat on. As he came directly toward me, I was forced to pull my mount to one side quickly to avoid being run down. When he got within reach, I raised my rifle as if to strike him, but it was menace only; I had no intention of clubbing him. The look he gave me as he passed was most appealing to my risabilities, and I burst out in a loud guffaw. Nothing short of a big pine or a mountain cliff could have arrested him just then. But I did not blame him. Only a week previously I had done some running from an imaginary danger myself. . . .

When General Forrest appeared on our line, encouraging us to hold on, our friends in the brush opened up on the cavalcade with all they had big guns and little, and yet not a man went down. I never could account for it to my own satisfaction fully. I have often read of the General's fearlessness and contempt of danger. In this instance, he showed not even the least excitement. I could see no trace of any emotion whatsoever about him, and he passed within two feet of me. By my side stood a stripling of my own age who had just rammed home a cartridge in his "Minie" and was fumbling for a cap as the General came up to him, and, stooping down, patted the boy on the shoulder in a fatherly way and said to him: "Go it, my little man!" "Bob" looked up surprised and seeing who was addressing him so familiarly started for a big pine tree a few paces in front of the line, laid his "Minie" against the side of the tree, and blazed away at the brush. Perhaps the General never laughed — I have never heard of his doing so — but I certainly thought I detected a grin on his face. The whole incident was comical to those near by and we had a hearty laugh over it then and afterwards. But "Bob" remained as sober as ever. What added to our hilarity was the fact that the night previous Bob's horse happened to step on the rifle barrel and his weight caused it to bend so that a charge could with difficulty be rammed home, and the bullet would hit fifteen degrees to the left of the object aimed at and he would take no other gun.

. . . The whole Federal line opened on us again, and "hell broke loose." If we had been subjected to a hot fire before, we were now subjected to a whirlwind of missiles, big and little. They gave us all they had and even borrowed from their neighbors to hurl at us. The air was full of lead, dust, and gravel. Woods was on his way back to his place near me (side by side we'd held until then), and I was looking toward him when I saw a small cloud of dust rise from his left thigh (our clothes were filled and covered with yellow dust), and he dropped the butt of his now empty Enfield to the ground as a support. Seeing him hardly hit, I rushed to him and offered to help him down the hill to a shelter but he declined my aid, saying that his leg wasn't broken and by using his gun as a support he could get to the surgeon all right. To prove it, he started on down toward the mill with a cheery, "good-by, old boy." With a gripping at my heart, I gave him the same and he disappeared down the hill, slowly and painfully. I never saw him again. He died in Texas many years ago.

I went back to my post and for a while did the best possible firing into the brush, lying prone until a bullet struck the ground directly in front of me and threw a handful of dirt and fine gravel full in my face, blinding me. I sat up and began to dig the dirt out of my eyes and before regaining my sight, the firing suddenly ceased. The regiment was behind the crest again. Only about a dozen men and officers remained on the line, and I was much relieved to find that the enemy had not left their ambuscade. They were by far the more numerous and they had bayonets; we had none, besides being weaker. It was then that looking from our elevation through the tree tops to the left we saw Wilson's Georgia Brigade of Infantry marching in battle line up the slight incline of a corn field (now wooded land). The enemy drew a regiment from his left, or center, to re-enforce his right, and these were the first of them I saw with the exception of one man alone during the three or more hours our little brigade had been holding Croxton's twenty-five hundred or more in check. We threw up our dusty hats and yelled our relief. Wilson's right came to the corner of the field less than one hundred yards from where I stood alone, pushed off the top rail, kicked off the lower rails, stepped over to the wood side, lined up and started to advance while at less than one hundred yards back lay a double line of blue waiting. When the gray line had advanced about forty yards the blue line rose and delivered a double volley. The gray line stopped short, like a man receiving a staggering blow in the face. Men fell in their tracks one against another. To me who was watching them with "my heart in my throat," it appeared that fully one-third of the line fell. But not a man of them turned his back. An instant later was heard the voice of a Stentor order: "Fire! Fire at Will!" and then the gray line blazed with fire and with fearful effect. The blues had fired down hill without taking time to aim and in consequence overshot. For a few minutes ten or fifteen at most this close range fire continued and then the same stentorian voice rose above the dire: "Cease firing! Forward!" the gray line threw its rifles over the right shoulder and moved as one man at a quick step without fear or falter, and then at thirty yards distance came a single word: "Charge!" the grays dropped to "Charge bayonet!" and bleeding at every step leaped forward with a yell such as the old woods had never heard. Looking on this, we expected then to witness a mix up with bayonets but when Wilson's men got to within but a few yards of the blue line, it gave way and disappeared in the woods, but still leaving a trail, as I saw next morning the fallen gray lying on top of fallen blue. At that point the havoc in Croxton's line had been fearful. I could have walked on the bodies as far as could be seen there, for twenty-five yards or more without putting foot on ground. Poor fellows! With the advent of Wilson our part in the affair was ended.

Wilson's loss in this and a subsequent action, four hundred yards farther on was 99 killed, 426 wounded, and 80 captured, most of whom were wounded and recaptured with a Federal field hospital. The total loss for the day was 604 out of 1,200 taken into action. [3]

When Wilson's Brigade was mentioned, it proceeded into battle just before the Tenth Texas and Ector's Brigade and took up position on the Texans' left to attack one more time. A participant in the melee gave his account of the arrival of the Tenth Texas:

And the fight was "on" in earnest. As quickly as this information was made Forrest called to Pegram: "Hold this position, Pegram, until I can bring up reinforcements. Pegram answered, "I'll hold it if I can. General." And hold it he did for I never knew how long as time has or had no existence for me when a fight was going on. At one time our whole line fell back slowly and in order, as if by command, except Huwald who double-shooting with canister, staggered their advance and drove them back. . . . Riding to the battery where the writer had left the General, he saw the most welcome sight of the head of a column of gray infantry from the front of which a tall officer, detaching himself, rode out and called out: "Harry, where are they?" This was Capt. Ryland Todhunter, of Lexington, Ky. An old neighbor and friend of the writer's. A quick hand grasp and, "Get into line, Ryland, and move forward and you'll find them" was the last greeting between two friends until the Louisville Reunion brought us gladly together.[4]

Captain Todhunter was leading the Tenth Texas, with Ector's Brigade, to the battlefield. Todhunter was wounded five times in the war and had five horses shot from under him. As a religious man, when he heard Stonewall Jackson had been killed, he said, "We are gone, God is not on our side." As he led Ector's Brigade up to the line of battle, he was about to have his horse killed under him and be seriously wounded.[5]

A member of Ector's Brigade relived his impression of the first charge with Wilson's Brigade on their left:

> We marched nearly all night on the 18th arriving at Chickamauga just at daylight. We waded the creek and halted for breakfast. I do not remember the hour exactly that the fight began; but I can never forget the first charge we made. A battery was in front of us and we started for it. Almost in the beginning of the charge our captain was killed and the command of the company devolved upon me. The guns were well served and their fire destructive. Four of my men fell in one pile, but we pressed forward and captured the battery that we started for.
>
> It is singular how little incidents trivial in themselves will be impressed on one's memory at such moments when more important ones are forgotten. Now I do not remember the number of guns we captured but I do remember as distinctly as if it were yesterday the position of one of the gunners as we rushed up. He was standing unconcerned by his still smoking piece, with his arm thrown over it as carelessly as if he had been "at rest" on dress parade, as much as to say: "Well, boys, I gave you the best I had, and here I am."
>
> Ector's Brigade went up against two heavy batteries of the enemy the first day. The last of these cut us badly late in the afternoon, but was taken by our brigade and Haskins Battery about sundown, when we were relieved by Cleburne's Division.[6]

As Wilson and Ector's Brigade attacked, a writer for the *Chicago Journal* wrote, "The enemy bore down upon (the Yanks) like a mountain torrent sweeping away a brigade as if it had been driftwood."

Another soldier shared about how the battle opened with their brave chaplain giving a pep talk:

> This same brave chaplain rode along with our brigade, on an old string haltered horse, as we advanced to the attack at Chickamauga, exhorting the boys to be brave, to aim low and to kill the Yankees as if they were wild beasts. He was eloquent and patriotic. He stated that if he only had a gun he too would go along as a private soldier.

You could hear his voice echo and re-echo over the hills. He had worked up his patriotism to a pitch of genuine bravery and daring that I had never seen exhibited, when fluff, fluff, fluff, fluff, FLUFF, FLUFF — a whir, a Boom! And a shell screams through the air. The reverend LL.D. stops to listen, like an old sow when she hears the wind, and says, "Remember boys, that he who is killed will sup tonight in Paradise." Some soldier hollered at the top of his voice, "Well parson you come along and take supper with us." Boom! Whir! A bomb burst and the parson at that moment put spurs to this horse and was seen to lumber to the rear and almost every soldier yelled out, "The parson isn't hungry, and never eats supper."[7]

The wife of a soldier from the Fourteenth Texas remembered what her husband shared about the first charge of the morning. For this battle, the Tenth Texas and Fourteenth Texas were consolidated. (Her description of the Rebel uniforms was probably an exaggeration, for this point in the war):

I shall write of a private in the ranks — little Jimmie Arnold, a fifteen-year-old orphan boy, a boy from our neighboring town of Carthage (East Texas), who was a member of Company G, of which company my husband was first lieutenant. This company left Texas for the war in 1861 with one hundred and forty men. Of this number, only thirteen returned to their homes. The bodies of one hundred and twenty-seven were left to molder into dust on the different battle fields from Corinth until they laid down their arms at Meridian, Mississippi in 1865. And now only six of that thirteen are left. Little Jimmie Arnold was the pet of his company and of his regiment.

They were proud of his courage and fidelity, and he was fond of each and every one of his comrades. Especially did he love and reverence his colonel. After months of hard service and privations, the music of the fife and drum, the glamour of battle, the glittering guns, bayonets, and swords, the plumed chapeaux, the handsome Confederate gray uniforms with the brass buttons, gold braid, and quivering epaulets of his officers — all were inspiring and still had a charm for the valiant young warrior, although he and a number of his comrades were ragged and almost barefooted, some with feet sore and bleeding, the blood running through the holes in their shoes; yet duty, with all of its appalling difficulties, still had its sweetness for him and was the lodestar of his existence. Nothing could daunt him, and danger was a word unknown to this hero of high ideals and loyalty to his country and to his friends. He was as brave as the bravest of any of their men, always ready and eager to go into a battle.

But one day, when a line was forming at the battle of Chickamauga, he had a presentiment that he would be killed if he went into it, and he said to Colonel Camp: "Colonel, you know I am not a coward and have always obeyed my officers' commands; but don't let me go into this fight."

"Why Jimmie?" asked Colonel Camp.

"Because if you do I'll be killed. Can't you find some excuse for sending me to the rear?"

"I can't think of any," replied the good, conscientious Christian officer.

"Let me take your horse to the rear, Colonel," pleaded the boy.

"I can't find any excuse for sending him back, Jimmie. Go on and do your duty, as you always have done."

There was a fearful, a soulful pause; but in a moment, with heroic determination and courage stamped on his face, the nervy boy replied emphatically: "All right, Colonel, I will; but I'll never come out of this fight alive."

In a few minutes a charge was ordered, and in ten minutes after Jimmie went into the bloody battle of Chickamauga, where Texas was proud to own her sons, he was killed — the dauntless, brave Texas boy, as brave as Leonidas, who defended the pass of Thermopylae with his three hundred Spartans against Xerxes's myriads of Persians. Who will say that his death was not as heroic as the Spartan king's? For he went into the battle facing death as did Leonidas in the narrow pass. Who will say that General Lee, Stonewall Jackson, Albert Sidney Johnston, Joseph E. Johnston, or any other of our brave leaders was a greater hero than the little orphan boy, Jimmie Arnold?[8]

Nearly all books that are written about Chickamauga make reference to a story told after the war by C.B. "Buck" Kilgore. Kilgore was a captain in Company G, Tenth Texas, before being appointed to brigade adjutant. Here was his story:

On Friday night, September 18, 1863, Ector's Brigade of which I was adjutant crossed Chickamauga Creek, and on Saturday morning, the 19th, formed on the extreme Confederate right, supporting General Forrest's cavalry, which was very heavily engaged. The fighting soon became fierce for us, and we were barely able to hold our ground.

General Ector became uneasy in regard to the protection of his right flank, and asked me to go to General Forrest and urge him to be very vigilant in his protection of it. I galloped up to where one of his batteries was engaged as I had been told he was there. He had on a linen duster with a sword and pistol on the outside of the duster and was exposed to very heavy fire of infantry and now and then a shot from the enemy's batteries.

I said: "General Forrest, General Ector directed me to say to you that he is uneasy in regard to his right flank." He replied: "Tell General Ector that he need not bother about his right flank. I'll take care of it." I reported to my commander and about an hour later news reached us that Wilson's brigade had been hard hit and driven back, and General Ector sent me again to Forrest to tell him that he was now uneasy about his left flank. I found him near the same spot right in the thickest part of the fight, the battery blazing away and every man fighting like mad. I told him what General Ector had directed me to say, and this time he got furious. He turned around on me and shouted loud enough to be heard above the terrible din that was in the air: "Tell General Ector that, by God I am here, and will take care of his left flank as well as his right." It is hardly necessary to add that we were not outflanked on either side.[9]

The interesting part of this statement concerns whether the Tenth Texas and Ector's Brigade were outflanked that day. It should be noted that the compiled service records of Kilgore show that he suffered a severe wound in the thigh and had his horse shot out from under him that day. If severely wounded in a wooded area, could Kilgore really be a credible witness for all the action around him at the same time? General Forrest, in his report, stated: "I must say that the fighting and gallant charges of the two brigades (Wilson on the left of Ector's) just referred to excited my admiration. They broke the enemy's lines and could not be halted or withdrawn until nearly surrounded."[10]

Another source used to see if Ector's Brigade was outflanked the first day at Chickamauga is a letter written by C.B. Carlton, Company I, Tenth Texas, to the father of John Templeton, explaining how John was captured that day:

After they found a line of Battle, Brigade was ordered to charge after charging about a mile they found they were flanked on the left & commenced falling back in confusion they had not fell back far before they were moved from between the two lines (Yankee lines) By the Right flank & since that time your son with four others of the Camp (Company I) has been missing & every one feels satisfied they

102

captured unhurt the Boys were Scattered pretty Badly & when the Order was given to move By the Right flank it Supposed they went on over the hill into the line Yankees that had got in their Rear there was Several of the Brigade captured at the same time & place that has since made their Escape & state that there was some of our camp among the Prisoners of our Brigade could not give any names & cannot believe but what the Boys were all captured unhurt for the last time they was Scene they were going in the Direction of this line that had gained their Rear But the Boys was unaware of the Yankees being in our rear.[11]

In his official report, the Northern commander stated his battle line formed an obtuse angle with the opening toward the Southerners. The two Yankee regiments on Ector's left were lying down and were apparently not seen until Ector's Brigade drove back some others on the right. This left the group of prone Yankees to the left and rear of Ector's Brigade. Their commander reported that they were pouring double charges of canisters in front and on the flank of Ector's Brigade at a distance of less than forty yards. Union reinforcements came on the scene just as the line was breaking apart. The Yanks took a small number of prisoners. In reference to the Texans, the Northern commander pronounced, "They fought with great obstinacy and determination, only retreating when fairly swept away by our overwhelming fire." The Yank commander also noted that the Rebs had captured some artillery but they recaptured it.[12]

Based on the number of prisoners the Tenth Texas and Ector's Brigade lost, and the letter to Templeton's father, it seems clear the Yanks got in behind Wilson and Ector before Forrest could react. This would explain Forrest's statement that he could not halt them.

Pvt. John Davis, Company E, was wounded in the right thigh on the morning of September 19 while charging and retaking a battery. He was captured, but because the bone in the leg was broken, the Yanks sent him back. He recovered and was later wounded at the Battle of Atlanta.[13] By Davis stating that they were retaking a battery, he implied that it was one of General Forrest's cannons. Forrest was well known for bringing his cannons up on the front lines to get maximum effect. He used them like large caliber shotguns. One of Forrest's cavalry officers said, "It was hard to bring away the cherished guns of the Confederate batteries. . . . All the horses of one gun were killed or wounded." This was probably the gun that Davis mentioned.[14] Forrest was also famous for utilizing his cavalry as mounted infantry, similar to a modern general using motorized infantry. Later, at the Battle of

Nashville, the Yanks started copying Forrest's tactics.

On Saturday night, September 19, Cleburne's unit attacked the Yanks after dark. This attack was to the left of the Tenth Texas position. This soldier characterized the night attack:

> On the night of the first day the woods took fire, and the cries of the wounded were dreadful to hear. At the close of this fight the Fifth Georgia Regiment had fallen back and taken a position behind the brow of a small hill and it was almost certain death for one to

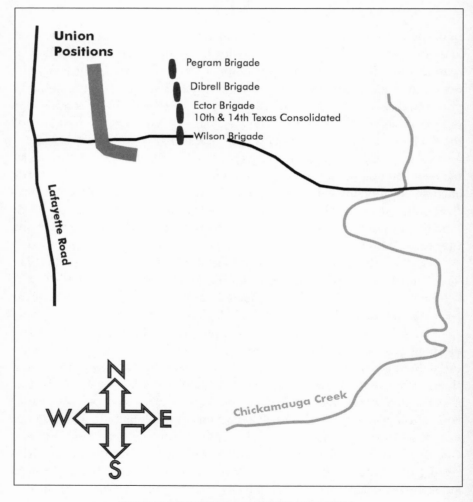

THE BATTLE OF CHICKAMAUGA
First Day, September 19, 1863

raise his head above the hill as the sharpshooters of the enemy kept up an incessant firing in that direction. One poor fellow of Company B thoughtlessly raised his head above the hill, when a shot struck him in the forehead and he fell back a corpse. That ball whizzed in close proximity to my head; so near did it pass, I felt the wind caused by its passage.

While the Command was behind this hill and about twilight the steady tramp of Gen. Pat Cleburne's men was heard advancing and as these heroes passed us we gave them a shout. In a little while we to were up and advancing to their support. (Cleburne, Texas, was named after Pat Cleburne.)

Then came the "Fire of Hell" in the dark woods upon the banks of the Chickamauga, "The River of Death." As the battle wave surged to and fro that fateful autumn night, the boom of the cannon, the rattle of musketry, the shouts of the advancing Confederates and the cries of the wounded made an impression upon the minds and hearts of all those who were engaged in the bloody work that will last as long as life.[15]

The "Fire of Hell" was a forest fire that consumed many of the wounded between the lines. Ironically, Chickamauga is an Indian word that means "River of Death."

As the fighting raged on for the second day, debate lingers as to which units were responsible for the Confederate victory. General Longstreet had arrived from General Lee's army on the night of the 19th. It can be argued that the ferocious and relentless attacks by the Tenth Texas and Ector's Brigade on September 20, along with the Confederate right flank, scared the Yank's commanding general into making a tactical error. To reinforce against these assaults, he pulled a unit out of his opposite wing. Unfortunately for the Yanks, he started the movement of this unit just as Longstreet stormed in with his troops. This action broke open the Federal right wing and the chase was on.

On Sunday, September 20, 1863, because the Tenth Texas had been seriously bloodied by the charges into the enemy's artillery positions the previous day, they were held in reserve. Here, they had their first good luck of the campaign. A Reb general asked for a brigade out of reserve to make an attack. He refused Ector's Brigade because he had not heard of them and instead took Gist's Brigade. (It should be mentioned that Gist's full name was States Rights Gist. Maybe that was the reason the general had heard of them because it would be difficult to forget that name.) Gist's Brigade was ordered into a frontal attack against the Yanks, who had built log breast-works the night before. A war correspondent for the *New York Herald* said the Yanks were behind piled up rails and logs breast high.[16] It has been said that a force behind breastworks triples its strength compared to being in the open.[17] To add to the problem, because of the wooded terrain, the attacking Rebs hit at an angle with the left of the line hitting first. This allowed the Yanks to shoot from the flank into the angled line of Rebs. Gist's Brigade lost one-third of its men in a matter of minutes. Multiple charges were then ordered, with the brigades of Ector, Gist, and Wilson all getting intermingled and confused. This lasted for about forty-five minutes, with the Tenth Texas pushing through the two other heavily engaged Rebel brigades in a tactical maneuver known as a "passage of lines." The disorder of the existing units, with their wounded soldiers and the intense close-range firing of weapons, apparently caused confusion in the ranks of the Tenth Texas. This neutralized the thrust of their attack.

The Tenth Texas struck around 10:00 Sunday morning because this was the time that Pvt. Jim Watson, Company G, stated he was wounded. He suffered a severe wound to the stomach. While lying in front of the Yankee breastworks, Pvt. Jeff Rosson, also of Company G, braved the withering enemy fire and pulled Watson to safety. Watson described how they took a silk handkerchief, soaked it in whiskey, tied it to a rifle ramrod, and pushed it through the bullet hole. Then, they cauterized the wound. Luckily, he did not have internal damage or this would have promptly finished him.[18] After getting resupplied with ammo at 4:00 in the afternoon, the Texans charged the enemy positions and the route started. In Gist's report he says, "Loud cheers went up to heaven."[19]

A Texan retold the action of September 20:

During the last day of this fight we drove the enemy back. Three of Captain Howze's men were killed together. That night taking a few of the company he went back to the spot and buried them.[20]

Another soldier explained what happened after the battle was over:

When the struggle had been to the death for quite a while, and many had met it, the Confederates saw light ahead and then with shot and shell they overwhelmed the confused and terror stricken ranks of Rosecran's magnificent army, as it retreated in the direction of Chattanooga.

When this was done there was a Rebel yell that went up from Bragg's Army the like of which has never been heard before nor since on this earth. The mountains and valleys seemed to take it up and echo it and re-echo it, as if the thunder of the great mountains was giving praise to the great God of battles for this grand victory.[21]

A Rebel described the Yank yell as a weak "HOO-RAY" with emphasis on the "RAY." The Reb yell was "WOH-WHO-EYS" with the emphasis on the "WHO-EY" given the effect of a "whee."

General Bragg, the Reb commander, was heavily criticized after the battle for not more aggressively pursuing the defeated Yanks. To convince him of his victory, a Reb that had been captured and then freed was brought before Bragg to tell him of the Yank retreat. Bragg, not believing him, asked, "Do you know what a retreat looks like?" The soldier looked at him and said, "I ought to General, I've been with you during your whole campaign."

As the Battle of Chickamauga ended, General Forrest had his horse shot in the neck while chasing the retreating Yankees. He plugged the wound with his finger and when the pursuit had ended dismounted his horse, pulled his finger from the wound, and his horse died.[22]

Gen. William Bate of the Confederate Army was also prominent at the Battle of Chickamauga. His future in the war was tied closely to the Texans. As a matter of fact, he blamed Ector's Brigade, including the Tenth Texas, for the defeat at the Battle of Nashville.

Two soldiers told of Bate's wounding at Shiloh and the three horses killed under him at Chickamauga:

> There under a crucial test he advanced in front of the regiment on the magnificent steed, and was shot through the leg, both bones being broken the bullet passing through the saddle and entirely through the horse. Col. Bate grew so faint from the loss of blood that he dropped the reins and was holding the pommel of the saddle, when the horse deliberately returned to his proper place in the rear of the regiment. Col. Bate was carried to a little cabin over a hill and out of immediate danger. The horse followed put his head in the door and whinnied then turned away and soon afterward was dead. . . .
>
> It was some months before Col. Bate had recovered sufficiently to enter service again, and then he went on crutches. He had to use them until sometime after the war. However, he never missed a battle except when confined with wounds and in the various incidents of horses being killed at Chickamauga he had to be lifted each time upon another horse, being unable to mount alone.
>
> He was my commander at Chickamauga. . . . He went into that battle with wounds received at Shiloh not yet healed. On horseback

he carried his sword in one hand, his crutches in the other, and the rein of his horse's bridle between his teeth. One horse after another was shot from under him until three were killed and none other was to be procured. In this dilemma did this proud indomitable soul falter? No; but like the lionhearted hero he was, he hobbled on through the fight upon his crutches until he led his men to victory, leaving fifty-eight percent of his entire command wounded or dead upon the field which his valor had won.[23]

From events related later, it appeared the 58 percent left on the battlefield were all his brave boys. In 1864, on the trip to Nashville, some of the survivors did not have the stomach to fight.

Another of General Bate's men witnessed Confederate President Davis' trip across the Chickamauga Battlefield:

After the battle, President Davis came out and went over the battlefield and at the sharp point he saw a horse lying dead with an officer's trappings on. He asked his guide whose horse it was, and the guide told him it was Brig. Gen. Bate's of Tennessee. This was the old sorrel. They went on some three hundred yards farther and saw a little black mare lying dead, and the President asked whose horse that was. The guide said it was Brig. Gen. Bate's of Tennessee. They went on further, and lying across a little earthworks was another horse, a mouse-colored, bobtailed artillery horse and the President asked whose horse that was; and again the guide said it was Brig. Gen. Bate's of Tennessee. The President turning to the party of general staff officers with him said: "This man Bate must be a gallant fellow."[24]

One Confederate soldier expressed the details he saw on the battlefield at Chickamauga eight days later:

About eight days later I was called back to my regiment. In passing back over the battle field I saw wounded and dead Federals lying in a space not larger than twenty-five feet square who had never been touched by nurse or doctor. They were crying, "Water, water, water," their long hair standing out in all directions, glued together with blood. The dead among them were swollen twice or three times their natural size. But I noticed no dead or wounded Confederates. I was anxious to know why the Federals had not looked after their men; but when I passed by a very large tent flying the United States flag, I saw wounded Federals lying as thick as could be placed. And this was war, and "war is hell."[25]

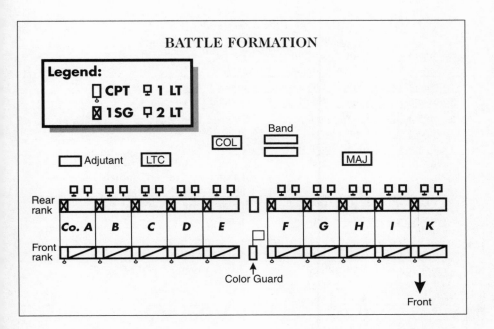

BATTLE FORMATION

Legend:
- ▯ CPT
- ⏄ 1 LT
- ☒ 1SG
- ⏄ 2 LT

Band

COL

Adjutant   LTC   MAJ

Rear rank   Co. A   B   C   D   E   F   G   H   I   K

Front rank

Color Guard

Front

The author, besides having one great-grandfather in the Tenth Texas Cavalry Dismounted, also had another relative at Chickamauga on the Union side. Henry C. Carlock fought for Company C of the 113th Ohio and was wounded on September 20, 1863. One document said he had a shell wound on the left side of his face. On September 20, after double quickening for about four miles, he was wounded. He also was hit in the skin and muscles, fracturing his fifth and sixth ribs, which caused him to cough up blood. He laid on the battlefield in the woods for two days and nights. Apparently, having decided he would probably die just laying there, he got up and made his way to Chattanooga. Many of the other Yanks were not as fortunate.

The Battle of Chickamauga was the costliest two-day battle of the Civil War. The total dead, wounded and missing was 34,654 in two days. Only Gettysburg and the Seven Day Battle exceeded these casualties in total. The Seven Day Battle (for seven days) had 1,809 more casualties. Gettysburg, which had the most, was a three-day battle. The Confederates could not afford victories of this kind. A French newspaper had it correct when it reported, "The two armies meet and fight and slaughter each other with the utmost fury. Then they fall back and reorganize for another general massacre. Positively, the war will end when the last man is killed."

The records show the Tenth Texas started with 272 men and had eleven killed, eighty-four wounded, and twenty-five missing. This was a 44 percent casualty rate.[26]

10th Texas Cavalry
Company Commanders at Chickamauga

Company A	Capt. J. Wright	Wounded "severely"
Company B	Lt. J.W. Cannon	Killed
Company C	Capt. W. McGee	Wounded "knee"
Company D	Capt. R. Smith	Wounded "face severely"
Company E	Lt. W. Young	Wounded "slightly"
Company F	Capt. Booty	Wounded "thigh"
Company G	Lt. G. Tramwell	Wounded "slightly"
Company H	Lt. R. Lyles	Wounded "slightly" — he was wounded, then captured, then recaptured from the Yanks (Templeton letter)
Company I	Capt. J. Hall	Wounded "arm"
Company K	Capt. T. Gibson	Wounded "head"

10th Texas Cavalry
Killed at Chickamauga — 11 men

Company A	J. McMillian	9/20/63, wounded at Murfreesboro
	M.C. Hilliard, Assistant Surgeon	
	T.W. Greene	9/20/63
Company B	J.W. Cannon	
Company C	C.C. Weir	9/19/63
	A. Hamilton	9/20/63
	J. Neal	9/20/63
Company F	J. Bowlin	9/20/63
	J. Shivers	9/20/63
Company G	B. Lay	9/19/63, wounded at Murfreesboro
Company I	J. Holmes	9/19/63

One interesting fact was that every company commander was killed or wounded at Chickamauga, but at Murfreesboro, which was just as devastating in casualty numbers, not a single company commander was even wounded. The Civil War combat formation for a regimental unit shows the company commander located to the right front of his company's front rank. The combat alignment shows the lieutenants behind the company ranks. It is possible that at Murfreesboro the company commanders brought up the rear in the lieutenants' spot.

At Chickamauga, the Tenth and the Fourteenth Texas were consolidated into one unit. Of the ten company commanders of the Fourteenth, only one was wounded and one missing. There is the possibility that the battle formation was aligned so that the Tenth Texas fronted into the enemy's artillery batteries that they were attempting to overrun.

Tenth Texas Cavalry
Wounded at Chickamauga
Never Returned to Duty — 25 men

Company A	J.J. Wright	Gunshot to the iliac region
	J.M. Shipp	Arm wounded
	A.J. Waldrip	
Company B	A. Garrot	Thigh
	Jack Huggins	Mortally wounded — died 9/29/63
	R. Lindley	Wound to spine
	F.M. Rogers	Mortally wounded — died 9/24/63
Company C	J.W. Kelly	Mouth — severe
Company D	R.W. Smith	Shot in face — bullet in neck muscles
	H. Morris	Thigh
Company E	W. Melton	Knee
	G. Berry	
	J. Eaton	
	A. Kelly	Leg
	W. Matthews	Slight wound — died 10/20/63
	E. Oliver	Ankle
	W.B. Turner	Leg amputated
Company F	J. Gray	Foot — transferred to cavalry unit
	S. Fite	
	C. Wall	Died of wound
Company G	J. Anderson	Arm amputated
	W. Smith	
Company H	D. McBride	
Company I	J. Loden	Leg
Company K	E. Wooten	

Tenth Texas Cavalry
Prisoners of War at Chickamauga
All captured 9/19 — 25 men

Company A	J.R. Butler	
	W. Essay	
	S.C. White	
Company B	C.J. Millsaps	
Company C	J. Spratt	
Company D	E. Shrum	
Company E	D. Melton	
	J. Terry	
Company F	W. Cogswell	
	J. Murphy	
Company G	T. Ward	
	W. Butler	
	J. Hicks	
Company H	W. Allen	

	A. Gilbreth	
	P. Smith	
	W. Sosby	
Company I	J. Burk	
	G. Egbert	
	C. Odom	
	J. Templeton	
	M. Walters	
Company K	W. Coker	
	C. Downey	
	J. Slemmer	
Note: At this time no prisoners were paroled.		

General Ector suffered minor wounds four times and had two horses killed under him at Chickamauga.[27] During the course of the entire war, Ector had a total of eight horses killed under him. He was wounded a total of eight times, three times in the left leg. The third time he was wounded in his left leg, at Atlanta, it was completely severed.[28] All of Ector's Brigade's mounted officers had their horse killed or wounded. Of the total Texas units in Ector's Brigade, they took 831 into the battle and had 383 killed, wounded, or missing for a casualty rate of 46 percent.[29]

CHAPTER 11

"Wearing their hog killing suits"

EVENTS CONCERNING MEN
CAPTURED AT CHICKAMAUGA

MEN CAPTURED during or after the fierce encounter at Chickamauga suffered different fates. During this period, Union forces were using a policy of attrition, and no prisoners were paroled except for those who were seriously wounded. With respect to one prisoner of war, the compiled service records must be falsified or at least in error. Pvt. James Terry, Company E, Tenth Texas, who enlisted at age seventeen, was a true Rebel hero at the Battle of Murfreesboro. His name appears on the Confederate Roll of Honor. He would have taken part in the charge that General Forrest said "excited his admiration." But the records contain an obvious error when they state that, after he was captured, he became a Yankee. It states he joined the Fifth U.S. Volunteers! (The Rebs called guys like him "Galvanized Yankees.")

A prisoner of war from the Tenth Texas, John Templeton, wrote about the disaster that befell them on the trip to the federal prison in Chicago. They had been placed in an unfinished hotel at Nashville called the Maxwell. Five members of Company I were at the hotel that day. Templeton wrote:

> The building was in an unfinished condition, the stairs being the old-fashioned kind called winding stairs and reaching the fifth story from the ground floor. There were over a hundred prisoners gathered around the head of the stairs on the fifth, or top, floor, waiting their turn to go down for the morning meal of fat meat and "gungerbread." Suddenly without warning the stairs, floor and all gave way, the sleepers snapping off owing to the immense weight going downward with its human cargo until it reached the bottom. It was understood at the time that fourteen prisoners were killed outright. I myself fell on top of the mass of humanity and was rescued at the third floor from the top of the stairs.[1]

Another prisoner at the Maxwell Hotel recounted the incident:

Quicker than thought and with a noise almost deafening we went downward a confused mass of humanity. Fortunately owing to the fact that I was on the outer edge of the crowd I fell on top and with a few others was rescued before falling entirely to the bottom of the stairs. In the scramble I lost my hat and requested one of the guards to go with me down another stairway to try and get either my own or some one else's. This he politely did, when on reaching the bottom of the stairs a sight met my eyes that I shall never forget. Several poor fellows were already laid out dead while many others were so badly hurt they were dying. Some were between the floors and were mashed almost to a jelly. The patriotic women of Nashville were soon there and gave the Yankees a good round of abuse for placing the prisoners in a trap to kill them rather as they stated than meet them on the field of battle. I never placed any censure on the Yankees for the unfortunate occurrence as it was purely accidental and unexpected. The stairway was temporary and like the building at that time unfurnished. Owing to this fact it could not sustain so much weight, hence the fall through.[2]

After the war the Maxwell Hotel was known as the Maxwell House. Supposedly President Teddy Roosevelt, while drinking coffee there, stated it was "good to the last drop." Someone then started selling the coffee with that advertising slogan.

As a prisoner, Templeton sent his one and only letter back to Texas in 1864:

> Camp Douglas Chicago Ill.
> August 5th/64
>
> My Dear Father,
> Having an opportunity I write you a few lines to let you know that I am yet alive and in good health. I was captured the 19th Sept at Chickamauga Ga. . . . Mose Walters was captured with me, also Geo. Egbert Neill Odom & John Burk of my company. The last three are at Camp Morton Ind. . . . Father I would like to hear from you all again, and if you would write I would be very proud. I may see you when the war ends but not any sooner. Let Frank know where I am and give my love to Grand Pa, Ma, the children and all friends. Your obt. Son. J. Allen Templeton. Barracks No. 17

This letter had to be delivered by flag of truce by a blockading ship off the coast of Galveston, Texas.

A prisoner with Templeton wrote about a planned prison escape while at Chicago in the P.O.W. camp:

In September 1864 a great plan was organized among the prisoners at Camp Douglas, which if successful would have been one of the greatest feats of the war. There were a great many Southern sympathizers in Chicago called "copperheads." We had secretly organized the whole prison of 11,000 men into companies, regiments, and brigades and on a certain day in October we were to make a dash from the prison and go into Chicago. It had been arranged with the "copperheads" to join us to take the arsenal and arm ourselves and go over to Rock Island release 10,000 prisoners there and join Kirby Smith in Arkansas. But one of our number (Shanks from Texas) who was elected a colonel, betrayed us. He was given a sutler's store by the Yankees for the betrayal.[3]

There was a Rebel "poet" at Camp Douglas with Templeton. After eating one of the Yanks' dogs, he put a sign up: "For want of meat, the dog was eat!"[4]

At the prison camp, all the Rebels had to be careful or the Yanks would force them to ride "Morgan's mule." It was a wooden structure about fifteen feet high, built like a carpenter's sawhorse. The unfortunate prisoner was placed on a board one inch wide. Having heard Lincoln had been killed, a certified Rebel said, "A damn good thing, he ought to have been in Hell long ago." The Yanks promptly put him on the mule and tied a coal burning stove to each leg. They offered to let him down if he would retract his statement, but he said he had spoken the truth. The Yanks then killed him with their bayonets.[5]

Pvt. John Burk of Company I was wounded and captured at Chickamauga. He was moved to a Yank hospital and from there to a Union POW camp. He did not care for the POW camp so he just left. Unfortunately, he was recaptured and spent the rest of the war as a guest of the abolitionists.

Pvt. John Hicks of Company F did not dislike the Federals as bad as John Burk. He was wounded and captured at Chickamauga, and then was exchanged and sent to a Reb hospital in Virginia. He preferred the Union hospitality so much, he deserted the Reb hospital for a Yank hospital in Maryland.

After the war, John Templeton became a famous man thanks to his friend H.C. Thruston, a cavalry man in the Fourth Missouri Confederate Cavalry. One thing sure was that Thruston could not ride a short legged horse; he was 7 feet, 7 1/2 inches tall and nicknamed the "Texas Giant." He shot a Yankee major one day and the man lived long enough to say that he saw the man that shot him and the man was standing on a stump! Thurston lived until he was seventy-nine years old.[6]

Another Reb chronicled an event in prison that personified what a true Rebel felt about the Yanks:

The legislators of Indiana and Governor Morton, with their wives and daughters went on a visit of inspection to the prisoners. . . . The confederates were called out for dress parade and were made to look as well as possible. The distinguished body rode in fine carriages. One lady had her carriage stopped about ten feet from the line. Opening the side door of the carriage and pushing her head out asked: "Why do you Rebel soldiers dress so poorly?" Crockett Hudson of Eagleville, Tenn. replied: "Gentlemen of the South have two suits one that they wear among nice people and one that they wear when killing hogs, and that is the one in which we are dressed today." She ordered the carriage to move on.[7]

CHAPTER 12

"Almost makes me weep to think of your situation"

WINTER OF 1863-64
CAMPLIFE AND MILITARY OPERATIONS

ON SEPTEMBER 22, 1863, only two days after the Battle of Chicka-mauga, Ector's Brigade, including te Tenth Texas, was ordered back to Mississippi. The Tenth Texas was fortunate they were moved to Mississippi and missed the fighting around Chattanooga. During the winter, they changed locations several times in anticipation of the Yanks attacking east out of Vicksburg. The Union troops did not attack until February 1864. By this time, Private Littlejohn had returned to duty after his severe wounds at Murfreesboro:

Meridian, Miss., Oct. 6th, 1863

Dear Sallie,

This leaves me in the enjoyment of good health. I arrived in camps night before last. The boys were talking about me when I came. I had written them sometime before that I thought I would be able to return to camps by the 1st Oct. I have not been put to duty yet, but I do not believe I can ever march to do any good. I have not shown my papers to the officers of the company yet but I will do it soon and see what disposal they will make of me. There are two or three men in the Company who was wounded at the same time who are not doing any duty. I wish I could get a transfer to John's regt. of Cavalry.

I have no news of interest to write you. We are not yet whipped on this side of the river, that is, the soldiers. The people of the country have been very despondent since the fall of Vicksburg and the reverses in Penn. But I think the victory of our forces at Chickamauga will somewhat revive their spirits. . . . Our Brigade was in the fight and suffered considerably. Our Company lost 16 or 18 killed and wounded, one being killed dead on the field, B. W. Lay, whose father lived near Jamestown. Poor Jim Hudson was killed dead on the field without knowing what hit him. He was shot through the neck. It will be distressing news to his wife and mother. . . .

Write to me soon. I remain your true and affectionate, Elbridge.

Littlejohn later described life in a Civil War winter quarters:

>Camp Cannon, near Meridian Mississippi Oct 15th, 1863
>. . . We don't have much to do but cook our scanty rations and eat them. But it seems like we are always engaged at something or other; either policing our yards (that is cleaning them off), or cleaning up our guns, which takes a good deal of rubbing.
>
>Well, we have no news in camps, all is quiet, and nothing to disturb the monotony of camps. There is some talk of our officers having a picnic here tomorrow. All the ladies in the County are invited, as I understand. I don't suppose we privates will be allowed to participate in the festivities of the day. It will be attended by officers and ladies alone."

A. J. Fogle of Ector's Brigade sent a letter home from winter camp about the men wanting to return to Texas. (He probably could have come up with a more tactful way to tell his girlfriend her brother had been killed.):

>Camp ner Meridian Missippi, October the 18, 1863
>Dear Miss . . .
>I saw avery bad sight the other day: their was threve men shot for Desertion those men was marched out in a old field and their Coffins was set in a row and each man set on his Coffen and their was twelve men to each one with their gunes and tuck a shot and they all fell ded. hit looked worse to me then to see thousens shot on the batle field their has bin severl that has Deserted from our Regiment That is one thing that I nevr expect to do: their is severl more talks of Deserting we had one to leave our compney.
>
>. . . I am end hope that I will get to com home in the corse of two or three years longer if I should live that long but life is very on sertan and Deth is shore and Miss Loo if you should meet with a good Chanse to mary you mout do well to not let hit Slip: for you are left a lone your brother is ded he got shot up in kentucky and hit al most makes me weep to think of your situation.
>
>We had a man shot out of our compney to day hit was dun axey Dentley but I dont think hit is seresely, A.J. Fogle.

It has been said that executions are a sure sign that an army is breaking up. These executions were clearly traumatic to the viewing soldiers and no doubt they could be effective in making soldiers fight to the death.

On October 20, 1863, Ector's Brigade was put in French's Division and remained a part of it to the end of the war. On October 27, 1863, the Commander of the Tenth Texas went on leave back to Texas because he "should be of service in collecting or bringing back to the brigade men on the other side of the river." Apparently, he did not bring many back. According to the official records, not a single one could be identified as returning. Several men went home and had doctors send statements that they were too sick to return to duty. Several men also joined Texas units stationed in Texas and never returned to the Tenth Texas. On November 6, the Tenth Texas moved from Brandon, Mississippi, to Meridian, Mississippi. The weather was cold, and the Tenth Texas had no tents and just a few blankets. When soldiers are not kept busy, morale and discipline break down. On November 16, Littlejohn described the wickedness in camp:

> None of us at home knows how long we are going to live; but here in camp, life looks much more precarious, beset with many more dangers, and the allurements of vice and wickedness are more apt to lead us astray. Wickedness in all its deformity reigns with unlimited sway in the soldiers' camps, and moral rectitude is a word which almost becomes obsolete in his lexicon. I often consider my own case to see if I have in any degree degenerated from my old courses. I don't profess to have lived up to all the commandments, but I hope that I have not been as morally wicked as a great many whom I have seen. Sometimes I fear I am losing sight of the right track. The temptations are great here, but I hope that I will be able to withstand all.
>
> This morning is quite cool, and I can't write much. Lieut. Wynn from our Company will be coming in a few days by whom I will write again at more length. . . . Robert Ligon from Tyler has been court marshalled and sentenced to work on the fortifications at Mobile during the War for cowardice. He was first condemned to be shot, but his punishment has been commuted.
>
> We have just had an inspection of arms and our company got the praise of being the finest in the regt. I have a tolerable nice gun myself. We all have a good supply of clothing and blankets. . . . Sallie, if you can have your likeness and the baby's taken, please do so and send them to me. It could be a great consolation to me in my lonesome hours. I often look at the one I have, though it is not a good one. I will send you one of mine when I can have it taken. We are getting very short rations now. Scarcely anything but coarse meal and a little beef. I don't have to do any hard duty now, nor do I believe I

ever will be. I will make an application for some detail after the winter is over. Probably I may get a transfer to the cavalry.

Enclosed you will find one piece of the bone that came out of my hip, the largest piece. I remain as ever your true and affectionate husband, E. G.

Robert Ligon was with the Third Texas Cavalry. As far as the records show, no one from the Tenth Texas was disciplined for cowardice. They did have numerous soldiers go AWOL. Lieutenant Wynn, referred to in the letter, was later shot in the neck at the Battle of Nashville and was captured.

When Littlejohn mentioned the "morally wicked," it resembles a story that was told about a young recruit who was given a dollar to buy food and drink. He bought ninety cents of whiskey and ten cents of food. He was berated for wasting so much money on food!

Littlejohn notes in the following letter that he was not serving normal guard duty. Instead of stopping people from getting into camp stealing things, his duty was to stop the thieves from bringing stuff into the camp.

Camp near Meridian, Miss.

My Beloved Sallie,

To while away a few of the solitary moments this evening while I am on guard I conceive this to be the most agreeable way in which I could spend the time. All the rest of the company have gone out to the woods to build the houses in which it is said that we are going to spend the winter. But I fear that even before we get them completed we will be ordered to leave them for some other field of action. As I sit writing on my humble desk of blankets and knapsacks with the ground for my chair, let me imagine you to be sitting in the entry of your Pa's house, with my Dear little Boy fondling in your arms, where we so often imparted to each other tokens of our love and esteem for each other; and where we have spent many pleasant hours of happiness, which none can appreciate but those who have participated. My memory oft recurs back to those times, and the straggling dew-drops of tears start from my eyes before I am aware of it. Perhaps while I am writing this you may be thinking of your far distant ever-mindful husband; between whom and yourself many miles, an insolent and inhospitable enemy, and the broad rolling waters of the Mississippi intervene to cut off all intercourse of communication, and if possible would sever forever those links of love, which nothing but death itself can separate. It does really seem as if the cruel and relentless fates were against me all the time; but I trust in God that he will bring all things out right at last, according to His holy will.

. . . Well, as I said before, I am guard today. We have no duty to do except the latter, which is merely around the camps to keep the boys from bringing in hogs and other things which they sometimes go into the country and steal. We have some mighty bad boys. They will take anything in the world they can lay their hands upon. We are two miles from Meridian in the Piney Woods. You may guess our appearance when you consider that we have to burn a great deal of pine wood, which smokes us pretty black.

As I told you, we are building houses to stay in during the winter, as we have but very few tents. It is my opinion that we are going to be kept here as a place of rendezvous in order to intercept any raids that the enemy might attempt to make through the state. We have been run about more than any other Division in the service and I think they ought to let us rest awhile. It is thought by some that we will be transferred across the river in the course of six months, but I fear very much it will not be the case. A good many of the boys from the brigade attempted to come anyhow a week or so ago. Some of them made it, but others were caught and brought back. I can't tell what their punishment will be. There were some boys from our own company who would have tried to come if they had had money. I don't like the idea of running away, and I don't believe you would want to see me coming home in that way, would you? No.

Well, I guess you think it is time I was drying up, but I have not anything else to do until night, and I recon you will pardon me for intruding upon your patience thus. We have no amusements in camps at all, but reading sometimes. Some of the boys employ their leisure in playing marbles. We have preaching on Sunday twice and prayer meetings three times through the week, and a debating society once a week. It is quite an imposing scene to look upon a group of men seated around the rudely built altar, upon the ground for the seats, and the heavens for their covering. It is truly a solemn sight. There are some very strong and able men in the brigade, who seem to take some interest in the welfare of the poor soldier. I never go there but what I think of you. We have a chaplain from our Com. who is young, but I think he will make a very good preacher. But there is a great deal of wickedness prevailing in camps. . . .

Elbridge

The chaplain mentioned by Littlejohn was George Birdwell. Another soldier gave his impression of religion in the camps:

> Late one afternoon I asked to go with me, to a secluded spot, a young comrade, who had been my schoolmate, classmate, and intimate associate, whose conversion a few days previous had caused his face to be changed so that he exhibited a meekness which was not natural to him. He was thoroughly converted. I sought an interview with him, that I might get comfort. We left our place of conference just before dark, to go directly to the night service. . . .
>
> After the sermon I was off in the dark in an agony of prayer that something would arouse me to realize the uncertainty of life. My friend had remained in the altar place, talking and praying with penitents. Suddenly there came a heavy, dull thud, like the falling of a tree in the forest, as indeed it was, an old oak that had been burned off at the roots. But the tragical part of it was, that it struck in its fall a file of young men who were in its path, of whom ten were killed by the stroke, and lay dead in a row under the huge trunk. They were all bright young fellows, full of life and promise. Of the number was this life-long friend, whose sweetest counsel had been given me just before that service. I was his only watcher that night. Profanity, which is so common among soldiers, was almost entirely given up. There were no scoffers at the religion that had such a hold upon the army.[1]

On December 4, Buck Kilgore, who was severely wounded at Chickamauga, headed home to Texas. He was captured attempting to cross the Mississippi River.

The following are excerpts from a letter by Henry Watson, Tenth Texas:

> Camp near Brandon, Miss, Dec. the 8th 1863
>
> Dear Sister Catherine,
>
> We built houses at Meridian, Miss for winter qua and about we get them finished our houses we received orders to come to Brandon but I do not no what the move was for we understood that the yankees were crossing Big Black River in a large force I guess we will go back to our houses as soon as we drive the yanks back across the Big Black. . . .
>
> I would like very much to see you all but I see no probability of getting to come soon they will not grant any more furloughs in our Co unless Newte Fite comes back and we dont expect him back any more. . . . Henry Watson.

Henry Watson was correct in that Newte Fite never returned. Newte Fite was listed in the records as N.O. Fite. He must have been an old man because he had six sons fighting for the Confederacy. The three sons in the Tenth Texas all suffered severe wounds at different battles. Apparently, Newte decided he had done his part.[2]

On December 9, 1863, a near riot occurred at Meridian, Miss., over a fight and subsequent arrest. General McNair, who was at the Battle of Richmond with Ector's Brigade, ordered the brigade on a train to stop any problems with the provost marshall's people. General McNair admitted in his report that the Texans cheered when he called the provost marshall's people "conscripts."[3]

Littlejohn sent home a letter to someone other than his wife and mentioned the various movements made by the Tenth Texas:

> Camp Harper, Brandon, Miss., Decr. 22, 1863
> The army in Miss. is resting quite easy. The enemy seems to have no desire to penetrate far into the interior of the State, their operations being confined chiefly to the narrow limits of the river bank (occasionally they scout into the country to forage a little). We have had quite an easy time since I came back to the regt. Tis true we have had to move several times, but it has been by railroad altogether. When I wrote to Sallie the time before the last, we were just on the eve of moving from our houses at Meridian. We had just completed them with a great deal of hard labor. We left them with much regret, as they were much more comfortable than sleeping in the open air and on the ground. But that is the fate of war and we ought not to expect more. I expect we will remain here for some time.
>
> I suppose you would not care to know what we are getting to eat. Well, I'll tell you in a few words. We get plenty of corn meal and for a few days past have been beef aplenty. Now this is what we draw. We have been buying potatoes until lately, at high prices. But they are all gone now in the country. We have been making hominy, and yesterday we made a potful, as good as you generally see if we only had some lard to fry it in. But we are all of us fat as you ever saw boys that live on buttermilk and butter. As for clothes, I am doing very well at the present. I drew a pair of pants yesterday but they are not much account. I have plenty of shirts and socks and upon the whole I have plenty to last me this winter. . . . Let me tell you what the Georgia *gals* done for our company. A week or so ago, one of our Lieuts. went up there on a visit and the Ladies, taking compassion

on our desolate condition, sent a pair of socks to every man in the company, many of whom stood in need of them. Now, I think this is an example worthy of imitation. And this is not the first time they have done so. If the men were half as patriotic as the women, I think our cause would prosper more. E.G.L.

Littlejohn's opinion of Georgia gals was a little different from another soldiers' opinions. He said, "The women smoke, chew tobacco, and drink whiskey and almost half of the women in the vicinity of the army, married or unmarried, are lost to all virtue."[4]

On February 3, 1864, General Sherman marched out of Vicksburg to destroy the Southern transportation center at Meridian, Mississippi, and the metal foundry at Selma, Alabama. Sherman destroyed Meridian but could not get to Selma. There was no real battle fought. Meridian was a major railroad center for the Confederacy. Two railroad tracks crossed there.

On February 8, 1864, the Tenth Texas was involved in heavy skirmishing around Morton, Mississippi.[5] The Tenth Texas was spared from a large battle by heavy rains and swollen streams. The Yankees, under Sherman, were to meet up with another Union army that did not arrive at Meridian to attack toward Selma, Alabama. It should be added that many soldiers felt skirmishing (picket fighting) was below the dignity of civilized nations. They said it was learned from the Indian tribes. However, from a shooter's point of view, it was certainly safer. The author's great-grandfather, Alvin Finley Hamilton, Company B, Tenth Texas, was wounded during the Yankee movement called "the Meridian, Mississippi, campaign" from February 3 to March 5, 1864. The only war story remembered, that he shared, was that he was shot in the leg while filling his canteen at a creek. He spent the months of March and April 1864 in the hospital at Marion, Alabama. He then spent a month making shoes before he was sent back to the war. A.F. Hamilton lived to a ripe old age. He made up for his horse being taken away during the war by riding a horse quite often. He was thrown from one and died of his injuries in 1932 at the age of ninety.

On March 24, 1964, 3rd Sgt. W. M. Coats, who was captured at Murfreesboro and paroled, was switched from Company B, Tenth Texas, to Company K, Third Texas Cavalry. The Third Texas then moved J.W. Johnson over to the Tenth Texas. J.W. Johnson was shot in the right groin at Atlanta. He also had his right index finger shot off. He surrendered with the Tenth Texas at the end of the war.

On March 26, 1864, Pvt. Marcus Turner of Company C, Tenth Texas, transferred to the Third Texas Cavalry because an ulcer on his leg hindered his walking ability. His letter requesting transfer was signed by the surgeons from the Tenth Texas, Ninth Texas, and Thirty-second Texas.

Littlejohn actually received a furlough, went home to see his son, and shocked everyone by returning to duty. On the journey back, he jotted down a series of short notes to the folks he once again left behind:

Shreveport, La., April 13th

My Dear Sallie,

You see that I have got here. Just been to Kirby Smith and got a pass to cross the river. I will proceed immediately and try the River about Rodney. I met a man yesterday who has just crossed. Says he had no difficulty. Had to swim his horse. Experience no uneasiness about me. I will try to take care of myself.

The news from the other side of the river is encouraging. I will write you again as soon as I cross the river. My horse does very well. I think will stand it. Spring has fairly opened down here and everything else seems to be gay, which only conspires to make me think of *the dear ones at home so much* the more.

Take care of Little Bridge and kiss him twice for his Papa, and accept the same for yourself. My respects to the family and friends. From your devoted, Elbridge

5 miles this side of Miss. River, *undated*

My Dear Wife and Friends,

Knowing that you are anxious to hear from me I will just say to you that I crossed the river last night (22nd) at St. Joseph. I had to lay over two days in the swamps, had to sell my horse, when I came to the river. And it being so rough I was afraid to try to swim him. Got $400 for him. I met with ten of my regt. who did not cross with their horses. The river was very rough indeed. Be not uneasy about me. I am out of danger of the river. I have no envelope and will just send this so.

I remain as ever, your Elbridge

During an inspection on May 2, 1864, "the Texas Brigade of Ector was poorly armed and not well clothed, but still presented a most soldierly appearance."[6] The Thirty-ninth North Carolina Infantry joined Ector's Brigade and would remain with it to the end of the war. The regiments in Ector's Brigade were the Ninth Texas Infantry, Tenth Texas Cavalry, Fourteenth Texas Cavalry, Thirty-second Texas Cavalry, and the Twenty-ninth and Thirty-ninth North Carolina Infantry.

Tuscaloosa is in northern Alabama close to the Tennessee River. Once he arrived at camp, Littlejohn explained both the cost and difficulties of trying to return to war after furlough, showing why many men simply did not return:

Camps near Tuscaloosa, Ala., May 5th, 1864

My dear Sallie and Friends:

I suppose you have read the little notes I wrote you; one before I crossed and the other just after crossing the river. But for fear you did not get them I will give you a short account of my trip.

After leaving Shreveport I was overtaken by Lt. Buckner of Rusk Co. He was apparently a clever man, and his company served to dispel the gloom of mind which would have been natural for me to experience otherwise. . . . Nothing of interest transpired until we got within twenty miles of the river. We found the man who was to put us over, but said he would not do it for two days. We laid over in the swamps in the night and employed ourselves by fishing in the daytime. The time arrived for us to go into the river, got to the river about 9 o'clock at night. The river was so rough he would not cross horses. So I concluded to go over anyhow. I sold my horse to a man belonging to our Regt. who was afoot, for $400 — that is I got $300 and I saved one hundred in ferriage, which is equal to $400. I crossed and left the balance of the crowd on the other side, who did not get over for four days later. I walked till I came to the cars, a distance of one hundred and sixty miles. I took the train and came to Randolph in Bibb Cty, Ala., and there took the stage for this place, which I reached the 3rd May, having been on the road twenty-three days. The boys were not looking for me back and of course were disappointed. Nothing was said to me about overstaying my furlough, although I was a little uneasy about it, as they had arrested one of our com. who is now under guard. The boys were or seemed to be glad to see me back again. I found them all well; the trip cost me $180, one hundred for crossing the river, without my horse. . . .

There is quite a talk in our camps of our being mounted again. Col. Young of the 9th Texas has gone to Richmond now with some strong documents, from Gens. S.D. Lee, Polk, French, and others. I hope he will be successful in the attempts, but is more than I expect, at least. I guess we will know shortly what will be the result.

We are camped on the bank of the Black Warrior at Tuscaloosa. The boys have been catching lots of fish in traps. One night before I came into camps they caught 3,000 lbs. We are all tired of fish. We are getting rather slim rations now. I had nothing but cornbread for breakfast this morning. Although the boys said that during my absence they were fed splendidly. I was on guard yesterday and last night. I could have got off from standing for several days by going to the Col. but I did not mind it. . . . The furloughing system has been stopped in this Brigade for awhile.

I remain as ever, your affectionate husband and friend, Elbridge.

The reason the furlough system stopped was due to the fact the Rebs needed all their men to meet Sherman's attack on Atlanta.

*Johnny Reb (A.F. Hamilton),
and his son (Charlie Hamilton),
l. to r., the author's great
grandfather and grandfather.*

CHAPTER 13

*Can't sleep with artillery shells
shining "through his closed eyelids"*

ATLANTA CAMPAIGN UNDER GENERAL JOHNSTON

DURING APRIL 1864, while the Tenth Texas was in Mississippi, General Sherman was preparing to move against the Army of Tennessee. Gen. Joe Johnston had taken over from Bragg with the Confederate army located at Dalton.

One soldier depicted the greeting General Johnston received from the troops and why he had such a greeting:

> After the battle of Chickamauga, General Bragg dissolved Cheatham's Division and gave him a division of troops from other States, allowing him to retain one Tennessee brigade upon the ground that so large a body of troops from one State in one division promoted too much State pride at the expense of pride in the Confederate States. When General Johnston assumed command of the army at Dalton, one of his first acts was to restore the old organization. The order to this effect created unbounded enthusiasm in the division. With one impulse the men marched to army headquarters with a band of music and called for General Johnston. General Cheatham escorted him from his room to the front door and presented him to his command with heartiness as genuine as it was unmilitary. Placing his hand upon the bare head of the chief of the army, he patted it two or three times and looking at the men, said: "Boys, this is Old Joe."[1]

In reference to the Atlanta Campaign, the subsequent definitions are relevant. When fighting from dug-in trench-like battlelines, the following items were used at various times. During the Atlanta campaign, all were used:

- Abatis: crude barrier of felled trees and branches.
- Chevaux-de-frise: portable logs with wooden spikes about three feet long imbedded on four sides.
- Palisade: a fence made of sharp spikes.

- Fraise: sharp stakes pointed out at forty-five degree angles.
- Head logs: logs elevated several inches above the ground in front of a trench. This was so a soldier could fire under it and it would protect his head from rifle fire.

Abatis was used extensively in the Atlanta campaign. Felled trees with the branches sharpened and intertwined were as effective as barbed wire. Swords and Bowie knives were needed to hack through the obstruction. By this stage in the war, many soldiers decided that hiding the head and body behind something and slowing down the enemy advance by using obstacles was the way to survive. Too bad not all of the generals figured this out.

On May 4, 1864, Sherman swung his forces into motion. On May 11, he outflanked Johnston and forced Johnston to retreat to a battle line around Resaca, north of Atlanta.

A grandson of a Texan in Ector's Brigade recounted an interesting story about the movement of the brigade to the battles around Atlanta. Some members of the Tenth Texas would have been in the hospital. His grandfather wrote part of the following:

> On our march to Atlanta I was taken sick and sent to Texas Hospital at Auburn. I had been there about two weeks and had become convalescent when a report came in one evening that there was a small scouting party of Federals coming in the direction of Auburn. We officers at the hospital immediately called a council of war and

Rebel fortifications at Atlanta. The rack looking devices are chevaux-de-frise. A yank told a rebel that he didn't want to eat his fodder from those racks.

decided to fight them. It was then late in the evening. I was appointed to take charge of a scouting party and ordered to try and find out the strength of our enemy forces and where they were coming to strike the Montgomery and West Point Road.

A one-armed Texas Colonel was appointed to take charge of the convalescent men who were able to go out and meet the enemy. There was also someone appointed to take charge of the sick and disabled who could fight from the windows of the hospital. After we were fully organized we found we had but few arms but we telegraphed for more to be sent to us on the next train. After all of the above arrangements were perfected I proceeded to organize my scouting party. I got orders from the Commander of the post to press horses for my expedition but I found good horses very scarce around Auburn. By the time I had procured 5 horses it was dark and we could see fire and smoke rising from a tan yard about three miles down the railroad. . . .

We, of course, had to move out. We kept a pretty safe distance ahead of the enemy occasionally returning fire and giving them a volley in their face to show them we were not scared.

By the time we reached the depot they were crowding us pretty close and the next thing we knew we received a volley of fire from the regiment coming in from the North. This created a panic in my ranks so I gave the command "every fellow for himself." I think most of the boys kept down the railroad and made their escape but I concluded that I should go through the town. The enemy pressed me close firing from behind me but I was on a good horse and thought I could get away from them. But to my utter surprise and astonishment when I ran into the square at Auburn there was the 9th Ohio regiment formed in line of battle not more than 30 yards from me. They hollered for me to halt but I had a horror of northern prison and had at other times ran out of some very close places so I thought I would take chances. I lay flat on my horse and applied the hickory vigorously but my plan was a failure. The whole regiment fired at me, my faithful horse fell turning a complete somersault with his head to the enemy and 10 bullet holes in his faithful body; I heard a mighty scream from some ladies in a house just opposite me. The yankees picked me up more dead than alive and carried me to a church nearby.

They gave me water and washed the blood and dirt off me — I don't know just how long we stayed in the church but they told me I must go with them down to the railroad where the depot was on fire and where troops were tearing up the railroad tracks. I asked the Lt. what they were going to do with me. He said he was going to take me to Col. Hamilton who would dispose of me. So they got me a couple of sticks and I hobbled down to where Col. Hamilton was sitting on his horse. The Lt. told him here was a prisoner they had captured. He asked me if I had been fighting them. I replied that I had. He then asked me what command I belonged to. I told him I belonged to Ector's Brigade and the 32nd Texas Regiment. He asked what I was doing in Auburn. I told him I was a patient in the hospital. His reply was "a patient in the hospital and out fighting." He pointed his sword in the direction of the hospital and said to me "do you see that yellow flag waving over your hospital?" I told him I did. He asked if I knew what it meant. I told him it meant protection for the inmates I supposed. I told him there was no flag there when I left town and I did not know of it until he called my attention to it. He said to me, "Do you know that according to the laws of nations you have forfeited your life." I told him that I had not knowingly violated the laws of nations. He said to the Lt. make a detail and have me shot immediately. . . . I was scared but after a little private talk with Col. Hamilton I was much relieved. He told me to go back to the hospital and behave myself and I should not be molested. (Grandfather said that he had revealed to the Col. that he was a Mason and so was the Col. and so he got a good break.)

I thanked the Col. and wended my way back to the hospital more dead than alive and fully convinced that I would not do for a General.[2]

On May 11, 1864, part of Ector's Brigade, the Thirty-ninth North Carolina Infantry, arrived at Resaca. On May 13, the Battle of Resaca began and went on for two more days. After again being outflanked, Johnston was forced to withdraw on May 16. One of his staff related an event at Resaca:

At Resaca General Johnston, surrounded by some thirty men, stationed himself at the side of a hill exposed to the enemy's sharpshooters. A ball of some kind took off the head of a man near by, and his brain was sprinkled over me. We all wanted safer quarters, but no man in that group had the temerity to suggest it.[3]

The Tenth Texas arrived at Rome, Georgia, on May 7 and had another skirmish with the Yanks.[4] As Johnston withdrew towards Atlanta, the forces clashed at Cassville. The Tenth Texas joined the Army of Tennessee on May 19 and suffered its first casualty of the Atlanta Campaign at Cassville.[5] The casualty at Cassville was Pvt. Joseph Pool of Company K. He was a man that suffered extreme turns in luck. He was left sick in Kentucky after the Battle of Richmond, and was captured, then paroled. He was "mortally" wounded at Murfreesboro but did not die. He sustained a foot wound and maybe that slowed him down enough that he was captured at Cassville. He was somehow granted another parole, then his fortunes really went down when another man from the Forty-eighth Tennessee Infantry "substituted" himself for Private Pool. He was finally sent back to a hospital in Mississippi.

The Battle of Cassville was fought on May 18 and 19. With a series of movements by both armies, and limited attacks by the night of May 19, it was determined that the Federal artillery was located on higher terrain, thus dominating the Confederate positions. This especially affected French's division which included the Tenth Texas. They arrived just in time to get hammered by the artillery. Luckily for them, General Johnston elected to advance to the rear. Johnston's army withdrew to a solid defense line that ran through New Hope Church on the right, and to Dallas, Georgia, on the left. Sherman confronted this line on May 25. Between May 19 and May 25, continuous skirmishing at times approached full battle conditions.

The Battle of New Hope Church was a violent four-day event. It also represented a new phase in the war. For survival's sake, both sides attempted to fight behind earthworks and log breastworks. The battle started on May 25, 1864. The Tenth Texas had one killed and seven wounded at New Hope Church. One of the soldiers wounded was C.M. Gingles of Company C. A rifle ball struck him between the eyes and knocked him unconscious. Fortunately, it was a spent round that hit him. He made it to Nashville where he was wounded for the third time. At this battle, General French's map showed Ector's Brigade to be in front of the actual church building. He said the Yanks had a position to his front that they named the "Hell Hole." It was a Yankee rifle pit where the Rebs shot twenty-one Yanks, one after the other.[6]

On June 2, poor General French had a rough time sleeping. The glare of enemy artillery shells flying over shined through his closed eyelids. Also, General Ector was wounded.[7]

On June 4, Johnston moved his Army to a battle line from north of Kennesaw Mountain on the right, to Lost Mountain on the left, with the center of the line over Pine Mountain. It took the Tenth Texas seven hours to travel six miles to the new battleline because of the mud.[8] On June 7, the Tenth Texas could not dig in because all their entrenching tools had been confiscated.[9] On June 14, Confederate General Polk was killed on Pine Mountain. A monument was erected on the spot where he was killed, stating:

Folding his arms across his breast, he stood gazing on the scene below, turning himself around as if to take a farewell view. There standing a cannon shot from the enemy's side crashed through his breast and opened a wide door through which his spirit took its flight to join his comrades on the other shore. Surely the earth never opened her arms to allow the head of a braver man to rest upon her bosom; surely the light never pushed the darkness back to make brighter the road that leads to the Lamb; and surely the gates of heaven never opened wider to allow a more manly spirit to enter therein.[10]

On June 17, 1864, Sherman again advanced and again Johnston withdrew. After the war, Johnston explained that the reason he retreated so often was that he knew many of Sherman's troops' enlistment periods ran out in June. He was just buying time until the number of Northern soldiers was reduced. Unfortunately, the reduction never materialized. This time, Johnston withdrew to a defense line in front of the Kennesaw Mountains. This line was called the "Mud Creek Line" by many, but the Tenth Texas called it "the fight at Latimore House." They had twenty wounded and one killed here. It appeared most of the action was an artillery duel. (The Texans made like a jackrabbit in a West Texas hail storm; they just hunkered down and took it.)

The Latimore House was at the point of an angle in the Confederate line, and the Yanks, with three divisions, attempted to crush the line at the angle. By bringing their superior artillery up on both sides and the front of the angle, they began to batter the defenders. French's division had Cockrell's Missouri Brigade, Ector's Texas Brigade (even though it had two North Carolina units attached) and a Mississippi brigade under Sears. The Federals got in behind the Missouri unit's skirmish line and forced Ector's skirmish line back to the main defense line.

A Missouri soldier told how they fought their way out of the encirclement:

During forty days or more rains fell in torrents day and night. The Missouri troops, together with others were stationed in fortifications a few hundred yards north of the Latimore farm. North of this farm was a dense and thick tanglewood. Our rifle pits were north of the plantation and in the midst of a forest where we stood waist-deep in water in those pits. One dark, dismal, foggy morning an advance was made upon our outposts. Company E, at that time being in the densest part of these woods, was left in ignorance of the advance by the enemy and the retreat of our forces. Our first information of this was heavy musketry firing in our rear. Making a hasty retreat, we found ourselves cut off, with thousands of the enemy between us and our works. Our captain, George W. Covell, as brave and undaunted a man as ever commanded a company, regiment, or brigade, said: "Boys, I see no way out of this save to surrender." Then it was that the superior military genius of Lieutenant Faulkner was displayed when, with the permission of our captain, he took charge of the company and, by deploying them to an immense extent (charging, firing, falling, and reloading, together with the Rebel Yell), scattered the thousand between us and our lines, bringing the company safely to our regiment with the loss of one killed and two slightly wounded, the writer being one of those wounded.[11]

J.M. Spinks of Company G, Tenth Texas, said he carried the orders from division headquarters to the Tenth Texas to withdraw. He recalled at least a hundred shots fired at him and had the job of bringing back the pickets at two in the morning.[12]

General French declared:

The way being clear, the enemy soon advanced in line of battle, and with many guns enfiladed my line all day. The constant firing never ceased, but I could not induce them to come out and make an assault on my front with infantry, and ere night came, my loss was 215 men. Captain Guibor's Battery lost more men today (13) than it did during the entire siege of Vicksburg.[13]

On the night of June 18, the Rebel army withdrew to the Kennesaw Mountain defense lines. The Kennesaw Mountain line extended about eight miles. The northeastern part of the line crossed Kennesaw Mountain, which consisted of two humps with the so-called Big Kennesaw (about seven hundred feet high) and Little Kennesaw (about four hundred feet) and a small spur, Pigeon Hill (about two hundred feet). It was about two miles across the mountains. Another two miles south was a point in the Confederate line called the "Angle" where the line bent back southeast in front of what became known as Cheatham Hill.

The Tenth Texas, with Ector's Brigade, was on Little Kennesaw. Burnt Hickory Road ran east and west just south of Pigeon Hill directly through the Confederate line. This road could give the Union forces a direct route through the Confederate lines and a straight shot to Marietta.

The Confederates had a battery of artillery on the north end of Big Kennesaw and one centered on the top. They had nine guns behind the Tenth Texas on Little Kennesaw and a battery on Pigeon Hill. The Tenth Texas struggled in getting the artillery to the top of the mountain. One hundred soldiers were used to pull each gun to the summit.

One soldier described an event at Kennesaw Mountain:

Our brigade line on Kennesaw Mountain extended from a dirt road near the eastern foot of the mountain nearly halfway to the top. . . .

Marietta, a very pretty town, is near Kennesaw, and there were quarters of the various officers who furnished our supplies, quarter-masters, ordnance officers, and their clerks. They usually dressed well and were the beaux of the place. Of course, they were held in sovereign contempt by the rank and file, who never lost a chance to guy them about their looks, clothes, and so on. . . . The young officer was handsomely dressed and had a big mustache, waxed and point-ed. He rode past a regiment drawn up in line, standing perfectly silent. As he came by one of the men remarked in a casual way: "Swallowed a rat. See his tail stickin' out?"

That started it. Another remarked in a deep bass voice: "Yes, swallowed a rat."

The next man in a clear tenor repeated: "Swallowed a rat."

Then a shrill treble said: "Swallowed a rat!"

Thus, it went down the line with every variety of voice and tone to the end: "Swallowed a rat."

The victim was furious, and he complained bitterly to the colonel that a man couldn't pass his regiment without being grossly insulted. The colonel was a kindly, good-natured man. He scolded the men roundly for their rough manners and told them that the young man whom they had insulted was a brave officer; that he would be going back in a few minutes and they must apologize, give him three cheers, or give some greeting that would show they didn't mean to insult him. He gave them the officer's name, and they promised to make it right with him. So as he got opposite the regiment on his return they were standing like so many graven images at present arms, every man looking straight ahead.

As he passed the end man remarked in a sepulchral voice: "He did not swallow a rat."

The next man in penitent tones said: "No, he did not swallow a rat."

The third spoke in a kind of meditative way: "No, he didn't swal-low rat."

And thus many took up the refrain, some of them very emphatic: "No, indeed, he did not swallow a rat."

But this was more than flesh and blood could stand, and the young man put spurs to his horse and fled, followed by: "Come back, sonny, and see us when you have more time to spend with us. Good-bye."[14]

On June 19, Sherman started feeling out the Confederate's new defense line with extensive clashes along the whole front. While the Tenth Texas was off the skirmish line, Pvt. C. E. Dale carved his name in the Kennesaw Mountain granite. (The carving "C. E. Dale, 10th Texas" can still be seen today.)

ATLANTA CAMPAIGN—100 DAYS FIGHT

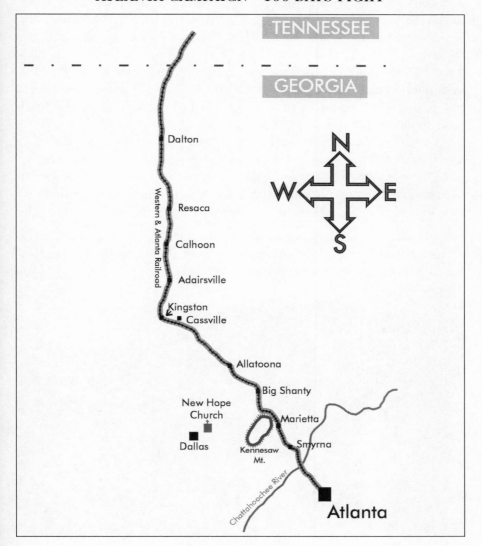

Private Dale was killed several months later at Allatoona and was noted in the official records for his bravery.

On the morning of June 27, after a fifteen-minute artillery prep that started at 8:00, the Yanks attacked north of Pigeon Hill and south of the hill along the Burnt Hickory Road with fifty-five hundred men.

A Northern correspondent said afterwards that the mountain showed no signs of life and looked as if even a mouse could not have remained alive under the bombardment. While the artillery fire was still furious, one of the Southerners ran by the battery and shouted: "You battery men better get to your guns, the Yankees are going to charge us!"[15] In this segment of the battle, the Yankees had seven Regimental Commanders fall. One was killed within thirty feet of the Rebel lines.[16] They also made a violent attack on the angle in front of Cheatham Hill.

On June 27, Ector's Brigade had the Ninth Texas Infantry in the skirmish lines. Because of the heavy attack on Pigeon Hill, General French had J.M. Spinks of Company G, who was assigned to his staff, guide the Tenth Texas to Pigeon Hill to help repulse the attack.[17]

A tragic mistake was made along the Burnt Hickory Road that morning. Experienced fighters knew that in a major attack, the skirmish lines retreated to the main line. The skirmishers south of Burnt Hickory Road were in an inexperienced Georgia Regiment that had never been in a major fight. As they started to retreat, someone ordered the rest of the regiment from the

Photo from Union positions showing Little Kennesaw in the center and Pigeon Hill on the right. During the Battle of Kennesaw Mountain, the Tenth Texas moved from Little Kennesaw to reinforce the Rebel positions on Pigeon Hill.

National Archives

main line out to the skirmish line. The Commander of the Ninth Texas reported he saw "a heavy line of the enemy appear at the edge of the woods immediately at the fire-pits, and could be distinctly seen firing down into the pits." A hundred men were killed as they crouched in the rifle pits or attempted to escape.[18] Naturally, the generals all blamed each other for the cause of the needless slaughter. In one rifle pit, nine of the Georgians were bayoneted. Another Reb said the Yanks clubbed the men with their guns.[19]

Littlejohn noted some of the action. The Tenth Texas must have been upset when General Polk was killed because he had promised to put them back on horseback:

Line of Battle, Kennesaw Mountain, Georgia July 2, 1864

At New Hope Church we laid in the ditches about ten days. Most of the time it was raining. One day we had to stay in the ditch. The ditch was full of mud and water and yet we had to stay in it close to keep from being shot. The fighting commenced about 9 o'clock A.M. and we laid in the ditch until dark, the mud and water being half leg deep. Three of our boys were wounded that day, Arnold, Howel, and Jeff Rosson. None of them dangerous. Hale was shot in the thigh but broke no bones. Rosson was slightly wounded on the same arm that he was wounded in before. Jeff is well again. We have been on the top of this mountain about fifteen days. It is about two miles west of Marietta and in plain view of the town. On the west side of the mountain is plainly to be seen the vast numbers of the enemy scattered around as far as the eye can reach. Our lines are not more than six or eight hundred yards apart and our pickets much nearer. Last night I was on picket duty and stood not more than two hundred yards from the Yanks. I was close enough to see the flash of their guns. I was behind a tree which they hit several times. But in the meantime we make them lye low too. Sometimes when we can get a safe position, we have considerable fun shooting at them and seeing them dodge. And not a doubt that we hit many a one. Last Monday morning I thought as everyone else did, that we were going to have a general engagement but it turned out otherwise. Our Brigade had been held in reserve for several days. About ten o'clock heavy cannonading and musketry commenced along the lines of our Division at the foot of the hill. Our Brigade was called to go down to the foot of the hill to assist the Missouri Brigade, which is a part of our Division. The enemy made a feeble attempt to take our works but failed in the attempt. Some of them reached within forty yards of our works but were driven back. . . . Not a great many of ours were killed or wounded, the Missourians suffering the worst. . . . But all these things a sad misfortune has befallen the Confederacy as well as our corps in the loss of the lamented Gen. Polk, of which you have heard before this reaches you. On the 14 June, while riding around the lines in company with Gen. Johnston and others he was instantly killed by a shell from the enemy which struck him in the breast, almost severing his back in two. He was deeply lamented by all the soldiers of his command and all feel as if they had lost their best military friend. By and through the instrumentality of him, we all expected to be carried back to Mississippi as soon as this command or campaign is over and furthermore to be mounted in the fall, which he had promised us he would do. But alas: Our expectations are blasted. We will no longer be known as the Army of Mississippi but will be united with the Army of Tennessee. . . . Since the campaign set in we have lost a great many men. Several from our Regt. have been killed. Our Lieut. Col. Craig was wounded. Besides what I have written many incidents have occurred that I could relate had I the time and chance. Our boys are all in fine spirits yet and anxious for the fight to come off. We are almost worn out with fatigue and marching, etc. We get plenty to eat most of the time, cornbread and bacon. I am very dirty and lousy, not having changed clothes for nearly two months. But I keep them picked off pretty well. I drawed me a good shirt the other day. I have clothes at the wagon (Ruben's) but I can't get a chance to get them; and if I could they would be as bad as these I have on in two or three days. I have the pants on that I wore from home, but they are worn out on the seat. Remember me to God in your prayers daily. E.G.L.

Interestingly, Littlejohn recalled the Federals moving to within forty yards of the Rebel lines instead of the thirty feet mentioned by one of the Yanks. Littlejohn says the enemy made a feeble attempt to attack these lines. French's division lost nearly as many men as did the Rebel units fighting at the Dead Angle. The Dead Angle was on the southern end of the battleline. Apparently they did kill a lot more Federals at the Angle.

Another soldier gave his impression of the Battle of Kennesaw Mountain:

We had cut down and placed in our front hundreds of black jack saplings as abatis, cutting off the tips of the limbs with our jack-knives and whittling them so sharp and close it would have been an uphill business for a rabbit to creep through. At any rate, enough to cause the Yanks to *bide a wee.*

I should also mention that in the valley or depression between the lines was a grove of pine and black jack, the ground being thickly strewn with leaves and pine cones, which were like tinder.

About 10 a.m. we could see quite a commotion across on the Yankee side, line after line apparently marching and countermarching. They seemed to be assembling mainly from their rear, massing just behind their breastworks. This meant for us *every man to his place and fix for business.* Line after line of Yanks mounted their works, and simultaneously their ordnance opened on us. Cannon — big, little, old, and young — made such a din that their muskets sounded like squibs. . . .

Well, the Yanks got as far as the gully in the ravine, which seemed at that time the healthiest place. One would imagine Vesuvius had moved over to the Confederate States of America and opened up business on Kennesaw.

As mentioned, our cannon were placed for execution. Their redoubts so low, the cannon's mouth nearly on the ground, and at every discharge a blaze of fire sprang out among the dry leaves, which were soon ablaze and eating their way toward the gully, which was full of a mass of human beings, squirming around and still piling on each other. Ah, but little can a peaceful citizen imagine the horror of war. Just one glimpse of that seething mass of weltering human beings, the flying, burning sticks and every discharge, flames leaping from limb to limb, the everlasting roar of cannon and small arms, not counting our usual Rebel yell.

At this stage our colonel, Will H. Martin, sang out, "Boys, this is butchery," and mounting our head logs, with a white handkerchief, he sang out to the Yanks as well as to our own men: "Cease firing and help get out those men." It is needless to add that the Feds never once refused to comply with this request. Our men, scaling the head logs as though for a counter charge, were soon mixed with Yankees, carrying out dead and wounded Feds with those who, a few minutes previous, were trying to "down our shanties." Together, the Rebs and Yanks soon had the fire beat out and the dead and wounded removed to the Federal side of the fence.

Now I will say this: The Yankees who were really engaged in this little matter were fully appreciative or our action, and I can't begin to mention the nice things they said to us. A Federal officer presented to Colonel Martin a brace of fine pearl-handled pistols, making quite a feeling little speech, not lengthy but to the point.[20]

141

The next soldier illustrated the danger of going after ammunition. This is the unit that the Tenth Texas moved to support during the battle:

And now I will answer some inquiries that I have read during the last thirty years concerning two Confederate soldiers who on the 27th of June, 1864, crossed over the summit of Kennesaw Mountain, bringing into our lines a supply of ammunition. After all had been exhausted, when bayonets, stones, and bludgeons were alone left for

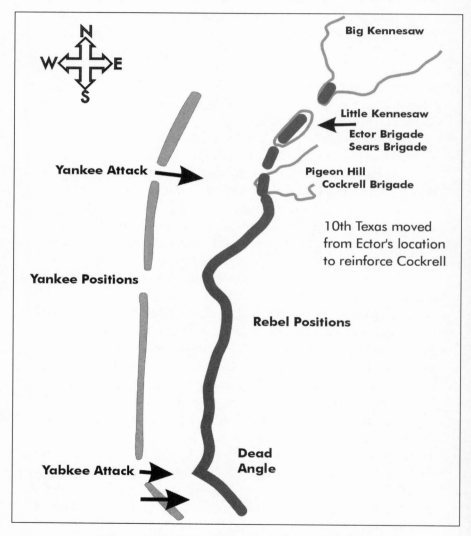

THE BATTLE OF KENNESAW MOUNTAIN
June 27, 1864

the defense of our works, which were situated on Pigeon Hill being played upon by fifty pieces of artillery in the valley below us — on the summit to our rear we had a battery of four to six guns, which were soon disabled and silenced by superior numbers and a concentrated fire. Our ammunition in the trenches was exhausted; a cry went up for a supply from all along the line. Col. James McCowan said: "Gentlemen, I will make no order for a detail to cross the summit of that [Kennesaw] mountain for ammunition, to go where I would not go, but will gladly accept volunteers." Our ordnance department was in a gorge on the eastern slope of the mountain near the base.

In looking over the situation with all of its perils and yet of our needs, I said to our captain: "I will volunteer for one, and if spared will return with some." Then, to my sorrow my brother said: "I will go." Side by side we climbed the rugged heights of Kennesaw Mountain under fire of small arms and of fifty pieces of artillery. We crossed over the summit and reached with safety the ordnance train, asking for three thousand rounds of Enfield ammunition. We found red tape there. The officer wanted a requisition. We had no time to comply. An old and loaded musket stood near by. I picked up the old and familiar gun, which was loaded and capped, and said: "Here is my requisition. Give us three thousand rounds now, and do it quickly." It was done. We took one box each on our shoulders and one between us. We climbed the rugged heights from the east and began the decent to the west. Two or three hundred feet from the summit a shell from some one of the fifty guns, coming from the front, burst between us (front or rear, I know not which) and scattered us thirty or forty feet apart, the box between causing a lively miniature battle. It all exploded as so many firecrackers in a barrel, but more terrific.

When the shock was over, I asked John if he were hurt, and he answered that he was not. In the midst of bursting shell we gathered each one thousand rounds; and if today, at the age of seventy-four, I could move with the celerity I then moved down the rugged and western slope of Kennesaw Mountain, I would feel that the days of Methuselah were promised me. Once in line, ammunition distributed, the orders in front were to fall back. Reinforcement (10th Texas) was received. At the hour of eleven that night we brought within our lines a Major Mullin, commanding the 121st Ohio Regiment, if I remember correctly. He had more wounds than any man I ever saw. He died soon after, and was buried on the morning of

June 28,1864, with Masonic honors on the eastern slope of Kennesaw Mountain, where so many of our noble dead lie buried in unknown graves, awaiting the judgment day. Major Mullin will not arise from the tomb with a halter around his neck, because he never burned or desolated the homes of widows and children.[21]

Another soldier recounted events at the Dead Angle. Union soldiers hid behind cracker boxes and shot ramrods at them:

The enemy formed a line of battle under the brow of the hill, and a more gallant charge was never made. . . . We reserved our fire till they were in a few yards of us, when we opened with a full line of infantry and an enfilade fire of artillery. They rushed right up to our works. Their colors were repeatedly shot down, but each time they were taken up. Finally the ensign stuck their colors on the works, but failed to get them away and our boys got them. At last, finding that they were "up against the real thing," as Cheatham's boys were there, they fell back under the brow of the hill and began to fortify. We could hear them at work, as they were only a few yards distant.

The next evening Gen. Cheatham sent out a flag of truce that they might bury their dead and take care of their wounded. We talked with the Yankees, moved some of their dead that lay against our works, swapped canteens with them, traded them tobacco for coffee, and one of our boys who had left his pocketknife on a large stone a few days before, where he had killed and dressed a sheep, was lucky enough to get it back from the Yankee who had found it. One of the Yankees during the armistice came up to our works. Reaching up and taking hold of a string in the *chevaux de frise*, he said: "I would not like to eat fodder out of that rack."

Having entrenched themselves under the hill, the work of advancing slowly began. They filled cracker boxes with dirt and kept them in front of them to protect their scalps, and worked day and night, digging and throwing the dirt behind them. When we evacuated the "Dead Angle," they were in about sixty feet of us. It was rumored the day before we evacuated that Gen. Cheatham had ordered hand grenades and troughs, that we might roll the missiles into their works; but we did not get them.

During our fighting there (for it was kept up every day), a Yankee shot his ramrod at our line. It struck a sapling, breaking it in two, and one piece about eight or ten inches long stuck through the leg of one of our boys and had to be pulled out.[22]

Another soldier was in the fighting at the Battle of Kennesaw Mountain:

The balls passing over in a constant, unending stream, gave forth every kind of sound. Some seemed to be mad, some sad, some laughing, some sorrowful, some mournful like a sighing breeze, some screaming like the ghosts of the dead. Every one seemed to say, "Look out, Johnnie Reb; I'm heading for you! Lie low, boy!"

I don't know how many pieces the Federals had in our front, but there must have been several million, judging by the way they shelled us. It appeared that the very foundations of the solid earth were being shaken. Sulphur and smoke and fire filled the air. Grim-visaged war seemed to laugh in all his pride and pomp and to have turned loose all the demons of destruction to join the dreadful havoc. It was like some terrible convulsion of nature wherein all the rough elements were at war and howling out their last requiem of terror and slaughter.

On that awful day the sun rose in a clear and cloudless sky; the heavens seemed made of brass and the earth of hot iron. As the sun mounted toward the zenith, everything became quiet; no sound was heard save a lone woodpecker on a neighboring tree hunting a worm for his dinner. We all knew that it was but the dead calm before the storm. On the distant hills we could plainly see officers darting about hither and thither and the Stars and Stripes moving to and fro, and we knew that the Federals were making preparations for a mighty contest. We could hear the rumbling sound of heavy guns and the distant tread of a marching army as a faint roar of the coming storm which was soon to break the ominous silence with the sound of conflict such as was scarcely ever heard on this earth. It seemed as if the angel of death looked on with outstretched wings while all the earth was silent.

All at once a hundred guns from the Federal line opened upon us, and for more than an hour they poured their solid and chain shot, grape and canister right upon this salient point. Then our pickets jumped into our works and reported the Yankees advancing. The witty man said: "Yes, yonder come forty lines of hard-tack and coffee, and I'm as hungry as a dog." At the same time a solid line of bluecoats came up the hill in our immediate front and seemed to hesitate and waver. I discharged my gun at the column, not more than ten paces away, and, happening to look up, there was the beautiful flag of the Stars and Stripes flaunting right in my face. I heard some

145

soldier say: "Look! Look at that flag! Shoot that fellow and snatch the flag." I raised up with my gun loaded, and there stood a pale, beardless boy, the flag bearer of his regiment, looking as white as a sheet. His flagstaff was planted in our earthworks. God bless the boy! I did not want to kill him. I thought I must have met him somewhere before. There he stood like a statue. Our eyes met. He gazed at me in a kind of mute entreaty. . . .

In fact, the whole force of the Federal army was hurled against this point; but they no sooner mounted our works than they surrendered or were shot down, and soon we had every gopher hole full of prisoners. Yet still the blue waves came, and it seemed impossible to stop the onslaught. The sun was beaming down on our heads, and a solid line of blazing fire right from the very muzzles of their guns was being poured in our very faces, singeing our hair and clothes. The hot blood of our dead and wounded spurted on us, the blinding smoke and stifling atmosphere filled our eyes and mouths, and the awful concussion caused the blood to gush out of our noses and ears — above all, the awful roar of battle, making a perfect pandemonium.

The ground was fairly piled with dead and wounded Yankees, and I learned afterwards from the burying squad that in some places they were piled up like cordwood, twelve deep.

But yet they continued to come. Our officers beat them in their faces with their swords and threw rocks and sticks; the Yankees did the same. But the Yankees kept on coming, line after line, to be mowed down, and seemed to be in no hurry to get away from the terrible slaughter. They seemed to walk up and take death as coolly as if they were devoid of fear. They were brave men, and our boys did not shoot for the fun of the thing. It was verily a death grapple, and the least flicker on our part would have been sure death to us. We could not be reenforced on account of our position, and we had to stand up to the rack, fodder, or no fodder. Here were also our dead, dying, and wounded almost filling the ditches of our earthworks.

I had just discharged the contents of my gun in the faces of two Federals, one right behind the other, and was reloading when another rushed upon me, having me at a disadvantage, saying: "D___n you! You've killed my brothers, and now I've got you." Everything that I had ever done rushed through my mind. I heard the roar and felt the flash of fire as I saw my more than friend, Billy Hughes, rush forward and grab the muzzle of the Yankee's gun; but, alas! too late, for in grabbing the muzzle he received the whole contents of the gun in his hand and arm, mortally wounding him. He died for me; in saving my life he lost his own. When the infirmary corps carried him off, he said: "Tell Sock to write to Florence and tell her how I died." It was the last time I ever saw him; but up yonder, beyond the clouds, tempest, blackness, and night above the blue vault of heaven, where the stars keep their ceaseless vigils, in the city of God, I hope to see him again.

After the Yankees were time after time beaten and driven back, they were at last enabled to fortify a line under the crest of the hill, only thirty yards from our line. In the meantime the woods had taken fire and during the nights and days of all that time continued to burn, and at all time of day or night we could hear the shrieks and screams of the poor fellows who had been left upon the field; and a stench so sickening as to nauseate both armies arose from the dead bodies left lying on the field. On the third morning a flag of truce was raised, asking an armistice to bury the dead; not for any respect they might have for the dead, but to get rid of the sickening odor. Long and deep trenches were dug and the dead piled therein. After they were all buried, the firing began again on both sides.

For several nights they made attacks upon our lines, but in every attempt they were driven back with great slaughter. They would ignite the tape of bombshells and throw them over our works. "Old Joe" sent us a couple of chevaux-de-frise, and a detail was to roll them over the works. Although it was a solemn occasion, every one of us was convulsed with laughter at the ridiculous appearance of the detail and their actions in the matter. All three of the detail knelt down and said their prayers. Two of them were religious boys and simply knelt down with their hands clasped, their eyes closed, and their faces looking heavenward. "Old Ten," on the detail, said his prayers too; he said his outloud. "O Lord," he prayed, "this is rather a ticklish and dangerous undertaking; and as bullets are said to have no eyes, I pray thee not to let one hit me on this occasion, if you please, sir. Now, O Lord, I've never been in the habit of calling on you before; an if you will just shield me and take care of me this one time, I'll never call on you again. Amen."

The boys had to roll the chevaux-de-frise only about three feet; but ah! in that three feet was death. I can laugh now whenever I think of the ridiculous appearance of that detail, but to them it was no laughing matter. They had no sooner gotten over the works than the alarm was given that the Yankees were advancing. Every man began yelling at the top of his voice to "Shoot! shoot! shoot!" On the alarm both the Confederate and Federal lines opened with small arms and artillery, and it seemed that the very heavens and earth were in one grand conflagration, like the day of judgment, when "the heavens shall be rolled together as a scroll and shall pass away with a great noise, and the elements shall melt with fervent heat, the earth also, and the works that are therein shall be burned up."

At the time the assault was raging in its fury the adjutant came running down the line to the left of the point where our regiment was stationed, with orders that we were to move to the right and fall in behind his regiment, which was out of ammunition. We were ordered to move by the flank, which was done amid a perfect shower of lead, and as we went we stooped very low.

During a part of this engagement General Cheatham, by flag of truce, offered a cessation of hostilities so the enemy could care for his dead and wounded. The reply came that they would "have possession of the field in time to bury their dead and care for their wounded"; but the next evening they asked for and obtained permission to bury their dead. Many of their wounded had died before getting any attention. The pickets were marched to halfway ground between the contending lines; and when they met they "about-faced" and stood back to back, each facing toward his own comrades. The Federals then scooped holes by each dead body, rolled them in, and covered them up. Those of us in the ditches the day after the battle could never forget the stench arising from those dead bodies.[23]

A Reb related his condition after the battle:

After we had abandoned the line, and on coming to a little stream of water, I undressed for the purpose of bathing, and after undressing found my arm all battered and bruised and bloodshot from my wrist to my shoulder, and as sore as a blister. I had shot one hundred and twenty times that day. My gun became so hot that frequently the powder would flash before I could ram home the ball, and I had frequently to exchange my gun for that of a dead comrade.[24]

One source said the Yanks came forward at Kennesaw Mountain like "a great blue cloud of Egyptian flies."[25] More Northern soldiers were piled up dead at Kennesaw Mountain than the British piled up dead at the famous Battle of New Orleans during the War of 1812.[26]

A Yankee gave his perspective of the fighting at Kennesaw Mountain and how the Rebs "cheated" by throwing cold "corndodgers" at them instead of rocks:

The Rebels commenced fighting by throwing stones at us, hurting some men, sometimes sending over a cold corndodger. Our men would say to them, "For God's sake throw rocks, but none of those corndodgers." Our men would throw over a hard-tack and say: "Take that; it's Uncle Sam's bread." They would reply: "Yank, send over some more." . . . We are getting our tunnel well under their works. This night the Rebs kept throwing over turpentine balls, keeping up a bright light, thinking we were going to charge them. We intended to mine under their works (at a point about thirty feet north of the angle) and blow them up on the Fourth of July.[27]

The writer went on to explain how a spy reached the Greybacks to warn them about the tunnel:

The spy, no doubt, furnished the information that Col. Dan McCook's Brigade had such close proximity to Cheatham's line that they had already tunneled under his breastworks, and that they had experimented as to the fact reported by laying pebbles and buckshot on a drum in the trench. They noticed the rattle on the drum at every stroke made by the sappers and miners in the tunnel beneath.[28]

A Reb detailed the lightning bug fight at Kennesaw Mountain. There were several New Hope Churches around and this was not the same location where the Battle of New Hope Church occurred:

Many of the boys, both Yanks and Johnnies, remember the lightning bug fight at New Hope Church. It may seem odd that lightning bugs could get up a fight, yet it is a fact. Our line ran by New Hope Church, and my brigade was in reserve, one hundred yards or more in the rear of the trenches, in a small depression caused by a ravine. Millions of lightning bugs were flashing their phosphorescent light in the balmy breeze and a summer night, when either a Federal or Confederate picket fired his gun and gave the alarm that a charge was being made. Two great armies turned loose every piece of ordnance they had, consisting of artillery, musketry, etc. That was one night when "h__ broke loose in Georgia."

In conversation with a Federal soldier many years after, who was in that fight, I asked him what harm was done to his side, and he replied that "you d__ fellows killed nearly all our horses and mules hitched to our commissary wagons, as we were at that time, 2 A.M., drawing our daily rations."

I passed New Hope Church in the fall of the same year, 1864, on our return march to Tennessee, and found every tree between the lines dead from shot and shell. The forest looked like a great deadening.[29]

General French, division commander of the Tenth Texas, could tell that war was hell. He could not sleep at New Hope because the cannonballs were shinning through his closed eyelids. Now, at Kennesaw, the abolitionists blew up his cooking utensils:

Last night I heard a peculiar "thud" on my tent and a rattle of tin pans by the side of my cot, and this morning my negro boy cook put his head into my tent with the pans in his hands and said: "See here, master Sam, them fernal Yanks done shot my pans last night. What am I going to do bout it?" A rifle ball, coming over the mountain, had fallen from a great height and perforated the pans and penetrated deep into the earth.[30]

On July 1, the Yanks went back to shelling the Reb positions, especially French Division positions, which included the Tenth Texas. The Tenth Texas was on the western end of Little Kennesaw where the artillery duel was fought:

Everything quiet up here until about five o'clock this evening, when Sherman got mad about something and commenced to throw shells at us. We bore the insult for twenty minutes or more, until Lieutenant Murphy, who was in command, a man of great patience, to the astonishment of all, was suddenly wrought upon and lost his usually good temper and said: "Boys, those Yanks want a fight, and let's give them what they want." And this decision brought on what I think was the greatest artillery duel in history as to the number of guns (52) focused upon a few (3) for several hours without intermission. Many of the enemy's guns were of large caliber, certainly none less than our three ten-pound Napoleon bronze field guns.

We were soon ready, and our three guns belched forth in response to their challenge, and the duel was on in dead earnest until nearly two hours after dark before Murphy ordered us to cease firing. Our guns were so hot that loading was dangerous. It has been a warm evening, and we boys are hot, thirsty, hungry, and wearied. There were many new guns brought into the ring against us this evening, and the odds were so great that nothing but the mercy of God saved our lives. We did not have a man killed, only a few slightly wounded. How wonderful that such could be the case amidst such a tornado of bursting shells and rain of iron and flying rocks! Yet we are here and ready for another round tomorrow.

General French speaks of this duel in his history of "Two Wars," and as he had a taste for the sublime, I will quote what he says of this artillery duel: ". . . but it was only in the darkness of the night that the magnificence of the scene was displayed. Grand beyond imagination, beautiful beyond description, Kennesaw, usually invisible from a distance at night, now resembles Vesuvius in the beginning of an eruption. The innumerable curling rings of smoke from the incessant bursting of shells over the mountain top, added to the volumes belching forth from our guns, wreathed Kennesaw in a golden thunder cloud in the still sky, from which came incessant flashes of incandescent light from shells like bursting stars. The canopy of clouds rolling around the peak looked softer than the downy cotton, but ever changing in color. One moment they were as crimson as the evening clouds painted by the rays of summer's setting sun, and the next brighter than if lit by the lightning's flash or bursting meteors."[31]

Surely the Tenth Texas soldiers only "enjoyed" the artillery fight because they were pinned down, caught in the middle. After the Battle at Kennesaw Mountain, the great Union General Sherman wrote his wife, "I begin to regard the death and mangling of a couple thousand men as a small affair, a kind of morning dash."[32] It would be "a small affair" as long as it was not you being the one getting mangled. On July 2, Sherman outflanked the Kennesaw battleline, and Johnston withdrew to a line along the Nickajack Creek, six miles south of Marietta. Johnston was immediately outflanked and withdrew to six miles of entrenchments north of the Chattahoochee River where he prepared to engage in the decisive battle. The Texans fought on July 4, 1864, at Rottenwood Creek. One of the Texans called it a battle.[33] On July 5, the Tenth Texas had four wounded and two captured at an engagement at Smyrna, Georgia. A Texan wrote of the fighting around July 4 through 8:

Near Chattahoochee River, Ga., July 8, 1864
Dear Ma: Another chance offers itself to write to Texas, and according to my promise I do so, although I have not much to tell you. You see by the heading of this that we have again fallen back. Fall back and fight, fight and fall back, is the order of the day. God only knows how this thing is to terminate. No one can tell the end of this campaign, and I am beginning to think it will terminate as did that of last year, which ended with Chickamauga. In my last letter I wrote you of the armistice we had made with the Yankee skirmishers. The next day I was on the skirmish line and loafing around in the woods,

when the Yankees broke through the armistice. You should have seen me "skeet" for our picket lines. The Yanks acted fairly with our boys, telling them to look out before firing a volley into the tree tops. After the first round they shot close, so a fellow had to keep covered. The firing lasted about half an hour when both parties ceased firing and the rest of the day passed off quietly. Since then I have been in but one fracas, and that was on the 4th. The Yankee band had been playing all day, and about one o'clock one of their buglers sounded the charge. We all looked to the front, and soon saw our skirmishers just tearing through the woods. Company A was ordered out to support them, and we went at double-quick. It was about four hundred yards to the skirmishers' works, and we were anxious to get there before too many Yanks got into them. When we arrived within one hundred yards of the works we saw that some of our skirmishers were trying to form a line. It was in an old field. The Yanks were in our works and some of them behind trees between us and the works. We deployed, raised a strong yell, and went at them. When we got to the works all we found was two Yankee knapsacks, two guns, and a haversack full of hard-tack and bacon. We did not get a man hurt in the charge. All remained quiet until about six o'clock in the evening, when the Yanks concluded to try us again. They came with the best yell I ever heard come out of Yankee throats, and at first I really thought they meant to interest us but when they came within a hundred yards our boys answered with a shout of defiance. This angered the Yanks, and the officers commenced shouting: "Forward, men! Forward!" Our men answered by shouting: "Come on, boys! come on!" Just then a Dutch officer shouted to the Yanks, "Trow avay de knapsacks!" and our men shouted not to throw them off, as we wanted them. The Yanks could not stand it any longer and they hid down in the bottom of a gully. The last command given by the Yanks was to hold that line. We knew where they were, and commenced firing on them, and about five minutes later the Yanks had gone and our videttes were in about a hundred yards of our works. One dead Yank and another who was mortally wounded fell into our hands. The one killed was as brave a man as ever lived. He was within seventy yards of us, loading his gun, perfectly cool, when five or six of the boys pulled down on him and killed him. The Yank that was wounded, as soon as he fell, shouted out to us that it was useless for us to fight them as they were too strong for us, but we soon showed him his mistake. He died in an hour or two, having been shot through the body.[34]

152

On July 8, Union troops, under Schofield, outflanked the Rebs to the east and crossed the Chattahoochee River. They were unopposed and had a clear path to Atlanta. Johnston withdrew on July 9 to Peachtree Creek, which is only six miles from Atlanta.

One of the Texans said they burned the railroad bridge across the Chattahoochee River.[35] Skirmishing along the river, the Tenth Texas had nine men wounded, one killed, and two captured.

Another soldier wrote describing the action around the Chattahoochee River. The writer was killed shortly afterwards:

We are now on picket on the bank of the Chattahoochee. Our whole division is out here in front of the army watching the enemy and keeping them from crossing the river. Our line is on one bank and the Federals on the other. We have established a kind of friendly picketing, and there is no shooting done. I was on picket duty the other night when a hard storm came up, blowing down a great many trees, one of which killed one of the boys who was on duty with me. We were under shelter trying to keep dry, and the wind was blowing so hard that some of the boys had left the shelter to get out of the way of the trees. I had just started when the alarm was given, and I made good my escape. We had to stand out and take the rain, wind, and hail.

Everything seems to be at a standstill with both sides. The soldiers seem to have the utmost confidence in Johnston. They think it will all be for the best, and all seem confident of success. I think when the time comes for a regular open field fight we will whip them very badly.[36]

CHAPTER 14

"All the bravest men have been killed"

ATLANTA CAMPAIGN AFTER
GENERAL HOOD TAKES OVER

O N JULY 17, Johnston was replaced by Gen. John B. Hood. One of the main reasons was that Johnston allowed the Blue Coats to cross the Chattahooche River virtually unopposed. Now, the Army of Tennessee and the Tenth Texas were in great peril.

Replacing Johnston with Hood may have been one of the biggest mistakes of the Civil War. Johnston might have been able to hang on to Atlanta until after the presidential elections in the Union. With a strong anti-war candidate against Lincoln, the election might have been different thus affecting the course of the war. Instead, Hood came out swinging and so weakened his army that he had to abandon Atlanta. The military victory by Sherman ensured Lincoln's victory. Lincoln, as late as August 23, 1864, told his cabinet he would probably not be re-elected. Even with the capture of Atlanta, Lincoln won by only 200,000 votes.[1]

Confederate General John B. Hood was a man who relished combat. After losing a leg at Chickamauga and the use of one arm at Gettysburg, he had to be tied to his horse. It has been alleged that, because of his constant pain, his liberal use of Laudanum (opium) caused a euphoric state of mind and may have affected his judgment. It was said that, prior to the war, Hood bet $2,500 on a poker hand when he did not have a single pair in his hand. Obviously, he was a gambler at heart.

Gen. John B. Hood

A veteran observed Hood's ability as a commander concerning an exchange Hood had with General Hindman:

> After we had returned to something near our original line, Gen. Hood, with part of his staff, rode up and saluted Gen. Hindman, and, pointing to a hill somewhat to our left front, said: "Gen. Hindman, when you see the enemy crown that eminence, take your division and charge them off. Hindman replied: "Let me take my division and post them there, and the enemy will not crown that eminence." Hood replied: "Gen. Hindman, why is it that I can never give an order but that you have some suggestion to make?" Hindman replied: "Because you never give me an order with any sense to it."[2]

One Reb stated that when they heard "Old Joe" was relieved and Hood was the new commander, thousands of them were "squatting down by a tree or in a fence corner, weeping like children."[3]

Even the enemy (General Sherman) was pleased with the new Rebel commander. He stated concerning the appointment of Hood: "The character of a leader is a large factor in the game of war, and I confess I was pleased."[4]

Hood took active command on July 19 and attacked the very next day. This was the Battle of Peachtree Creek. The Tenth Texas was on the extreme left flank of Hood's attack and saw little action. The official report shows no casualties for the Tenth at Peachtree even though Henry Smith, Company D, had a gunshot wound "passing through chest" and S.S. Tillman, Company D, was seriously wounded. Also, M.V. Goode, Company A, and Ferdinard Williams, Company I, were captured and became prisoners of war.

On July 22, Hood again attacked. This is commonly referred to as the Battle of Atlanta. Hood was appointed to fight the Yankees and in four days he fought two major battles. His losses in this battle have been estimated at ten thousand while the North's loss was only thirty-five hundred. July 22 was the day that Yankee General McPherson was killed.[5] The Tenth Texas saw no action in this battle.

The Tenth Texas was in position to the northwest of Atlanta and southwest of the Marietta Road when the brigade commander, M.D. Ector, was hit by an artillery shell and lost his left leg. This was on July 27, 1864. The commander of the artillery unit was killed and a member of the unit was severely shell shocked by the events witnessed at the time the shell exploded. Ector was replaced by Colonel William Young from the Ninth Texas Infantry. Colonel Young was injured at Murfreesboro and severely wounded again, in the left breast, at Chickamauga. He would also finish the war minus a foot. After taking over Ector's Brigade, he was promoted to general.

Around this time, one Yankee picket shouted, "Well, Johnny, how many you got left?" A Johnny Reb replied, "Oh, 'bout enough for another killing." The problem was the Southerners did not have the men to keep charging the way they were. The Army of Tennessee had the reputation that they would "charge hell with a cornstick."[6]

Also in the action around Atlanta, Pvt. James Harrison of Company C, Tenth Texas, was hit by a rifle ball behind the ear, ranging downward and lodging in the windpipe. A good cough and the ball popped out of his mouth.[7]

As the Yankees attempted to move west of Atlanta, Hood again fought a battle on July 28, at Ezra Church. Since taking command of the army, Hood ordered them to charge into fortified enemy breastworks in three clashes in eleven days.

The Tenth Texas was again fortunate in that they left their positions at Atlanta and moved out as the Battle of Ezra Church commenced. At midnight, they marched back to Atlanta.[8] The Tenth Texas was only involved in some light skirmishes.

The following is part of a letter by the flag bearer of the Tenth Texas Infantry (not our unit). He told of the battle of Ezra Church. This letter was sent to his uncle, one of the founders of Baylor University:

We have been lying in the ditches near the city for something like a week. The enemy has almost quit shelling this portion of our line. It is said they are concentrating their forces on our center: for what purpose I cannot say. I hardly think that they will charge our works. I have heard repeatedly that the Yankee gents can't get their men to charge rebels' works, and I believe it from what I have seen. I have heard them blow their forward calls but could not get their men to advance.

We have had three fights with them, beginning on the 20th of July and lasting to the 28th of same. It seems that our Brigade is quite lucky to get into fights. We worsted them every time, but the last one, and I suppose we did then. I understand that our Gen. claims a victory even then. I will give you rather a detailed account of the fight of the 28th.

The enemy was flanking us on our right as usual. Our corps (Hardee's) was sent round to flank them and rout and drive them from their positions. We moved all night, and next day we came on them about noon and found them strongly fortified. We charged their works and carried some two lines of works. The enemy abandoned their artillery and wagons in our front. The Brigade on our right and left failed to come up as did our support, and we had to fall back. The Brigade on our left met with stubborn resistance but carried two short lines of works (rather, the enemy's front works), and captured all that was in them. Those in our immediate front fled before our battle-line engaged them. They said that our Brigade captured some 15 or 16 pieces of artillery, two 20 pound Parrots among them but lost some of them by not having support at the right time. Late in the evening of the same day, we were sent on another charge, pretty much over the same ground. But the enemy fought with great courage and no doubt but what they had marked their forces: at all events, we failed to carry their works. I suppose I get in 10 paces of their works with the colors of the 10th Texas Regt. but could not stay there, from the fact that the men did not come up. I suppose that there was not more than half a dozen men with me. The men were badly scattered and many exhausted from the loss of sleep and warm weather and long marching. . . .

I suppose that you have heard, or will before this reaches you, that Gen. Hood is in command of this Army. For what reason Johnston was released it is more than any of us know. The army had the utmost confidence in Genl. Johnston, and I will say that I have not heard a man say anything about it but what regretted his being released. All that I hear say anything about Genl. Hood say that he is too fond of charging the enemy's works. We had rather not charge them, but would rather be charged by them, until our number equals theirs. And then we would be willing to meet them in open field. We are all quite tired of this war but will stay as long as life lasts or see the end of this cruel war.

Father (John Garrett) is in the enemy's lines. How they have treated him I cannot say, as I have not heard from him in more than a month. I suppose that they have taken all that he had, for I understand that they take even the ladies' wearing apparel, also that of helpless children.

I can't believe that God will let such a people go unpunished. I believe that the day for their overthrow is not far distant. I have heard that they cut the throat of every wounded man that they came across in Miss. They drove Forest back the first day 5 miles, and this is the treatment that our brave soldiers, wounded at that, received at their hands. And I heard that some of our men found some of their wives tied to stakes and dead from the cruel treatment that they received from their foul hands. If such as this will not make men desperate, what will? . . . I remain as ever, A true friend and nephew, Hosea Garrett, Jr.[9]

After listing all the casualties, the letter went on to state, "All the bravest men have been killed!" When men believed the atrocious stories as found in this letter, it was simple to get them to fight to the end.

Pvt. Jeff Rosson, Company D, Tenth Texas, the hero at Chickamauga, had been wounded at Murfreesboro and Latimer Farm. At Atlanta he was hit in the leg by a twenty-four-pound artillery shell. Luckily, it was a glancing blow and did not knock the leg off.[10]

After Hood fought these battles the action died down for several days. On Sunday, July 31, 1864, it was so quiet that a Baptism was done in a pond just behind the front lines of the Tenth Texas.[11]

Littlejohn recorded his memories of the action around Atlanta:

> Atlanta, Ga., Aug. 6/64
> I am at our Div. Hospital myself, have been here three days, but expect to go back to the front tomorrow. . . . I have not been very sick but worn out with constant diarrhea and fatigue. I am not stout but able to return and try it again as long as I can.
>
> I have no other news that would interest you. We are so hemmed in here in Atlanta that it is next thing to impossible to hear anything at all except the constant firing of artillery at some point along the lines, almost every minute of the day, and . . . small arms which are waiting to fill up the intervals between the artillery. It is so general and has lasted so long that we do not pay any attention to it unless it is directed at us. Occasionally some of our men get shot. Last night our Regt. went on picket in front of our works. This morning the authorities wishing to make a feint on our part of the lines, our regt. had to deploy in front and advance. While in motion Maj. Redwine & Charles Birdwell were both severely wounded, both in the left foot and by the same ball. I think that both of them will be disabled from the service. Two more of Regt. were wounded soon after, in the arm, but as yet none have come into the hospital dangerously wounded. We have had ten or eleven of our com. wounded in this campaign, none killed, but one died, Arnold, a boy beliked by all the com. who knew him. Sam had his arm shot off just below the elbow by a fragment of a shell. Others of the company have been seriously wounded in the many little skirmishes we have had. The loss of our regt. has been as great as it would have been in a general engagement. . . . I have great confidence in Johnston, and rely equally as much on the ability of Gen. Hood. He has called into service all the details in the numerous workshops of Ga. and also the militia, which strengthens our lines considerably. I

am glad to see all these *"play outs"* put into the service, but I do hate to see old grey headed men lying in the ditches taking the mud and water as it comes. We have very strong works around the city, which the enemy have assaulted a few times, but have gained nothing. I think we would be able to hold the ditches against great odds if they would only charge our works. I think we could make the ground blue with them, and should they ever try it they will find it so. . . . E.G.L.

Henry Watson, Company H, Tenth Texas, told his folks about the Atlanta action. The two men noted killed, and two of the three noted wounded, had just dropped off the roster of the Tenth Texas. No further entries were made concerning service. J.J. Langley survived and surrendered at the end of the war. Ben Birdwell was shot in the "right front" at Richmond, Kentucky, and was discharged from the military. He came back to fight again:

> Camp in the Field near Atlanta, Ga.
> August 9th 1864
>
> Dear Father and Mother, as I have an opportunity of writing you a few lines I will do so Mr. Benjamin Birdwell is a going to start home day after tomorrow and I will write by him well I have no good news to write to you we have had a hard time for about sixty-seven days we have been in line of Battle and a skirmish fighting with the yanks every day and night during this time. . . .
>
> We have been very lucky since we have been in this Campaign our Brigade has not been ary Genl engagement Since we have been on this Campaign although we have lost a great many men killed and wounded out of our Brigade I do not no how many men has been killed out of our Brigade we have had Two killed and four wounded out of our Company Winslow Corley and W.H. Daniels was killed and Thos. Hodges wounded in the head (A.M.) Fite was wounded in the elbow his arm will be always stiff Eli Banks was wounded in the ankle and J.J. Langley was slightly wounded in the hip I have been fortunate enough not to get touched with a ball. . . . The Bum Shells and Minnie Balls are constantly flying over us but the Boys are a getting sorty ust to them but once and a while one gets hit. Henry Watson

Another Texan from Ector's Brigade wrote home. (They should have been warned to not play with the explosives.):

> August 25, 1864
> Atlanta, Georgia
>
> We hafent got but Ten more left in our compney now and we hafto go

to Picket to morow and then we surely loos severl more we are nevr saft her no plase. their was two of the boyes that was a fooling with a bum shell that the yankes had thron over at us and hit dident burst and while they were Pateren with it exploded and cild one and wounded the other ones their is more or less that is cilld and wounded evey day and knight as the bum shelles a flyen ovr so that I shell hafto stop for this time. A.J. Fogle.[12]

A soldier in the same division as the Tenth Texas describes the withdrawal from Atlanta:

General Hood began moving his army to the left, leaving our brigade before Atlanta and stretching out our line until the men were thirty feet apart. . . . In the meantime our brigade, after leaving a few men in the entrenchments, was in the city destroying the government and railway property. At 2 a.m. our brigade left Atlanta at a rapid gain, and just as we were leaving the suburbs the explosion of the magazines shook the city from center to circumference. As we marched along the streets, it seemed that every woman and child in Atlanta was standing in the doors or yards with sad faces and in tears. About four o'clock next evening we succeeded in swinging clear around the army and took our position at Lovejoy, on the Charleston and Memphis Railroad, and very soon all of the Confederate troops that had been engaged in Jonesboro took their position in line with us. The campaign was at an end, and Sherman and his army took possession of Atlanta.[13]

The following is a listing of Tenth Texas casualties for the one hunded days fight:

List of Killed, Wounded, and Missing, Since Joining Army of Tennessee, May 19 to September 5, 1864

Resaca			Cassville			New Hope Church			Latimer House			Kennesaw			Smyrna		
K	W	M	K	W	M	K	W	M	K	W	M	K	W	M	K	W	M
					1	1	7		1	20		1	11			4	2
Chatta-hoochee			Peach Tree Creek			Atlanta			Lovejoy's			Total			Aggregate		
K	W	M	K	W	M	K	W	M	K	W	M	K	W	M			
1	9	2		2	2	3	19			1		7	73	7	87		

K = killed; W = wounded; M = missing.

The detailed personnel records, which were not updated toward the end of the war and reflect only the following casualties:

Tenth Texas
Killed in Action at Atlanta

Company F	W.W. Cauley	
	W.H. Daniels	
Company G	S. Mitchell	
Note: Last entry in personnel records showed present 4/5/64. Watson letter showed them as KIA.		

Tenth Texas
Wounded in Action in Atlanta
Never Returned to Duty

Regimental Staff	Ras Redwine	Hit by cannon ball
	W. Craig	Hospitalized for wound
Company D	B.F. Goss	Absent at Lovejoy's Station due to wound
	H.L. Smith	Gunshot wound through chest
	S.R. Cox	Gangrene — died 8/25/64
Company E	F.P. Hardin	On wound furlough
Company F	J.J. Scott	Of wounds received in battle?
	A.M. Fite	Wounded — arm stiff
	E. Banks	
	I. Hodges	
Company G	C. Birdwell	Wounded — received discharge
	B. Birdwell	
	J. Whitfield	Gunshot wound — left hand
	H. Hale	
Company I	T. Stafford	Gunshot wound — right hand
Company K	A.T. McDonald	Gunshot wound to lung — POW —survived

Tenth Texas
Members Taken Prisoner in Atlanta Campaign

Company A	M.V. Goode	Captured at Chattahoochee River
Company G	J.H. Wade	At Atlanta — claimed to be loyal deserter
Company I	F.L. Williams	Captured at Chattahoochee River
	J.P. Goodson	Captured at Chattahoochee River
Company K	J.W. Allen	Captured at Chattahoochee River
	J.W. Pool	Captured at Cassville, Georgia

Hood abandoned Atlanta on September 1, 1864. The Tenth Texas was marched from Atlanta to a place called Lovejoy's where the Army of Tennessee was already massed. They arrived at 3:00 p.m. on September 3. In the action there, the Tenth Texas lost one soldier due to wounds. The Tenth Texas, with around 150 soldiers present for duty, lost eighty-seven killed, wounded, or missing in the one-hundred-day fight. Hood succeeded in having 20 percent of his army put out of action from July to the end of September.

A Texan described the retreat from Atlanta:

On the 5th at Lovejoy Station the old 14th Texas was called on in another emergency. We were bringing up the rear, the enemy pressing us hard. A part of our line rested across an old field, and we had orders to hold our position at all hazards. Captain Howze had ordered his men to pile up some rails and throw dirt over them for protection. The enemy began to fire on us with what we called six-pound Parrott shells. Several times they hit our works, knocking the rails over us. Then came a shell under the rails, killing W.S.P. Wallace and breaking First Lieutenant Doyle's thigh; but still we held our position. Next came a shell and fell in our ditch with the fuse smoking. Captain Howze seized it in a moment and threw it over the works before it exploded. We were then ordered to a danger-ous retreat, as the Federals could see us until we reached the timber. The two armies who had fought each other day and night for four months took different directions.[14]

A Texan communicated a little about "black-hearted" people:

Camp at Lovejoy Station, Ga., Sept. the 17th, 1864
We have left Atlanta and are now between 20 and 30 miles down the Rail Road towards Macon. We left Atlanta the night of the first of this month and the Yanks are in the place. Old Sherman has driven all the people out of the place. There is a truce going on now between the two armies along the Rail Road bringing the families out of Atlanta.

The army is increasing rapidly every day. The teamsters are being sent to their commands and negro's put in their places except ambulance and ordinance wagon drivers. We are getting a plenty to eat at this time such as beef, corn bread and peas and we got molasses once and sometimes rice.

The Regt. drawed money yesterday. I have assigned a pay account and have sent for some cloth to make me some clothes. I will have some money in a few days and I would send you some the first opportunity, but I suppose that confederate money has become worthless in Texas by the State refusing to take it for taxes, and if it would do you no good I do not deem it necessary to be at the trouble of sending it. If it is so that the State of Texas has refused to take the currency of the country for its tax, I look upon it as a very disgrace-ful act of the legislature. I thought that Texas was too patriotic to send men to the legislature that are so black hearted. I think that they every one ought to be driven out of the State.

Our army is generally in good spirits and determined to be free or sacrifice their lives trying.[15]

When the Texan wrote about the state refusing to take the currency of the "country," he might have meant "county." The counties of Texas were printing their own money and, by this stage of the war, all of it was basically worthless.

As General Sherman started his pillage through the south, one Reb felt Sherman was entitled to abode forever in the bottomless pit of Satan's kingdom.[16]

After leaving Lovejoy, the Tenth Texas, with Ector's Brigade, marched to Palmetto, Georgia, to prepare for Hood's attack into Tennessee.[17]

While at Palmetto the president of the Confederacy came calling:

An illustration of the feeling of our men over the removal of General Johnston occurred after the fall of Atlanta. Mr. Davis visited the army, and it was drawn up for review. Our colonel was an enthusiastic man, and several who knew his temperament warned him not to call for cheers for the President. They told him that our men would not do anything to insult him, but they would not cheer him. So they urged the colonel to remain quiet in his position while the President passed, and the men would present arms and salute. He promised to do as advised. The President passed the Mississippi Division and was greeted with ringing cheers. Our colonel's enthusiasm got away with him. As the President came opposite us our colonel spurred his horse out of the line and, swinging his hat about his head cried: "Three cheers for our President!" But there was no response. The men were as silent as the grave. I never pitied a man more than I did the crestfallen colonel as he got back into line. We all loved him, for he was a grand man and a lovable one, but the men felt that they had warned him. Mr. Davis passed on as if not noticing, saluting as he rode by.[18]

President Davis later denied making the statement, but the newspapers at the time reported it and supposedly General Sherman read it. Davis told Cheatham's Division of Tennesseans, "Be of good cheer, for within a short while your faces will be turned homeward and your feet pressing Tennessee soil."[19] By being printed in Southern newspapers, the quote notified the Yankees of the Rebel intentions.

Here Hood formulated his plan to strike into Tennessee. On October 4, 1864, he ordered French's Division to attack the Yankee garrison at Allatoona to cut Sherman's supply lines. The Tenth Texas was still in French's Division. French was ordered to proceed up the Western and Atlantic railroad destroying any bridges and then to fill in the ravine in the Allatoona

Mountains through which the railroad tracks ran. Hood also ordered all stragglers and able-bodied men called back into the combat ranks.[20]

It should be pointed out that Sherman wisely bypassed Allatoona Pass. He built better fortifications and reinforced them with more troops than the Rebs had previously stationed there. Hood now ordered a frontal attack by the Tenth Texas.

Left, ruins of Atlanta depot, blown up on Sherman's departure
Right, Gen. Sherman at Federal Fort No. 7, Atlanta.

CHAPTER 15

"Magnificent courage"—all the brave boys aren't dead

BATTLE OF ALLATOONA PASS, GEORGIA

THE BATTLE OF ALLATOONA PASS has been described as a battle made famous for no real reason. One Union general stated, "Looking to the numbers engaged, this was no doubt one of the most desperately contested actions of the war."[1] It was a battle that reflected the advantages and disadvantages of having little or no supplies. The enemy cannot be burned out without matches, and someone cannot be asked to surrender without a white flag. There was also an advantage to having no food to eat if one happened to get gut shot. No food in the intestines might help solve the problem of infection.

After the war, a staff officer of General French questioned why the division, including the Tenth Texas, was assigned the duty of capturing and destroying Union supplies at Allatoona Pass:

> Now, why was it that Gen. Hood directed French's Division, the farthest from the objective point, to march by the divisions of Walthall and Loring to Allatoona, when Loring's Division, double in strength, and fully six miles nearer, could have been marched to Allatoona, surrounded the fort by dark or a little thereafter, and completely isolated the garrison at Allatoona from all possibility of being re-enforced, as it was that night by a portion of the division of Gen. Corse?
>
> The order of Hood directing the movements of the divisions of this corps was of such an astounding character that I hardly know how properly to characterize his action as a general commanding troops in active operation in the field. The order to French's Division without the possibility of being reenforced by the troops under his command which occupied the old lane at New Hope Church — certainly was an unjustifiable order; one more unjustifiable for a general commanding an army cannot be found in the history of the late war than that given by Gen. Hood to French on this occasion.
>
> Never was an assault made with more gallantry, determination, and rapidity than that of French's Division up the mountain

sides of Allatoona on that October morning in 1864, and it can be said with equal truth that the Federals with equal determination fought and defended their lines until the assaulting troops were mingled indiscriminately with those in the fort. It was the only time within my knowledge and observation that bayonets and clubbed muskets were used.[2]

It is possible Hood assigned the division this mission because they had not been as bloodied in his short but violent battles around Atlanta as some of his other units. The Battle at Allatoona was a conflict over fixed fortifications. The Rebs drove in a heavy battle line of skirmishers, then after crossing a long line of abatis, overran the second line of defense. These were fortified with entrenchments (ditches). The capture of the third line of defense involved hand-to-hand fighting, which left the ditches littered with the dead. The Yanks were then pushed back in a star-shaped fort.

The Tenth Texas and French's Division marched all day, October 3, 1864. They worked all that same night tearing up railroad tracks to cut the supplies to General Sherman. They labored all the next day, and on that same afternoon received the order to march and capture the Yank position at Allatoona.

General French furnished details about the movement to Allatoona Pass:

I left Big Shanty about 3:30 p.m. and marched to Acworth, a distance of six miles, arriving there before sunset. There I was detained awaiting the arrival of rations until 11 o'clock at night. As I knew nothing of the roads, the enemy's works, or position, it was important to procure a guide, and at last a young man, or rather a boy, was found who knew the roads and had seen the position of the fortifications at Allatoona, he being a member of a cavalry company. . . . From an eminence near Acworth the enemy could be seen communicating messages by their night signals from Allatoona with the station on Kennesaw, and to the east of us were the fires of a large encampment of the Federals. . . . Continuing the march the division arrived before Allatoona about 3 a.m. Nothing could be seen but one or two twinkling lights on the opposite heights, and nothing was heard except the occasional interchange of shots between our advanced guards and the pickets of the garrison in the valley below. All was darkness. I had no knowledge of the place, and it was important to attack at the break of day. Taking the guide and lights I placed the artillery in position on the hills south and east of the railroad. . . . This being done I proceeded with the guide to gain the heights or ridge crowned by works of the enemy. Without roads or paths the head of the line reached the railroad, crossed it, and began the ascending and descending of the high, steep, and densely-timbered spurs of the mountains, and after about an hour's march it was found we were directly in front of the works and not on the main ridge. The guide made a second effort to gain the ridge and failed, so dark was it in the woods. I therefore determined to rest where we were and await daylight. With dawn the march resumed, and finally by 7:30 o'clock in the morning the head of the column was on the ridge, and about 600 yards west of the fortifications. . . . Here the fortification for the first time were seen, and instead of two redoubts there were disclosed to us three redoubts on the west of the railroad cut and a star fort on the east, with outer works, and the approaches defended to a great distance by abatis and nearer the works by stockades and other obstructions. The railroad emerges from the Allatoona Mountains by crossing this ridge through a cut sixty-five feet deep. . . . So rugged and abrupt were the hills that the troops could not be got in position until about 9 a.m. when I sent in a summons to surrender.[3]

One of the disadvantages of not having a lot of supplies was that, in order to ask an enemy to surrender, a white flag was needed to send the message. Here is the story of the white flag:

(Major Sanders, assistant to General French) related as an interesting anecdote of the battle of Allatoona and the demand made on the Federals to surrender the garrison, that the flag of truce which he bore in making the demand consisted of a handkerchief fastened to the butt end of a musket. The division had been so constantly in the field that when a search was made for some white material with which to fabricate the flag of truce none could be found until a negro servant of Major Sanders produced a white handkerchief, bearing the name stenciled thereon "A. Coward," which had belonged to a Colonel Coward, whose regiment had been with French's Division in North Carolina during the winter of 1862-63, and which the negro had evidently appropriated.[4]

Mr. A. Coward survived the war and was superintendent of the Citadel for many years. The message delivered and the message returned was:

Commanding Officer United States Forces, Allatoona,
Sir: I have placed the forces under my command in such positions that you are surrounded, and to avoid a needless effusion of blood I call on you to surrender your forces at once and unconditionally.

Five minutes will be allowed you to decide. Should you accede to this you will be treated in the most honorable manner as prisoners of war. I have the honor to be, very respectfully yours, S. G. French, Major General Commanding Forces, Confederate States.

To which General Corse made the following reply:

Headquarters, Fourth Division, Fifteenth Army Corps, Allatoona, Georgia, October 5th, 1864.
Major General S. G. French, Confederate States Army, etc.:
Your communication demanding surrender of my command I acknowledge receipt of, and respectfully reply that we are prepared for the "needless effusion of blood" whenever it is agreeable to you. I am, very respectfully, your obedient servant, John M. Corse, Brigadier-General Commanding Forces, United States.[5]

As Major Sanders returned to the Reb lines after waving his "A. Coward" flag, a soldier asked, "Is it surrender or fight?" Sanders replied, "Fight!"

Around 10:00 a.m., the sound of rifle fire signaled that Sears' brigade had attacked the eastern fort. Orders were shouted to begin the attack on the western fortifications. The Missouri brigade lead the attack with Ector's brigade in support. Ector's brigade was aligned with the Tenth Texas on the left, Fourteenth Texas in the center, and the Ninth Texas on the right. The Thirty-ninth North Carolina Infantry and the Thirty-second Texas were left with the artillery and the Twenty-ninth North Carolina Infantry were temporarily lost in the woods. The Twenty-ninth arrived in time to participate in the attack at the third defense line. The Missouri brigade overran the first Union fortifications but stalled at the second defense line. The Texans, after passing through the abatis, aligned their formation at the first defense line that the Missouri brigade had captured. General Young gave the order for the Texans to charge and they swept the second defense line and cracked the Yanks' heads with rocks and rifle butts. The surviving Federals ran to the third defense line with Rebels mixed with and behind them. Retreating Yanks and Rebs ran into the third defense line together. The Yanks with the fifteen-shot Henry rifles were hindered from firing them because of the confusing mixture of Yanks and Rebs. The fight at the third defense line was again rifle butt, rocks, bayonet, and Bowie knives. Lt. M.W. Armstrong of the Tenth Texas saw a Yankee carrying a United States flag. General French, in his report, says Armstrong overpowered the flagbearer and brought him out with the flag. One soldier claimed Armstrong bashed the Yank with a rock and had a Rebel private carry out the flag.

The Texans found themselves standing in the ditch behind the third line of Yank works. The ditch was packed with the dead and wounded from both sides. A withering fire opened upon the Confederates from the last fortified position less than forty yards away. Stunned, they took cover in the ditch, behind tree stumps and logs, and began to return the fire. The only way to take the last line of fortifications was to win the rifle duel, suppressing the abolitionist fire so the Greybacks could move forward.

Capt. Mortimer Flint, on the staff of General Corse, had this to say about the Texas charge:

> Now from out [of] the woods and up from the valley they came; a solid mass of somber brown and clouded gray; no vacant places in their steady ranks; their artillery on each flank keeping up a constant roar.
>
> . . . Our artillery answers theirs. . . . They open with musketry and we reply. . . . Oh, that Sherman or night might come! The Springfields were getting so hot that they could scarcely be handled and those who manned the parapets were taken off in relays so that one half could continue the firing and the others allow their guns to cool. Young hurled his brigade of Texans on Rowett's command. Well for us that their attack was on the 7th Illinois, who were armed with the Henry rifles, a fifteen shot magazine gun, which the rebels declared were loaded up on Sunday, and fired the rest of the week. They were the personal property of the men who had purchased them at $51 each. They had both a destructive and mortal effect upon the enemy, who were now thrown into confusion and for a moment wavered, but soon rallied and with magnificent courage again breasted the storm.[6]

The Tenth Texas charged straight on to the Seventh Illinois. On average, one could fire a musket about three times a minute, the Henry repeating rifle could be fired fifteen times in eleven seconds. A Spencer repeating rifle fired about eight times in twenty seconds. (No wonder one member of the Tenth Texas had twenty-six holes in his clothes and himself.)

The Texans held their position in the Union third line for three hours, trying to outshoot the Yankees and silence their fire coming from their last fortified position. Finally, the Yank fire began to slacken, and the men of the brigade steeled themselves for the final attack.

General Young was wounded so Colonel Earp of the Tenth Texas took command of the brigade and ordered a charge to capture the final Union fortification. They made it to the ditch in front but were hit down the flank by canister fire. This was the last charge of the battle.

Todhunter, on the staff of Ector's Brigade and the man that led them onto the battlefield at Chickamauga, related the action. It should be mentioned that the third defense line of the Yanks was called a "fort" by the Rebs:

This was the most terrible and sanguinary battle ever fought by any division of the Army of Tennessee up to that time.

The Confederates numbered less then twenty-eight hundred effectives. The fort of Allatoona was defended by General Corse (Federal) with about an equal number of men behind the most formidable breastworks protected by every modern impediment known to scientific engineering. This battle was of about three hours' duration and consisted of repeated charges on the Federal works. To charge those gallant Federals behind such splendid fortifications of almost impassable abatis of felled trees and up a rugged mountain was a frightful undertaking.

The Confederates succeeded in capturing Fort R, and all its redoubts with a fearful loss to both sides, fighting hand to hand with bayonets and guns clubbed. It was simply horrible. The trenches in this captured fort were filled with dead and wounded Federals. Just as the last fort was captured, having expended what ammunition we had, and before we could get supplies from our ordnance train, some distance in the rear, we were ordered to withdraw, as Sherman, with

Soldiers from the Seventh Illinois pose with their Henry repeating rifles. The Tenth Texas drove them out of their ditches at Allatoona Pass, Georgia. Private Sam Birdwell, Tenth Texas, had 26 holes in his clothes and body from charging the repeating rifles.

a large army, was near at hand, advancing with troops to the rescue of Corse, which would have cut French's Division off from Hood's army stationed near New Hope Church.

The brigade officers at the time censured General French for not awaiting the arrival of the ammunition in order that they might take the Star Fort, as the Federals were crying, "Cease firing!" "Surrender!" etc. Sherman's proximity proved General French's withdrawal correct. The losses to the Texas Brigade up to this time were: Gen. W.H. Young, who was promoted to the command of this brigade for General Ector; Col. J.L. Camp, of the 14th Texas, one of the best colonels in the army; also two majors, Purdy and McReynolds, seven captains, eleven lieutenants, and one hundred and ninety men from nine hundred of the best soldiers on earth.

It is seldom that a well-fortified fort is ever taken. During our four years' fighting I cannot now recall a single fort being taken, if properly manned, either by Federals or Confederates. For instance, Atlanta, Vicksburg, Kennesaw Mountain, Franklin, and others. Allatoona was far better fortified than any of those mentioned. It is estimated that one man behind the works is equivalent to five in front charging. And yet to show the desperation of this battle the forces on both sides were nearly equal.

Sherman, who was near at hand with his large army, advancing to the rescue of Corse, sent him repeated signals, such as "Hold the fort; I am coming!" "Near you." "Sherman working hard for you!" "Sherman moving in force!" "Sherman says, 'Hold the fort, we are coming!'" P.P. Bliss, the great evangelist, the first Sunday after the battle had this song, "Hold the Fort," sung in his tabernacle at Chicago. It was caught by a thousand voices, and from that day to this it has been a standard gospel lyric:

> Ho! my comrades, see the signal
> Waving in the sky;
> Reinforcements now appearing,
> Victory is nigh.
> Hold the fort, for I am coming,
> Jesus signals still;
> Wave the answer back to heaven,
> By thy grace we will.

The Federals reported a heavy loss of officers and men, nearly equal to ours, in this battle. The Federal officers recklessly exposed themselves in order to encourage their men to fire over the works at us, as many were crying, "Surrender!" "Cease firing!" General Corse, their commander in chief, stationed in the center fort, was badly wounded; also his other fort commanders, General Rowett and Colonel Tourtelotte, were severely wounded. Encouraged, as they were, by General Sherman's repeated signals to hold out, they fought with desperation. This battle should not have been fought. It was a useless expenditure of life of the best soldiers on earth. Confederates were misinformed as to the strength of the Federals, as General Corse's command from Rome, Ga., arrived in the night preceding the battle.[7]

Apparently the real message Sherman sent was, "Hold fast, we are coming." It sounded better to say, "Hold the fort, we are coming." Sherman was sending messages using the "wig wag" system (waving signal flags).

A Texan with the Ninth Infantry, which was located to the right of the Tenth Texas on the assault, said the Missouri unit drove the Yanks from the first fortification, then they fell back and Ector's Brigade took the lead. He related:

We went with our guns loaded, or rather ran like we were in a foot race, to the edge of the ditch and shot down on them, then clubbed our guns and had a regular hand-to-hand fight.[8]

During the Battle, General French said the Yanks were crying out "Cease firing!" They cried "surrender" with some playing dead. He said the Yank General Corse, after being shot, used a Yank body as a chair.[9]

Photo of Allatoona Pass taken during the war. The Tenth Texas did its fighting on the hilltop on the left

The Yanks had fired 164,750 rounds at the Rebs and reported only having 250 rounds left.[10] A Yank boasted about "busting caps" on eight Rebs at the "pulpit":

> After one early assault the Southern sharpshooters took possession of a pulpit that the Reverend Sylvanus Allen, serving as a private in the 4th Minnesota, had built, weeks before, in a gully. On many a Sunday, Allen had preached from this glory-box, and it angered him now to see the enemy use it as a vantage point from which to kill his comrades. Alonzo Brown of the same regiment observed how Allen trained his rifle on the pulpit and waited. "He gave his attention to it and during the afternoon killed eight rebels in his gospel shop.[11]

The Thirty-ninth Iowa was the northern unit from which the Tenth Texas took the flag. This is the unit shown on the cover of this book:

> The most vulnerable spot in the earthwork was a break made by a ditch, and here a fragment of the 39th Iowa under Lieutenant Colonel James Redfield took its stand. A bullet broke Redfield's leg, but he stayed on, crawling about with his leg dragging, shouting encouragement to his soldiers, who fired so fast that they had to discard their hot pieces for the cooler weapons of dead comrades. A private brought Redfield a chair and he sat in it facing the full blast of the Confederate fire. More balls kept hitting him, but still he sat there, firing his revolver, shouting to his men, till one final bullet shot the last flicker of life out of him and he slid down to the ground, dead at the foot of his throne.[12]

The Texans were commanded then by Gen. W.H. Young who was wounded in the ankle and had his horse shot out from under him. He was captured while he was in a wagon ambulance on the way to the hospital. The Yank doctors amputated his foot at the ankle. Command of Ector's Brigade was then assumed by Col. Julius Andrews from the Thirty-second Texas Cavalry.

A Texan mentioned the capturing of the flag. He claimed Armstrong used a rock on the offending Yank:

> When we lost Gen. Ector at Atlanta, Ga. Gen. Young, then being senior colonel, took command of the brigade, and so continued until the battle of Allatoona, where in that desperate charge his horse was soon shot from under him, but he continued leading his men until wounded himself. Guns were clubbed, bayonets and rocks were used, a lieu-

tenant knocked down the Yankee flag bearer with a rock and a man of my company, John Hardy, brought the flag out on the retreat.[13]

Many sources said the Rebs were minutes away from capturing the last fort. The Yanks were attempting to surrender. This soldier from the Missouri Brigade to the right of the Texans swore they would have needed thirty minutes with crow bars and pick axes to dig the Yanks out:

> The fort to be attacked was built on the top of the hill, immediately by the side of this railroad cut. The fort was a casemated block house,

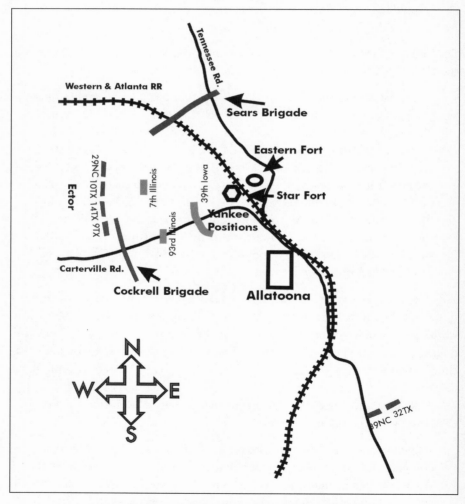

THE BATTLE OF ALLATOONA PASS
October 5, 1864

constructed and roofed with hewn logs. A ditch, about sixteen feet wide and six feet deep, had been cut around the block house at a distance of some forty feet from its walls, and the dirt taken therefrom had been thrown against its walls for an embankment, and also on top of it, so as to render it practically proof against light artillery or an infantry attack. Outside of this ditch for some distance a strong abatis had been constructed of heavy brush and sharp spikes driven in the ground, and trimmed and pointed outward, so as to obstruct the advance and break the force of an attack. . . .

When the charge was ordered, Cockrell's Missouri Brigade had much the shortest distance to advance and much the smoothest ground to pass over. . . . It was worse than madness to attempt to cross this heavy abatis and big ditch under the heavy fire; and could this even have been accomplished, we could not then have penetrated the fort probably in less than thirty minutes had we been armed with crow-bars and pick-axes, especially so with six hundred men inside firing on us with sixteen-shot Henry rifles and about a half-dozen pieces of artillery. . . . In order to withdraw from our position we had to retire over the same ground over which we had advanced, and which was strewn with our dead and wounded. In withdrawing, the moment we left the position we then occupied we came in full view of the enemy and were exposed to the same terrific fire to which we were subjected while advancing, with this difference, perhaps, that we made better time coming out than going in. So great was the danger of withdrawing, that many of the men were inclined to remain and surrender, rather than take the risk of getting away. In the writer's efforts to have every man of his own command started out, he was among the very last to leave, and was consequently far in the rear of most of them, and subjected to extraordinary risk. He may not have gone in with extra rapidity, but it would have taken a "stepper" to pass him coming out. . . . We lost perhaps one hundred and twenty-five men who remained and were surrendered, rather than undergo the danger of withdrawing.[14]

A Union soldier from Iowa was amazed when he walked over part of the Allatoona Pass battlefield in October 1864. According to him, when the battle was over, they found an Iowa soldier dead, lying face to face with a dead Southern soldier. The men had run their bayonets through each other. The Iowa unit was in front of the charge of the Texans, and this was where the Tenth Texas captured the U.S. flag. The Iowa Regiment entered the fight with 280 men and sustained 170 killed and wounded. The Illinois unit, equipped with the Henry rifles, suffered almost as many casualties.[15] A soldier with the Mississippi unit under General Sears remarked:

> In less than five minutes after our entrance into the battle, every field officer in the Regiment lay upon the field dead, together with two hundred and fifty others.[16]

J.M. Spinks, Company G, Tenth Texas, wrote:

> I carried a dispatch to General Sears and met Sam Birdwell wounded on a Yankee horse, and he bartered me to swap horses, Sam had twenty-six bullet holes in his clothes.[17]

Fearing Sherman was sending reinforcements to cut his division off, General French ordered a retreat. French's troops marched off to escape Sherman, but left a skirmish line in position until 3:00 p.m. to cover the stretcher parties collecting wounded outside the Union works. The stretcher parties worked quickly. They had orders to take only the lightly wounded, leaving all the worst cases to be captured.

Pvt. Henry Pool, of the Tenth's Company K, recounted what happened to him:

> At Allatoona Mountain I was shot between the eyes and they were about to leave me but I was determined to get in the ambulance. I was carried down the mountain and I guess I fainted for I paid no attention to what they were doing until I looked up as best I could and saw that they were putting those in the ambulance who were only slightly wounded. I raised up and told the doctor that I was going too and he said that there was not room for anyone else, but I told him if he did not let me go, I would never fire another gun. They thought I would die, but I got up and ran to the ambulance and got in and got away.[18]

The Tenth Texas had no official report after the battle. The report of the Ninth Texas Infantry had an interesting comment in it. It stated that C.E. Dale was the first to mount the enemy's works and was shot dead. C.E. Dale had carved his name in rock at Kennesaw Mountain and claimed he was with the Tenth Texas. No records were found confirming his assignment to the Tenth Texas.

The Tenth Texas suffered forty-four men killed and wounded and six missing out of approximately 125 men. The casualty count for the Tenth Texas was arrived at by taking the Ector's Brigade total and subtracting the other regimental casualties. It is clear that many casualties were not noted in the personnel records. This would account for many of the eighty-nine men shown present in April 1864 but who were not present at the surrender.

Tenth Texas
Killed in Action at Allatoona Pass

Company I	J.R. Jones	Mortally wounded
Company K	Q.K. Gibson	Death noted in official report

Tenth Texas
Wounded in Action at Allatoona Pass
Never Returned to Duty

Company C	D.B. O'Bryan	Wound noted in official report
Company H	R.S. Lyles	Wound noted in official report
Company I	P.R. Jones	
Company K	H. Pool	Shot between the eyes
	S. Birdwell	26 holes in him and his clothes

Tenth Texas
Members Taken Prisoner at Allatoona Pass

Company G	R.S. Brownlow	
	T.L. Gladney	
Company K	W.R. Glenn	

Henry Pool, Company K, was the brother of James F. Pool, also of Company K. Henry, after being shot between the eyes at Allatoona, made his way to another brother's unit that was mounted cavalry. This brother gave him his horse and Henry promptly headed home to Texas. [19]

Another drawback from fighting with limited supplies was that when the Rebs first attempted to burn the Yank's supply depo, they found that they only had three matches. None of them would light. Apparently, a Reb from the Sears Brigade did get a pine knot torch lit, but he was shot as he attempted to race to the supply depo. A Yank noted this incident was after the battle was over and two thousand Yanks were all shooting at the man. He was buried south of Allatoona. [20]

The Yank general sent the following message the next day:

I am short a cheek bone and one ear, but am able to whip all hell yet. My losses are very heavy. A force moving from Stilesborough on Kingston gives me some anxiety. Tell me where Sherman is. [21]

One Yank viewed the aftermath at Allatoona:

The scene in that ravine [in front of the Star Fort], after the battle was ended, was beyond all powers of description. All the languages of earth combined are inadequate to tell half its horrors. Mangled and torn in every conceivable manner, the dead and wounded were everywhere, in heaps and windrows. Enemies though they were, their conquerors, only a few minutes removed from the heat and passion of battle, sickened and turned away, or remaining, looked only with great compassion, and through tears, upon that field of blood and carnage and death, upon that wreck of high hopes and splendid courage, that hetacomb of human life.

Their dead and wounded were scattered through the woods and ravines and gulches all around and were continually found, and the dead buried, from day to day, until the 22nd of October. One Yank flag had one hundred and ninety-two bullet holes in it.[22]

There was at least one advantage of not having supplies. If you are "gut shot" and your intestines are empty, you have a chance of living. In the book *Two Wars* by General French, he states:

Texas will mourn for the death of some of her bravest and best men. Capt. Somerville, Thirty-Second Texas, was killed after vainly endeavoring to enter the last work, where his conspicuous gallantry had carried him and his little band.

Capt. Somerville was shot through the intestines and because he had had nothing to eat for more than 24 hours prior to being wounded, lived to arrange parole for his group of fellow hospital inmates in a conference with Gen. Sherman. . . .

Prior to him being shot, Co. K had been in a forward position for more than a day and night, or at least Capt. Somerville had been. Rations were supposed to have been issued before going forward, but were either not available or held up by some blunder. A scout reported there was a barn serving as a commissary storehouse for Federals which could be easily captured; to reach it, the Company would have to circle behind some Federal fortifications.

There was a cover of small brush and low places between ridges or some uneven contours. In a group discussion, Co. K decided to get food from that storehouse. That was the "GALLANTRY"; pure old hunger. At the storehouse, Co. K filled canteens from whiskey barrels and hurriedly grabbed food, mostly hams, cheeses, and boxes of crackers. Some of the men ate as they made their get-a-way. Capt. Somerville did not eat. On the way out, Co. K had to deviate from the route taken on the way in. The men had to pass close to Federal fortifications of logs and dirt. The rear and sides of the fortifications were unprotected. Co. K was at the side of and slightly behind the line of fortifications, in enough cover so they could fire and not be readily seen. The Federal troops were very busy with a group of Confederates who were firing volleys at the fortification. Company K was in a good position. They were so close to the unprotected side and at an angle to the back of Federal troops, so that each shot made should kill a man. They took cover and began shooting, timing their volley with that of the Confederate front.

Then the Confederates in front of this particular unit retreated. Co. K had no way of knowing this, so that their small volley rang loud and clear in the sudden cessation of noise from the front. There was no immediate reaction from the Federal troops, who had already fired in a volley and were preparing to reload. Then one man, described as a tall, gawky country-looking fellow who must have been an Illinois farmer, turned and pointed in Co. K's direction and began yelling. The remainder of the Federal troops about-faced in what Capt. Somerville described as a parade type maneuver. The men of Co. K picked up their stolen rations and began running, all except the one man called "Bill." Bill figured prominently in a number of stories; he was a good fighter but invariably goofed at the most inopportune time. Now he was trying to reload in time for one more shot. Capt. Somerville, trying to make sure none of his troops were left behind, turned around to yell at Bill just as the Federal troops fired. A slug hit him in the abdomen. His reaction was numbness and disbelief; he had been in combat so long that he had forgotten how vulnerable he was. He could still move. Fighting to remain conscious, he made his way to an abandoned building which was to be a rendezvous. He knew he would be late, and that his own men might shoot him as he came out of the brush. This was almost the case. One man almost shot him, then was so startled at recognition that he froze with the gun still aimed at him, so that another man had to push the gun barrel down before danger was past. Co. K was now in full retreat, trying to rejoin the other Confederates. Someone found the bullet had passed through Somerville's body and was almost out near his backbone. The bullet was dug out and placed in his pocket; it contained a metal alloy "bore cleaner" which supposedly caused gangrene if left in the wound.

In later years, Somerville often remarked on the lack of first-aid training, especially on the fact that no one, including himself, thought of making a simple stretcher by blanket and poles. A blanket was simply placed under him and the men grabbed a corner, with no poles being used, so that the blanket sagged in a most uncomfortable manner. In this way he was carried to an old mill. Here the Confederates tried to make their wounded comfortable before leaving them.

Another officer, a Texan, was placed beside Capt. Somerville. He also suffered a "gut shot" and knew he would die in pain. He begged his men to return his pistol so he could quickly end his misery but they refused. During the night, he did indeed die in pain. Sometime during the night or next morning, Federal troops and doctors began to tend the Confederate wounded. In the hospital, Somerville was treated amazingly well. For one thing, the doctors were proud of having saved the life of a man who sustained a "gut shot." For another thing, he was not an American; he was a Scots-Irish, a Presbyterian, and was born in Elphain, Ireland. He migrated to Texas via New York, and most importantly, he was a Mason. Federal officers who were Masons visited him in a brotherly fashion, seeing that he was well cared for. Presbyterians took a special interest in him. Irish Catholics, glad to see someone from the "Old Country," dropped in to talk about people and places at home. He was placed on his honor as a Mason and given some freedom of movement when he became better. He visited those necessary to help arrange for parole of prisoners from Allatoona Hospital. By this time, the War was almost over and surrender was only a matter of time. One man, who lost both legs above the knees, left Allatoona Hospital on crutches, his legs padded by heavy leather at the amputations. Capt. Somerville often wondered if he got home.[23]

General Hood, in his book written after the war, concerning Allatoona stated, "Our soldiers fought with great courage." The author believes this feeling by General Hood saved the Tenth Texas and its sister regiments from disaster. Hood had them guard his pontoon brigade during the Battle of Franklin.

CHAPTER 16

"Corn hauled up and issued out to us like we were horses"

MARCH TO TENNESSEE

GENERAL HOOD spent several weeks trying to prepare for his push into Tennessee. He requested that the railroad from Corinth to Tuscumbia arrange to move provisions for his troops on their march northward. Because of the twin problems of inclement weather and major repairs to the rails, Hood delayed the crossing of the Tennessee River by three weeks. Once he was ready to forge ahead, Hood had to change his plans again. Forrest's Cavalry was unable to traverse the river at the shortest and most direct route because it was too high at that point. Without Forrest and his troops to defend him, Hood decided to march west and meet up with Forrest. They would then be able to move into Tennessee together. The days wasted allowed the Yankees valuable time to assemble troops and prepare a defense.

A soldier from French's Division, which included the Texans, wrote about the "great" food they had on the trip up to Tennessee and about fighting to get something better:

> The army resumed its march northward on the morning of the 8th of October. The three days' march following was made with great rapidity, the incentive for which could not be surmised, unless it was that Sherman was marching in one direction and we in another. The march of the third day (October 10th) was continued until 10 o'clock at night, and up to that hour the army had marched twenty-nine miles that day, and received no rations for two days except two ears of corn daily to each soldier. The road was rough and the men weary and exhausted almost beyond endurance. The excessive long marches and ear-corn rations had lead the army to style itself "Hood's Cavalry."
>
> The army had just halted, stacked arms, and was preparing to parch some corn, when a courier approached me with an order to take my command and advance three miles further, and put out pickets for the protection of the army. The order seemed a great

hardship at the time, but in a few minutes we were ready to renew the march. I am candid to admit if there was a Christian in the regiment then, there was nothing in his language to indicate it.

We had marched about two miles further in the dark, and on the railroad track, when we were greeted with a volley of shots, which whistled over our heads. I at once filed the regiment to the right under cover of a small hill, put out pickets, and sent a courier back to brigade headquarters with advice to the effect that we had encountered what was supposed to be a Federal garrison of some kind.[1]

The soldier continued his story after the order to attack was received:

A moment before the charge was ordered I suggested to the command the probability of our coming in possession of a fine lot of Federal stores, both to eat and drink, in the event of our success. The suggestion proved a trump card. The advance was ordered, and if the success of the Confederacy had been staked on the result, it could not have produced more zeal than the prospects of those Federal stores. . . . We advanced under their fire to within sixty yards of their works, at which time we had reached the foot of the hill on which the fort was situated. Not one of the enemy was to be seen — nothing but the fort and the fire from their guns through their port-holes was visible, and it was readily seen that we could not carry the works by brute force, but must resort to some kind of strategy. . . .

An inquiry was made from the fort as to what command had attacked them, when I informed them it was the advance of Hood's Army, and thereupon demanded their surrender, with the assurance that I had them surrounded, and that if they did not comply we would soon open on them with a couple of Parrot guns, which had been ordered up. . . . In less than ten minutes word reached me that the garrison had surrendered and was in charge of two companies of the regiment. I returned to the spot as quick as practicable and found the command had fallen on to the supplies promised them, which up to their hearts' desire — sugar, coffee, bread, bacon, crackers, canned meats, and fruits of every description, condensed milk, etc., besides two barrels of what then seemed the best whiskey a soldier ever tasted. Campfires had also been started, and the men were going through these good things with a gusto that knew no equal. . . . The eating and drinking lasted until daylight, and my word would likely be discredited were I to attempt to state how much those Confederates ate and drank. Suffice it to say, in the meantime the two barrels of whiskey were pretty well absorbed, and I can say, without fear of successful contradiction, that they were the most promiscuously and universally drunk set of men in my opinion that ever occupied the same amount of territory, the writer, of course, excepted.[2]

On November 17, 1864, the Tenth Texas was at Tuscumbia, Alabama, building forts and breastworks. Littlejohn wrote home on this date. He noted in his letter that there was a paper shortage in East Texas and the price of paper for letters was over six times higher than in Alabama:

We have suffered more for the want of something to eat on this campaign than on any previous one, having been compelled to eat parched corn right ahead. On one occasion our generals had corn hauled up and issued out to us like we were horses or hogs and they (Gens.) also were short. I recollect of seeing Gen. French one day sitting by the roadside cracking hickory nuts like a good fellow. But I don't mind to do without when I know it can't be had, or that the Generals are doing without. E.G.L.

One Texan knew how to handle his ration of corn. He drank it. Three times a day he parched it brown, crushed it, and made coffee from it. He then ate the grounds.[3]

Another Texan, A.J. Fogle, writes to Miss Loo:

Florance Alabama November 18th 1864

Dear Miss . . .

I would like very much to send you a long letr but I hafent got the paper we have bin on a long mach and had to go threw so much rain and waid the creeks that hit is imposable to cary any thing of that sort James williames left us sum time ago and if he gets home safe he can tell you all the late nese he can tell you who was kild and who was wounded. I would of liked very much to have writin and hent by him but he was on the march and we couldent stop and I hafto write this in such a hury I dont expect that you will ever wread hit We have stoped her on the bank of Tennessee River a few dayes to bill wum brest works so we can leave a small forse their to guard the pon toone Bridg whilest the rest of the arms makes a raid up in to Tennessee and I guess we will see a hard time of hit for the wether is a geting cold and the roads is a geting very much.

So farwell Miss Loo, A. J. Fogle

Ector's Brigade was left behind temporarily to guard the pontoon bridge equipment because of their heavy casualties at the Battle of Allatoona Pass. This gave them a chance to regroup and saved most of their lives because they did not participate in the great slaughter at Franklin.

When the forces of Hood and Forrest met up, Hood's headquarters sent Forrest an order reducing the army's number of mules per wagon and ordering that all surplus animals be turned over to Hood's transportation quartermaster. Forrest ignored the directive, and when Maj. A.L. Landis arrived the next day to inquire why no mules had been sent, he was given a tongue-lashing certain to cause talk at headquarters. According to John Morton:

> The atmosphere was blue for a while. Stripped of General Forrest's bad words, he said to Major Landis: "Go back to your quarters, and don't you come here again or send anybody here again about mules. The order will not be obeyed; and, moreover, if [the quartermaster] bothers me any further about this matter, I'll come down to his office, tie his long legs into a double bowknot around his neck, and choke him to death with his own shins. It's a fool order, anyway. General Hood had better send his inspectors to overhaul [his] wagons, rid them of all surplus baggage, tents, adjutant desks, and everything that can be spared. Reduce the number of his wagons instead of reducing the strength of his teams. . . .[4]

Forrest's refusal of the order may have saved the Army of Tennessee. Hood attempted to pull heavily loaded wagons with either two and four mules. The muddy and frozen roads, with jagged rocks in the roadbed, severely damaged his mules. The ice and rocks actually tore the hooves from their feet. Forrest, using six mule teams, had mules in good condition and allowed them to be used on the retreat to move the wagons hauling the pontoon bridge material. One soldier said, after crossing the Tennessee River during the retreat, that there were hundreds of horses and mules standing with hooves gone, just waiting to die. The Yanks also reported that the hooves were falling off their cavalry horses, and they were not pulling weight behind them.[5] Another soldier recounted the trip up to the Tennessee River. During this period, the Tenth Texas was in Stewart's Corps:

> The three corps, Cheatham's, Stewart's, and Lee's, marched by separate routes, each of which was designated by specific marks on the trees, that "straggles" might be able to follow their respective commands. One evening after having bivouacked General Cheatham ("Old Frank," we called him) came along and called for the "bare-

footed boys." He went with them to the slaughter pen and had them to take the beef hides and cut moccasins and hang them on their feet, turning the hairy side in. However ridiculous it may have looked, those moccasins served a good purpose.

Do you remember boys, how we used to charge the "sorghum patches" and carry with us the stalks for that delicious juice, and how we would climb the persimmon trees and eat the fruit thereof, which would sometimes make our mouths assume the position of that of the "Whistling School Teacher?" Don't some of you remember that one day we halted to rest near a dwelling which stood near the roadside, a double log house, and that three young ladies in the yard sang, "I am a Rebel soldier and fighting for my home," and that when they had finished the Old Rebel yell thrilled every one present?

After marching across Sand Mountain and going down into the valley, Cheatham's old division was detained near Decatur, Ala., to watch the Yankees, while the main army, with the wagon train, moved on down the river to Tuscumbia. All of that division will remember how hungry we were while there. While we remained there, all the rations we drew was an ear and a half of corn to the man. It was reported that a load of fodder was on the way, but the wagon broke down before it got to us. We picked up the grains of corn that the artillery horses lost and roasted them in the ashes, and parched all the acorns we could find under the oak trees, of which we made coffee or ate. Then we broke camp and followed the other part of the army on to Tuscumbia, where we waited a few days for the pontoon bridge on which to cross over to Florence.

. . . One night some of the boys killed General Gist's milk cow, and after dividing out the beef put the cow's head on a pole and stood it up front of the General's tent.

We then marched for Tennessee. The weather was very bad. We encountered rain, snow, ice, and mud. Orders were very strict. We were forbidden to straggle, forage, kill any hogs, or visit any henhouses, yet some such things were done. Two boys who killed a hog which they said "tried" to "bite" them were overtaken by one of our generals, who made them carry the hog suspended from a fence rail all day. . . . One day we heard cheering in front of us; and when we got to the State line, we found suspended from one tree to another across the road a canvas with the inscription: "Tennessee, a Grave or a Free Home." Then we knew what the cheering meant. Proudly we marched across the State line under the canvas, thinking whether it would be a grave or a free home. We marched the quickstep to Columbia.

A sad accident happened on the way. Three men were riding on a caisson when the friction caused the powder to ignite, blowing them high into the air and killing all three instantly.[6]

One soldier thought that using green (uncured) rawhide to make shoes did not sound too bad. However, after two or three days, they became two inches too short, they had a terrible stink, and he had to carry a bush with him to beat away the flies.[7] Luckily, the men going into Tennessee had cold weather to keep the flies away from their new shoes.

A soldier from French's Division wrote about the trip into Tennessee after crossing the river:

On the 20th of November we crossed the Tennessee River on pontoons and marched through Florence on a cold, rainy day. The mud was thinned by the rain and snow to the consistency of gruel. The roadbed was macadam and our footing sure, but we waded through this awful mess for several miles before reaching the point where we were to bivouac. It took the best part of the night to clean up and make ourselves comfortable.

After a few days at Florence we started north with the army for Middle Tennessee. The morning we moved out on the road was gloomy and cloudy. Presently a snowstorm set in, the first heavy snow of the season. The men set up a shout and hurrahed for Missouri. "This is the kind of weather we want, regular old Missouri weather. This is none of your Southern rains; this is something decent. Hurrah for old Missouri! We are on our way home." After several hours the sun came out. We had by this time reached the pike road, and from that time on we had delightful weather and most excellent roads — very little rain, the nights cool and slightly frosty, the days warm and pleasant. This march was kept up for several days. We were received everywhere with great enthusiasm and kindness by the people along our route. We passed through the finest farming country we ever saw, and, to the enemy's credit, there were no signs of destruction to private property such as we saw in Georgia and Alabama.

We had several brushes with the enemy during our advance, but they were only skirmishes and did not give us any concern until the morning of the 30th of November.[8]

CHAPTER 17

"The path to glory leads but to the grave"

BATTLE OF FRANKLIN, TENNESSEE

HOOD HAD A CHANCE to trap a Yankee army under Schofield, south of Franklin, but the army managed to escape, and there is still confusion over who was responsible. Again, the Tenth Texas was not at the Battle of Franklin.

General Hood was furious over Schofield's troops' escape. He was subsequently spoiling for a real fight at Franklin, Tennessee. The open terrain, the enemy's repeating rifles, and the enemy's well positioned artillery were not going to deter General Hood from utilizing his outdated Napoleonic tactics. His anger apparently clouded his judgment.

One soldier from French's division gave this account of the Battle of Franklin on November 30, 1864:

> While we were in line of battle someone in the company impressed with the scene, quoted Nelson's famous order at Trafalgar: "England expects every man to do his duty." Sergt. Denny Callahan took it up at once, saying: "It's damn little duty England would get out of this Irish crowd." Nearly all the company and regiment were composed of Irishmen or their descendants. The laugh Denny raised on this was long and hearty. They were noble fellows, indeed, laughing in the face of death. Four years of war hardens men, and yet there were few in the command over twenty-two years of age.
>
> About four o'clock the corps of Lee and Cheatham were ready for the grand assault. The sun was going down behind a bank of dark clouds, as if to hide from sight the impending slaughter. His slanting rays threw a crimson light over the field and entrenchments in front, prophetic of our fate. Our brigade was in the rear, formed in the same order as at Allatoona's bloody field, recollections of which were so many thrilling reminders that it was no boy's play to charge this veteran Western infantry when well entrenched. General Cockrell gave orders to march straight for the position in quick time and not to fire a shot until we gained the top of the works; then when the

decisive moment arrived, in clear, ringing tones came the final command: "Shoulder arms! Right shoulder shift arms! Brigade forward! Guide center! Music! Quick time! March!" And this array of hardened veterans every eye straight to the front, in actual perfection of drill and discipline, moved forward to our last and bloodiest charge. Our brass band, one of the finest in the army, went up with us, starting with "The Bonnie Blue Flag" changing to "Dixie" as we reached the deadly point. The enemy instantly opened heavily with musketry and artillery in front and an enfilading fire from a battery on our right, on the far side of the Harpeth River, which was deliberate and deadly, as we fired not a shot in return. Men commenced dropping fast from the start. The distance we marched from our position where we first formed line of battle to the enemy's works was, I remember, about nine hundred yards. In that space our flag fell three times. Joseph T. Donavan, ensign, of St. Louis, was the first to fall, badly hurt by a fragment of shell. Two other members of our regiment were killed a few moments later while carrying it. Sergt. Denny Callahan was the last bearer, and this brave Irish boy carried it successfully to the works, where he planted it, and was wounded and captured, the flag falling into the hands of the Federals when we were forced from the position.

Advancing in echelon (stair step) order, our long, swinging step soon brought us abreast of Cleburne's Division, just to the right of the Franklin Pike, and with that superb command we crossed the enemy's advance line of rifle pits, raised the glorious old yell, and rushed upon the main works a frantic, maddened body with overpowering impulse to reach the enemy and kill, murder, destroy. On and on we went right up to the murderous parapet, delivered one smashing volley as General Cockrell had directed, and the line rolled over the works with empty guns, the bayonet now their only trust. I should have said what was left of the line, for the ground in the rear was all too thickly covered with the bodies of our comrades.

As we crossed the rifle pits our line was delayed a moment, when, finding myself alone, I cried out: "Who is going to stay with me?" I made a stroke at a bluecoat, felt my leg give away, and fell on top of the works. He was too quick for me, my sword flying from my hand. In another second our men were on top of the parapet. The enemy's fire ceased abruptly, and I crawled forward and picked up my sword; then, finding that I could walk a little, I started back to hunt for a surgeon, but my wound was too severe, and I fell. Two slightly wounded men of the 5th Missouri assisted me off the field and placed me in an ambulance.

But our triumph was very short. With empty guns, without officers, out of breath, our thin line rested a few seconds, when it was assailed by the enemy's second line. The scene inside the fatal fortifications of Corinth was repeated, a solid wall of blue infantry advanced at the double-quick and poured in a volley. It was too much. Our brave fellows came out of the works as quickly as they had entered them and sought refuge behind the rifle pits a short distance back. . . . Night put a stop to the slaughter. During this last firing nearly all our wounded lying in front were killed by the enemy's fire. Poor fellows! Their cries for help and for water could occasionally be heard; but no one could reach them, and they were gradually silenced by the fire from that awful parapet. After midnight the enemy withdrew, leaving his dead and severely wounded in our possession. Following the custom of Federal authorities in similar battles, this might be claimed as a Confederate victory. I can safely say that just two such victories will wipe out any army the power of man can organize. Surely "the path to glory leads but to the grave."

Our appalling loss was not generally realized until next morning, when a ghastly sight was revealed to those still living.

Our army was a wreck. Our comrades were lying in the embrace of death. So many young hearts were stilled forever which a few hours ago beat high in the prospect of soon being at home in Missouri! The sad news quickly reached our people, and many, many families of Missouri friends bowed their heads in sorrow for the poor boys laid low on the ill-fated field of Franklin.[1]

Another soldier from French's Division relived the action at Franklin:

In the famous charge made by the Missouri Brigade I was seriously wounded in my right leg, which was amputated next day on the field near the Federal breastworks close to the cotton gin and not far from the Carter House. My wound was so serious that I could not crawl or get away, and while thus prostrated on the ground I was shot through the forearm, the ball shattering both bones, and a few minutes thereafter I was again shot in my shoulder.

In this awful condition, with my clothing saturated with blood and with hundreds of dead and wounded Confederate soldiers lying almost in a heap about me, I beheld the dead body of Col. Hugh Garland, commanding the 1st Missouri Regiment in the battle, who was killed by a second shot while prostrated on the ground. Many other Confederates were shot all around me, and died, weltering in their own blood. . . .

About ten o'clock at night, when the battle was somewhat over, the roar of cannon and small arms had in a measure ceased, and nothing could be heard but the wails of the wounded and the dying, some calling for their friends, some praying to be relieved of their awful suffering, and thousands in the deep, agonizing throes of death filled the air with mournful sounds and dying groans that can never be described.

While in this pitiable condition and shivering with cold and almost dead from the loss of blood, I beheld a sight that I can never forget. Colonel Carter, whose home was at the Carter House (as I afterwards learned) and who commanded a regiment in the Confederate army, was shot and killed in sight of his own home, and his sisters in some way had heard of his sad fate and went out on the battlefield about one hundred yards from his home with lanterns in hand and found him dying. They carried him to his own sweet home amid the groans, the weeping, and the wailing of thousands of wounded Confederate soldiers, and he died just as they reached the house. The battle of Franklin, Tenn., November 30, 1864, was the worst slaughter pen and the most bitterly contested of all of our battles, with greater loss of life on the Confederate side for the number engaged than any battle of the Civil War.[2]

A Yankee gave an account of the action from his side:

Our colonel, George W. Smith, called out to "fall in." As soon as we did so, Gen. Opdyke, commanding the brigade, took the lead and called out: "Forward to the works." As we started, we saw the Confederates inside the works. The first sight that caught my eye was a Confederate with the butt of his gun striking a 16th Kentucky soldier and knocking him down. Another of the 16th Kentucky then clubbed the Confederate with his musket and knocked him down. By this time the 16th Kentucky soldier, who was knocked down, was up and put a bayonet on his musket, turned it upside down, and plunged the bayonet in the Confederate, who was on the ground. Then we had troubles of our own to look after, and I saw them no more.

We charged up to the works, and there one of the severest struggles that falls to the lot of any men but once in a lifetime took place. We used bayonets, butts of guns, axes, picks, shovels, and even Gen.

Opdyke picked up a gun and clubbed with it. We had a Capt. Barnard, of Company K, in the 88th Illinois, who used a little old four-barrel pistol and even a hatchet that he always carried with him to assist in putting up his tent. At last the Confederates who were inside the works surrendered.[3]

The Battle of Franklin would have been considered a Confederate victory because they held the battlefield and the enemy left many of their wounded behind. However, this victory finished off Hood's Army. His bravest men were continually being wounded or killed.

The day before the Battle of Franklin, the Tenth Texas was in a skirmish. Lt. David Oppenheimer, Company I, was wounded in the thigh. He was left at Franklin and captured by Union soldiers on the retreat back to Dixie.

On December 4 and 6, 1864, the Texans got in a shoot-out with some Federal gunboats at Bell's Mills, Tennessee, on the Cumberland River, about four miles by land from Nashville.[4] The commander of Ector's Brigade, Col. Julius Andrews, former commander of the Thirty-second Texas, was wounded. He was replaced by Col. David Coleman of the Thirty-ninth North Carolina Infantry, which was part of Ector's Brigade. The Texans briefly captured some Union vessels but were later driven off by the gunboats. Ector's Brigade had one man killed and fourteen wounded in actions around this date.[5]

On December 6, General Forrest's Cavalry and General Bate's Infantry marched to Murfreesboro to see if they could capture the city. When the Yankees attacked, parts of Bate's Infantry broke and ran. Forrest galloped up to the retreating flag bearer and shouted, "Rally men — for God's sake, rally!" When the flag bearer did not stop, Forrest pulled his pistol and shot him.[6] Interestingly enough, Bates, who was undoubtedly one of the bravest soldiers around, had the same troops break and run ten days later. Also, even after they had run at Murfreesboro on December 6, Hood stationed them in the key part of his defense line at Nashville.

One Rebel described the march from Franklin to Nashville prior to the big battle:

After the wounded were cared for and the dead buried who fell in the battle of Franklin, Tenn., in the evening and night of November 30, 1864, we took the road to Nashville. We found a good many of the enemy dead, left on the side of the road unburied.

Near Nashville, on December 2, we formed line of battle south of the city and dug ditches. It was very cold and began to snow. . . . We dug little fireplaces in the rear bank of our ditches which were a great help in keeping us warm. It continued snowing for over twenty-four hours, then sleeted about twelve hours and froze solid as it fell. The weight of our cannon would not break through it. During that time the enemy assaulted us and Pettus' Brigade was ordered to move to the left to reinforce the line where it was needing support. Imagine how we traveled over that slick, frozen sleet. When we started down grade the only safe way was to sit down on the ice and slide to the bottom, then crawl on all-fours up the hill on the opposite side. The enemy was shooting at us with every cannon that could reach us. In many places the cannon balls broke the ice for us and killed and wounded several of our brigade, but we kept them from breaking our line. That night we fell back to a better position and dug ditches. For several days there were artillery duels. The weather turned warm enough to melt the ice, thaw the ground, and turn the face of the earth into one big mudhole. The men, wagons, artillery, and horses worked it until it was knee-deep in some places. For several days there were artillery duels occasionally, but the enemy was getting reinforcements every day, but we were getting none.[7]

CHAPTER 18

"Lord, direct these bullets!"

BATTLE OF NASHVILLE, TENNESSEE

O N DECEMBER 9, 1864, Ector's Brigade had 569 soldiers ready for action.[1] On December 15, it was reported they had seven hundred men effective and ready to fight. They would need them all and then some.

The Battle of Nashville was two days of combat that destroyed the Army of Tennessee. Bad weather, lack of supplies, and the slaughter at Franklin all contributed to the rout of the Rebel army. The abolitionists, on both December 15 and 16, hit the left flank of the Southerners with overpowering force. Most sources, especially the soldiers involved, blamed General Bates' unit for starting the debacle. One soldier said "they made off like a big flock of birds." A Rebel ordnance officer reported only fifteen thousand Rebs actually armed and fighting while the Yanks had fifty-five thousand engaged.[2] Hood completely mishandled and was totally outmatched in planning this encounter. Nearly all sources state that the only Rebel troops not routed at Nashville were under Gen. S.D. Lee. From the official report of General Walthall, the eulogy of Private Scurlock, Company I, Tenth Texas, the statement of J.M. Spinks, Company G, Tenth Texas, the soldier that said Stewart's men enabled part of the Rebel army to get through the gap, and Lieutenant Tunnel's statement, there were certainly a few Texans that still had some fight in them.

A Rebel soldier gave the positions at Nashville and detailed a good overall description of the major movements of the action on the first day of the battle, December 15, 1864:

> Stewart's corps was on the left, covering the Granny White and Hillsboro Pikes, leaving on Hood's left to the river on the west an open space or distance more than equal to the front occupied by his entire army, from the Hillsboro Pike to the river (west). . . . This large area was covered by one brigade of cavalry under Gen. Chalmers (about 1,000 strong), and for a little while one brigade of infantry (Ector's) on the Harding Pike. Gen. Hood had strengthened his left flank by five redoubts on both sides and to the west of the Hillsboro

Pike. . . . Two of these redoubts west of the pike were from a mile to a mile and a half from the left of Gen. Stewart's Corps, and occupied by artillery and small garrisons of from 150 to 200 men. . . .

These were the relative positions of the two armies on the evening of December 14 preceding the battle. The weather had been intensely cold, and sleeting from about December 9 to December 14.[3]

One Rebel cavalry soldier described the Yankee army that was sweeping to attack the Tenth Texas (fighting approximately one hundred men) on December 15, 1864, to open the Battle of Nashville:

We soon became hotly engaged with the enemy's skirmish line, which lasted for some time. We rested quietly for a little while, when suddenly someone exclaimed: "Look, look! Just look at the Yankees!" Springing up and looking over our rail piles we beheld a sight which filled us with awe. About half a mile away, but in plain view, there appeared an immense number of the enemy's infantry as we supposed coming over the hills and marching with quick step down the slope toward us forming into one, two, three, four, five, or six lines of battle — how many, I could not say — and marching as steadily as on dress parade. Their line of march was not directly toward us, but across our front, so that when they got opposite us we were squarely on their right flank and about three hundred yards or less away. In fact, they seemed to have ignored us and to have directed their attack against a line of our troops directly in their front and apparently running nearly at right angles with us. We stood quietly looking on at the masses of the enemy nearly passing out from feeling helpless.[4]

The soldier was describing the Yanks as they attacked the Texans. The Tenth Texas, as part of Ector's Brigade, was the far left flank infantry unit of Hood's Army. Smith's whole army corps, plus Wilson's horsemen, hit Ector's Brigade.[5] The Union force attacking the seven hundred men of Ector's Brigade was twelve thousand men of Smith's corps and about eight thousand cavalry men under Wilson. The cavalry men all had seven-shot Spencer repeating rifles.[6] With twenty thousand against seven hundred, it was time for a retrograde movement to the rear!

A Texan to the left of the Tenth Texas recalled the opening attack:

On the morning of December 15 the brigade was camped on Harding Pike with a picket line in front extending across the pike at the mouth of a lane, in charge of Capt. Howze, of the Tenth, on the right and the writer on the left. We soon discovered a vast body of cavalry maneuvering to our left front, and a little later we saw a large brigade of infantry advancing upon our left front in line of battle followed by a battery of artillery. We reported to Col. Coleman, who came to our line and examined the situation. He instructed us to hold the line until forced to retire, then to fall back over the ridge in order, and make a run of about two miles to the Hillsboro Pike, where we would find him with the brigade. The enemy threw forward a skirmish line and moved slowly but steadily forward. Our thin line in rifle pits gave them a warm reception. When they got uncomfortably near, we hastily fell back, but in order, over the ridge. We then made a run for the brigade, fearful of being cut off by cavalry.[7]

The Union troops reported they captured some shovels and picks that the Texans left behind.[8] The lack of these tools may have later influenced the outcome of the battle, according to General Bates.

Martin Clary, Second Lieutenant, Company K, Tenth Texas, was captured on December 15, 1864. Several others were captured the first day of the Battle of Nashville. Curiously, he was previously declared "mortally" wounded in the breast at Murfreesboro. To have been declared mortally wounded in the chest, one wonders if Lieutenant Clary's wound hindered him from running as he was chased by twenty thousand Yanks the two miles back to the Rebel lines.

An artillery man recounted the first day's action:

From the left of Hood's line to the Cumberland River, below Nashville, there were several miles of farming country crossed by the Harding and Charlotte Pikes, which were picketed by Gen. Chalmer's Cavalry, of about one thousand men, and Ector's Skeleton Brigade (seven hundred strong). Gen. Hood had ordered five redoubts to be built to protect his left; three of them at the end just in the rear of his intrenched line and the other two about a mile in rear of his extreme left, the troops occupying these latter two being ordered to "hold them at all hazards." These two redoubts were numbered four and five.

About December 9, Lumsden's Battery was ordered to occupy Redoubt No. 4. The battery consisted of four 12-pound smooth bore Napoleon guns that at six or eight hundred yards could be used with fair accuracy. Arriving at our position, we found that a slight trench, indicating the position of the guns and with a shallow ditch on either side for the infantry that were to support us, was all the fortifications that had been made. The weather was extremely cold from the 9th to the 14th; snow, sleet, and ice, with the ground frozen every morning.

The sleet and snow had melted by the morning of the 15th and a heavy fog concealed everything. Scattering shots and an occasional wounded man (from Ector's Brigade) coming from the front told us that the enemy was on the move around Hood's left flank.

It was about 11 a.m. when Ector's men passed us in retreat, going on both sides of our battery, leaving the bushy hollow in our front and to our right front full of Federal sharpshooters. Capt. Lumsden called to the officer to rally his men and help us hold our position, stating that we were ordered to hold it at all hazards. "It can't be done sir; there is a whole army in your front," was the reply, and away they went. Three eight-gun batteries took position on a ridge about six hundred yards from us and opened fire on our battery. "Cannoneers, to your posts! Load shell six hundred yards! Battery, ready! Fire!" were Capt. Lumsden's orders, and at it we went with four smoothbore guns behind the slight breastworks mentioned against twenty-four rifled pieces.

Corporal Ed King, of my gun, soon got the range, but was wounded by a splinter, and I was ordered to "take the trail." This suited me, for I had been gunner during the whole years work, from Dalton to Atlanta, and was glad to get back in my old place again. The dirt, chunks, and stones were knocked in showers about us by the twenty-four guns of the enemy. For two hours we kept up the fight with that Yankee battery. Twice Capt. Lumsden had sent word back to Gen. Stewart telling him the situation: that a charge would sweep us off at any moment. The only reply was, "Hold them back as long as you can." It was about one o'clock when suddenly, and square off to our left about five hundred yards, another Federal four-gun battery opened on us, completely enfilading our position. My gun, being our left piece was ordered to open to it, and the next gun to me was ordered to open it, and the next gun to me was withdrawn sufficiently from the embrasure to give it range across the rear of my piece, and with solid shot we began to pound them. It was not long before we drove them off and again turned our attention to those in front. In whirling my gun back I broke off the rear pointing ring on the trail, but quickly looping it with a trace I soon had her "barking" again through the embrasure.

Just then Private Horton, No. 3 of my gun, went down, with a shot in his groin; he was carried to the rear, and that night we buried the poor fellow near the Franklin Pike. Helm Rosser, a lad of seventeen, the youngest of three brothers that belonged to the battery, had his head shot off by a shell, scattering his brains in the face of Capt. Lumsden. Shortly after this the captain shouted: "Look out, men! Give them canister!" They had, unobserved, worked around our left under the hill and were making a rush on us. One more discharge through the embrasure and one to my left were all I had time for before they were on us. I ran to my right, and as I did so the piece next to me was whirled to the left and pointed toward the Yankees, swarming a few feet away from my gun. "Look out, Jim," shouted the gunner, and I fell directly under the muzzle, the discharge passing over me. The gun was loaded again with a double charge of canister, and Capt. Lumsden ordered, "Fire!" but the primer would not work, and, as the Yankees were almost in arm's reach of us, the captain told us to look out for ourselves. One of the men had another charge of canister in his hand when this order was given, and he threw it into the muzzle of the gun as he turned to run. I learned afterwards that when the Yankees turned it on us it exploded. . . .

That night I was pouring water from a canteen for Capt. Lumsden to bathe his face and hands. I noticed that he would pick something from his beard, and I asked what it was. "That is poor Rosser's brains, Maxwell," he replied.[9]

Another soldier from Ector's Brigade depicted the action the rest of the day on December 15. He mentioned that the brigade did go into a redoubt to fight (not the one that had Lumsden's Battery), and the Yanks went around them. If darkness had not fallen, they would have been captured:

We found our brigade near the Hillsboro Pike in line of battle fronting west. Very soon a large regiment of cavalry galloped up in front to the foot of the hill, probably a hundred yards distant, and halted. Col. Coleman, called to them to show their colors, for as the morning was gloomy he could not determine whether they were Federals or Confederates, but they made no response. Then Col. Coleman gave the command to fire. They returned the fire, but soon retreated at full speed. Their loss was pretty heavy, especially in horses killed. If we had any loss, I did not hear of it. In another minute or two our brigade was ordered into a redoubt near the pike. About this time we heard a heavy battle in front and to our right. Very soon we could see the Confederate lines moving to the rear and to our right, but fighting desperately as they retreated. They and the Federals, that were pressing them, passed our fort and left us in the rear. A prompt retreat was ordered, and we moved at a double quick on a line parallel with the movement of the troops in the battle. When we got to the Brentwood range of hills, Gen. Hood and his staff were on the hill. Gen. Hood rode down the line saying to all the soldiers as he passed, "Texans, I want you to hold this hill regardless of what transpires around you," and the spontaneous answer was: "We will do it, General." Our line was formed on the brow of the hill fronting west. In the meantime the battle reported above had ceased and Gen. Bate was reforming his lines to our right and in plain view of our line. Soon they attacked him again, and for a time we stood watching a terrific battle. A battery of artillery close in the rear of Bates's Infantry on a little eminence did splendid work. The lines of infantry wavered back and forth as long as we saw the fight. Before very long, however, a strong force of infantry attacked our line and made a desperate, but unsuccessful, effort to drive us from the hill. Night closed the conflict with our line unmoved. Our losses were pretty heavy.[10]

A soldier told the fate of General Sears, who commanded Mississippi soldiers in the same division as the Tenth Texas:

He removed his field glass from its case and began his inspection. While seated upon his horse and with the glass to his eyes, the enemy fired a shell at him. It carried away one of his legs below the knee and it also killed his horse. The General was a man about sixty years of age, the ground was frozen hard and was covered with deep snow. And it seemed the coldest as well as the saddest day I had ever experienced. No surgeon was near to administer to his pressing need; everything was in confusion and in the midst of all the sad surroundings and heart rending scenes of a fierce battle the grand old hero stood upon one foot and with tears running down the cheeks like a child exclaimed: "Poor Billy! Poor Billy!" He did not seem to notice his own sad condition but his whole attention and sympathy were directed toward the faithful steed which he had ridden during the entire war.[11] (After the war, General Sears became a professor of mathematics at the University of Mississippi).[12]

The action at Nashville continued:

Well, on the 15th of December, (the Yanks) with an overwhelming force, turned up, certainly very unexpectedly to me. It was Thursday about eleven o'clock. I had slept late and was on my knees grating some corn to get meal for my breakfast, when all at once the order came to get into line at once. Away to our left, to the west, there were firing and yelling. Our barefooted men, fifteen, or sixteen of our regiment and maybe sixty or seventy in all from the brigade, were ordered to the top of the hill. The remainder were sent at double-quick along the pike northward toward the city and took position behind a stone fence on the slope of a long, gentle rise. As soon as I could gather up my blanket, haversack, and frying pan I followed as fast as I could the part going along the pike. By the time I got started the artillery fire was becoming quite heavy, so I ran along on the side of the road, where it was considerably higher than the general level. This fill of the road formed a good protection to me. As I ran a cannon ball struck the surface of the road, plowing a rut through it and passing just over my head. It may be supposed that my speed was quickened until I reached the men behind the wall.

Meanwhile the Federals in their advance reached Compton's Hill. They literally swarmed up the hill and overwhelmed the little garrison, which surrendered only after killing and wounding many of the enemy. Some of our men dashed down the hill in a shower of bullets and escaped. I was told after the war the details of the surrender by one who was captured. He said that the Union soldiers rushed up the hill shouting and firing, but their shots passed over the men's heads. When they reached the top and demanded the surrender, our men threw down their arms, and some of them dashed down the hill, followed by a volley or two which overshot them. The Yankee soldiers were boasting a great rate of their exploit, when Mike Crantz, of Robertson County, Tenn., replied to their taunt, "Well, you needn't brag; we killed more of your men than there are of us," pointing down the hill, where they lay thick. Instantly one of the Yankees ran him through with a bayonet, saying: "You shall not live to tell it." Mike was placed against a tree, and before he died he gave to a comrade for his mother a little bible that I had given him.

Let the name of the man who murdered Mike Crantz rot in forgetfulness. . . .

Pretty soon three batteries of artillery were turned loose. The line of their fire crossed just at the little spring where I lay with the doctors. For a few minutes it was the hottest place around Nashville. We all developed a marvelous fondness for mother earth and hugged her closely. I stuck to the ground as closely as a postage stamp to a

THE BATTLE OF NASHVILLE
Dec 15 and 16, 1864

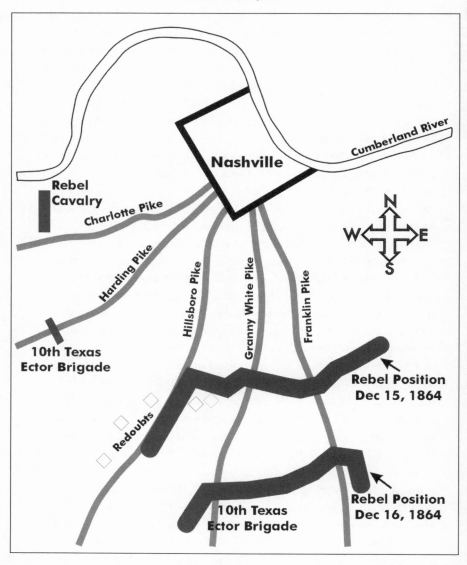

letter. In a little while (the Rebel line) gave way, our line was turned, and most of our men were captured. Reynolds (Brigade) was retreating in good order, firing back at the enemy.

The only thing for the surgeons and me, if we would escape capture, was to run. So we set out to reach Reynolds as he fell back. We were thus exposed to the cross-fire of our own men and the Yankees.

As we ran through a dense hazel thicket the bullets seemed to cut every twig. Three years afterwards I was passing along the Hillsboro Road, and I turned aside and went across a field to the thicket, and every bush bore the marks of that fierce fusillade. Yet we were not touched by a bullet or a shell. I think the prayer of a soldier in the battle of Shiloh would have been appropriate: "Lord, direct these bullets." He did it.

My running mate was a young doctor six feet four inches tall and very slender, a veritable "Slim Jim." I was built on far shorter and broader lines. As we toiled through the muddy fields he distanced me. I could see Dr. Gupton's feet loaded with mud, looking like Saratoga trunks, as they rose and fell with the strides he made. As he got ahead I would call out: "Wait for me, Gup." He would stop for a moment, calling back: "Come on, parson. Hurry!" And then a particularly vicious volley would start us again on our wild race. After we got through the thicket, we ran through a field over which a brigade had retreated. They had thrown away or lost portions of their equipment. Among other things many frying pans were lying around loose. My old pan was about worn out. I especially coveted one with a good long handle, and here was my chance. But alas! I was too fastidious. I would see one that I liked, and as I stooped to pick it up I would see another just ahead that suited my fancy better. But as I rushed forward to get it a sudden volley from the yankees hurling by made me feel that I could do without that pan just then, and I continued my flight with my eyes fixed on another pan, and the former experience was repeated, until I had passed completely beyond the zone of frying pans and had failed to get one. It is not best to be too fastidious when one is too hurried for time to make a careful selection.

To this day I look back with fond regret to the assortment of cooking utensils and my failure to supply myself when they were to be had just for the taking. . . .

The fighting was heavy in front of General Cheatham's position. There the boys for the first time saw negro troops make a charge. I was told that they came on in fine style as if in holiday parade, but at the first volley, when they saw their comrades falling by the score, they broke and fled. It was said that the white Federal troops were behind the negroes with bayonets fixed and forced them to go forward, and the poor creatures were shot down "like dumb driven cattle." I do not vouch for this report, but I heard the version given by an old negro man belonging to one of our neighbors. Steve had come to Nashville "to jine de Yankees," and they put him to driving a wagon; but the scenes he saw in this battle frightened him so that he ran away and didn't stop running until he got home to Charlotte, forty miles away. He told my mother his experience: "Mistis, I is done wid dem Yankees, sho'. Why, dey jes' make breas'works of dem niggers. Dey took a brogan of niggers, dem Yankees did, and driv' 'em up to dem Rebels, and de Rebels shoot 'em down: and den dey driv' up another brogan of niggers, and de Rebels dey shoot dem down. Den I lef'. And here I is and here I stays.[13]

Most of the frying pans used by the Rebels had thin handles so they could be carried on the marches by sticking the handle into their gun barrels.

The Rebel battle lines on the second day were two miles long, while the first day they had reached six miles in length.[14]

A soldier complained of living conditions in the trenches in front of Nashville, and how on the second day, December 16, 1864, Bates' units broke like a flock of big birds. The soldier also mentioned a narrow escape by getting through a gap in the hills. This was a gap held open by the Texans:

We slept together like pigs, and when one turned over all of us had a turn. . . . Our picket line was several hundred yards in front of our breastworks, and beyond us were open fields to the Federal lines. It turned bitter cold a day or so after we established our line, and it was no picnic doing picket and vidette duty out there in our threadbare and ragged clothes. . . .

All night long we could hear the enemy's columns moving to our left, and next morning (December 16) we could see a stream of them passing not more than half a mile in our front. About noon the Federals made a most desperate attack on our center (which was held by General Stewart's corps), bringing up several heavy double lines against him, in which were two lines of negro troops in front (I saw no negroes in our front). General Stewart's line was holding magnificently, his infantry and artillery inflicting fearful losses on the Federals. But about three o'clock a determined attack in heavy force on Shy's Hill, which was held by Maj. Gen. William B. Bates's division, forced that line to give way, thus making our whole line untenable. From our position on the left we could see General Bates's line very distinctly, and when it broke the men seemed to rise like a flock of big birds and fairly fly down the hill. Many of them were cut off and captured. Our division did not become engaged at all, but we had a narrow escape from capture by getting through a gap in the hills behind us and thence to the Franklin Pike. General Stewart stemmed the tide in the rear and enabled those who had gone through the gap to escape being captured. When I reached the pike it presented a scene of wild confusion. Commands were scattered, and there was no organization except General Stewart's men. We went as far as Brentwood that night, remaining until the next morning, the 17th, when we moved on to Franklin, resuming our retreat on December 18.[15]

A Nashville reporter, following the attacking Union soldiers, described what he witnessed on the battlefield near the right extremity of the Confederate line:

This scene before the Rebel works was awful. Dead men, black and white, were strewn over the ground and piled upon each other in indescribable confusion. In some places . . . five deep.[16]

The battle of December 16 was tough enough especially when the constant rain became a downpour in the afternoon.[17]

The Nashville newspapers were very tacky with their headlines:

Hood's Army Demoralized and Full Retreat.
The Rebels Completely Routed. They Flee in a Perfect Panic.[18]

CHAPTER 19

"Ragged, barefooted invincibles
sprang forward like hungry tigers"

FIGHTING REARGUARD ON
THE RETREAT FROM NASHVILLE

A S THE SECOND DAY of the battle raged at Nashville, Hood played what has been called "his last card." In order to keep the Union cavalry off his rear, he pulled the Texans from Shy's Hill and double timed them to a hill west of the Granny White road. Hood had his cavalry units defending his rear on the opening of the battle on December 16. The Yanks drove them from a hill to the south of the Rebel battleline and captured about seventy-five of the Reb cavalry men. Hood sent the Texans south, and they attacked up the steep hill in the face of the Yanks' fire from repeating rifles. The Tenth Texas and Ector's brigade reclaimed most of the captured Rebel cavalry men. They then charged the Yanks four times but failed to drive them. The enemy's repeating rifles were too much to overcome.[1] The Yanks then used ropes and men pushing the wheels of two artillery pieces to the top of a hill higher than where the Tenth Texas was located. They shot fifty artillery rounds at the Tenth Texas, which had to hunker down and take it.[2]

By holding this hill, the Texans allowed the Rebel ambulances to pass down the road during the fight.[3] The Texans then withdrew to a hill further east. The Yanks reported taking 150 prisoners. The Reb cavalry unit was still with Ector's Brigade, and it is unclear how many of Ector's people were captured. The records reflect possibly three men captured from the Tenth Texas on December 16. Around 3:00 p.m., Hood sent Reynolds' Brigade to the Texans' assistance. The Texans had been pulled from Shy's Hill just as the Yanks started a massive attack led by artillery. Had the Tenth Texas been left on Shy's Hill, the vast majority would have been killed or captured. Again, the Tenth Texas was blessed with good luck. This was where General Bates' unit took off in an undignified retreat.

General Bate blamed Ector's Brigade for all his problems. Hood had placed the Texans in the key spot then pulled them off to guard his rear. Bates claimed that Ector's men did not dig the trenches deep enough on the night of December 15 and early morning of December 16. Remember, the

Yanks captured picks and shovels from Ector's men earlier that day. Also, Bates said that in the darkness, Ector's troops dug and built fortifications too far back from the front slope of Shy's Hill. This made it impossible to see the enemy until they were nearly up the hill.[4] General Walthall stated in his official report that Major Foster, an engineering officer, laid out the defense line at 2:00 a.m. It can be assumed that Ector's Brigade dug the line where they were told to dig it.

As the Reb lines fell apart and the left wing of the Army of Tennessee retreated, Reynolds and Ector's Brigades held open a country road that allowed the soldiers to retreat to the Franklin Pike. Reynolds was on a hill three hundred yards east of the Granny White Pike. Ector's Brigade was on a hill southwest of Reynolds. Between the Brigades down the country road, the left wing of the Rebel army retreated.[5]

General Walthall in his official report referred to both brigades: "Both of which did valuable service in holding the only passages through which many detachments of the army were able to retreat."[6]

Lieutenant Tunnell, Fourteenth Texas, described the action on December 16 and how they charged at dusk to drive back the Yanks, which allowed the left wing of the Army of Tennessee to escape:

> About noon our (Ector's) brigade was ordered to the left, nearly due south, at a double-quick, to head off a flank movement of the enemy over the range of hills. When we arrived at the place, their skirmish line was in possession of the hill, but we climbed the hill, which was very steep, and drove them off. We held this hill till late in the evening, when we were ordered down to an old country road running down the narrow valley. When we got to this road we found a column of troops marching in quick step down the valley, when we learned that Hood's entire army was in full retreat, and we were ordered to follow. Soon a brigade of Federals attacked our retreating column from the west, and Ector's Brigade was called on to drive them back, which was done by a vigorous charge just at twilight. We hastily gathered up our wounded and carried them to some farmhouses nearby and continued our march, intersecting the Franklin Pike, which we found full of retreating troops.[7]

A member of Hood's staff, in a Masonic funeral eulogy years later, remembered who held the Yanks back at that point. James Scurlock was a private in Company I, Tenth Texas. He was severely wounded at both Murfreesboro and Chickamauga.

My Dear Brothers:

At your request, I pen the following statement in regard to our deceased brother James W. SCURLOCK, whose body, we as Masons, consigned to the dust from which it came, and the Spirit to God who gave it, on yesterday.

I had a higher regard for Brother SCURLOCK, than for most men aside of the incident I have given, he had many of the virtues that go to making up vaulting manhood. He was a member of ECTOR'S Texas Brigade in the Army of John B. HOOD. On the march into Tennessee after the fall of Atlanta in 1864, I was temporarily attached to the staff of General HOOD, and in command of the secret service, acting as an aide in the engagements on that campaign.

On the morning of the 16th day of December, 1864, the federal army began to move out of their works around the City of Nashville upon our army before the intensely cold day. . . . While the attack was hardly a surprise, it was sudden; and in overwhelming numbers they came with unparalleled fury broke the Confederate lines.

Amid a confusion indescribable, the staff officers endeavored to rally the broken columns. Scarcely light enough to distinguish friend from foe, a Division gave way and fled that occupied a key area. In desperation I was entreating threatening to get men to rally, when I came upon a squad of men and in reply to my question as to who they were, and the whereabouts of the Command, one answered: Texans, ECTOR'S Brigade. I announced to them that I was a Texan, and for the love of God and country to rally and show me their command.

Under fire this man we buried yesterday responded with patriotic alacrity, with a gallantry to be admired, and ECTOR'S Brigade filed into the gap and held it until relieved by the Corps of Stephen LEE, and the panic was ended. Men for less service than this have been knighted and donned the star and garter.

I will state that I never know the name of the man who aided me that day until four years since, when he told me of the circumstances, having never met him since the war and up to that date in perfect ignorance of his name. But of, and only of, such material are heroes made, and may God in His wisdom and mercy give him the reward he so richly deserves.

"Requiescatin pace"
John C. Claiborne

J.M. Spinks, Company G., says while a courier, he rode backward and forward across the road halting every man that had a gun until French's division came in regular order.[8]

After Ector's Brigade and Reynolds' Brigade held the Yanks back on the side road, General S. D. Lee was rallying a rear guard. A little drummer boy told of the General's actions forming the initial rear guard and also the fighting from a square formation as used years before by European armies:

Late in the evening of the 16th Gen. Bates's division on the extreme left gave way. That caused the Federals to turn our left flank so they could form a line across our left and charge our line on the flank, which compelled the right to give up the ditches and fall back. The ground was so boggy we couldn't run. The stoutest soon got ahead. I think I was among the hindmost with my drum on my back when a Federal not over fifty yards away called me, saying: "Stop, you little devil, with that drum!" I jumped behind a tree, looked back, and saw that he was going in a different direction. I went as fast as I could to a rock fence and clambered over it. I was then on the road and could travel faster. I did not go far until I met Gen. S.D. Lee on his horse with a battle flag in his hands appealing to the men to form a line there. He told me to beat the long roll. I did so and expected to receive a bullet, but to my surprise the Federals began to retreat. They thought it was our reserve being called into line of battle when they heard the drum. Our brigade and Cumming's Brigade rallied to General Lee and in a little while a battery of artillery joined us on a run. I never saw cannons discharge canister shot as fast during the war. . . . The Federal cavalry tried hard to capture us. The second day, late in the evening, a cold rain was falling. General Pettus called his brigade to attention and told us we were surrounded. "What must we do?" Someone in the ranks told him we would try to do what he commanded us to do, as we always had done. He gave the command to fix bayonets and form a hollow square with guns loaded and go in position to guard against cavalry. We had not formed the square but a few moments before they charged us. Our men did not fire until they got close up to us, as the breech of our guns was on the ground and the men's right knees also on the ground with fingers on the triggers and bayonets raised to a level with their heads. I never saw as many men and horses killed at one volley. The remainder of that cavalry did not bother our rear any more. We made fires not far from there. I put on a new Federal suit of clothes and slept under two blankets, I got off of a Federal horse I captured when the rider was shot off in forty feet of me. I also got his rations and made coffee in his coffee pot and drank it out of his cup. I hope he was prepared to die and is in heaven now.[9]

A Reb cavalry soldier witnessed the brutality of some of the fighting in the retreat:

The enemy's cavalry swooped down upon us with drawn sabers, cutting and slashing us from right to left. Three soldiers assaulted Gen. Buford at one time. One he shot; another he struck over the head with the butt of his pistol, knocking him from the saddle, but breaking his pistol; and the third he grabbed by the hair and pulled from his saddle and thus escaped. They swarmed around me like a flock of blackbirds. How I got out of it with a whole skin, I do not know. My face was powder-burned and my hair was scorched from a pistol shot thrust in my face at the moment of discharge, and I found myself with two severe bruises on the shoulder from saber strokes.[10]

A prisoner told the Yanks that Hood's army was greatly demoralized and nearly half had thrown away their guns.[11] One man detailed the formation of the main rear guard under the command of General Forrest:

On the morning of the 20th of December, 1864, General Hood sent a member of his staff to General Walthall, near Columbia, with the urgent request that he call at army headquarters immediately. General Walthall at once rode to headquarters, and the writer accompanied him. On the pike, as Walthall approached army headquarters, he met General Hood. . . . Hood said to Walthall substantially as follows: "Things are in a bad condition. I have resolved to reorganize a rear guard. Forrest says he can't keep the enemy off of us any longer without a strong infantry support, but says he can do it with the help of three thousand infantry with you to command them. You can select any troops in the army. It is a post of great honor, but one of such great peril that I will not impose it on you unless you are willing to take it; and you had better take troops that can be relied upon, for you may have to cut your way out after the main army gets out. The army must be saved, come what may, and if necessary your command must be sacrificed to accomplish it.

Walthall, in reply, said: "General, I have never asked for a hard place for glory nor a safe place for comfort, but take my chances as they come. Give me the order for the troops, and I will do my best.

Being the youngest major general in the army, I believe, my seniors may complain that the place was not offered to them, but that is a matter between you and them.

General Hood said in reply: "Forrest wants you, and I want you."

General Forrest rode up during the conversation in time to understand what had been said, and he remarked: "Now we will keep them back."

Hood gave verbal orders for Walthall to take any troops he desired, and he selected eight brigades, estimated at three thousand effective, as follows: W.S. Featherstone's, J.B. Palmer's, D.H. Reynolds', O.F. Strahl's (commanded by Col. C.W. Keiskell), Smith's (commanded by Col. C. Olmstead), Maney's (commanded by Col. H.R. Field), Ector's (commanded by Col. D. Coleman), and Quarles' (commanded by Brig. Gen. George D. Johnston). These brigades reported to Walthall, who had them inspected and a report of effectives made. The eight brigades numbered one thousand six hundred and twenty-one effectives.

The field return of this command's effectives was as follows: Featherstone, 408; Reynolds, 528; Palmer, 297; Field, 298; total, 1,621.[12]

Ector's Brigade and Reynolds' Brigade were consolidated under the command of Gen. Reynolds. These were the two brigades that Walthall in his official report had said kept the road open so a large part of Hood's army could retreat. Of the rear guard infantry, out of 1,621 men who were effective to fight, three hundred had no shoes.[13]

The number of effective soldiers under Reynolds was 528. This included Ector's Brigade. Reynolds had 263 effective soldiers after the Battle of Nashville, which leaves Ector with 315. This means Ector's Brigade lost nearly 385 men at Nashville. Out of seven hundred men, 265 were left after the retreat.[14]

As for Forrest's infantry with no shoes, he emptied some of his wagons for them and made them "motorized infantry." These wagons for the soldiers explain how the Tenth was able to save the number of wounded they brought back in the severe weather conditions. Forrest also started hooking up oxen to his mule teams to get more rapid movement over the bad roads.[15] He also lent some of his mules to Hood to move the heavy pontoon boats and materials.

One soldier mentioned that Hood asked for volunteers.[16] But other sources state that Hood volunteered the soldiers. The furlough question after the retreat nearly caused a mutiny, but Hood did attempt to give his Trans-Mississippi men a furlough:

He asked me if the brigade would volunteer for that service. I replied: "We are soldiers, General." He then said: "You will report to Colonel Field. I know no soldiers upon whom I can rely with greater confidence that the work will be done well than you Tennesseans." He then ordered those without shoes to go to the wagon train. I recall, however, that some soldiers without shoes remained with the reserve.

An incident here illustrates the freedom of speech between the men and their officers. General Hood, upon being asked when he would give the boys a furlough, said, "After we cross the Tennessee," adding, "The cards have been fairly dealt, for I cut them and dealt them myself, and the Yankees have beat us in the game." Thereupon a soldier of the 19th Tennessee said: "Yes, General, but they were badly shuffled."[17]

Another soldier gave a good description of the rear guard under Forrest's command:

The Federals crossed Duck River during the night of the 21st and started pursuit of our forces. Jackson and Buford covered the rear while Chalmers protected the right flank (all cavalry units). The Federals overhauled Buford about four miles south of Columbia and opened fire with twenty or more cannon. The shells passed over our troops, roaring and bursting high in the air, while fragments of iron whizzed and whirled through the trees and ricochetted along the ground. It was enough to demoralize veterans even. Having a company of skirmishers to keep the Federals at respectful distance, Forrest continued to fall back toward a more favorable position, about seven miles from Columbia. The road was through a gorge between two high ridges, and about two-thirds of the way through the cut the direction changed — that is, the road assumed the shape of an elbow. The high ridge through which it passed was rough and irregular, covered with ice and sleet as it was on that occasion there was no opportunity to flank the place. Forrest planted four guns on an eminence commanding the approach to the gorge, and near the south end of it he had the remaining eight cannon posted so as to sweep the road after making the turn. Walthall posted his men on the brink of the bluffs, overlooking the road, while the cavalry formed rearward, and all awaited the Federals. Capt. J.H. Goodloe, of the 8th Kentucky Cavalry, was left in the rear with orders to skirmish with the advance guard of the enemy until the Federals approached the cut, then fall back in a full run and pass beyond. Then very soon the Federal cavalry raised a shout, and, dashing forward, followed Goodloe through the defile. Fully, six hundred men and horses had entered the cut when our guns gave signal for the terrible slaughter. Walthall opened with a volley, while the grape was raking the cut, and men and horses tumbled in heaps, blocking the road with dead men and horses. Those in front who escaped the first fire could not retreat on account of the dead and the struggling, wounded horses obstructing the road. The scent was appalling — wreck, ruin, and disaster. Men cut off struggled over the bodies of the dead in an effort to escape, and fell from the shot of Walthall's men. Every man who passed into the cut was killed, wounded, or captured. It was a desperate work, and the Federals who had not entered the cut fled in disorder.

There was no further attempt to dislodge the Confederates. The dreadful slaughter in the gorge made the enemy very careful. We held the position until the afternoon of December 23, and fell back to Lynnville. The dead men and horses were frozen and blocked the road through the hills and had to be moved before the Federals could pursue; but soon after reaching Lynnville, they made a savage attack, which was maintained for two hours or more. Forrest then fell back behind Richland Creek, where he found a favorable position for artillery. Chalmers and Buford were posted on the right, while Walthall held the center. Armstrong supported six cannon on a hill which swept the pike. The road had been made impassable almost by Hood's cannon and wagon train, and furthermore was frozen. After reaching the vicinity the enemy opened at long range with cannon, but, gradually and cautiously moving forward, advanced the line to within about four hundred yards of our position.

The boom of cannon and rattle of rifles was deafening, but the Confederates held their position. Finally the six guns supported by Armstrong were directed upon one of the Federal batteries and dismounted two of the guns. The effect was grand. The enemy, greatly confused, withdrew their batteries, while our men cheered. After some little time, Forrest found that the Federal cavalry was attempting to turn his position and, all wagons having passed beyond the reach of the enemy, he fell back to Pulaski.

By this time the enemy realized that whatever was done must be attended to quickly, otherwise Hood would escape; and yet there was the dreaded Forrest to overcome. The Federal cavalry continued their efforts to flank us, while their infantry pressed vigorously on the pike. Throughout the past thirty or forty hours Forrest's men had been fighting with little intermission, and every officer and man acted as if the fate of the army depended on his conduct. There never was, and can never be, manifested higher qualities of soldierly conduct than were exhibited by that heroic band under Forrest, and this refers to Walthall's infantry as well as to Forrest's own men.

The roads were well-nigh impassable; it was very difficult for a wheel to turn in the frozen mud. So much so that General Hood had a lot of wagons burned at Pulaski. We passed through Pulaski fighting over every inch of the way, but slowly falling back, until we reached Anthony's Hill, seven miles south, and about forty miles from Bainbridge, Ala., where the army crossed the Tennessee River.

General Hood notified Forrest that several wagons containing pontoons had not reached the river, and much of the infantry was still enroute. Forrest knew, that the enemy's cavalry in great numbers was pressing him, besides 25,000 infantry was close at hand.

General Wilson, with 12,000 cavalry, was making strenuous efforts to flank him. Therefore, in order to prevent the total annihilation of Hood's army, it was necessary to make even stronger efforts than before. He must delay the enemy two full days, a task which no other man that ever lived would have had the confidence to undertake. The approach to Anthony's Hill for more than two miles was through a valley. Two high ridges, which came together at the south, formed a very steep and tall hill. The ascent was sudden, and both ridge and the hill were covered with timber. John Morton's Parrott guns were planted at the top of the hill, from whence he could sweep the valley and the road; while along the ridge, Featherstone's and Palmer's brigades of infantry were formed. Further south Jackson's two brigades of cavalry, dismounted, took position, while Reynolds's (10th Texas included) and Fields's brigades of Walthall's command formed a reserve. The men hurriedly threw timber and rails together for breastworks.

Chalmers was sent to the right to prevent a flank movement. The timber was so dense and the country so rough that the Confederates were easily concealed. There could not have been a better position nor troops deployed to better advantage. . . .

About 1 p.m. the Federal cavalry forced our rear guard into the passage and followed us closely and viciously. Before reaching the foot of the hill the Federal commander suddenly halted, dismounted his men and formed, and began to push up the elevation. He had two pieces of artillery moved forward by hand.

The two companies which the enemy drove through the defile galloped over the hill, leaving the impression, doubtless, that Forrest had continued the retreat. The federal line climbed the hill in fine order to within forty yards of our skirmish line. Nothing warned them of the proximity of a foe; not a gun was fired, and there was no evidence of danger. Suddenly the deathly silence was broken. Morton fired double charges of canister into their front, while the infantry and dismounted cavalrymen poured a galling fire from rifles into their flank. It was a complete ambuscade, which shocked the enemy more than any previous contretemps. Those not killed fled down the hill in the wildest disorder, and, regardless of each other, rushed headlong over those in the rear. Words cannot picture that scene. The Confederates sprang forward with yells and charged down the hill after them. There was no order given to charge, but, with a common impulse, the ragged, barefooted, hungry heroes sprang forward. They acted like fresh troops that sought to win applause. There can never be a more surprising scene than that.

Those of the enemy who escaped did not halt until they had passed beyond the range of our guns. It was with difficulty that the officers could restrain the Confederates in their eager pursuit. We captured about two hundred prisoners and killed and wounded some three hundred, besides taking two fine twelve-pounder Napoleon guns and teams of sixteen horses. Toward evening Forrest ascertained that the enemy was making an effort to flank him, and fell back, taking along the prisoners and captured cannon. The roads could not have been worse. The infantry was frequently waist deep in ice-cold slush and mud. The artillery horses had to be actually pushed along. The sleet and ice hung to the men's clothing and on their hair. No other body of men could have endured the hardships with so little complaint. We reached a beautiful creek about midnight where a halt was made. The men waded into the clear, icy stream, with pebble bottom, and spent half an hour washing the mud and sleet from their clothing. Then big fires were built and everybody rested until daylight. Early the following morning the Federals began to press our rear guard, and Forrest, falling back slowly, met an officer from General Hood who said that the teams hauling the pontoons had all broken down and that they were being pulled by hand. The situation was desperate. I think General Hood feared the worst. It was therefore necessary to make another stand and defeat the enemy, otherwise Hood's army would be destroyed before it could cross the river.

Forrest was the only man on earth who could save it. He selected a ridge on Sugar Creek commanding the ford and which was approached by a narrow ravine through which the road runs. He threw together rails and logs, and secreted the infantry. . . . There was a heavy fog, and it was impossible to see more than a hundred yards away. The enemy came within thirty paces of our line and were met by a terrific fire, which threw them into confusion. Walthall's old ragged, barefooted, invincibles sprang forward like hungry tigers and rushed into the enemy's ranks, using their guns as clubs, and yelling like demons. The enemy ran in disorder and, passing through their lines of horse holders, stampeded the horses, increasing the confusion and panic. The enemy plunged into the creek wherever they found it without reference to the ford and were followed by Walthall and his dauntless heroes.[18]

Regarding the soldier's description of the frozen horses and dead men blocking the road through the hills, the men of the Tenth Texas claimed to have killed four hundred Union horses there. Several hundred horses were captured.[19] At Sugar Creek, 350 Yank horses were captured.[20]

Another soldier related events of the rear guard fighting:

About eighteen miles south of Sugar Creek, was formed a line of battle, and the Tennesseeans, under Field, and the Arkansans and Texans, under Reynolds, were on the front line. The Federal officer was approaching with his forces. Forrest called Reynolds, Fields, and the regimental officers, including Colonel Heiskell and myself, together on a little knoll in front of our line and said: "The Yankees are coming. We are going to have a fight; and when the infantry break their lines, I'll throw Ross's Cavalry on them." Fields, a wiry, brave soldier, misunderstanding Forrest, with a stutter in his speech said: "We have got no such infantry, General. They will not break our lines." Forrest, laughing, said: "I don't mean when they break our lines, but when we break theirs." Fields instantly said, "That's the kind of infantry we have, General," which created a big laugh all around.

Another incident occurred just before the Sugar Creek fight. General Forrest told the infantry soldiers that when the Yanks were put to flight every infantry soldier that captured a horse might ride it; and the boys believed it, and did capture several. Mounted on their steeds, they rode toward the Tennessee River with much glee.

Arriving at the river, however, they found a guard at the pontoon bridge, who accosted them with: "What command do you belong to?" . . . . Then came the woeful order: "Get down off that horse," and they had to do it, as it appeared that the cavalry needed all the horses; but that fact did not keep the boys from criticizing the act all the same. [21]

On December 23, the Yanks had a spy tell them that Forrest's artillery had oxen hooked on them to move then through the mud and his rear guard infantry were without shoes and would surrender if pushed. The spy might have been correct about them being shoeless, but he was certainly wrong when he said they would surrender.[22]

On the morning of December 26, Reynolds (including the Tenth Texas) and Field captured nearly all the horses of a dismounted regiment and some prisoners.[23]

The Texans, having been promised any horses they captured, were understandably upset when, after securing the horses to ride home on furlough, both the horses and the furloughs disappeared:

On Christmas day we left Pulaski, setting fire to the bridge there when we left. The rascals came up, put the fire out, and crossed over and attacked us on the first hill. We gave them a good drubbing, however, capturing some of their artillery. We made a forced march then to Sugar Creek, only a few miles from the Tennessee River, wading the creek in a late hour of the night and bivouacked at the edge of the valley, half a mile or more from the creek.

At daylight we were aroused and informed that the Yankees were on our side of the creek. A dense fog rested upon the valley. After waiting some time for them to make an attack, which they failed to do, we were ordered to charge them, and did it very successfully. In trying to cross the creek on their big cavalry horses, the banks on our side were so high they could not ascend them, and our boys captured many large, fine horses. When they were driven across the creek, Gen. Ross's Cavalry Brigade charged and drove them for miles. Our brigade got a good Yankee breakfast from the saddle pockets in horses killed and captured. From there to the pontoon bridge on the Tennessee River our brigade (including the Tenth Texas) was largely mounted.[24]

Still another soldier had a different perspective on the retreat:

. . . It had snowed and sleeted the day before, and the ground was as slick as glass. We reached a steep hill, and I rode on to its top with the troops. General Cheatham remained at the foot of the hill, and he knew they were going to have terrible times with that train of his approaching with ordnance stores, quartermaster's stores, etc. He sent word to me to pick out a hundred well-shod men, and send them to help push the wagons up. I dismounted and gave my horse to the courier. The fellows soon found out that I was after men with shoes on, and they were highly amused. They would laugh and stick up their feet as I approached. Some would have a pretty good shoe on one foot and on the other a piece of rawhide or a part of a shoe made strong with a string made from a strip of rawhide tied around it, some of them would have all rawhide, some were entirely bare-footed, and some would have on old shoe tops with the bottoms of their feet on the ground. I got about twenty or twenty-five men out of that entire army corps, and we got the teams up the hill.[25]

Another soldier related details of the retreat and how to spot a Reb soldier:

Finally daylight came, and surely it was welcomed as it never was before. Looking across to the west, we could see troops on the Columbia Pike, but we could not decide whether they were friends or foes. We plodded along as best we could, endeavoring to ascertain the identity of the travelers on the pike. After awhile I saw a possum tied on to a fellow's gun, which indicated to me that he was a Rebel. We cautiously drew nearer the pike and saw evidence unmistakable that they were friends. That "a friend in need is a friend indeed" was proved by their proposal to swap me some skinned pork for a piece of corn bread. I had neither, consequently I was out of the market . . . .

We passed on through the mud and slush until we finally came in sight of the Tennessee River, with its wide expanse of murky waters bearing down the stream drifts of logs, trees, brush, and everything imaginable. We could see, too, a rickety pontoon bridge hastily and insecurely built. It was serpentine in shape, about twelve feet wide and half a mile long, covered from end to end with all kinds of beasts, wagons, and, in fact, you could see everything in the shape of humanity except women and dogs. Besides this, there was a Yankee gunboat half a mile or more down the river throwing bombshells, trying to break the bridge; but the shoals prevented it from getting near enough to do any damage. The north end of the bridge had a promiscuous mass of humanity and animals all trying to get on and over the bridge at the same time. Finally my time came, and I went forward in great fear that the cable would break and let us all go down into eternity together. But the Lord was surely with us and permitted us to reach the southern shore without the loss of one. I turned my eyes toward the northern bank, and O what a sight! Just then I agreed for myself and all concerned that I would no more cross that river in the interest of secession.[26]

General Walthall issued the following circular to the "infantry forces of the rear guard" :

December 28, 1864, 3 a.m.:
Featherstone's Brigade will move promptly (without further orders) at daybreak across the bridge, to be followed by Field and Palmer.

General Reynolds will withdraw his command from Shoal Creek in time to reach the main line by daybreak and leave a skirmish line behind for a half hour. He will follow Palmer. Ector's Brigade will cover the road until the whole command has passed, and then will follow, leaving a line of skirmishers behind until the rear of the brigade has passed on to the bridge.

It is important that the movements be conducted with promptness and good order.

By command of Major General Walthall.[27]

The place of honor in a fighting retreat is the last unit. Colonel Coleman commanding Ector's Brigade rode over last. Nearly the whole Tenth Texas was mounted on fine Yankee horses, but they were taken away.

Union General Thomas, in his official report dated January 20, 1865, said this of Hood's rear guard:

He had formed a powerful rear guard, made up of detachments from all his organized forces, numbering about four thousand infantry, under General Walthall, and all his available cavalry and artillery under Forrest. With the exception of this rear guard, his army had become disheartened and a disorganized rabble of half-armed and barefooted men, who sought opportunity to fall out by the wayside and desert their cause to put an end to their sufferings. The rear guard, however, was undaunted and firm, and did its work bravely to the last.[28]

A soldier gave a brief summary of what happened on Hood's trip to Tennessee:

On the retreat near Pulaski, the roads were muddy and crowded, and every soldier was pulling along as best he could. General Hood and staff were passing, and as they were about to crowd an old soldier out of the road, he struck up this song, where General Hood could hear it:

> You may talk about your dearest maid,
> And sing of Rosa Lee,
> But the gallant Hood of Texas
> Played hell in Tennessee.[29]

Ector's Brigade started at Nashville with seven hundred men. Only 315 men were still effective to fight the rearguard on the retreat. By the time they entered Mississippi they only had 265. Based on these numbers, they lost 55 percent at the Battle of Nashville, and 16 percent on the retreat for a total casualty loss of 62 percent on the Nashville campaign. Many sources estimate that Hood's Army lost more than 60 percent of their total manpower on the trip into and out of Tennessee. Based on the personnel records of the Tenth Texas, and the apparent lack of record keeping at this late date of the war, the following listed men are all that can be identified as serious casualties:

Tenth Texas
Killed in Action at Nashville

Company I	B. Carlton	Disappeared — supposed dead
	R. Payne	Thought to have died in Tennessee

Tenth Texas
Wounded in Action at Nashville
Never Returned to Duty

Company A	T.G. Turman	Admitted to hospital 1/19/65 for wound
Company B	L. Hay	12/17/64 gunshot wound, left hip, died 12/18/64
	J.P. Smith	Admitted to hospital 1/7/65, gunshot wound
Company D	S.T. Wilson	Admitted to hospital 1/28/65 for wound
Company E	C.M. Johnson	Admitted to hospital 12/17/64, died 12/25/64, gunshot to left thigh
Company G	I. Martin	Captured returning from Tennessee after being left wounded
Company H	W.J. Wilson	Admitted to hospital 1/7/65 for wound to hand

Tenth Texas Cavalry
Members taken Prisoner at Nashville and on Retreat

Company B	F.A. King	POW — died 12/27 or 28/64
Company D	I.P. Cherry	POW — near Nashville
	J.A. Milner	POW — Franklin, Tenn., 12/17/64
Company F	A. Pierce	POW — Egypt Station, Tenn., 12/28/64
	J.J. Wells	"Supposed to be captured"
Company G	R.V. Irvin	Surrendered at Columbia, Tenn., 12/18/64

	J.R. Monk	POW — near Nashville, 12/16/64
	R.W. Wynne	Wounded 12/15/64 neck; POW — Franklin, 12/17/64
Company I	D. Oppenheimer	Gunshot wound to the right thigh — captured Franklin 12/18/64
Company K	M. Clary	POW — near Nashville, 12/15/64

The rear guard that fought to the Tennessee River continued to defend the rear of Hood's army until it reached Tupelo, Mississippi.[30] On January 3, 1865, General Hood, as promised, wrote to President Davis asking permission to send the Trans-Mississippi men home for one hundred days.[31] Hood stated that he did not have two thousand troops left from Texas and other locations west of the Mississippi River. The secretary of war replied:

War Department
Richmond, Va., January 8, 1865
General J. B. Hood, Tupelo, Miss:
The proposition to furlough the Trans-Mississippi troops cannot be entertained; the suggestion is regarded as dangerous; compliance would probably be fatal; extinguish the thought in the troops, if practicable."

J.A. Seddon
Secretary of War[32]

The secretary of war knew that if all the Texans left, they would never come back.

On January 11, 1865, it was reported that nine-tenths of Ector's Brigade were barefooted and "naked." Also, they expected to be furloughed as a brigade.[33] By January 14, 1865, Hood had to keep cavalry close to his army to run down deserters, and he took the soldiers' guns away from them to stop "depredations" (stealing food).[34] He also issued an order to execute any of his hungry soldiers found shooting livestock (biting hogs and etc.) or plundering private property.[35] General Forrest furloughed a large percentage of his soldiers, but the inspector general of the Army of Tennessee put out orders to arrest them and bring them back. By January 16, 1865, General Beauregard approved a judicious system of furlough to prevent disorder and desertion.[36] Even though the numbers are not available, General Robert E. Lee had 779 men desert from February 26 to March 8, 1865, and it can be assumed Hood was losing them at the same steady rate. One Texas cavalry unit had 180 men take the "owl train" home to Texas. This was a term used for running from the law.[37]

The Yanks were aware of the large number of deserters crossing the

Mississippi River heading west. They put out orders to let them cross peacefully. Even they knew the war was over.[38] On January 22, 1865, Hood reported losing his entire pontoon train, eighty-three boats and 150 wagons, because most of the soldiers guarding the equipment went home.[39] One can only imagine what the Tenth Texas survivors thought about Hood and the Confederacy after they were promised a furlough for fighting the rear guard out of Tennessee. Also, after being told they could keep any captured horses and then having them taken away, they must have been heartbroken. The horses were the transportation to be used on their furlough. There was no need to worry over what never happened. Soon, they had to prepare for a real battle!

CHAPTER 20

"Many others will bite the dust"

SIEGE AT SPANISH FORT

FOLLOWING THE RETREAT across the Tennessee River, the Tenth Texas camped near Verona, Mississippi. Littlejohn sent a letter from there:

> Encampment near Verona, Mississippi Jan. 22/65
> My dear Wife and Friends,
> Three of our Company, C. Birdwell, Hale, and Johnston, who were wounded last summer at Atlanta, are coming home on furloughs, by them I will send this letter. They are yet unable for duty and have been furloughed for sixty days. The rest of the company have drawn. There will be eight or ten men from our company on furlough when they all get off. Since I wrote you by Birdwell we have finally settled down in regular camps at Verona, five miles from Tupelo, the first time since last Spring. Rest feels very comfortable and agreeable to us who have been constantly on the move the last nine months.
> General Johnston is the *only man* to put confidence in the soldiers about arming and putting the negroes in the field. I am firmly of the opinion it will be done in the spring. All, or at least, some of the first men of the land are favoring the plan. General R.E. Lee, Jeff Davis, and a great many are in favor of the move. I believe the majority of the soldiers oppose the measure, saying they do not think it is right to adopt a principal which they have been fighting against, and moreover do not like to go in ranks with our sable brethren of the South. I have heard many say they would quit this service if such a measure was adopted by Congress. E.G.L.

The Confederate Congress passed a law in February 1865 to recruit blacks into the army. The Union already had one hundred thousand ex-slaves in their army.

The Tenth Texas moved to Mobile for its final big combat action, which was also the last large combat of the Civil War. Littlejohn said the following:

> Camp near Mobile, Ala. Feb 9th, 1865

. . . There are some very strong works here, and many a one of them will find a watery grave if he attempts to come to land. And many others will bite the dust for his last time if he should ever try the land route to this city, while as many brave and dauntless hearts remain to guard the works of this city, so well executed. But we are all encouraged to think that we will not have much of that business to do while here, and hope we may get to stay here and rest.

We are camped four miles from the city, west in a few hundred yards of the bay. The enemy's vessels, four, are very plain to view. There was some firing yesterday but I could not tell what at.

Mobile is not the place it was four years ago, very little business going on. Everything in price is beyond the reach of a private soldier. Small biscuit is selling at $4.00 per doz., eggs $5.00, butter $10.00 per lb., pies $1.00 for a slice as broad as your two fingers, and tapers to a point in the middle. A man can eat a month's wages in a day and not half try. But we are getting very good rations now, better than for a long time before, getting some fat beef and flour. I just finished building me a little chimney to my shantee last night, built us a little pen of logs, covered it with a fly. We have nothing at all to burn but green pine. We have learned to burn it finely. We have had a great deal of rain lately, but not much cold weather. My best wishes to you and my boy.

Yours affectionately, E.G.L.

Jim Watson (Company G) had his views about the soldiers and men that did not fight:

Mobile Bay, Ala, February the 22nd, 1865

Dear Father,

. . . There are a great many traitors in our land now. The country swarms with deserters. I never want you to feed a deserter nor a play-out. If a soldier calls at your house I want you to call for his papers and see whether he is all right or not before you give him anything to eat. There are a few men fighting the battles of our country, and the majority are playing out of service. I think the citizens ought to drive all of the skulkers and playouts to the front. Tell all that you see playing out to go and stand by their comrades and fellows in the hour of trial. If the people at home would not countenance men that are playing out there would not be so much of it going on. In your letter you seem to be despondent. That is all stuff. There is no use for men to fret out their days for nothing. I am for fighting this war to the end. The Negro question is up pretty high. Some of the soldiers are in favor if it and some are opposed to it. I am in favor of anything before subjugation.

J.M. Watson

Andrew Fogle from Ector's Brigade writes to Miss Loo:

Mobile, Alabama March 12th, 1865

. . . I sense of duty and the impulse of my heart enduses me to write those lines I may be unknowen to sum but I am knowen to my comreds in armes we have bin introduced to each other fifty times in line of batle we went forth in the befining at the first note of the fife and drum to sustain the name and fame of our country in this strugle for self-government while other sons of freedom were called to armes through fatigue and hunger and thirst and cold and heat and sickness and [ ] and the [Rage] of battle when the deth [ ] fly thick a round us and meny fell to rise no more but our harts are fixed as steel and we risk all and dair all for independence all this and more we have boren with cheerfulness But their is one thing that we cant well bar and that is A cowerdly ignominious and base spirit of submission on the part of the people of our confedrecy their is lots of men that is redy now to sub mit to lincon (Lincoln) they have got Charlston and Columbus South Carolina and if they get all of our towns and sities and then we will fite them on we neve will giv hit up as long as we are able to muster Fifty thousen men: I neve was in favor of secessing nor nevr will I be in favor of subugation and if evry man would com out and do his part we would sune have pease. but evry when their is a bagle to be faut their is one half of the army back in the Rear dooing nothing and as long as they do that we will neve gain a victry. Andrew Fogle 9th Texas Inf

The Tenth Texas, along with Ector's Brigade, was ordered to Fort Blakely near Mobile. The fort was located on the east side of Mobile Bay on the Blakely River. Later, most of the Tenth Texas was sent to Spanish Fort located five miles south of Fort Blakely. At this time, Col. Julius Andrews had recovered from his wound and was commander of Ector's Brigade. Capt. Jacob Ziegler was commanding the Tenth Texas. Colonel Earp was on ninety days leave to bring back recruits. Both Lieutenant Colonel Craig and Major Redwine were still recovering from the wounds they received at Atlanta.

The defense lines at Spanish Fort were described as looking like a horseshoe spread open. The Yanks were able to move artillery up to each end of the horseshoe shaped line and shoot down the trenches. With three Yank ships in the rear firing at them from behind, it is easy to see why the men of the Tenth Texas considered this their most dangerous fight. Spanish Fort was garrisoned by twenty-one hundred men, and Fort Blakely, five miles above, by twenty-six hundred. Nearly thirty thousand Federal troops were engaged in the siege of the former. When Spanish Fort was evacuated (midnight of April 8), they were joined by twelve thousand more. The whole force proceeded to attack Fort Blakely, which was bombarded, assaulted, and captured on April 9.[1]

Ector's Brigade arrived at Spanish Fort on March 29. The commander at Spanish Fort said of the Texans:

> The brigade was ragged and battle scarred; there was not 500 of them left, but there was an honest scar for every one of them.[2]

On March 31, 1865, the commander at Spanish Fort encouraged his men to "dig, dig, dig, nothing can save us here but the spade."[3] The problem was that no one can dig a hole in a swamp. The defense line at Spanish Fort was about thirty-five hundred yards long. On the left was a swamp that Ector's Brigade was assigned to defend. Even the Yanks said it was an "almost impassable swamp, thickly strewn with fallen trees and brush and in which water and mud was very deep."[4]

Spanish Fort had six redoubts (forts) built into it. Old Spanish Fort was called Redoubt No. One, and Fort McDermot was Redoubt No. Two. Ector's Brigade defended Redoubt No. Six with the North Carolina troops on its right and the Texans to the left. Based on casualties and numbers of captured men, the Ninth Texas Infantry and the Tenth Texas were next to the redoubt and not in the swamp on the last day of the siege.[5] The Texans task was to build defense lines in the boggy conditions. It extended to the waters of Bay Minette and was supposed to be protected by the guns from the Rebel gunboats, the *Nashville* and the *Morgan*. The Fourteenth Texas and the Thirty-second Texas were on the left in the furtherest reaches of the swamp. Unofficial records reflect that the Fourteenth Texas nearly had all their men captured or killed when the Yanks forced their way through the marsh in the final attack.

The abolitionists assaulted the left on April 2 and April 5. On April 5, they used marine tactics by attempting to storm the beach (really a swamp). They came out of the bay with three barges of troops, but the C.S.S. *Nashville* drove them off, aided by the Texans' rifle fire.[6]

The men of the Tenth Texas thought Spanish Fort was the worst fight they were in during the Civil War. This artillery man explained some of the action. When the soldier referred to the defense works not being completed on the left, the Texans would build up a breastwork in the swamp at night, and the Yanks would blow it down with cannon fire during the day:

Behind the breastworks, dense with men, hung the ever-changing, fluttering battle flags, floating from every point. The illumination by the mortars was beautiful, but of course dangerous as by day. After the siege guns's last report came the crack of the sharpshooters in our redoubts and the enemy's musketry poured in. . . .

Our artillery was served under galling fire. Wooden embrasures and iron screens were imperatively demanded. When the guns were ready to run out the "curtain" was withdrawn for an aperture to let our cannon speak. At each opening the enemy's riflemen improved their opportunities, but we plied our guns while the enemy's sharp-shooters were within three hundred yards.

Sunday, April 2, opened clear and was bland. By sunrise can-nonading was heard in the direction of Blakely. Soon the boom of heavy guns and screeching shells blended with continuous musketry. It was a peculiar sort of Sunday. The sky was rimmed with fire. Strains of music from brass bands of the enemy were borne in at times by the wind. "The heavens were rimmed with fire and the earth was banded with brass." Much of this band music was unfamiliar to us.

During the day our works were struck thirty-eight times, five being killed and twenty wounded. Fort McDermot suffered severely. Its parapets were badly damaged, and the carriage of a Brooke's rifle was disabled by an eight-inch mortar shell, and a twenty-four pound how-itzer was dismounted. The firing on this formidable line was general, and we all had a share in the pernicious activity of this shell game. One battery — the First Indiana Heavy Artillery — paid us special atten-tion. It was located in the rear of a Yank division, and had our left under enfilading fire while we were nine hundred yards distant.

The night was passed in repairing damages, and our men "resumed business" at daylight.

With all their fearful three-minute rounds with ninety guns the enemy were steadily building batteries on the right, center, and left. They were constantly adding to their equipment from the affluence of invention and production — waxing stronger almost hourly.

It was good for us that our bombproofs were well constructed, and we had some surcease; human nature otherwise could not have stood the strain. . . . We awaited from day to day the final assault. The enemy's fire grew in weight and execution, while there was a failing fire from our relays and reinforcements. Mortar shells were thrown into our garrison throughout the night with perfect periodicity. A ten-inch mortar shell is a fraction under ten inches in diameter, and weighs very near ninety pounds. An eight-inch shell is nearly eight inches in diameter, and weighs about fifty pounds. Some idea can be formed of the noise they produce in exploding and their fatal effect when they chanced to strike near troops. On this day a ten-inch shell from the (Yanks) struck inside Redoubt No. 5 (Phillips's battery) and penetrated six feet of earth and three layers of pine logs, literally burying twenty-six men, of whom one was killed and five wounded. It was marvelous, we thought, that while this man was hurled twenty feet in air and every bone was broken when he fell he sustained no mangling whatever.

The last Monday of the siege, as it proved (April 3), we awoke feeling as though heavily pounded. All night long the hideous shells had kept up their din and glare with musketry interspersed to give the mortar men a chance to rest. Such digging as our enemy accomplished! We had fighting all day and digging all night. Gen Liddell records on the 29th of March: "The enemy's skirmish line of yesterday is a line of battle to-day."

A remarkable feat of the Washington (Rebel) Artillery Saturday, April 1, is worthy of record. The Fourteenth Indiana Light Artillery was worrying over our columbiad with its fifty-pound shells. About 10 A.M. one of the shells struck a limber of this Hoosier Battery, and as it carried eighty pounds of power ignition was instantaneous, and the limber chest flew to pieces, killing one and wounding five. My schoolmate, Corporal Charles W. Fox, sighted this columbiad ("Lady Slocomb").

The enemy had in position against us thirty-eight siege guns, including six twenty-pounder rifles and sixteen mortars, and thirty-seven field guns, and in all ninety. Each gun was ordered to fire every three minutes. The enemy bears witness to the earth's actual trembling from the effect of the mighty firing. . . . The ditch in front of the breastworks was five feet deep and eight feet wide, but in front of Fort McDermot it was deeper and wider. In front of the batteries were also detached rifle pits for sharpshooters, and along the entire front was a line of abatis fifteen feet wide. On the extreme left the works were unfinished. Toward the interior the surface continued undulating and wooded but no spot was so commanding as the bare crest of McDermot.

After reporting to Gen. Gibson I returned to Redoubt No. 3. The enemy's artillery had not slackened, and the casualties of April 3 were eight killed and sixteen wounded. Just as I began telling my comrades my experiences a shrapnel struck the calf of my right leg. The boys rushed out and brought me under shelter. While lying on the ground I noted the awe inspired by the hissing trajectories athwart the dark sky, and the ground itself quivered.[7]

The Tenth Texas survivors were treated to a real light and fireworks display at Spanish Fort. They might have enjoyed it if it had not been so deadly. A Federal mortar gun shell was like a great meteor with a flaming tail about forty or fifty feet long. The sound effects were created by the screaming of the artillery shells lead ring around the shell that formed the seal between the shell and the gun barrel. The Rebs called the elongated Yank shells "lamp posts."

A soldier relived the adventure of just passing behind the Spanish Fort defense lines:

After a generation of peaceful life I cannot forget the terribly systematic work of the enemy which impressed us as we traversed the continuous line of breastworks and redoubts in order to visit (a New Orleans artillery unit called Washington Artillery). Not a yard of ground or a house had escaped the iron and leaden scythes; the very grass was mowed. We only knew of the general range of our artillery boys near the center of the line, and we devoted ourselves to diligent study of course and distance unpiloted. There were long, swampy flats over which we had to crawl upon prostrate pine trees felled for trailing — the only way of crossing these miry, treacherous "stretches." The bullets kept pelting, throwing mud, and now and then dropping down boughs and branches in startling proximity; but nimble limbs and a happy humor gave us rapid transit until the flats were passed and the breastworks reached about the right center of the line, and here we drew draughts of air, inflating our lungs prodigiously. In fact, we presented a tableau, for we embraced the soil of Alabama and uttered the legend of the seal of State: "Alabama — here we rest." There were no troops here, but near by we saw a tent and an officer standing near the works examining the enemy's line with field glasses. As we approached he turned and told where the Washington artillery was located, and invited us to sit down beside him. He was just about to walk in the direction of that company, and would show the way. Unmindful of the bullets, he raised his glasses to survey the enemy with characteristic nonchalance for several minutes. A bullet angrier than the others skipped past his ear, over our heads, and struck the tent at about the height of a man seated in a chair. Out came the inmates to see what was going on outside, and from them we learned that we were under jurisdiction of no less an officer than the commander of the fort, Brig. Gen. Randall L. Gibson. . . . Our destination was one hundred and fifty yards away in front, and the enemy was on the alert. Farewell to the General was uttered, and he wished us a happy arrival, and returned to his line of observation. We made a good time and reached the earthworks, and were at home with the Washington Artillery. Just as we entered there was a cry, and two members of the company fell wounded. Lieut. Abe I. Leverich and Serg. James F. Griffen were both struck by the same bullet from a sharpshooter's rifle, which penetrated Leverich's cheek and lodged in Giffen's shoulder. . . . The wounds were not fatal.

We were now taken to the bombproof, or "gopher hole," where the boys slept and ate. This was a log house covered with three layers of pine logs and six feet of earth to protect the inmates from explosion of shells and rifle balls.

One incident (like half a dozen experienced by the boys) seemed a performance made to matriculate us in the school of war. We were counting up the missing, and became absorbed, when a crash at the door brought an end to roll call, and lo! a fuse shell had come to see us, and was about two feet within the door of our "gopher." Not a syllable was uttered, but such a display of nimbleness was never equaled before football came around, and there were more artillerist in the flesh and spirit stowed into one corner than Armour, Swift, or Morris (meat packing companies) could pack in an hour. Here we huddled — minutes? no, seconds. But New Orleans boys are always equal to the emergency. Orderly Serg. John Bartley seized the unwelcome tongue-tied visitor and threw it out.[8]

Along with the enemy trying to kill the Texans, they also had to contend with "gas warfare." A herd of cows got between the lines at night and was killed by both sides believing it was an attack. A Yank said the Rebs pulled back their positions because of the smell.[9]

A Reb soldier remembered the action at Spanish Fort:

I went through the fight at Missionary Ridge and New Hope Church and other hard battles, and from the time the fight at Spanish Fort commenced until the end it was as hard as I was ever in. We fought two days before they forced us back to the ditches. For sixteen days we had a hard time. I well remember the night when three lines of battle charged our picket line, but we forced them back. At daylight they were two hundred yards in our front, behind stumps and logs. By 11 A.M. they had killed or wounded all in my pit but myself. . . . Three of them climbed a sweet gum tree, the only tree in front nearer than one mile, and at one o'clock they fired on us. We located them by the smoke of their coming out of the leaves. We fired on them, and two fell out like squirrels; the other came down and ran as I never saw a man run before.[10]

One soldier described how the commander made plans to get his troops out of a bad situation:

Maj. Gen Maury, commanding the district of the Gulf, had most ingeniously arranged for the safety of the garrison of Spanish Fort when it should become untenable, by constructing bridges across the marshes and streams between them and deep water, so that when the abandonment was made necessary the troops were marched by this route to where steamers were held in readiness to transport them to Mobile.

The Confederate gunboats were unable to render much service in these operations on the eastern side of the Mobile waters, but they kept going along the shore and did occasional execution against the entrenched lines of the enemy. In this work the Nashville and Morgan were conspicuous. The Federal craft were very actively employed, and no less than eight of them were sunk by torpedoes.[11]

The bridges across the marshes were really a treadway about eighteen inches wide and about a mile long.

At 5:30 on the evening of April 8, the entire Union artillery strength in front of Spanish Fort opened fire. Fifty-three siege guns and thirty-seven field guns pounded the Confederate positions. As many of the guns as could be brought to bear concentrated their fire on Ector's brigade. Covered by this fire, an assault force poised in the farthest-forward Union trench moved ahead in a two-pronged attack. One force came around the left of Ector's brigade, through the swamp. As that flanking force reached each Rebel strong point, the other group of Yankees came to its aid in a frontal attack. The Union commander wrote:

One thing that was very much in our favor was that the enemy's works from their extreme left for a considerable distance consisted of a series of small pits without direct connection with each other. This enabled us to attack them in detail, and we had carried a considerable portion of their works before their main force was aware that we had turned their left. We here witnessed the spectacle of dying in the last ditch, as quite a number of the rebels refused to surrender and were shot in their ditches, and on the other hand quiet a number of them who were taken prisoners ought, in justice to our men, to have been killed, as they would first fire at our men after being ordered to surrender, then throw up both hands and surrender.[12]

In the official report, one of the Federals clearly did not hear the Texans correctly. After getting around and through the left flank in the dark, he said a heavy column of Rebs approached calling out "we surrender." When they were within thirty or forty yards the Rebs opened fire on them.[13] If any of the Texans said "we surrender" then opened fire on the Yanks, it could be said that this was a survival instinct learned during a brutal war. While this action did not happen that often, each side commonly blamed the other for "false" surrenders.

One of Ector's men with the Fourteenth Texas wrote of the action of Spanish Fort:

We retreated back to Verona, Mississippi and remained in quarters there a short time, and then Ector's Brigade was sent to Mobile, Ala., where we remained in winter quarters a month or two. While in camp there we had a great revival of religion. The Spirit of God entered the camp, and hundreds were converted. I remember the fervent prayer that went up from the camp for souls and for our bleeding country. I do believe God answered those prayers, for the war closed in a short time. About March 1, 1865, we were taken over to Spanish Fort, opposite Mobile, and thus began our last campaign. The war was near its close. . . . During this siege the enemy's pickets had gotten so near our lines that not a man dared to raise his head above the works. There was a call for a volunteer force to drive the enemy back. Any good soldier will go when he is ordered, but to volunteer in such a crisis — few will do it. Captain Howze said if he could pick his men he would do it, and he had his men selected when the order was countermanded. It was thought too dangerous to hazard men's lives. A few days after this, about dusk, the enemy massed their forces on our left and drove our boys from their works, at the same time opening fire from their batteries and gunboats all along

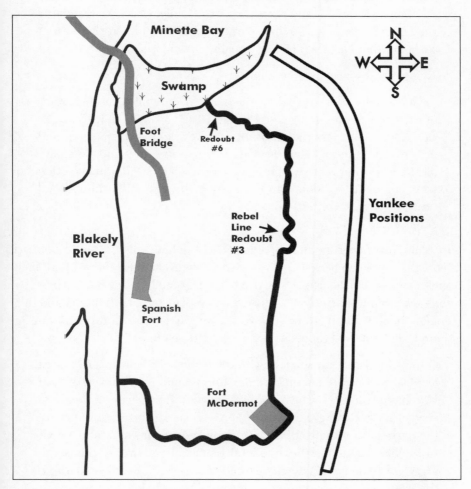

SEIGE AT SPANISH FORT

Fort McDermot and Redoubt #3 were built on high hills.
The large guns at Redoubt #3 were called "Lady Slocomb" and "Cora Slocomb"
The coehorn mortars were called "Peanuts" and "Louise"

the line to keep us from reinforcing our left. Our line was driven back in great confusion. The moon was shining brightly, and we were in close proximity. I heard Captain Howze's well-known voice call out to rally around the flag. Some twenty or thirty men from different lots of the old 14th answered to his call. He gave the word to charge, and the boys gave the Rebel yell and charged. Here I saw our brave young flag bearer, Billy Powers, go down. This checked us. Some one gathered up the colors and we retreated. This was the last gun we

235

fired. When we reached the other part of the command, they were retreating in great confusion, every man pretty much his own commander. We waded in the marshes of Mobile Bay, sometimes in mud and water up to our knees and waist, and we were finally picked up by a blockade runner and carried over to Mobile, where we evacuated the city and retreated toward Meridian, Mississippi. On this retreat we heard that General Lee had already surrendered.[14]

The Reb general summarized the battle:

> The defense of Spanish Fort was the death grapple of the veterans of the Confederate and Federal armies. They brought to it the experience of four years of incessant conflict, and in the attack and defense of that fort demonstrated every offensive and defensive method then known to war. It is not too much to say that no position was ever held by Confederate troops with greater hardihood and tenacity nor evacuated more skillfully after every hope of further defense had gone.[15]

Fort Blakely was overrun after Spanish Fort. A soldier told of the final action at Fort Blakey. When he referred to subterra shells, he was talking about land mines. At this battle, the Rebs used hand grenades and land mines. At Kennesaw Mountain, the Yanks pushed up cracker boxes full of dirt and dug trenches behind them. Here they rolled up barrels full of dirt and dug in behind them and used them as part of their trench line:

> On April 9, 1865, my services with the Confederate army terminated at Blakely, Ala., about fifteen miles from Mobile. . . . On the 28th of March our works were invested by a strong force of Federals, and the siege was on. During the night of April 8 Spanish Fort was evacuated, the garrison coming to Blakely through the swamps and taking boat to Mobile. Then the whole Federal forces, about twenty thousand, attacked Blakely. Our works extended in a half circle about three thousand yards, each flank on the river. We had about twenty-seven hundred men, many of them the old and young reserves, from Alabama; these last occupied the right of our works.
>
> About 5 P.M. on Sunday, April 9, 1865, the attack was general. The Missouri troops were sent to the left on two occasions to help repulse some negro troops attacking there. About this time the Federals came over the works on our right and moved down toward the left. When we saw this, many made their way to the river; but there was little or no means of escape except in a few old boats and

on planks, by which means about one hundred and fifty men escaped. About this time I was at the field hospital, being detained by the surgeon in charge (I forget his name) to assist in amputating the leg of a wounded man, which I was required to hold above the knee. The delay was prolonged because of the time it took to get the man under the influence of chloroform.

As soon as I was relieved the hospital steward and I made a run for a wharf to get planks to escape upon, I throwing down four planks. The steward took two, and I ran down to get my planks, but another fellow was floating off on them. By this time the Federals were on the bluffs of the river about two hundred yards off, and were firing at every object in the river. Some of the shots struck quite near me. I concluded not to take a plank ride just then, and was busy fastening a twenty-dollar gold piece in the lining of my cap and dropping my watch into my bootleg when a Federal called out: "Say, you fellow with a green shirt on, come up or you will get hulled [shot] next time."

I obeyed making my way to the bluff where others of our men were. In a short while a Federal corporal with one man took another officer and me and started for the rear. When we got to the works, there were several explosions. Some of the incoming victorious troops had got upon the subterra shells that we had placed in front of the works and were more or less injured. They talked very ugly toward us, so our guard had us sit down a little on one side until the troops had passed. On our way to the rear we stopped at a wagon train, and our guard got us some coffee and crackers. While there a Federal abused us for being Rebels, etc. Our guard told him to stop; but he did not until the guard gave him a slap, which rolled him over, and told him to go off and attend to his mules. We were then taken to where the other prisoners were bivouacked for the night.[16]

This ended the last large ground combat of the Civil War.

By this time of the war, personnel records were poorly kept. Several men were captured that were returned to the Tenth Texas prior to the surrender. Littlejohn's friend, Roe Spinks, was one of them.

Tenth Texas Cavalry
Killed in Action at Spanish Fort, Alabama

Company B	J. Benton	
Company G	J. Becton	
Company I	A.A. Blakey	

Company E	Wilson Prior	Gunshot wound
Company H	J.F. McEnturff	Flesh wound left shoulder, hip and back shell wound
Company I	A. Glass	Fracture right arm, shell wound

Tenth Texas Cavalry
Captured at Spanish Fort, Alabama
Never Returned to Duty

Company E	B.F. Rushing	
Company G	W.H. Hollingsworth	
Company I	C.B. Carlton	

Littlejohn wrote his last letter home. He covered some of the action at Spanish Fort and eloquently closed his last letter expressing the uncertainty of the future:

Encampment, Meridian, Mississippi
April 18th, 1865

. . . On or about the 26th or 27th of March orders came for us to take the boat and go to Blakely on the East shore of the Bay, 12 miles from the City. As the enemy were approaching from Pensacola in force. We got on the boat about 9 o'clock Saturday night and everything being made ready we started. Had not gone more than five or six miles up the Mobile River when we run into another steamer, the Gertrude, going down the river from Demopolis, laden with government supplies and having several passengers on board. Nearly all on our boat had gone to sleep but myself. I had reclined on my elbow and was meditating on the Past and the Future, when all of a sudden I felt a considerable shock and perceived that our boat had hit something. Being in the after part of the boat, I could not see before, I thought we had run aground. Soon I heard someone awakened by the shock exclaim "the boat is sinking." Upon this everyone jumped up and running to the same side of the boat came very near sinking ours. Our boat being large and heavily laden had knocked a hole about mid way of the other. She whirled around and went down in four minutes. But before going down all the passengers got on our boat. Several ladies jumped up in their night clothes and jumped fearful on ours. One lady threw her baby on our boat and it was caught by a soldier of our regt. Several women perhaps would have fallen into the water but by the timely aid of the soldiers all were saved. One beautiful young lady in her fright rushed to the edge of the boat and seeing no other means of escape, fell into the extended arms of a young soldier. No lives were lost but the boat load consisted of beef cattle, hogs, flour and a good many other things. It was an exciting scene, and it was a lucky thing that no one was drowned.

We proceeded on to Blakely and next morning went out five or six miles, camped for the night. Next morning the enemy were pushing our advance heavily and finding they were too strong we began to fall back to our works; however, a main part of the Div. had fallen back to Spanish Fort. The Yankees soon closed in around them and began to ditch. From Blakely we could hear heavy firing. After we got back to the works at Blakely it was not long before a dispatch was recd from the Commdg. Gen. at Spanish Fort asking for reinforcements. Our regt. being the largest, it fell to our lot to go down there. . . . We did not lose a man in getting to the works. There was hardly any fortifications on the left. We took position in the center where the works were tolerably good. But soon our luck changed. Every day we lost some, more or less by their artillery and sharp shooting. One day we had four men killed and some wounded by the explosion of a shell. After this we moved on the left where we worked day and night on the works. By this time they had brought up their siege train and began to work on us heavy with their mortars, pitching the shells right into our ditches. They had ditched up to within two hundred yards of our works and they kept us awake night and day almost by throwing their 120 pounder shells. One or two evenings the cannonade was terrific and said to be, by some the heaviest ever heard. By these we lost one brave boy, severely wounded. On the evening of the 8th April they sought to try our lines on the extreme left and meeting with no resistance, came right through. On the extreme left was a marsh of two hundred yards in which we had nothing only picquets (pickets), it being impossible for men to stay there. They turned the left of our lines about sundown, and as soon as our boys heard it, it spread like electricity among them, and they became alarmed for fear the enemy would get between us and our getting out place and had they known our situation they could have caught the last one of us. A narrow plank bridge had been made across a portion of the marsh, about a mile long. We walked on this till we got out of hearing of them and then we split the mud. The mud was from knee to waist deep. I got into one place from which I had to be pulled, not being able to extricate myself. I waded for about a mile and then got

239

a skiff and went to a blockade runner launched in the river. Many of the boys trudged six miles through that mud. It was an awful time. . . . . We lost several from our regt. About half our Brigade was captured and killed. . . . After going on the boat we, the garrison from Spanish Fort was taken to Mobile. The city was taken very easily and with but little loss to the Yankees. They lost one or two gunboats. We met many a sad face on our return to the city. The ladies wept bitterly. They were kind to us as they could be. In many instances they gave our boys money, clothing, hats and everything. I could hardly refrain from shedding tears myself. We left many a true Southern heart in Mobile; and many a traitor.

A great many soldiers stayed in the city and gave up to the Yanks. We did not lose much government property. True, we had to burn a great number of the finest canons I ever saw. We left Mobile on Monday and the Yankees came in next morning. I learn that a train has gone to Mobile after the prisoners, which I understand are to be paroled. I hope many whom we considered dead will yet come in. Our men are very much demoralized and a good many are running away. . . .

It is common report now, but not credited now, that Genl. Lee and Johnston have been whipped, that Lee had surrendered himself and whole army to Grant. There is no doubt about Richmond being evacuated and that some troops were lost, but it is not believed that Lee surrendered the finest army in the world ever saw to Gen. Grant. I expect there had been some very heavy fighting in N.C. but as communication is interrupted we can get nothing straight. . . . We have also recd telegraphs to the effect that Lincoln and Seward have been assassinated in Washington, that Lincoln was shot through the head in the theatre and lived a few hours, and that Seward's throat was cut, supposed to have been done by some northern man. We got all this news by Yankee paper. It may be so and it may not. As for my part I don't believe any of it. But I wish to the bottom of my heart that the last report was true. Though it does not show a spirit of Christianity to rejoice at such wickedness. . . .

Since we have left Mobile we have been here at this place doing nothing. There has been considerable excitement about consolidating our brigade. I am in favor of the act if done right. The Commanding Gen. wants to consolidate our four Texas regts. into one and put it into an Alabama Brigade. To this we are not willing, from the fact that it should be humiliating to put us, after having made a name for ourselves, into another brigade, who has no history. If they would put us with other troops from Texas none would object, but numbers of the boys say they will quit if the other takes place. I think they might please us now and then. I want a chance to get new officers, our old ones are of no account in the world, regular sot drunkards, the most of them. They were all dog drunk when Spanish Fort was given up, and it is the same all the time when they can get it. . . .

I would like much to be with you again but do not know whether I ever shall be or not. I have escaped well so far, for which I thank God. But I hope I may be spared to get home again honorably. Some of the boys are going without papers, but unless my notion changes I shall never come until the Brigade comes or the Army ceases to be an organized Command. I will never run away. . . .
Your Husband, E.G.L.
P.S. Direct to the Army of Mississippi etc. as you have done heretofore

Encampment, Cuba Station, Ala. May 4/65
Oh! My Country! My Country! What a deplorable condition Thou art in; what future destiny awaits thee I can't tell, but necessity knows no law. Her sons, though numerous, have forsaken thee. No longer will be a free people, no longer have our rights, but must submit to the cruel relentless yoke of Yankee Tyranny. Far better to have fell on the Glory battle field than to witness what is now going on. Thrice happy are they whose bodies bleach on the plains of Shiloh, Manassas, Murfreesboro, and Chickamauga, and whose spirits now rest from strife. They will be remembered with all honor, praise and reverence.

Littlejohn wrote this the day the Tenth Texas surrendered.

CHAPTER 21

"They shucked their part of the corn"

CONCLUSION

THESE MEN MARCHED to the war with high spirits looking forward to a "great adventure." Their morale wavered when they confronted sickness and death from disease early in the war. They then complained of the incompetence of their officers and the lack of and quality of the food just as all soldiers do. These mostly subsistence farmers had no stake in slavery. The South could make better arguments for secession than the colonies could from England. This would be enough by itself to get these men to repeatedly fight to the death. One of the reasons the Tenth Texas fought until the end of the war was that they had the advantage of fighting against what they perceived as an invader. They were fighting for their homeland. As their flag stated, "Fight for your altars and your homes."

Another strong influence that caused the Tenth Texas to stay in a fighting mood until after most of the others had "blew off the hounds" was a good dose of propaganda. Many of the letters in this book refer to the brutality of the Yankees. Their anger at the stories of bringing in the Dutch (Germans) and Irish to fight them added fuel to the fire. Camp life of the Rebs rebounded with rumors of the enemy shooting Rebs after capture, the wounded with throats cut, the use of poisoned bullets, and the abuse of women. One letter in this book mentioned Union soldiers stealing the clothes off the women. The South made good use of a written order by the Yank's Commander at New Orleans when he wrote that if the women kept up being disrespectful the Yanks would treat them as harlots. Certainly the propaganda, as in all wars, had a potent effect on the fighting spirit. Another reason the Tenth Texas fought to the end was the pride that came with their rural religious upbringing. As Littlejohn said in one of his letters, he could not stand to be the subject of talk, as some were who had gone AWOL.

Certainly the fall of Vicksburg and the defeat at Gettysburg were almost the death blow to the Tenth Texas. From the subsequent number of desertions, and their sister unit, the Fourteenth Texas, having the "Hell or Horses" rebellion, it was clear the Tenth Texas was in serious trouble. One soldier stated that General Walker thought they were so worthless they should be discharged from the military. That same general apologized after the battle at Chickamauga.

The fall of Vicksburg and seeing their way home blocked would have demoralized most military units. After the retreat from Nashville and the fighting of the rear guard, it is amazing the Tenth Texas continued to struggle against all odds, especially after being promised that the war was over for them. A general furlough home for all soldiers would have been the end of the Tenth Texas. One of the old soldiers wrote concerning Ector's Brigade and Tenth Texas:

> I deem it a duty while esteeming it a privilege to say that we never met a foe in open field whom we didn't drive, nor did we ever meet a foe who could drive us. In some battles a brigade or command on the right or left of ours gave way, it was necessary to move by the flank in retreat. In that event firing of small arms did not cease, nor did the enemy's loss lessen. In many battles — notably Richmond, Kentucky, Murfreesboro, and Chickamauga, Ector's Brigade was among the first of the infantry to open and the last to close.
>
> The Regiments comprising this brigade entered the Confederate service over eight thousand strong, and surrendered . . . only five hundred and forty men nearly all of whom were battle-scarred.[1]

An elite unit has an indescribable inner force that keeps a military formation fighting after others have given up the struggle. The Tenth Texas endured many battles fought at close quarters, hand-to-hand, rifle butts to heads. They fought a hard and uncompromising war that is difficult to comprehend. As the war progressed, all military units of the south had casualty lists of the bravest and most willing for self sacrifice. As the most fearless were killed and maimed, the fighting qualities of the units diminished. The Tenth Texas proved at Allatoona, the retreat from Nashville, and the siege at Spanish Fort, that they had many courageous men left to the end.

An elite unit has a sense of comradeship that realizes its strength is in its loyalty to each other. At Nashville, Lieutenant Tunnel from Ector's Brigade made a point that, when the weather was horrible and the tactical situation was out of control, the Texans still took time to shelter the wounded. Based on the information available, the Tenth Texas proudly conducted themselves as a military unit to the very end. Some of the Confederate units that retreated from Nashville and were sent to South Carolina "behaved shamefully" and "there was not an officer that could do anything with them."[2] Some of the other Texas cavalry units had large numbers leave for Texas.

Littlejohn, in his last letter of the war, made it clear that the units in Ector's Brigade had made a good name for themselves. They would not tolerate being put into a unit without a fighting reputation. Their achievements against great odds for the entire war are irrefutable evidence of the unit's distinctive status. To the author's knowledge they were the only unit in the Civil War that overran a fortified enemy position with the enemy firing Henry repeating rifles at them.

One of the Texans wrote the following:

The simple fact of my having been a private soldier during that fearful struggle covers the whole ground as effectually as if I should write a volume. My life, like that of thousands of others, during that period was a continuous succession of hard, wearisome marches with blistered feet; with scant clothing and food; exposed to all kinds of weather practically unsheltered, and to conflicts with the enemy in which it was the duty of the private soldier to kill — and, perchance, ere the termination of the struggle, to get killed.

While the duties, dangers and hardships incident to and inseparable from the Confederate soldier's life, shared alike by my comrades and myself, were such as to tax to the utmost the manhood, courage and physical endurance of all of us who faced the enemy in deadly conflict, I can now recall no circumstance in my own experience in the field that would entitle me to greater honor than should of right be bestowed upon my comrades in arms; I merely "went with the crowd," never halting short of the firing line and faithfully "shucked my part of the corn.[3]

The entire Tenth Texas had indeed "shucked their part of the corn."

APPENDIX A

LIST OF ENGAGEMENTS, BATTLES, SIEGES, AND SKIRMISHES
OF THE TENTH TEXAS CAVALRY DISMOUNTED

May 1862 . . . . .Engagement at Farmington,
Siege at Corinth,
Engagement at Boonesville, all in Mississippi

August 1862 . . . . .Engagement Mount Zion Church, Kentucky
Battle of Richmond, Kentucky

December 1862 . . . . . . .Battle of Murfreesboro, Tennessee

July 1863 . . . . .Skirmishing at Big Black River, Mississippi
Battle of Jackson, Mississippi

September 1863 . . . . . .Battle of Chickamauga, Georgia

February-March 1864 . .Engagements against Sherman's Meridian,
Mississippi Campaign

May 1864 . . . . .Engagement at Rome,
Battle of Cassville,
Battle of New Hope Church, all in Georgia

June 1864 . . . . .Engagement at Pine Mountain,
Engagement at Lost Mountain,
Engagement at Latimer House,
Battle and siege at Kennesaw Mountain, all in Georgia

July 1864 . . . . .Engagement at Smyrna,
Engagement at Nickajack Creek,
Engagement at Rottenwood Creek,
Skirmishing at Chattahoochee River,
Battle of Peachtree Creek,
Battle of Ezra Church, all in Georgia

August 1864 . . . . .Siege of Atlanta, Georgia

September 1864 . . . . . .Engagement at Lovejoy's Station, Georgia

October 1864 . . . . .Battle of Allatoona Pass,
Skirmish at Resaca,
Skirmish at Dalton, all in Georgia

December 1864 . . . . . . .Skirmish at Bell's Mills, Tennessee
Battle of Nashville, Tennessee
Rear guard on retreat of the Army of Tennessee
back to Mississippi

March-April 1865 . . . . .Siege of Spanish Fort and Fort Blakely, Alabama

May 1865 . . . . .Surrender at Citronelle, Alabama

APPENDIX B

SCHEDULE OF PERSONNEL

Total that served with the Tenth Texas 1,334

Less number that never left Texas 99

Total that served East of the Mississippi River 1,235

Less total discharged (26 at time of officer election, May 1862) 253

Total died — non-combat 291

Absent without leave (some were wounded or on leave
and sent medical statements — not able to return) 86

Transferred, assigned or detached duty 63

Released because of Conscript Act 19

Killed, wounded, and prisoner
(never returned to duty) after the listed battles:

                    Richmond 40

                    Murfreesboro 67

                    Chickamauga 61

                    Atlanta 25

                    Allatoona 10

                    Nashville and retreat .19

                    Spanish Fort 9

In the hospital at the end of the war:

                    Sick 19

                    Wounded 1

Present 4/5/64 and undocumented* 89

Other (see Appendix C for details) 24

Number that surrendered at the end of the war 159

---

*Of these eighty-nine men, probably twenty-five to thirty were on furlough when the war closed. Littlejohn noted in a letter that eight to ten from his company would be on furlough shortly before the end of the war. The Tenth Texas was operating with three companies at that time. The rest would have been men killed or seriously wounded at Atlanta, Allatoona Pass, Nashville and the retreat, and at Spanish Fort. Just at Atlanta, the official reports show five more men killed or captured than the personnel records reflect. This does not count the extra fifty-seven wounded at Atlanta with many of them who would not have ever returned to duty.

APPENDIX C

SCHEDULE OF SOLDIERS LISTED UNDER "OTHER" CATEGORY

Andrews, J. . . . . . .Court-martialed two times — dropped from the roster.

Birdwell, G. . . . . .Furloughed at the end of the war.

Booty, A.J. . . . . . .Captured while crossing the Mississippi River on leave.

Boykin, R.S. . . . . .Captured while crossing the Mississippi River on leave.

Cornelious, J.M. . . .Captured while crossing the Mississippi River on leave, died in prison camp.

Davis, W.P. . . . . . .Got out of the army by paying a substitute.

Earp, C.R. . . . . . .After the retreat from Nashville, he was given 90 days of leave on Jan. 19, 1865, apparently to go recruit new soldiers — did not make it back for the surrender.

Farmer, E.O. . . . . .Left sick in Mississippi in May 1863, captured and died in Yank prison.

Flournoy, R.R. . . .As the Tenth Texas moved to Chickamauga, he was "killed by the cars (railroad) at Meridian."

Garner, W. . . . . . .Detailed to Provost Guard, captured near Tilton, Georgia, October 1864.

Holt, J.J. . . . . . . .Went home sick.

Kilgore, Buck . . . .Captured while going home on leave because of his wound. Had a lot of Littlejohn's money with him when captured.

Lloyd, T.B. . . . . . .Apparently captured crossing Mississippi River returning from leave.

May, J.S. . . . . . . .Went AWOL in 1863 and joined a Reb unit west of Mississippi and surrendered with them at the end of the war.

Mobley, A.H. . . . . .Killed by J.L. Lowery, private in Company C, April 11, 1863. Apparently Lowery hung around for four days before he disappeared.

Nail, W.W. . . . . . .Shown as deserted July 21, 1863. Captured by Yanks and died in prison camp.

Neal, D.L. . . . . . .Hired a substitute and got out of the Tenth Texas.

Newberry, J.H. . . .Became sick, shown as AWOL, and was captured on way home to Texas.

Phillips, C. . . . . . .Apparently on his way home or on his way back to the Tenth Texas when war ended. Surrendered in New Orleans.

Prior, G.W. ......A man with bad timing, he was crossing the Mississippi at Vicksburg and was part of the big surrender July 4, 1863.

Ransom, H.B. .....Captured at the first skirmish of the Tenth Texas and was then moved to Ohio and paroled at Vicksburg. Apparently, he was then released from the military.

Smith, H.V. ......Deserted July 17, 1863, and stumbled into the Yanks around Vicksburg. Was not freed until 1865 while in bad health.

Smith, L. ....Shown as captured in 1862, paroled to Vicksburg and arrived on the steamer *Metropolitan* and was marked as dead on arrival.

Trout, W.S. ......Gen. Hood on August 18, 1864, sent him to Texas to round up absentees. Never made it back.

APPENDIX D

COMMANDERS OF TENTH TEXAS CAVALRY DISMOUNTED

Col. Matthew Locke

Organized and commanded the unit as it left Texas. Resigned March 6, 1863, for "affection of the spine, asitis, and chronic hepatitis." The official reports show him commanding at the Battle of Murfreesboro even though he was not in command at the previous battle (Richmond). A soldier says Col. C.R. Earp was in command at Murfreesboro.

Col. C.R. Earp

Commanded the Tenth Texas in its first battle at Richmond, Kentucky, and there is some doubt as who commanded at the second large battle at Murfreesboro. Earp's two majors, Ras Redwine and William Craig, were both wounded in the battles around Atlanta. He was given a leave of absence on January 19, 1865, to go to Texas to bring back absentees. He did not make it back for the last action at Spanish Fort.

Capt. James Howze

Per Lt. Tunnell of the Fourteenth Texas, Captain Howze was in charge of the Tenth Texas or at least a detachment of the Tenth Texas at Nashville. Howze was with the Fourteenth Texas and never appears on the Tenth Texas records. Howze was friends with many people in the Tenth Texas because he was from Rusk County. His company's flag was made by Lucy Kilgore, the sister of Buck Kilgore. His company's name was "The Rusk Avengers."

Capt. Jacob Ziegler

Was commanding the Tenth Texas at its final battle at Spanish Fort, Alabama.

APPENDIX E

COMMANDERS OF ECTOR'S BRIGADE
(CALLED ECTOR'S TEXAS BRIGADE)

Gen. Matthew D. Ector

Commander from the formation of the Brigade prior to the Battle of Murfreesboro until July 27, 1864, when he lost his leg from a cannon ball hit at Atlanta. He previously was the commander of the Fourteenth Texas Cavalry Dismounted, which was part of Ector's Brigade.

Gen. William H. Young

Commanded Ector's Brigade after Ector had his leg shot off until the Battle of Allatoona in October 1864. His horse was killed under him and he was shot in the foot. He was loaded in an ambulance, which made a turn on the wrong road where the Yanks captured him. He previously was the commander of the Ninth Texas Infantry. This was his sixth wound of the war. His foot had to be amputated.

Col. C.R. Earp

Commanded the Brigade for the last charge at the Battle of Allatoona after Colonel Young was wounded. He was commander of the Tenth Texas.

Col. Julius Andrews

Commanded from October 5, 1864, after the Battle of Allatoona, until December 4, 1864, when he was wounded near Nashville. He was previously the commander of the Thirty-second Texas Cavalry Dismounted, which was part of Ector's Brigade. Commanded the Brigade at the last large land battle of the Civil War at Spanish Fort, Alabama.

Col. David Coleman

Commanded the brigade through the Battle of Nashville and the retreat. He was given the place of honor for fighting the rear guard on Hood's retreat from Tennessee. He was the last man to cross the pontoon bridge over the Tennessee River. He was the commander of the Thirty-ninth North Carolina Infantry Regiment, which was part of the Brigade.

APPENDIX F

TENTH TEXAS ROLL OF HONOR
BRAVEST OF THE BRAVE

Sgt. Andrew Sims, Company D

At the Battle of Murfreesboro, the Yank flag bearer was waving his flag taunting Sergeant Sims by "costing it forward, and, by various motions." Sims pressed forward with incredible speed, grabbed the Yank flag, and both Sims and the Yank were shot dead. This would have been the first flag captured that day (of three taken) by the Tenth Texas.

Pvt. Thomas "Jeff" Rosson, Company G

Wounded at Murfreesboro — right arm.
Wounded at Latimer House — right arm.
Wounded at Atlanta — right leg — hit by cannon ball.
At the Battle of Chickamauga on the second day, he braved the fire of hundreds of Yanks to rescue Jim Watson. In Vietnam it would have been said he was working on a CMH (Congressional Medal of Honor). Some of the author's friends would have said he was working on a CMH (Casket with Metal Handles).

Lt. M. W. Armstrong, Company I

At the Battle of Allatoona, he charged up to the enemy's breastworks and captured the Yank flag and flag bearer. Another soldier says he cracked the Yank's head with a rock and had a private drag out the flag and the enemy soldier.

Pvt. John W. Davis, Company E

Shot in the right thigh while charging a Yank artillery position at Chickamauga. With the broken thigh bone the Yanks sent him back. He returned and was wounded again during the Georgia campaign.

Cpl. S.S. Tillman, Company D

Suffered two serious wounds, one in the left thigh at Murfreesboro and again at the Battle of Peachtree Creek. He came back to fight at Spanish Fort.

Pvt. C.M. Gingles, Company C

Suffered four wounds in the war. At Murfreesboro he was wounded in the arm, at New Hope Church was struck between the eyes with a spent round knocking him out, wounded in the left hand at Nashville, and hit in the head and suffered a scalp wound at Spanish Fort.

Cpl. James T. McGee, Company C

Picked up the Tenth Texas flag at Murfreesboro after Sergeant Simms was killed and only made it a few paces before he, too, was killed. He was the last of the color-guard left standing. He "fell to rise no more until aroused by the trumpet of God to come to judgment."

Pvt. J.O. Manning, Company H

He picked up the Tenth Texas flag at Murfreesboro after all the color-guard was killed or wounded and carried it the rest of the day. He died two and a half months later, and it is unclear if a wound caused his death.

Pvt. Ben Birdwell, Company G

Shot in the "right front" at Richmond, Kentucky, and discharged, then returned to fight at Atlanta and was wounded again.

Pvt. J.H. McGee, Company C

Discharged for pthis-pulmonalis, then five months later re-enlisted and fought for the duration of the war.

Pvt. Sam Birdwell, Company K

Made the Confederate Roll of Honor at Murfreesboro and had 26 holes shot in him and his clothes at Allatoona Pass, but was still able to capture a Yank horse and ride off.

Pvt. E.H. Oliver, Company E

Discharged for burned hand in June, 1862. Re-enlisted January 1863 and was shot at Chickamauga which ended his military career.

Pvt. Wilson Prior, Company E

Discharged September 1962 due to chronic rheumatism after walk across Tennessee and Kentucky. Re-enlisted in January 1863 and fought the rest of the war, to be shot in the last battle at Spanish Fort.

Cpl. James Loden, Company I

Discharged November 1861, re-enlisted and was severely wounded at Chickamauga.

Pvt. Jack Wall, Company F

Discharged June 1862, reenlisted in March 1863 and fought the entire war.

APPENDIX G

MEN WHO SURRENDERED WITH THE UNIT
AT CITRONELLE, ALABAMA, MAY 4, 1865

Company A

(Consolidated) Commanded by Capt. J.F. Hall

Company	A	8 men
	F	21 men
	D	12 men

41
1 Capt. Hall
42

Company B

(Consolidated) Commanded by Capt. J. Ziegler
(acting Tenth Texas Commander)

Company	B	16 men
	G	15 men
	K	12 men

43
1 Capt. Ziegler
44

Company E

(Consolidated) Commanded by Capt. W.F. Young

Company	E	6 men
	I	15 men
	H	11 men
	C	16 men

48

Another group surrendered at Citronelle, which was called Co. F (Detachment of Ector's Brigade). It was commanded by Lieutenant Armstrong (the Tenth Texas hero at Allatoona Pass). It included fifty-six men from Ector's Brigade and three, including Armstrong, from the Tenth Texas.

Total who surrendered per the surrender rolls was 137 men. Per the compiled personnel records, 159 men surrendered at the end of the war with the Tenth Texas. For some reason, the twenty-two men did not get their names on the surrender rolls.

Private Littlejohn, a teetotaler, in his letter referred to his officers — Ziegler, Hall, Young, and Armstrong — as "sot drunkards." Based on the author's combat experience, it could be assumed they were good old boys that enjoyed a stiff drink, while they discussed "busting caps" on the Yanks. Armstrong would have enjoyed describing the Yank that he bashed in the head with a rock at Allatoona Pass as he drug him and his flag out of the fortifications. Armstrong lived to the age of eighty-one. At his burial in 1922, only three members of Company I were still alive.

REGIMENTAL STATISTICS BY COMPANY

	Total	Never Left Texas	Discharged	Died Non-combat	Absent Without Leave	Detached Duty or Transferred
Staff	26		5	1		5
Company A	128	8	24	34	15	3
B	186	43	16	31	17	9
C	152	16	31	40	6	6
D	123	9	28	24	10	4
E	111	5	18	22	15	3
F	137	6	32	25	8	9
G	144	7	27	25	6	10
H	107	2	26	31	4	
I	127	3	28	33	1	9
K	93		18	25	4	5
Total	1,334	99	253	291	86	63

	Released Conscript Act	Killed, Seriously Wounded, or Prisoner— Never Returned to Duty	Hospital End of War Sick and Wounded	Present April 5, 1864, No Longer on Rolls	Other (see Appendix C for details)	Surrendered
Staff		6	1	2	2	4
Company A	2	22		9	2	9
B	10	22	5	13		20
C	3	17	3	9	2	19
D	1	23		7	4	13
E		21	2	11	4	10
F	2	26	2	2	1	24
G		33	3	13	4	16
H		16		9	5	14
I	1	23	2	9		18
K		22	2	5		12
Total	19	231	20	89*	24	159

*See Appendix B for explanation.

APPENDIX I

PERSONNEL OF THE 10TH TEXAS CAVALRY DISMOUNTED

Most of the following information is found in the Compiled Service Records in the National Archives. Various other sources were also used such as letters and other casualty reports. Citronelle, Alabama (north of Mobile) is where the 10th Texas surrendered at the end of the Civil War. The following codes are used:

- (k) Killed
- (w) Wounded
- * Indicates original member of company
- ( ) Age is in parentheses when known
- ($) Indicates value of horse and equipment when available in the records
- POW Prisoner of War
- (d) Died

Original Field Officers:

*Colonel Locke, Matthew F. (37)
elected Colonel, 10/3/61; submitted letter of resignation, 3/6/63, on Surgeon's Certificate of Disability, signed by Surgeon A.B. Flint of the 10th Texas Cavalry-"affection of the spine, asitis and chronic hepatitis."

Lt. Col. Barton, James M. (43)
$250, $40; not stated as present or absent, January-February, 1862.

*Major Ector, Wiley B. (32)
$150, $35; not stated as present or absent. Promoted to Brigade staff.

Field Officers at the Reorganization, May 8, 1862:

Lieut. Colonel Earp, C.R.
originally 1st Lt., company D; elected Lt. Col., 5/8/62; 10/27/63-granted 45 day leave-"Col. Earp ... would be of service in collecting or bringing back to the brig. men on the other side of the river." 7/3/65-paroled at Marshall, Texas.

Major Craig, William deLafayette
promoted to Major at the reorganization, 5/8/62; (w), Murfreesboro, TN, 12/31/62, right arm, severe; (w), 6/18/64-Atlanta; surrendered at New Orleans.

Other Field Officers:

Major Redwine, Hulum D.E. "Ras"
(w) Atlanta 8/20/64, Atlanta, GA, as absent, General Hospital; absent due to wound.

Birdwell and he were hit by the same cannon ball.

Quartermasters:

*Winbray, John A.(35)
$160, $35; resigned, 9/10/62.

Durkee, A.G.
commissioned Quartermaster, 5/8/62; on detached service at Auburn.

Commissary, of Subsistence:

Scott, Spencer B.
not stated as present or absent, January, 1862; appointed Commissary, 7/7/62.

*Moore, E.P. (30)
$200, $30; shown as Captain and Chief of Subsistence, Ector's Brigade.

Surgeons:

*Francis, C.C. (27)
$150, $35; January-February, 1863; shown as POW.

Flint, A.B.
appears as Assistant Surgeon; 4/5/64-present; transferred to be Division surgeon.

Assistant Surgeons:

Hart, V.T.
promoted to Assistant Surgeon on 6/5/62.

Hilliard, M.C.
assigned as Assistant Surgeon; (k), Chickamauga.

Adjutants:

*Ransom, Henry B.
shown as Adjutant, January-February, 1862; POW, 6/3/62, Boonesville, MS.

*Jarvis, J.J.
originally Sergeant-Major of regiment; (w), Murfreesboro, TN, 12/31/62, left arm; recommended for disability discharge on Surgeon's Certificate.

Sparks, W.J.
(w) Murfreesboro 12/31/62, shoulder, (w), Chickamauga, slight, returned to duty; 11/21/64 at Ladies Hospital, Montgomery, AL.

Chaplain:

Stovall, S.K.
appointed Chaplain, 5/13/62; resigned, 7/28/62, due to "continued ill health ... dyspepsia accompanied with chronic diarrhea."

Birdwell, George P.
originally private, Company G: commissioned Chaplain, 8/7/63; present, 4/5/64.

Sergeant-Major:
Kelly, J.W.
acting Quartermaster, (w) Chickamauga, 9/19/63, mouth-severe.

Commissary Sgt./Sergeant Major:
Brown, J.S.
POW, Citronelle, AL, 5/4/65
(as Commissary Sgt.).

Quartermaster Sgt:
Cherry, Isham P.
appointed QM Sgt., 5/8/62.

Weir, R.A.
POW, Citronelle, AL, 5/4/65.

Ordnance Sgt:
Walton, T.O.
appointed Ordnance Sgt., 4/17/62; POW, Citronelle, AL, 5/4/65.

Hospital Steward:
Walker, J.F.
appointed as regimental Hospital Steward, as "temperate, honest"; 4/5/64-present; POW, Citronelle, AL, 5/4/65.

COMPANY A, 10TH TEXAS CAVALRY REGIMENT

Original Officers:
*Captain McKnight, C.D. (37)
$200, $35; dropped.

1st Lt. Barnes, R. H. (30)
$150, $20; dropped.

*2d Lt. Crabb, T.J. (33)
$150, $20; dropped.

*Jr. 2d Lt. Wright, J.J.T. (25)
$140, $25; (w), Chickamauga, severe "gunshot wound entering left side, ranging downward and lodging in the iliac region.

Original Non-commissioned Officers:
*Orderly Sgt. Riggle, John W. (24)
$150, $20; (w), Murfreesboro, TN, 12/31/62, detached gathering conscripts, arresting stragglers and deserters 9/10/64-on detached service.

*2d Sgt. Thompson, Simon (40)
$200, $30; January, 1862; no later record.

*3d Sgt. Hart, Samuel H. (18)
$175, $25; POW, Citronelle, AL, 5/4/65.

*4th Sgt. Rowland, J.R. (24)
$150, $25; POW, 9/8/62; deserted, July, 1863, at Jackson, MS.

*1st Cpl. Farbrough, James W. (24)
no later record.

*2d Cpl. McMillan, James W. (23)
$150, $25; (w), Murfreesboro, TN, 12/31/62, right foot-severe, (k), in battle, Chickamauga, 9/20/63.

*3d Cpl. Front, W.G. (20)
$225, $25; no later record.

*4th Cpl. Nash, John C. (29)
$100, $25; transferred to Douglas' Texas Battery, 10/1/62.

Others:
*Ensign Siseloff, James B. (23)
$100, $25; POW, Citronelle, AL, 5/4/65.

Privates:
Allred, John A.
(27) $160, $25; unfit for 60 days, due to arthritis. 6'3", fair complexion, blue eyes, dark hair. A farmer.

*Aired, Thomas M. (22)
$150, $25; (w), Murfreesboro, TN, 12/31/62, right thigh severe; "knee joint in fixed position, not fit for any duty;" 6'0", fair complexion, light hair, blue eyes.

*Bain, T.C. (29)
$135, $25; POW, Citronelle, AL, 5/4/65.

*Bateman, J.T. (30)
$135, $25; discharged due to phthis pulmonalis, 5'6", fair complexion, gray eyes, dark hair. A farmer.

Bates, E.M.
POW, Citronelle, AL, 5/4/65.

Baxter, E.L.
(d), Guntown, MS, 5/10/62.

*Baxter, E.M. (27)
$220, $30; no later record.

Benton, T.F.
absent sick, September-October, 1863.

*Byrd, James A. (28)
$125, $25; present, 4/5/64.

*Bratcher, John A. (21)
$150, $5; (k), Richmond, KY, 8/30/62; (d) of his wound, 9/2/62.

Bratcher, William
discharge, 11/13/63, due to chronic diarrhea.

*Bryant, Charles B. (18)
$125, $25; (d), Jacksonport, Ark., 4/10/62.

*Bryant, W.A. (16)
$100, $20; (d), Little Rock, 4/9/62.

*Butler, J.R. (18)
$100, $20; POW, Chickamauga, 9/19/63; (d), 4/25/64, of inflammation of the lungs.

258

*Byram, John (17)
$100, $25; deserted, 8/23/63 at Morton, MS.

Carter, Abraham (22)
$100, $15; (k), Murfreesboro, TN, 12/31/62.

*Case, W.L. (17)
$100, $20; no later record.

*Conder, R.T.
no later record.

*Cook, S.L. (19)
$100, $15; (w), Murfreesboro, TN, 12/31/62, right thigh severely; discharged due to "contraction of tendons."

*Cooke, Alex (19)
$140, $20; shown as missing at Murfreesboro, Tn, 12/31/62.

*Cooper, B.Z. (19)
$130, $20; POW, Citronelle, AL, 5/4/65.

*Crabb, S.F. (19)
$150, $20; (d), Holly Springs, MS, 6/30/62.

*Crow, William
deserted, 8/22/63,at Morton, MS.

*Davis, David B. (19)
$135, $25; (d), Macon, MS, 9/17/62.

*Dearborn, J.H. (31)
$200, $30; POW, Stones River, 12/31/62.

*Demet, John (21)
$100, $15; (d) Macon, MS, 6/5/62.

*Demmet (Dement), Charles (19)
$175, $20; 4/5/64-present.

*Demmet, George (17)
$110, $20; discharged 6/12/62.

*Essary, W.L., (18)
$125, $15; POW, Chickamauga, 9/19/63.

*Faulkner, A.J. (27)
$140, $35; (d), Jacksonport, AR, 4/3/62.

*Finley, Z.R. (23)
$80, $30; (w) Chickamauga, slight and returned to duty; POW, Citronelle, AL, 5/4/65.

Fisher, J.
(d), Little Rock, 5/30/62.

*Fletcher, William Lt. (23)
$100, $30; left sick at Barboursville, KY, POW-deserted in KY.

*Flournoy, R.R. (20)
$125, $25; "killed by the cars at Meridian, 1863."

*Flournoy, S.H. (19)
$185, $15; (d), Jacksonport, AR, 4/3/62.

*Fowler, W.H. (22)
$150, $25; left at Little Rock, 2/27/62, "on account of illness."

*Gholston, W.J. (21)
$125, $20; (d), Little Rock, 3/31/62.

*Goode, M.V. (23)
$150, $25; (w), Murfreesboro, TN, 12/31/62, head and shoulder-slightly; POW, near Chattahoochie.

Goode, T.G. (21)
discharged 7/31/62; age, 21; 5'6", dark complexion and hair, black eyes. A clerk.

*Graves, T.J. (20)
$125, $30; (d), Macon, MS, 5/28/62.

Greene, T.W.
(k), Chickamauga, 9/20/63.

*Hendricks, Martin V. (18)
$150, $25; (d) 8/15/62.

*Horton, C.L. (46)
dropped from roll, 7/21/62, by order of commanding general.

*Jones, A.A. (20)
$125, $20; discharged, 6/23/62, for pulmonary affection; 6'0", fair complexion, gray eyes, light hair. A farmer.

*Jones, A.H. (22)
$150, $20; present (as musician), 4/5/64-absent on detail.

*Jones, Clark (18)
no later record.

Kelly, J.L.O.
no later record.

*Kerr, W.M. (23)
$100, $20; (d), at Little Rock, 5/30/62.

Knox, William M. (21)
discharged as his measles "settled in [his] lungs." 5'4", dark complexion and hair, black eyes.

*Lindsey, J.M. (23)
$140, $25; (d) in hospital 9/19/63.

*Lindsey, W.P. (18)
$140, $25; (d), Memphis, TN, 6/25/62.

Livingston, Charles H.
transferred to the navy.

*Long, Thomas (22)
$140, $25; (d), General Hospital, Macon, MS, 6/12/62.

Maloney, W.H.
(w), Murfreesboro, TN, 12/31/62, right arm-severe; 4/5/64-absent due to wound.

*McBride, A.A. (30)
$200, $30; POW Citronelle, AL, May, 1865.

McGee, John A.
discharged 6/22/62.

*Miller, F. (36)
$125, $20; discharged at Readyville, TN
(Conscript Act), 12/17/62. 5' 10", dark
complexion and hair, black eyes. A carriage-
maker.

*Moore, A.J. (23)
$160, $25; (k), Murfreesboro, 12/31/62.

Moore, O.B.
deserted near Canton, MS, 6/1/63.

Murray, George
(d) at Fair Ground Hospital, Atlanta, GA,
2/19/63.

Murray, Robert A.
(d), Little Rock, 3/12/62.

*Murray, S.F. (26)
$150, $25; (w) Murfreesboro,TN, 12/31/62,
right thigh; 4/5/64-present.

Noyes, Robert
shown as chief bugler; (w), Chickamauga,
leg-slight, detached guard at Baker Creek
Bridge, on Muscogee Railroad, near
Columbus, GA, "to November 30, 1864."

*O'Keily, John L. (21)
$150, $25; also shown as nurse, 4/5/64-
present.

Parker, Jesse L. (46)
discharged, 12/17/62 (Conscript Act);
5'10", dark complexion, hazel eyes, black
hair. A blacksmith.

*Parker, L.F. (27)
$140, $20; detailed to drive wagon; no later
record.

Parker, W.L. (38)
"Chronic disease of stomach, atrophy of
liver." (d) 9/12/62 at Covington, KY; 5'8",
fair complexion, blue eyes, chestnut hair. A
farmer.

*Parris, E.V. (16)
$175, $30; no later record.

Patton, B.
deserted 8/23/63, at Morton, MS.

*Patton, Jacob (30)
$100, $20; no later record.

*Phillips, Houston (23)
$125, $20; deserted at Cynthiana, KY,
8/20/62.

Pierce, G.G.
"sent home with horses, not returned."

*Pierce, Thomas (19)
$140, $20; (w), Murfreesboro, TN,
12/31/62, left arm; deserted at Morton, MS,
8/23/63.

*Raines, George R. (20)
$125, $25.

*Rains, P.P. (24)
$165, $25; 4/5/64-present.

*Rains, W.F. (23)
$100, $25; (d), Guntown, MS, 6/10/62.

*Rainwater, B.F. (23)
$100, $20; (d), Chattanooga, TN, 7/13/62.

*Ratliff, B.Y. (41)
$50, $20; detailed to drive wagon; discharged 4/17/62.

*Ray, James L. (20)
$150, $20; 4/5/64-present.

Ray, John C.
name appears on rolls at Texas General
Hospital, Quitman, MS, as cook; POW,
Citronelle, AL, 5/4/65.

*Reed, B.M. (19)
$125, $25; (d) at Atlanta hospital, 2/24/63.

*Reeder, A.D. (17)
$150, $20; (d), Little Rock, 4/30/62.

*Reeder, A.N. (19)
$140, $25; deserted; 8/23/63, at Morton,
MS.

*Robertson, S.G. (23)
$100, $20; (d), Tupelo, MS, 7/16/62.

*Rushing, John C. (19)
$140, $30; deserted, 8/23/63, Morton, MS.

Sartain, J.F.
deserted, July, 1863, at Jackson,MS.

*Shamburger, W.M. (25)
$150, $20; (d), Little Rock, 3/31/62.

*Shipp, J.M. (18)
$140, $25; (w), Chickamauga, arm-slight,
discharged, 11/24/63, due to gunshot
wound, "entering upper 3d of arm, passing
across the elbow ..."

*Shuford, A.M. (30)
$125, $25; (d), Little Rock, 4/6/62.

*Slaughter, G.H. (18)
$125, $25; deserted at Bridgeport, TN,
11/20/62.

*Stuart, J.R. (19)
$140, $25; (d), Enterprise, MS, 7/4/62.

*Tharp, R.G. (24)
$125, $20; (d), Guntown, MS, 3/30/62.

Tollett, W.W.
deserted, 8/23/63, at Morton, MS.

*Trousdale, James (23)
$150, $20; (d), Enterprise, MS, 6/1/62.

Tumlinson, James R.
(d), Camp Barton, Texas, 12/19/61.

Trout, W.S.
detailed as body guard for Major Ector; paroled at Marshall, Texas, 7/9/65.

*Turman, T.G. (23)
$175, $35; (w) Nashville, admitted to Way Hospital, Meridian, MS, 1/19/65, for wound.

*Turman, W.H.H. (20)
$140, $35; shown as (d) of gunshot wound, Nashville, TN, 1/27/63.

*Turner, Frank (28)
$150, $30; (d), Macon, MS, 5/27/62.

Vannay, J.W.
discharged 6/25/62.

Wagner, Lisby (17)
"unfit for duty 60 days", due to pthis, pulmonalis; 5'10", light complexion, black eyes, dark hair. A farmer.

*Waldrip, A.J. (27)
$140, $25; (w), Chickamauga, slight; 4/5/64-absent due to wound.

*Ward, J.W. (24)
$140, $25; (d), Jacksonport, AR, 4/27/62.

*Warren, T.J. (23)
$125, $25; detailed to drive wagon; sent from Jacksonport sick, and [not] heard from since."

*Wheeler, G.W. (23)
$150, $25; discharged, 4/17/62.

*Wheeler, Henry (28)
$125, $25; (d), Little Rock, 3/30/62.

*White, A.E. (23)
$150, $25; (d), Enterprise, MS, 6/20/62.

*White, David Milton (23)
$160, $30; discharged 3/20/63.

*White, J.A.B. (26)
$160, $30; "sent home with stock/horses, not returned."

White, S.C.
POW, Chickamauga, 9/19/63.

*Williams, John P. (31)
$150, $25; 4/5/64-absent on furlough; AWOL in Wood County.

*Williams, W.F. (22)
$150, $25; 4/5/64-present.

*Wright, T.H. (18)
$125, $30; 4/5/64-present.

*Yarbrough, G.G. (25)
$140, $25; deserted, 11/20/62, at Bridgeport, TN.

Yarbrough, J.F.
(k) in the battle of Richmond, KY, 8/30/62.

Yarbrough, J.W.
(k) in the battle of Richmond, KY, 8/30/62.

*Yarbrough, W.M. (28)
$125, $25; (d), Little Rock, 4/19/62.

*Yoder, D.A. (26)
$140, $25; POW, Citronelle, AL, 5/4/65.

COMPANY B,
10TH TEXAS CAVALRY REGIMENT
"Wood County Rebels"

Original Officers:

*Captain Wilson, John W. (33)
$200, $30; 5/25/62; dropped.

*1st Lt. Cannon, Joseph W. (31)
(w), Chickamauga-(d) of his wound, 9/27/63.

*2d Lt. Stout, Henry
dropped; relieved from command, 5/25/62.

*Jr. 2d Lt. Rozell, James M. (28)
$160, $25; dropped—discharged from service, 6/13/62.

Original Non-Commissioned Officers:

*1st Sgt. Ziegler, Jacob (36)
$140, $30; (w), Murfreesboro, TN, 12/31/62, POW, Meridian, MS.

*2d Sgt. Austin, James M. (35)
discharged under Conscript Act.

*3d Sgt. Benton, F.M. (40)
$150, $30; discharged under Conscript Act.

*4th Sgt. Brown, John W. (18)
(w), Chickamauga, arm; AWOL; submitted application to be transferred to Company E, Brown's [35th Cavalry] Regiment.

*1st Cpl. Reinhardt, R.S. (21)
$150, $20; (d), 6/7/62.

*2d Cpl. Conger, Thomas Eli (19)
$100, $20; 4/5/64-AWOL.

*3d Cpl. Willingham, R.T. (22)
$80, $30; 4/5/64-present.

*4th Cpl. Bentley, John H. (22)
west of MS River, "against orders".

Other:

*Ensign Harris, David (41)
(d) or discharged.

*Bugler Rozell, G.W. (26)
$175, $20; (d), 5/19/63.

*Bugler Simpson, Christopher Columbus (21)
$200, $30; discharged 4/17/62.

*Farrier Duncan, Silas (39)
$120, $20; (d) near Loudon, TN, 8/5/62.

Privates:

*Adam, A.L. (34)
$125, $20; no later record.

*Angell, John W. (28)
$100, $20; POW, Citronelle, AL, 5/4/65.

*Bailey, S.P. (23)
$100, $25; (w), Murfreesboro, TN,
12/31/62, head "gunshot wound to the
head ... [which has] rendered me entirely
unfit for duty." Letter from Asst. Surgeon
A.J. Spencer-..."fracturing both cranial
plates of skull...frequent attacks of
apoplexy."

Attaway, E.L.
4/5/64
shown as absent sick.

*Attaway, David (19)
(w), Chickamauga, foot, 4/5/64-present.

*Ayers, William H. (18)
at Texas Hospital, Auburn, AL, dated
4/30/64.

Ayers, R.S.
no later record.

*Azbell, J.V. (19)
name appears on list of absentees, Ector's
Brigade.

*Azbell, H.M. (21)
AWOL, in Wood County.

Baird, Alex
name appears only on enlistment roll at
Quitman, Texas.

Bates, Daniel
4/5/64; "this man was detached as guard
for ordnance stores and was kept by Div.
Ord. Off. w/o notification to his command."

*Bates, William (22)
$100, $20; (d), 3/29/62.

Baxter, J.F.
no later record.

Bayles, Charles
discharged under Conscript Act, 6/25/62.

Belcher, J.W.
(k), 8/30/62 at Richmond, KY.

Bell, David
discharged 4/7/62.

Bell, G.W.
4/5/64-present; at Way Hospital, Meridian,
MS, 1/29/65 for wound. POW, Citronelle,
AL, 5/4/65.

*Bell, James A. (17)
$120, $20; (d), 10/25/62, Cumberland Gap,
TN.

*Benton, Jacob (26)
(k), $130, $20; POW at Murfreesboro; (k)
Spanish Fort.

Benton, John L.
4/5/64-detailed as teamster; 5'9", gray eyes,
brown hair, dark complexion.

Berry, Darius A.
appeared before the Hospital Examining
Board, Selma, AL, 2/25/65-disease:
"V.S.M.B."

Berry, William
appears only on enlistment roll at Quitman,
Texas, 10/5/61.

*Blalock, J.J. (22)
$160, $25; January-October, 1863; discharged 1864.

*Boyles, Charles (27)
$125, $25; no later record.

*Brewer, T.J. (28)
$140, $20; (w), Murfreesboro, TN,
12/31/62, left arm; 4/5/64-present.

*Brown, J.P. (22)
$160, $20; POW, Meridian, MS, 5/9/65.

*Brown, J.S. (21)
$150, $20; (w), Richmond, KY, 8/30/62,
(w), Chickamauga, slight-returned to duty
promoted to Regimental Staff.

Brumley, W.B.
name appears only on enlistment roll at
Quitman, Texas.

Burnett, W.C.
AWOL, west of MS River; POW at Brandon,
MS, 7/18/63
5'11" light hair and complexion, blue eyes.

Burton, Jacob
POW, Citronelle, AL, 5/4/65.

Butler, J.F.
(d), 6/1/62.

*Byramo, Cyrus J. (26)
$150, $25; (d), 5/22/62.

Campbell, Tim
discharged, 11/15/62, 6'0", fair complexion, blue eyes. A farmer.

*Clark, W.G. (26)
$100, $25; "AWOL in Texas, P.O. unknown".

*Clayton, John (20)
$120, $20; present, 4/5/64.

Coats, J.A.
(d), 4/25/62.

*Coats, W.H. (21)
$200, $25; POW, Murfreesboro, TN;
12/31/62; exchanged with J.W. Johnson of
Company K, 3d TX Cavalry on 3/24/64.

*Collier, C.R. (25)
$80, $20; AWOL, all rolls from March-October, 1863; POW; Vicksburg, 7/4/63.

*Conoly, J.P. (17)
$120, $20; discharged, 6/14/62, Conscript Act.

*Cook, J.W. (17)
$100, $20; discharged, Conscript Act, 8/4/62.

Cooper, B.F.
name appears only on enlistment roll, dated 10/5/61.

*Crumpier, D.A. (22)
$125, $20; POW, Citronelle, AL, 5/4/65.

Davis, B.P.
discharged, Conscription Act, 6/25/62.

*Davis, Isaac A. (19)
$120, $20; (d), 5/16/62.

*Davis, J.M. (19)
$125, $20; 4/5/64-AWOL since March in Alabama.

*Davis, John D., Jr. (46)
$80, $20; discharged 6/20/62.

Dill, J.C.
appears on list dated 8/5/61, Quitman, Texas.

Duncan, James
discharged for disability.

Duncan, J.M.R.
"AWOL, Hunt County".

*Etheridge, M. (21)
$120, $25; no later record.

*Evans, B.G. (27)
$120, $25; (w), Murfreesboro, TN, 12/31/62, thigh-slightly; discharged on 1/13/64 "paralysis of left leg ... caused by wound from a shell. 5'10", fair complexion, hazel eyes, dark hair. A farmer.

Fields, A.J.
4/5/64-present.

Fields, W.C.
(d), 4/9/63.

*Forbis, O.S.
AWOL; September-October 1863.

Forbis, W.J.
enlisted at Quitman, Wood County, Texas, 8/5/61 later record.

*Fowler, W.M. (25)
$140, $25; discharged on Surgeon's Certificate, 5'10", fair complexion, black hair and eyes. A farmer.

Freeman, W.H.
enlisted 8/5/61; no later record.

Frize, H.B.
enlisted 2/7/62; (d), 3/12/62.

Garrett, B.F.
missing at battle of Murfreesboro, TN, 12/31/62; "lost at Murfreesboro".

*Garrott, A.H. (20)
$150, $30; (w), Chickamauga-thigh, discharged, "gunshot wounds rec'd, in battle", 5'10", fair complexion, dark eyes, light hair. A farmer.

*Garrott, John D.
enlisted 8/5/61; no later record.

Goley, R.L.
POW, Citronelle, AL, 5/4/65.

Grant, A. J.
Enlisted 9/25/61; (d), 4/9/62.

*Greer, Daniel (37)
$125, $20; no later record.

*Greer, James (51)
$140, $20 (d), 5/1/62.

*Greer, John J. (20)
$120, $15; POW. Citonelle, AL. 5/4/65.

Gunter, Samuel
enlisted 8/5/61; (d), 2/12/62.

Gunter, J.J.(28)
(w), Murfreesboro, TN, 12/31/62, severely, in foot, discharged; 5'10", fair complexion, blue eyes, light hair. A farmer.

Gunter, W.W.
discharged, 11/14/62, due to "piles, and disease of the spine."

Guy, J.W.
4/5/64-present.

*Haldeman, E.E. (21)
$125, $17; (d), 3/20/62.

Hall, J.R.
name appears on list dated 8/5/61. No later record.

Hamilton, A.F.
enlisted 2/5/62 at Clarksville by M. F. Locke; present, all rolls from 3/1/62-12/31/62, January-October, 1863; 4/5/64-present and reenlisted; at General Hospital, Marion, Al, 4/25/64 (as patient); shown as detailed as shoemaker for Dashiell's Battery, 6/30/64; POW, Citronelle, AL, 5/4/65, as a member of Company B, 10th Texas Cavalry-paroled at Meridian, MS, 5/9/65. Residence: Wood County, Texas.

Hamilton, W.F.
left sick at Readyville, TN; POW,10/31/62.

*Hanson, John M. (26)
$150, $20; POW, Citronelle, AL, 5/4/65.

Hanson, T.S.
private, Company I, 2d Texas-transferred to Company B, 10th Texas Cavalry "now in Trans-MS Dept" shown as AWOL.

Hanson, William F.
(w), Chickamauga, slight-returned to duty; 9/10/64, Lovejoy's Station, sick at hospital, Auburn, AL.

Harrell, D.H.
name appears on list dated 8/5/61; no later record.

*Harris, W.J.
missing at battle of Murfreesboro, TN, 12/31/62.

*Harris, W.T. (26)
name appears on list dated 8/5/61; no later record.

Harry, John T.
(w), battle of Richmond, 8/30/62; 4/5/64-present.

Hart, W.H. (22)
$100, $20; "unfit for duty 60 days, due to chronic diarrhea"-6'0", fair complexion, hazel eyes, dark hair.

Hay, George C.
detailed as nurse at Atlanta hospital, 4/5/64-present.

*Hay, Levi H. (21)
$140, $20; (w) Nashville; admitted to USA General Hospital #15 at Nashville, TN, 12/17/64; for gunshot wound; (d), 12/18/64.

Hill, C. C.
4/5/64
present.

Howard, Isaac N.
appears on list October 5, 1861. No later record.

*Howard, Jesse (31)
$100, $18; deserted at Chattanooga, 7/25/62.

Hoyle, L.A.
POW, Citronelle, AL, 5/4/65.

*Huggins, John W. (24)
$100, $20; mortally wounded, Chickamauga, 9/19/63-(d) of wound, 9/29/63.

Ingrain, J.J.
shown as present and reenlisted, 4/5/64.

Jerrod, James
name appears on list dated 8/5/61.

*Johnson, J.M. (24)
$135, $25; POW, KY; POW, soldiers of divers companies/regiments (detached).

Johnson, J.W.
admitted to Ocmulgee Hospital, Macon, GA, on 9/12/64 for gunshot wound "ball, entering right groin, and emerged at right nates(?), with amputation of right index finger." POW, Citronelle, AL, 5/4/65.

Johnson, T.L.
name on list dated 8/5/61.

Johnson, Willis G.
name appears on list dated 8/5/61.

*Johnson, W.J. (20)
$150, $30; AWOL, July-August, 1863; present, in arrest; 4/5/64-present.

*Kinchelow, E.B. (33)
issued disability discharge, chronic rheumatism. 5'10", fair complexion, blue eyes, dark hair. A farmer.

*King, Franklin A. (21)
(w), Chickamauga, slight; POW at Nashville, admitted to USA General Hospital (Colored and Small Pox), Chattanooga, (d), December 27 or 28, 1864.

*King, J.W. (26)
no later record.

Landers, W.B.
after 4/5/64 POW, admitted to Stonewall Hospital, Montgomery, AL, 10/18/64, POW, Citronelle, AL, 5/4/65.

Leverett, Dr. T.J.
name on list dated 8/3/61.

*Lindley, Robert A. (19)
$120, $25; discharged, 1/26/64 due to gunshot received in battle; 6'1 1/2", fair complexion, blue eyes, light hair. A farmer. Admitted to Marietta Hospital, 7/9/64, due to gunshot wound to the spine-sent to Gen. Hosp., 7/9/64.

*Lyles, B.D. (24)
$100, $20; admitted to Breckinridge's Division Hospital #1, Lauderdale Springs, MS, 6/27/63.

*Lyles, J.M. (21)
$120, $20; deserted,1/28/64.

Lyles, Washington
(w) through both thighs, Murfreesboro, TN, 12/31/62.

*Mansell, S.K. (18)
$140, $20; POW, Citronelle, AL, 5/4/65.

McCord, W.M.
name appears on list dated 8/5/61.

McFarland, James C.
AWOL, 7/5/63.

*McLaren, F.R. (21)
$125, $25; (d), 4/30/63.

McLaren, G.W.
(d), smallpox, April, 1863.

McMillian, P.R.
name appears on list dated 8/5/61.

Millsaps, C.J.
POW, Chickamauga, 9/19/63.

*Minick, J.W. (24)
$150, $25; "[unable to read] in, battle at Chickamauga"; Certificate of Disability Discharge, "Tubercular deposit, right lung ... debility and emaciation." 5'10", fair complexion, hazel eyes, light hair. A farmer.

Moore, J.E.
(d), 3/21/62.

*Moore, T.J. (23)
(w) Richmond, KY at 8/30/62; discharged due to Richmond wound; 5'10', fair complexion, blue eyes, light hair. A farmer.

Morgan, M.D.
name appears on list dated 8/5/61.

*Moseley, J.H. (31)
$120, $20; (w), Murfreesboro, TN-12/31/62, slightly in foot; (d), 3/13/63.

Oliver, J.D.
4/20/62 at Memphis, by Col. Locke; (d), 5/30/62.

*Palmer, J.R. (23)
$130, $20; (d), 6/13/62.

Payne, J.T.
4/5/64-present.

*Payne, W.E. (18)
$125, $20; POW, Citronelle, AL, 5/4/65.

Phillips, Lemuel
name appears on list dated 8/5/61.

Pond, W.L.
name appears on list dated 8/5/61.

*Price, Gary D. (23)
detailed on Pioneer Corps by order of Gen. French.

Price, James
name appears on list dated 8/5/61.

*Price, Thomas D. (26)
$125, $25; (d), 5/10/62.

Puckett, Nat
name appears on list dated 8/5/61.

Rambo, John H.
appears on list dated 8/5/61; no later record.

Redding, H.R.
8/11/64; name appears on hospital list (no date), "diarrhea,. ch.-able to bear transp."

Redding, John B.
POW, Citronelle, AL, 5/4/65.

Reeves, J.J.
discharged 6/11/62.

*Reinhardt, M.A. (20)
$130, $20; AWOL, July-October, 1863; POW, provost marshal, Memphis, TN, 9/1/63-sent to Alton, IL, 10/3/63.

*Richards, J.W. (21)
$130, $25; discharged from hospital, 10/30/62.

Rogers, F.M. (19)
$100, $20; (w) at Chickamauga, died of wounds, 9/24/63.

Rounceville, J.R,
appears on list dated 8/5/61.

*Rozell, John W. (18)
$130, $20; discharged, 6/25/62 due to Conscription Act.

Rozell, Peter
deserted on 1/26/64.

*Setzler, John
(d) 4/3/62.

*Setzler, L.T. (22)
$130, $20; (d), 5/4/62.

*Setzler, W.H. (26)
$130, $20; (d) of wounds received in battle, 8/31/62 [Richmond, KY].

Shamburger, J.W.
name appears on list dated 8/5/61.

*Smith, J.P.
$125, $20; (w) since muster; absent due to wound, July-October, 1863; (w), Nashville, admitted to St. Mary's Hospital, West Point, MS, 1/7/65, due to gunshot wound-transferred, 1/7/65.

*Smith, Newton
$120, $20; admitted to Way Hospital, Meridian, MS, 1/18/65, for wound; POW, Citronelle, AL, 5/4/65.

*Starr, William (22)
$120, $20; (d), 3/28/62.

*Stephens, J.S. (26)
$130, $20; POW, Murfreesboro, TN; at Lumpkin Hospital, Rome, as nurse, General Hospital, Tuscaloosa, AL, sick.

Strickland, W.L.
(w), Murfreesboro, TN, 12/31/62, both thighs severe, discharged due to "wounds received in battle, both thighs and face, injuring sight of right, eye", 6'1 1/4", fair complexion, dark eyes and hair. A farmer.

Swain, M.R.
4/5/64-present.

Taylor, T.N.
discharge, under Conscript Law 6/25/62.

*Thompson, R.F.
$200, $30; no later record.

Tippett, William
appears on list dated 8/5/61.

Tritall, J.C.
(k) in battle, Richmond, KY, 8/30/62.

*Usselton, R.W.
shown as deserted, 2/27/64.

Vaden, Olerver
name appears on list, dated 8/5/61.

*Vickery, Daniel (28)
$120, $20; (d), 3/25/62.

*Vickery, James S. (26)
$100, $25; (d), 6/19/62.

Vickery, A.H.
name appears on list, dated 8/5/61.

Waters, J.M.
appears on list, dated 8/5/61.

Watts, W.G.
detached to Van Dorn's body guard.

*Weathers, W.M. (30)
on roll at Texas General Hospital, Quitman, MS; on roll at Texas Hospital, Auburn, AL; POW, Citronelle, AL, 5/4/65.

*Webster, A.S. (34)
$120, $20; discharged, 6/25/62, under Conscript Act.

*Weed, J.J. (23)
$120, $25; no later record.

Wheeler, W.H.
appears on list dated 8/5/61.

White, W.H.
appears on list dated 8/5/61.

Willingham, B,T.
appears on list dated 8/5/61.

*Willingbarn, Ed G. (24)
$120, $20; (d), 3/16/62 at Benton, AR.

*Wilson, C.C. (16)
$100, $20; discharged under Conscript Act, 6/25/62.

*Wilson, J.M. (33)
$100, $25; (d), 11/25/62, Marietta, GA.

Woods, J.J.
(d), 5/10/62.

Wright, J.A.C.
(d), 3/8/62.

*Yandell, Samuel (33)
$130, $30; (d), 3/3/62.

COMPANY C,
10TH TEXAS CAVALRY REGIMENT

Original Officers:
*Captain Rucker, James H. (40)
$175, $30; dropped.

*1st Lt. Holbert, Claiborne D. (36)
$160, $30; dropped.

2d Lt. McGee, W.G. (21)
$175, $30; (w), Chickamauga knee-slight; absent due to wound, admitted to Way Hospital, Meridian, MS, 1/17/65, 2/16/65, 3/7/65, for wound.

*Jr. 2d Lt. Hagens, W.B. (33)
$125, $30; POW, Citronelle, AL, 5/4/65.

Original Non-commissioned Officers
*1st Sgt. Griffin, John Bunn (22)
$160, $25; (w), Murfreesboro, TN, 12/31/62, right foot, severe, 3/9/63-foot amputated at ankle; gathering conscripts- "wounded and entirely disabled".

*2d Sgt. Earp, James (24)
$125, $25; discharge signed by Capt. McGee. 5'10", fair complexion, hazel eyes, dark hair. A farmer.

3d Sgt. Kaufman, John H. (26)
$130, $25; (d) at Memphis, TN.

*4th Sgt. Weir, C.C. (22)
$140, $30; (k), Chickamauga, 9/19/63.

*1st Cpl. Duncan, T.A. (27)
$125, $30; (d), Upshur County, Texas, 1/14/62.

*2d Cpl. McGee, James T. (22)
$150, $35; (w) in battle, Richmond, KY; (k) at battle of Murfreesboro, TN, 12/31/62.

*3d Cpl. Mobley, Alex H. (28)
$130, $20; killed by J.L. Lowery, 4/11/63.

*4th Cpl. Howard, Calvin (20)
$130, $30; (d), 6/1/62.

Other:
Ensign Dearmore, Thomas B. (23)
$150, $25; (d), 5/20/62.

*Bugler Jones, Samuel (20)
$140, $25; (d) of disease.

Privates:
*Allford, Erasmus L. (18)
$175, $30; POW, Citronelle, AL, 5/4/65.

Allison, J.N.
enlisted 10/7/61; $200 (mule). No later record.

*Allison, Thomas J. (38)
$150, $10; (d), 4/30/62 of typhoid fever.

*Andrews, John B. (22)
$140, $30; (w), Murfreesboro, TN,
12/31/62, thigh-seriously.

*Armstrong, William P. (21)
$175, $25; shown as POW, 10/17/62, 5'7",
blue eyes, light hair and complexion. (d),
Quitman, MS, 8/28/63.

Barnes, A.
enlisted at Quitman, 10/7/61; $330 (2
mules); no later record.

*Barton, James B. (22)
$125, $25; (d), 5/14/62.

Beasley, S.W.
enlisted 10/7/61; $175 (mule), no later
record.

*Black, Henry L. (32)
$150, $25; (d), 5/1/62.

Brooks, J.H.
"discharged in Texas, date unknown, by
Conscript Act."

*Brown, James H. (23)
$100, $25; discharged 10/7/62, 5'10", dark
complexion and eyes, black hair. A farmer.

*Brown, Thomas
-detached to drive wagon.

*Bryson, John A. (20)
$150, $25; POW, Citronelle, AL, 5/4/65.

*Bumpass, James (25)
$100, $25; discharged, 4/14/62.

Careman, C.B.
discharged.

*Castleberry, James (22)
$125, $25; (d), 3/4/62.

Christman, G.
enlisted 10/7/61, no later record.

*Clingman, F.H.
$100, $25; AWOL, July-October, 1863.

*Coffman, Caswell N. (23)
$140, $30; (d), 7/20/62.

Cox, A.H.
4/5/64-present.

Craver, David A
$250, $40; 4/5/64-present.

Craver, L.L.
(d), 2/19/63.

Craver, W.H.
(d), 5/29/63.

Croam, C.L.
left sick at Little Rock.

Crossley, P.G.
present and temporarily attached to
Company I, 14th Texas Infantry, 2/15/64.

*Davie, Seth M.
$175, $30; 1/24/64-shown at Eufaula, AL,
gathering conscripts, arresting deserters;
POW, Citronelle, AL, 5/4/65.

Davis, B.B.
AWOL, July-October, 1863.

Davis, W.H.
(k), Murfreesboro, TN; 12/31/62.

Dean, J.F.
4/5/64-present.

Dearmore, G.W.
(w), Murfreesboro, TN, 12/31/62, arm-seri-
ous; 4/5/64-present.

Dudley, James (21)
discharged. "Unfit for duty", 6'1", light
complexion, dark eyes, black hair. A farmer.

*Dudley, John T. (25)
$130, $25; discharged, 6/19/62; 6'1", fair
complexion, blue eyes, dark hair. A carpenter.

*Edwards, J.H.
mule, $75; no later record.

*Evans, Watson B. (26)
$130, $35; sick at hospital.

*Ferguson, James A. (23)
$140, $25; AWOL, July-October 1863.

Fincher, W.B.
(d), 7/3/62.

Fincher, W.S.
(d), 6/1/62.

Fisher, G.A.
POW, Citronelle, AL, 5/4/65.

*Flint, Abijah B. (23)
$150, $25, transferred to Regimental Staff.

Fox, John
no later record.

Furgason, A.R. (27)
$110, $30; (d), 5/30/62.

*Garrett, John W.
$175, $35; (d), 8/30/62.

*Garrett, Leonard H.
$150, $40; no later record.

George, C.A.
(d)-no date.

George, J.W.
no later record.

*German, W.C. (17)
$165, $25; (d), 5/3/62.

Garmand, C.B.
discharged, 7/8/62, due to gunshot wound
of left hand. 5'10", fair complexion, hazel
eyes, light hair. A farmer.

*Gillam, John C. (19)
$140, $20; no later record.

*Gillam, William II. (20)
$125, $15; (w), Murfreesboro, TN,
12/31/62, left breast, slightly; absent on
wound furlough.

Gingles, C.M.
(w), Murfreesboro, TN, 12/31/62, arm-seri-
ous; (w) New Hope Church-hit between the
eyes; (w) Nashbille-left hand; (w) Spanish
Fort-scalp wound; POW, Citronelle, AL,
5/4/65.

Gorman, William C.
$160, $45; no later record.

Gregory, Jonathan
mule, $225; no later record.

Halbert, L.E.
4/5/64-present.

*Hamilton, Archibald (17)
$125, $30; (w), Murfreesboro, TN,
12/31/62, head seriously; (k),
Chickamauga, 9/20/63.

*Harmon, Thomas (27)
$150, $25; 4/5/64-present.

*Harrison, James H., Jr. (19)
$120, $25; POW, Citronelle, AL, 5/4/65.

*Harrison, James H.
$140, $25; (d), 6/28/62.

*Hathaway, Pleasant (20)
$135, $25; discharged at Loudon, TN, for
pthis, pulmonalis, 5'9", fair complexion,
blue eyes, light hair. A farmer.

*Hilliard, John B. (22)
$140, $25; (w), Chickamauga, leg slight-
returned to duty; 4/5/64-present.

*Holmes, William Lt. (22)
$130, $25; no later record.

Holyfield, C.H.
4/5/64-present
Lee Hospital, Lauderdale, MS, as patient,
4/19/64.

*Honeycutt, E.B. (27)
$150, $25; (d), 5/10/62.

King, E.M.D.
POW, Citronelle, AL, 5/4/65.

*Lee, George (22)
$135, $25; (d), 6/17/62.

*Lee, Isham M.
$125, $30; (d), 12/1/61.

Lee, James J.
on list dated 10/7/61.

*Lee, Robert T. (25)
$150, $25; promoted to QM Sgt.

*Leroy, Gilbert (52)
$140, $30; discharged; 5'10", fair complexion, blue eyes, light hair.

Little, James D.(28)
(w) battle, Richmond, KY, 5'6", blue eyes,
light hair and complexion; absent, wound,
furlough to Harrison County.

*Lowery, James L. (21)
$140, $25; killed Alex Mobley of this company, AWOL, 4/15/63.

Lunsford, John H.
discharged due to fracture of right knee-
signed by Surg. Raisford, 5'9", fair complexion, blue eyes, black hair. A farmer.

Maddox, L.H.
(d), 5/12/62.

Marshall, J. H.
appears on list dated 10/7/61.

Massey, W.H.
appears on list dated 10/7/61.

*Moseley, Elijah R. (21)
$140, $25; POW, Citronelle, AL, 5/4/65.

McCutcheon, A.D.
AWOL in Texas, 8/31/62-12/31/62,
McCutcheon resigned due to "double fistu-
la, unfit 10 months."

*McCutcheon, James (51)
$125, $25; discharged (pulmonalis) age, 51.
5'10", fair complexion, hazel eyes, light
hair.

McGee, J.H. (18)
discharged (pthis, pulmonalis). 5'10", fair
complexion, dark eyes and hair. A farmer.
POW, Citronelle, AL, 5/4/65.

McGough, J.T.
POW, 5/4/65 at Citronelle, AL.

McGrill, W. B.
(d), 8/17/62.

McKinney, David (42)
discharged (Conscript Law). 5'11", fair
complexion, blue eyes, light hair. A farmer.

Miller, William Y. (24)
discharged, 6'6", fair complexion, dark eyes,
light hair. A merchant.

Mings, J.M.
discharged.

Mings, J.T.
(d), 4/27/63.

Mings, Wesley
(d), 4/17/63.

Montgomery, James N. (20)
(w), Richmond, KY. Discharged for "gunshot
wound through the ankle." 6'2", light complexion, blue eyes, black hair.

*Montgomery, R.J.
$200, $40; (d), Collin County, Texas.

Moore, Dudley
(w), Murfreesboro, TN, 12/31/62, foot seriously; 4/5/64-present.

*Morgan, Daniel M.C.C. (22)
$175, $25; admitted to Grant (small pox) Hospital, Atlanta; returned to duty, 4/16/64.

*Moseley, Alfred M. (18)
$130, $30; (d), 7/7/62

Neal, D.L.
"D.L. Neal's substitute and draws his pay"- name of J.W. Valentine appears in column of names present.

*Neal, John D. (18)
$175, $25; (k), Chickamauga, 9/20/63.

*O'Bryan, Dennis B. (25)
$175, $25; (w), Murfreesboro, TN, 12/31/62, thigh-slight; 4/5/64-present; (w) Allatoona.

Orton, William
discharged at Loudon, TN, 11/20/62, for pthis, pulmonalis. 5'10", sallow complexion, blue eyes, dark hair. A farmer.

*Pace, Cyon (Sion) (47)
$125, $20; discharged at Readyville, TN, 12/22/62; age, 48. 6'0", light complexion, blue eyes, auburn hair. A mechanic.

*Patrick, Charles R. (22)
$135, $25; (d), 3/21/62.

*Patrick, James H. (18)
$100, $25; POW, Citronelle, AL, 5/4/65.

*Phillips, E.S. (19)
$140, $25; POW Murfreesboro, TN, 12/31/62; (w), Chickamauga, leg-slight; POW, Meridian, MS.

Phillips, J.F.
(d), 5/15/62.

*Pierce, Silas M. (23)
$125, $20; shown as POW; (d), 1/27/63.

*Poer, Robert B. (18)
$140, $30; (w), Murfreesboro, TN, 12/31/62, head slightly; exchanged as Sgt. with Jeff Williams of 3rd Texas Cavalry.

Pritchert, J.M.
(d) 5/19/62.

*Ray, John W. (26)
$100, $30; discharged, due to "disc. of obercron, paralysis of hand"; 5'4", blue eyes, dark hair. A school teacher.

*Ray, William F. (21)
$125, $25; (d), Fairground Hospital, Atlanta, GA.

*Ridley, Robert H. (24)
$125, $35; (w) Murfreesboro, TN, 12/31/62, hand seriously; (d), 3/29/63.

Ross, M.V.
(d), 6/15/62.

Schooler, J.W.
on roll at Lee Hospital, Lauderdale, MS, admitted 8/19/64.

*Shepherd, James R. (28)
$100, $25; discharged, 8/23/63, at Morton, MS, due to "enlarged spleen, general pneumonia." 5'10", dark complexion, black eyes and hair. A farmer.

*Shepherd, William W. (21)
$120, $20; (w), Murfreesboro, TN, 12/31/62, arm seriously; .

Shields, J.H.
POW Citronelle, AL, 5/4/65.

*Simpson, George W. (23)
$150, $25; (d), 6/15/62.

Smart, W.W.
(d), 6/5/62.

Smith, D.A.
POW, Citronelle, AL, 5/4/65.

*Spratt, John J. (23)
$175, $35; POW, Chickamauga, 9/19/63.

*Stiles, A. Benton (20)
$125, $25; (w), Murfreesboro, TN, 12/31/62, arm seriously; admitted to Yandell Hospital, Meridian, MS, 4/5/65, for wound.

Stubbs, J.A.
admitted to Receiving/Wayside Hospital, Richmond, VA, 9/12/64.

Summerow, M.E. (19)
discharged; 5'10", fair complexion, hazel eyes, dark hair. A school teacher.

*Summerow, M.P. (25)
$140, $25; discharged; 5'9", dark complexion, black eyes and hair. A merchant.

Tally, W.J.
(d), 7/4/62.

Tanton, Nathan
(d), 3/25/62.

*Taunton, W.M.
(d), 3/22/62.

*Thomas, George (27)
$150, $30; (d), 5/1/62.

Thompson, H.P. (36)
discharged, due to chronic dysentery, camp fever; 6'2", fair complexion, gray eyes, dark hair. A physician.

*Turner, John R. (26)
$135, $30; shown as sick in Texas.

*Turner, Marcus D. (21)
$175, $30; transferred to Company B, 3d Texas Cavalry on 3/26/64, due to ulcer of right leg-letter signed by Surgeons DeAragon (9th Texas), McClarty (32d Texas Cavalry), and Flint (10th Texas Cavalry).

*Turner, Willis Benjamin (20)
$125, $30; absent in the Trans-MS-shown as AWOL.

*Walters, Phillip F. (or P.T.) (27)
$125, $25; detachment, dated 12/31/62; AWOL, July-October, 1863.

*Walters, Robert F. (20)
$100, $20; (w) in battle, Richmond, KY; 4/5/64-present.

*Watkins, James R. (42)
$140, $40; discharged, 6'1", dark complexion, blue eyes, black-hair. A farmer.

*Whitting, Jasper N. (-)
present, October, 1863. No later record.

Wilkes, John
name appears on list dated 10/7/61.

Williams, W.J.
POW, Citronelle, AL 5/4/65.

Williamson, Nathan H.
(w), Murfreesboro, TN, 12/31/62, knee seriously; (d) of wound, 2/7/63.

Williford, M.R.
discharged.

*Wilson, H.P. (25)
$130, $25; (d), 4/4/62.

*Wilson, William E. (30)
$135, $15; POW, Citronelle, AL, 5/4/65.

*Wright, Henry E. (23)
$125, $25; POW, Citronelle, AL, 5/4/65.

*Wright, John B. (27)
$125, $25; (w) Chickamauga, hand-severe; POW, Citronelle, AL, 5/4/65.

COMPANY D,
10TH TEXAS CAVALRY REGIMENT

Original Officers:

*Captain Earp, Alex (29)
dropped and resigned, 5/8/62.

*1st Lt. Earp, C.R. (34)
elected Lt. Col., 5/8/62.

*2d Lt. Smith, R.W. (24)
(w), Chickamauga, face severe; "gunshot wound to right side of face below the mala bone passing around the muscles of the neck and lodging in the posterior position where it now remains. Slowly regaining movement of his head and neck", paroled, Marshall, Texas, 7/3/65.

*3d Lt. Hefner, L.G. (24)
(w), Murfreesboro, TN, 12/31/62, leg and shoulder mortally; (d), 2/15/63.

Original Non-commissioned Officers:

*1st Sgt. Turner, W.W. (41)
$140, $20; dropped from roll.

*2d Sgt. Daniels, J.P. (21)
$15; (d), 6/1/62.

*3d Sgt. Morris, William (29)
$150, $15; (w), Murfreesboro, TN, 12/31/62; discharged on 4/13/63, due to gunshot wound. 5'8", fair complexion, blue eyes, dark hair. A farmer.

*4th Sgt. Matthews, W.B. (53)
$125, $20; discharged on 6/12/62.

*1st Cpl. Gage, Joshua (32)
$140, $20; (w), Murfreesboro, TN, 12/31/62, left arm; POW, Citronelle, AL, 5/4/65.

*2d Cpl. Sims, J. Newton (25)
$125, $20; (d), 5/19/63.

*3d Cpl. Daily, M. (18)
$75, $15; (d), 6/20/62.

*4th Cpl. Morris, H. (24)
$140, $20; (w), Chickamauga, thigh-slight; 9/20/63, in hospital."

Other:

*Ensign Davis, S.H., Sr.
"dropped from the roll, 7/20/62.

*Bugler Jones, L.G.S. (32)
$100, $10; discharged 6/13/62.

Privates:

Alston, J
discharged 6/13/62.

*Andrews, Johnson
$50, $20; present, with provost guard, September-October, 1863.

*Bailey, S.P. (23)
$100, $25; (w), Murfreesboro, 12/31/62, head slightly; "gunshot wound to the head ... rendered me entirely unfit for duty"; "fracture of both cranial plates of skull-frequent attacks of apoplexy."

*Bass, J.H. (22)
$125, $20; POW, at Citronelle, AL. 5/4/65.

*Bass, J.T. (18)
$20; POW, Louisville, KY, 10/31/62; (d), Vicksburg hospital, 11/26/62.

*Bassmore, J.L.
present, 4/5/64; paroled at Millican, Texas, 7/3/65.

*Bazemore, L.C.
shown as present 4/5/64.

*Beam, D.W. (25)
$100, $20; Arkansas, sick.

*Beaver, M.W. (24)
$75, $20; (d), 6/16/62.

Brown, William D.
AWOL, July-October, 1863.

*Burns, Samuel (22)
$100, $20
4/29/63, "very badly wounded."

*Cherry, Isham P. (28)
$80, $20; POW, near Nashville, TN, 12/15/64; 5'7", fair complexion, light hair, gray eyes.

*Cherry, N.J. (23)
$80, $15; (d), 5/24/63.

*Clinton, W.R, (24)
$100, $20; discharged, chronic diarrhea, 5'10", dark hair, eyes, and complexion. A farmer.

*Coffey, J.H. (21)
$80, $15; exchanged POW, Vicksburg, 11/15/62; (d), 5/8/63.

*Coker, J. (24)
$100, $20; no later record.

*Cope, A.H. (30)
$100, $15; POW, Citronelle, AL, 5/4/65.

*Cope, W.H.H. (21)
$80, $20; no later record.

Cornelious, J.M.
4/5/64-absent on furlough of 30 days, "now AWOL"; POW, Izzard County, 3/23/64; (d), 1/12/65 of variola.

*Coslet, A. (24)
$80, $20; no later record.

Cox, Sidney R,
(w) Atlanta, admitted to Ocmulgee Hospital, Macon, GA, 8/9/64 for "thigh-flesh, gang[rene] right"-transferred to Vineville, 8/25/64, (d) 8/25/64.

*Davis, G.W. (21)
$150, $20; missing at Murfreesboro, TN, 12/31/62; absent due to (w), July-August, 1863.

Davis, Samuel
discharged, 7/22/62, under Conscript Law.

*Davis, H. (60)
$80, $15; discharged.

Davis, J.J. (25)
$80, $30; (d), 7/9/62.

*Davis, J.M. (25)
$80, $15; on detached duty in Engineer Corps.

Davis, S.H.
left sick at Baldwin or Tupelo, MS, 6/4/62 (d), June, 1862.

*Davis, S.H., Jr. (18)
$125, $20; at Murfreesboro, sick.

*Davis, S.S. (20)
$80, $15; (d), 11/1/62.

*Dunnwoody, D.H. (41)
$150, $20; dropped from roll, 5'11", dark complexion and hair, blue eyes. A farmer.

*Earp, H. (18)
$125, $20; discharged, 6/13/62.

*Earp, J.C. (22)
$140, $20; (d), 5/18/62.

*Earp, R.M. (33)
$135, $30; discharged, 6/22/62.

Eaton, N.
detached service as wagoner by Gen. Walker-supply train for Walker's division.

*Ellis, M.C. (33)
$125, $25; (d), 12/17/62.

Farley, W.N.
POW, hospital attendant, paroled at Meridian, MS, 5/14/65.

*George, Arthur J. (20)
$150, $20; AWOL, 3/1/62-8/31/62; POW, 10/30/62, received at Vicksburg; AWOL; July-October, 1863.

*George, B.F. (22)
$125, $25; AWOL, July-October, 1863.

*George, Jairus H. (23)
$145, $25; (d), 5/10/62.

*Gilliland, A.F. (31)
$125, $25; "now absent in Trans-MS-Texas P.O. unk."

*Gilliland, H.C. (24)
$100, $15; present 4/5/64.

*Gilliland, S.G. (17)
$80, $20; (d), 7/15/62.

*Gilliland, W.H.
absent furlough to 2/16/62. No later record.

Goss, B.F. (28)
$140, $20; absent on detached duty in Conscription Dept., dated 8/20/64-(w), Atlanta, absent, at General Hospital; absent, due to wound.

*Goss, W.L. (22)
$140, $20; (w), Chickamauga, leg-slight, POW, Citronelle, AL, 5/4/65.

*Harper, W.G.
no later record.

Harrison, W.B.
left sick at Memphis, 4/25/62.

Hughes, J.H. (18)
$150, $25; appears on absentee report, Ector's Brigade.

Hurt, J.M. (20)
$140, $25; absent, sick.

Jones, F.M. (22)
$130, $25; (d), 6/11/62.

Jones, George W.Y. (27)
$125, $25; (d), 6/5/62.

*Jones, W.J. (20)
$80, $20; (d), 6/25/62.

*Jones, W.M. (22)
$135, $20; (d), of gunshot wound, 3/1/63 received at Murfreesboro.

*Lee, J.E. (23)
$160, $20; (d), no date given.

*Lilly, T.B. (32)
$125, $20; "dropped from roll", 7/21/62.

*Lindley, E. (23)
$140, $20; (d), 5/6/62.

*Long, John M. (23)
$130, $20; POW, Citronelle, AL, 5/4/65.

Manion, J.N.
discharged, 6/13/62.

Manley, M.D.
(d), 6/11/63.

Matthews, J.L. (20)
$125, $25; POW, Citronelle, AL, 5/4/65.

Mathews, W.N.
4/5/64, detailed as provost guard by Gen. Ector's order, dated 9/1/64-3/1/65-deserted in Tennessee.

Matthews, J.D.K.
3/20/64-detailed as orderly by Gen. Ector.

May, John S.
AWOL, July-October, 1863.

*McGee, W.Y. (25)
$100, $20; (d), 3/6/62.

*McKinney, C.A. (32)
$125, $30; discharged, 12/8/62.

*McMurtrey, W.C. (21)
$125, $20; present, September-October, 1863, no later record.

*McSpaddin, J.T. (26)
$125,$25; absent-sick. No later record.

*Merritt, D.D. (20)
$150, $25; (d), no date given.

*Milner, J.A. (24)
$150, $25; POW, Franklin, TN, 12/17/64; age, 27. florid complexion, light hair, blue eyes.

Murphy, H.D.
4/5/64-present.

Newberry, J.H.
7/5/63 absent-sick, now AWOL; name appears on POW roll, captured at Yazoo City, MS. Dark eyes and hair, 5'10".

*Porter, H.S. (20)
$80, $25; left at Murfreesboro, AR, sick. No later record.

Ringo, E.
(d), 7/12/63.

Ringo, Robert
(w), Murfreesboro, TN, 12/31/62, left arm-seriously; absent due to wound, discharged, 3/26/63, due to gunshot wound of left arm, 5'10", fair complexion, blue eyes, light hair. A farmer.

Ringo, Samuel
discharged, 6/12/62.

Robertson, J.T.
AWOL, July-October, 1863.

*Saunders, J.R. (19)
$80, $20; (d), 8/3/62.

*Shelton, W.V. (19)
$125, $25; AWOL, 3/1/62-8/31/62; POW, exchanged near Vicksburg, (w) Murfreesboro, TN, 12/31/62, head-mortally; (d), 1/31/63.

*Sherwood, —
(23)
$140, $25; no later record.

Shrum, Elisha
POW, Chickamauga, 9/19/63.

*Sims, Andrew (24)
$125, $25; (w), Murfreesboro, TN, 12/31/62, thigh and POW; (d), 5/1/63.

Sims, G.W.
AWOL, rolls of March-October, 1863.

Sims, J.B.
4/5/64-present.

*Smith, Henry L. (19)
$140, $20; (w), Murfreesboro, TN, 12/31/62, right thigh slightly; (w) Atlanta, gunshot wound passing through chest, 7/20/64.

*Smith, T.W. (39)
$100, $20; dropped from roll, 7/21/62.

*Smith, W.M. (23)
$150, $25; 4/5/64-present.

*Snider, W.F. (20)
$140, $25; 3/1/65-"deserted in Tenn."

*Speare, J.H. (22)
$125, $20; (w), left arm-seriously; shown as missing at Murfreesboro.

*Stapler, John T. (17)
$125, $20; (d), 8/1/62.

*Steelman, Alexander (19)
$100, $20; (w), Murfreesboro; TN; 12/31/62, left side, POW, Citronelle, AL, 5/4/65, 5'10", fair complexion, blue eyes, light hair. A farmer.

*Steehnan, J.A. (21)
$100, $25; POW, 10/16/62, Winchester, KY; 5'6", black eyes and and hair, dark complexion; 4/5/64 on detached service, west of MS River.

Tally, H.P.
POW, Citronelle, AL, 5/4/65.

*Taylor, G.W. (23)
$125, $25; no later record.

Taylor, T.W.
(d), 10/15/62.

Thornton, B.D.
sick, February, 1862. No later record.

Tillman, S.S.
(w), Murfreesboro, TN, 12/31/62, (w), Peachtree Creek, GA, 7/20/64, seriously; POW, Citronelle, AL, 5/4/65.

Trouell, Y.F.
discharged, 6/20/62.

*Tucker, J.M. (21)
$200, $30; POW, Citronelle, AL, 5/4/65.

Tuel, W. H.
POW, Citronelle, AL, 5/4/65.

*Turner, C.C. (22)
$160, $35; discharged 11/1/62; 6'0", fair complexion, blue eyes, light hair. A farmer.

Turner, G.W.
4/5/64-present.

Walker, W.J.
discharged, 6/13/62.

*Wallace, C.E. (29)
$150, $25; driving wagon.

*Warren, E.H. (21)
$125, $20; (d), 7/10/63. 5'6", light complexion, blue eyes.

Western, W.B.
POW, Citronelle, AL, 5/4/65.

*Williams, D.F. (17)
$140, $20; discharged, 6/21/62.

Williams, T.F.
discharged, 6/22/62.

*Wilson, S.T. (18)
$125, $25; (w), Chickamauga, face-severe; (w), Nashville, 1/28/65, for wound-furloughed.

*Wilson, T.C. (30)
$150, $25; no later record.

*Winn, T.H. (26)
$80, $15; no later record.

COMPANY E,
10TH TEXAS CAVALRY REGIMENT
"Bully Rocks"

Original Officers:

*Captain Redwine, Hulum D.E. "Ras" (24)
$200, $35; promoted to Major, 6/12/62; 4/28/64-absent on furlough; (w) Atlanta.

*1st Lt. Moore, William A. (37)
$140, $25; "not reelected as 1st Lt. at reorganization, 5/8/62-taken as substitute for W.D. Davis." October, 1863; present at Walker's Division Hospital, 4/5/64-present; admitted to Lee Hospital, Lauderdale, MS, on 4/19/64 as patient; name appears on roster at General Hospital, Marion, September, 1864, as patient.

*2d Lt. Brewer, W.T. (25)
$140, $25; 5/8/62-dropped.

*Jr. 2d Lt. Jones, Paul C. (26)
(d), Polk Hospital, Rome, GA, 7/23/63.

Original Non-commissioned Officers:

*Orderly Sgt. Van Sickle, E.S. (42)
$140, $30; no later record.

*2d Sgt. Cauley, John W. (19)
$140, $25; no later record.

*2d Sgt. Deason, J. Henry (21)
$140, $25; AWOL (as private), west of MS River, 8/31/62.

*4th Sgt. Melton, William (25)
$140, $25; (w), Chickamauga, knee slight; admitted to Way Hospital, Meridian, MS, for his wound, and furloughed.

*1st Cpl. Deason, John (18)
4/5/64-present and reenlisted, under arrest.

*2d Cpl. Engle, John (26)
$140, $25; no later record.

*3d Cpl. Cameron, J.M.
no later record.

*4th Cpl. York, William M. (30)
$130, $25; (w); Murfreesboro, TN, 12/31/62, leg seriously; POW, Citronelle, AL, 5/4/65.

Others:

Musician Wagoner, Daniel
(d), Columbus, MS, 6/15/62, of fever.

Privates:

*Arnold, M.V. (22)
$125, $25; POW, 5/4/65 at Citronelle, AL.

*Barber, John (22)
$160, absent, no later record.

Barker, S.D.
(d), 5/9/62.

Berry, G.W.
absent, AWOL, "left in KY", 4/5/64-absent
due to (w)-"supposed to be in Texas."

Berry, J.T.
enlisted 4/29/62 at Camp McIntosh, MS, by
M.F. Locke; discharged for disability,
5/17/62, Corinth, MS-"idiocy-incapable of
taking care of himself;" age: 28. 5'7", dark
complexion, black hair and eyes. A farmer.

*Berry, Samuel (21)
$150, $30; (k), Richmond, KY, 8/30/62.

Berry, Silas J.
POW, Citronelle, AL, 5/4/65.

Brewer, Leven
AWOL, west of MS River, January-April,
1863.

Buchanan, S.E.
AWOL, left in KY, 9/16/62; POW, name
appears on list of officers/men now in Trans-
MS-AWOL.

*Buckley, John (29)
$80, $15; 4/5/64-present sick, 5'11", light
complexion, blue eyes, dark hair.

Carr, W.L.
absent in Trans-MS-AWOL.

*Clay, William (17)
$100, $20; POW, Spanish Fort, AL, 4/8/65,
POW, Citronelle, AL, 5/4/65.

*Craig, Paul B. (18)
$140, $20; POW, surrendered at New
Orleans.

Culp, Henry (21)
(d), Pine Bluff, AR; 5'9", fair complexion,
blue eyes, dark hair. A farmer.

*Culp, L. William (24)
$140, $20; (d), Atlanta, May 17 or 23, 1863.

*Cunningham, James (22)
AWOL, May-October, 1863.

*Curbo, Thomas B. (19)
$125, $20; absent on furlough, July-August,
1863; AWOL, September-October, 1863.

*Curvin, Thomas (23)
$100, $20; absent-sick.

Davis, John W.
(w), Chickamauga, 9/18/63; POW,
Citronelle, AL, 5/4/65.

Davis, W.D.
discharged, 6/27/62-furnished substitute at
Camp Priceville, MS.

Deason, J.R.
(d), of the measles.

*Deason, R.C. (22)
$140, $25; (d), Macon, MS, of pneumonia,
5/31/62.

Deason, Walter
(d), Lauderdale Station, 7/10/63.

*Eachers, John A. (18)
$130, $20; discharged.

*Eaton, Joel (18)
$80, $20; (w), Chickamauga, slight; 4/5/64-
AWOL (as 2d Cpl.) since 11/7/63.

Floyd, Thomas J.
POW, Citronelle, AL, 5/4/65.

*Gatliff, Aaron (16)
$100, $25; surrendered at Citronelle, AL,
5/4/65.

*Gibson, Robert (33)
$75, $25; No later record.

Grigsby, G.W. (28)
discharged "shortening of one leg." 5'8",
dark complexion, black hair and eyes. A
farmer.

Hanack, Louis
"unfit for duties as a soldier," shown as
laborer at Selma arsenal, January-February
1864.

*Hardin, F.P. (37)
$140, $30; 4/28/64-name appears on roster
of commissioned officers of Ector's Brigade,
camp near Tuscaloosa, AL. (w), Atlanta,
absent on wound furlough.

*Hargroves, Edward (34)
$100, $15; absent-sick, May-October, 1863.

*Harvey, William H.H. (19)
$125, $15; (w), "Chickamauga, head;
4/5/64-present.

Hudman, Alvin
discharged, due to Chronic Rheumatism.

Hudman, Thomas
(d), Searcy, AR, of measles, 4/8/62.

*Hudson, Francis (18)
$150, $25; (d), of measles.

Hudson, Rufus
(d) at Little Rock, of measles.

Johnson, C.M.
(w) Nashville and POW—; admitted to USA

General Hospital #15, Nashville, 12/17/64-(d), of gunshot wound to left thigh, 12/25/64.

Kelley, John
POW, Citronelle, AL, 5/4/65.

Kelly, Anderson
(w), Chickamauga, leg, severe.

Kelly, J.M.
(w), Richmond, KY; July-October, 1863; shown as nurse at Buckner Hospital in Newnan, GA.

Kennedy, W.H.
absent (w) since muster, May-August, 1863; appears on roll at Texas General Hospital, Quitman, MS, 8/28/63.

*Langston, Nathan (36)
$150, $35; discharged for disability; age, 37; 5'8", fair complexion, gray eyes, light hair. A farmer.

Lewis, Sterling
(d), of consumption.

*Lloyd, Thomas B. (24)
$125, $30; (w), Murfreesboro, TN, 12/31/62, left leg; POW, 7/19/64 in Rodney, MS; 5'8 1/4", light complexion and hair, blue eyes.

Lloyd, W.E.
(w) Chickamauga; 4/5/64-present.

*Matthews, W.J. (28)
$150, (w), Chickamauga; (d), Flewellen Hospital, Cassville, GA, 10/20/63.

*Mayberry, George W. (21)
$130, $20; (d), Camp Van Dom, of congestion of the brain 3/30/62.

*Mayo, A.S. (25)
$140, $25; discharged, due to compound fracture of clavicle, upper shaft of humerus. Fair complexion, blue eyes, auburn hair. A farmer.

*McAnally, William (20)
$150, $30; (d), 5/11/63.

*McCarty, J.B. (28)
absent-sick.

*McCauley, James (22)
$140, $30; (w), Murfreesboro, TN, 12/31/62.

McCauley, John H.
4/5/64-present.

*McCauley, R.H. (20)
$130, $20; discharged on account of disability; 5'9". Fair complexion, blue eyes, dark hair. A farmer.

*McCauley, R.J.
$130, $25; 4/5/64-present.

*Melton, D.T. (27)
$130, $25; (w), Murfreesboro, TN; POW, Chickamauga, 9/19/63.

*Melton, J.T. (23)
$140, $30; discharged, due to pthis, pulmonalis, partial paralysis of lower extremities; 6', fair complexion, blue eyes, light hair. A farmer.

Moores, Alexander
4/5/64-present.

*Murff, Jerry (20)
$150, $30; shown as AWOL, west of MS River.

*Nelson, John (35)
$160, $30; AWOL, left in Kentucky, on 9/8/62; transferred to Company D, 14th Texas Cavalry.

*Nelson, J.W.C. (22)
$125, $25; hospital-sick.

Nelson, Taylor
(d), Jacksonport, AR, 3/31/62 (measles).

*Nevilis, P.J. (16)
$125, $25; left sick at Barboursville, KY, 8/29/62, "general debility following typhoid pneumonia-under age," 5'5", sallow complexion, hazel eyes, black hair.

*Oliver, E.H.
discharged, 6/24/62, due to burnt hand. Reenlisted 1/21/63 at Henderson, Texas; (w), Chickamauga, 9/18/63, 2/16/64, for gunshot wound-furloughed.

*Parrish, S.G. (18)
$80, $20; (d), Oil Trough, AR.

*Phillips, Caleb (22)
$100, $25; 4/5/64-present.

*Pinkston, Henry (19)
$140, $25; (d), Atlanta, GA, August, 1862.

Prior, George W.
POW, near Vicksburg, 7/4/63; 5'11 1/2", dark complexion, light hair, blue eyes.

Prior, William
(w), Murfreesboro, TN, 12/31/62, right thigh; POW Citronelle, AL, 5/4/65.

Prior, Wilson
discharged, due to chronic rheumatism. 5'10", fair complexion blue eyes, black hair. (w), Spanish Fort, admitted to Ross Hospital, Mobile, AL; for gunshot wound, 3/29/65.

Quaid, William Riley
(w), groin, Murfreesboro, TN, 12/31/62.

*Redwine, Rufus F. (26)
$140, $35; 8/31/62,-POW, (d), 12/1/62; 5'4". Blue eyes, light complexion, auburn hair. A physician.

*Riddle, Thomas (21)
$130, $25; no later record.

*Roundtree, J.H. (23)
$100, $20; (d), Jacksonport, AR, of measles.

*Rushing, Ben F. (19)
$150, $20; POW, Spanish Fort, 4/8/65.

*Rushing, Thomas (22)
$140, $25; discharged, 6/24/62; 5'9", fair complexion, blue eyes, dark hair.

Ryan, R.J.
(d), Enterprise, MS, of measles, 5/8/62.

*Sentel, John B. (26)
$150, $25; discharged 1/17/63 at Shelbyville, TN., on Surgeon's Certificate (sec., syphilis); 5'11", fair complexion, gray eyes, light hair. A farmer.

Skelton, A.W.
4/5/64-present.

*Smith, J.K. (22)
$175, $25; 4/5/64-present.

*Spence, Ira J. (24)
$150, $25; (w), Chickamauga, slight; 4/5/64-present.

*Stone, R,L. (19)
$125, $15; 4/5/64-AWOL since 2/15/64.

*Stone, W.J. (23)
$130, $25; 4/5/64-present, on extra duty as brigade teamster by order of Gen. Ector, 3/30/64.

Stovall, S.K.
resigned as Chaplain, 7/28/62.

*Summers, W.T. (23)
$125, $25; absent, west of MS River.

Taylor, J.L.
disability, due to "varicolle."

*Terry, James (17)
$150, $20; POW, Chickamauga, 9/19/63; enlisted in 5th U.S. Volunteers, 4/6/65.

Travis, W.W.
(d), of fever.

*Tucker, William W. (30)
$130, $30; no later record.

Turner, W.B.
(w), Chickamauga, leg amputated; name appears on roster of Invalid Corps.

Waggoner, Doc
AWOL, west of MS River.

Wagoner, Angus (18)
$100, $25; (d), of pneumonia, 5/18/62.

Wagoner, John (31)
$160, $25; discharged at Pittsburg, Texas, 12/22/61, due to sickness in family. 5'8",

dark complexion, black eyes and black hair. A farmer.

Welch, C.N.B.
(d), of measles.

*Welch, W.H.H. (20)
$125, $25; 4/5/64-present.

*Wimberley, Ezekiel A. (17)
$80, $25; 4/5/64-AWOL since 11/7/63 in Texas.

Wright, Silas
POW, Murfreesboro, TN.

*York, Jesse (28)
$125, $25; (d), 4/2/62, "choaking lungs."

Young, W.F.
(w) Chickamauga, slight; POW, Citronelle, AL, 5/4/65.

COMPANY F,
10TH TEXAS CAVALRY REGIMENT

Original Officers:

*Captain Craig, William de Layafette (44)
$175, $30; elected Major at the reorganization of the regiment, 5/8/62.

*1st Lt. Hull, Thomas P. (38)
dropped, no date given.

*Sr. 2d Lt. Garner, T.W. (40)
dropped, no date given.

*Jr. 2d Lt. Booty, A.J. (21)
$160, $25; (w), Chickamauga thigh; POW, in Tensas Parish, LA, 9/27/64.

Other Officers:

Capt. Smith, W.H.
"absent by permission since 2/12/63".

Original Non-commissioned Officers:

*O. Sgt. Walker, Sidney J. (23)
$125, $35; POW, Murfreesboro, TN, 12/31/62; paroled at Meridian, MS, 5/9/65.

*2d Sgt. Johnson, P.L. (33)
discharged, due to pthis, pulmonalis; 5'9", fair complexion, black eyes, dark hair.

*3d Sgt. Gray, James N. (23)
$130, $25; (w), Chickamauga, foot-severe; disabled for infantry duty due to wound-transferred to 3d Texas Cavalry, 11/10/63.

*4th Sgt. Hull, J.H.L. (18)
$135, $25; on detached duty, Gen. McCown's order.

*1st Cpl. Melton, Henry (19)
$130, $25; (w), Murfreesboro, TN, 12/31/62, left leg, sent to hospital; POW, Citronelle, AL, 5/4/65.

*2d Cpl. Bell, J.H. (29)
$125, $20; POW, Murfreesboro, TN, 12/31/62; admitted to CSA General Hospital, Charlotte, N.C. on 1/17/65, due to V.S. (gunshot wound), lower extremity.

*4th Cpl. Forsythe, James (20)
$140, $25; (w), Murfreesboro, TN, 12/31/62; POW, Citronelle, AL, 5/4/65.

Others:

*Ensign Hooker, James (43)
$140, $25; discharged.

*Bugler Hardy, J.F. (27)
$125, $25; AWOL, July-October, 1863.

Privates:

*Appling, C.C. (19)
$140, $20; (d) 5/25/62.

Armstrong, G.H.
shown as AWOL, July-October, 1863.

*Armstrong, R.B. (35)
$40, $25; discharged, 6/12/62.

Atkinson, G.F.
sent to Atlanta hospital, 4/18/63-(d), 5/20/63.

*Banks, Eli (19)
$120, $25; (w), at Atlanta.

*Barbee, C.L. (20)
$135, $15; (d), at Guntown, MS, 6/2/62.

*Bark, E.L. (30)
$130, $20; no later record.

*Benton, J.M. (18)
discharged, 6/20/62.

Bigger, Lee Theo.
4/5/64-detached as teamster for Military Court by Gen. Johnston.

*Bird, J.W. (28)
$130, $15; detached as wagoner.

Birt, A.L.
9/16/64-at Ocmulgee Hospital, Macon, GA; 9/18/64, for flesh wound left foot; POW, Citronelle, AL, 5/4/65.

Bowlin, James
(k) Chickamauga, 9/20/63.

*Brantley, J.S. (24)
dropped from rolls.

*Bryan, A.B.
appears on company muster-in roll; no later record.

*Campbell, D. (20)
discharged for disability; dark complexion, black hair and black eyes.

*Carriken, G.W. (21)
$200, $25; dropped from roll.

*Cauley, A.D. (24)
$120, $25; (k), Murfreesboro, TN, 12/31/62.

*Cauley, W.W. (26)
$130, $20; (k), Atlanta.

Cherry, H.J.
at Ross' Division Hospital, admitted 3/30/65 for contusis; POW, Citronelle, AL, 5/4/65.

*Clark, W.G. (22)
$80, $15; (d), Macon, MS, 6/2/62.

*Coats, J.A. (22)
$100, $25; POW, Citronelle, AL, 5/4/65.

Cogswell, W.V.
POW, Chickamauga, 9/19/63; (d), 12/13/63 (inflammation of the lungs), buried in grave #899, Chicago City Cemetery.

*Daniels, W.H. (21)
$80, $20; (k), Atlanta.

Fite, A.M.
(w), Atlanta

Fite, Monroe
discharged, Conscription Act; 1/1/63.

Fite, N.O.
10/13/63 for 45 days- "now in provost guard, Shreveport"; absent in Trans-MS-AWOL.

Fite, Smith L.
(w), Chickamauga, 9/20/63-at hospital; at Blackie Hospital, Madison, (GA).

*Flemming, G.F. (23)
$75, $20; no later record.

*Freeland, O.P. (27)
$80, $20; shown deserted near Morton, MS, July, 1863.

*Freeland, J.H. (27)
$100, $15; (d), Little Rock, 4/9/62.

Freeland, P.G.
deserted, 5/8/63.

*Freeland, W.J. (26)
$80, $15; (d), Memphis, TN, 6/7/62. 5'10", fair complexion, blue eyes, light hair. A farmer.

*Furgerson, W.J. (32)
$100, $20; (d), General Hospital, Macon, MS, 5/20/62.

Gary, Leroy
(d), Little Rock, 3/15/62.

*Greenwood, B.H. (17)
$130, $25; discharged, 6/12/62.

2d Lt. Gresham, W.W.
(w), Atlanta, 9/10/64, appears on

Inspection Report, (Lovejoy's Station, GA)-
absent due to wound; POW, Meridian, MS.

*Griffin, Alfred (30)
$135, $20; 4/5/64-present, and detailed as
teamster by Gen. Ector on 3/30/64.

*Hardin, T. H. (18)
present, 3/1/62-8/31/62; (k),
Murfreesboro, TN, 12/31/62.

*Harris, J.C. (37)
$135, $25; (d), Little Rock, 4/20/62.

*Harrison, J.H. (18)
$135, $25; discharged, 6/11/62.

Harrison, J.N. (22)
$75, $20; discharged due to dislocation of
right knee; 6'0", light complexion, dark
eyes, light hair. A carpenter.

Henry, R.D. (22)
$140, $20; no later record.

*Herron, J.L. (24)
$140, $25; (w), Richmond, KY., 8/31/62;
4/28/64-absent on detached service.

*Herron, L.F. (17)
$130, $15; discharged.

Herron, William
dropped from roll, 2/28/62.

Hill, W.H. (19)
$140, $20; admitted to Way Hospital,
Meridian, MS, February 4 and 6, 1865-fur-
loughed (Feb. 4-complaint: Diah.); 5'4",
dark complexion, hazel eyes, fair hair.

*Hilliard, A.C. (23)
$140, $20; (w), Chickamauga, hip, slight,
returned to duty; POW, Citronelle, AL,
5/4/65.

*Hilliard, C.T. (25)
$130, $20; POW, Citronelle, AL, 5/4/65.

*Hilliard, S.T. (21)
$100, $20; (k), Murfreesboro TN, 12/31/62.

Hinton, G.W.
(d), Tullahoma, TN, 12/9/62.

Hodges, C.M.
deserted at Des Arc, AR, 4/17/62.

Hodges, Thomas
4/5/64-present; at Lee Hospital, Lauderdale
MS, as patient, 4/17/64; (w), Atlanta.

*Hood, S.M. (27)
$135, $25; POW, Citronelle, AL, 5/4/65.

*Hooker, H.C. (23)
$140, $25; POW, Citronelle, AL, 5/4/65.

*Jackson, S.C. (33)
$80, $15; discharged, 6/20/62.

Kersey, John
(d), 4/17/62.

*King, C.W. (33)
$160, $20; (d), 4/5/62.

King, William
January, 1862-furloughed to 2/15/62. No
later record.

Langley, G.W.
POW, Citronelle, AL, 5/4/65.

*Langley, J.J. (21)
$125, $20; POW, Citronelle, AL, 5/4/65.

*Leach, L.W. (23)
$80, $15; appears on roll at Ross Hospital,
Mobile, AL, admitted 3/29/65, for gunshot
wound; POW, Citronelle, AL, 5/4/65.

Lewis, W.H.
(d), Aberdeen, MS, 7/1/62.

Loud, M.V.
dropped from roll.

Loud, James
(w), Murfreesboro, TN, 12/31/62, left ankle-
slightly; 4/5/64-AWOL "reported regularly
by surgeon's certificate as long as there was
communication between here and Texas."

Malar, J.W.
deserted 4/17/62, at Des Arc, AR.

Maynar, John F.
(d), Enterprise, MS, 6/11/62.

*McCann, Hugh (27)
$140, $25; (d), Priceville, MS, 6/27/62.

*McCaskill, C.E. (18)
$140, $25; name appears on report of
absentees, "to be found in Auburn, AL."

McCaskill, J.J.
(d), Corinth, MS, 5/15/62.

McClanahan, W.F.
(w), Chickamauga, slight; POW, Citronelle,
AL, 5/4/65.

*Metcalf, I.N. (16)
$100, $25; (w), Jackson-sent to hospital;
POW, Citronelle, AL, 5/4/65.

*Metcalf, L.R. (19)
$125, $25; admitted to Yandell Hospital,
Meridian, MS, 4/2/65; POW, Citronelle, AL,
5/4/65.

Moore, Jacob
discharged, 6/11/62.

*Morgan, A.J. (30)
$125, $25; 4/5/64-absent, furloughed for
15 days to Boonesville, GA, on 3/23/64.

Murphy, J.M.
POW, Chickamauga, 9/19/63; (d), 12/4/64,
due to small pox.

Pierce, Alfred
POW, Egypt Station, TN, 12/28/64.

Plemmons, G.F.
detailed as teamster, July-October, 1863.

Poag, Samuel
POW, Citronelle, AL, 5/4/65.

Pounds, D.T.
4/5/64-present and detailed as teamster, by order of Gen. Ector; POW, Citronelle, AL, 5/4/65.

*Pugh, B.D. (21)
$140, $20; (d), 5/20/62.

*Ramsey, O.F. (31 1/2)
$150, $25; dropped from roll.

*Reed, J.M. (20)
$150, $25; (k), battle of Richmond, KY, 8/30/62.

*Risinger, G.L. (28)
$80, $25; 4/5/64-present and detailed in January, 1864, as provost guard by Gen. Ector.

*Ritter, J.H. (18)
$130, $20; POW, Citronelle, AL, 5/4/65.

Ross, J.B.
discharged at Loudon, Tenn; 5'11", fair complexion, hazel eyes, light hair. A farmer.

Rowe, B.H.
(w), Richmond, KY; (d) 9/4/62.

Rowe, J.F.
(d), Macon, MS, 5/30/62.

Rye, B.L. (41)
5'10", dark complexion, gray eyes, black hair. A physician.

*Scott, John J. (23)
$125, $20; (w), Atlanta (d), Foard Hospital, Forsyth, GA., of wounds received in battle 9/24/64.

*Scott, T.J. (20)
$75, $15; discharged, 6/24/62.

Scott, William
discharged, 6/11/62.

*Scott, W.M. (35)
$145, $25; dropped from roll.

Scruggs, Lem
4/5/64
present.

*Shaw, W.P. (23)
$100, $20; discharged, 8/6/63, due to a "tubercular deposit", 5'10", fair complexion, blue eyes, red hair.

Shepherd, J.L.
shown as deceased, 5/20/63, at Rome, GA.

*Shivers, Jabel S.
$140, $2; (k), Chickamauga, 9/20/63.

Shivers, W.L.
(d), Little Rock.

*Sims, Thomas J. (20)
$100, $30; deserted from Morton, MS, July, 1863.

*Smith, G.W. (35)
discharged, 6/20/62.

*Sparkman, T.J. (20)
$125, $20; discharged, 1/29/63, due to accidental wound through hand; light complexion, blue eyes, fair hair. A farmer.

*Sweeden, L. (17)
$125, $20; discharged on 6/11/62.

*Stone, J.C. (34)
$160, $25; dropped from roll on 2/28/62.

*Stone, John N. (30)
$50, $25; appears on roster at Texas Hospital, Auburn, AL, dated 12/31/63 to 6/30/64.

*Taylor, W.H. (23)
$100, $20; (d), Corinth, MS, 5/17/62.

Thomas, W.M.
POW, Citronelle, AL, 5/4/65.

Thompson, E.F.
discharged on 8/5/62.

Thompson, J.C.
(w), Chickamauga, slight, returned to duty; 4/5/64 absent, detached as provost guard by order of Gen. Ector; POW, Citronelle, AL, 5/4/65.

Tims, John
dropped from records.

*Walker, J.F. (26)
$140, $30; detached as hospital steward, 12/30/63.

*Walker, N.H. (24)
$80, $20; (d), Guntown, MS, 5/3/62.

*Wall, C.H. (20)
$145, $25; (w), Chickamauga, severe; (d), dated 11/30/63.

Wall, Jack
discharged 6/20/62. Reenlisted 3/1/63 at Carthage, Texas; POW, Citronelle, AL, 5/4/65.

Ward, T.W.
POW, 9/19/63, Chickamauga.

*Watson, Henry L. (22)
$150, $20, 4/5/64-present.

*Watts, W.H. (19)
$100, $25; (d), Centerpoint, AR, 3/8/62.

Westmoreland, William
(d), Macon, MS, 6/5/62.

Wethington, G.H.
dropped from roll.

Whiddon, W.A. (17)
$80, $15; discharged on 6/11/62.

Whiddon, Seth
absent sick; (d), Columbus, MS.

Williamson, J.N.
POW, Citronelle, AL, 5/4/65.

Wills, John J.
name appears on report of absentees,
Ector's Brigade, dated 9/1/64 to 3/1/65
"supposed to be captured."

Womack, James (24)
$130, $25; (w), Murfreesboro, TN,
12/31/62, right knee; sent to Murfreesboro
hospital.

Yarbrough, James L.
dropped from roll, 2/28/62.

Yarbrough, G.W. (18)
$130, $25; no later record.

*Yarbrough, J.H. (27)
$140, $25; no later record.

*Yates, Sanford (24)
$140, $25; (w), Murfreesboro, TN,
12/31/62, left arm-slightly; AWOL, July-
October, 1863-"reported regularly by
Surgeon's Certificate as long as there was
communication between here and Texas".

COMPANY G,
10TH TEXAS CAVALRY

"Texas Troopers"

Original Officers:

*Captain Thompson, John M. (31)
$200, $30; present, February, 1862;
dropped, (no date given).

***1st Lt. Kilgore, Constantine Buckley
"Buck" (27)**
$125, $25; Present, February, 1862; promoted to Captain, 5/8/62; (w), Chickamauga,
thigh-severe; absent, due to wound,
September-October, 1863; POW, 12/18/63;
roll dated 4/5/64-"absent in captivity";
imprisoned at Johnson's Island.

*2d Lt. Mitchell, R.F. (38)
$175, $25; present, February, 1862;
dropped (no date given).

*Jr. 2d Lt. Leach, W.H. (37)
$150, $25; present (as 3d Lt.), February,
1862. No later record.

Other Officers:

Captain Barton, James M. (43)
$250, $40; appointed to Lt. Col. of regiment. Not reelected at regimental reorganization.

Original Non-commissioned Officer:

*Or. Sgt. Stroud, Ethan A. (25)
$250, $35; elected 1st Lt., 5/8/62; (d),
9/24/62.

*2d Sgt. Wasson, William S. (32)
$150, $25; detached duty by Gen. Ector as
brigade carriage-maker; discharged due to
chronic diarrhea, 6/9/63; 6'2". Dark complexion, gray eyes, black hair.

*3d Sgt. Whitfield, John R. (24)
$135, $35; (d), Sept. 1863."

*4th Sgt. Birdwell, Charles A. (21)
$160, $25; (w), Chickamauga, 9/19/63, leg-
absent; (w) Atlanta.

*1st Cpl. Richardson, William H. (26)
$140, $25; (d), on 5/4/62.

*2d Cpl. Trammell, George W. (24)
$200, $35; (w), Chickamauga, slight,
returned to duty; 4/5/64-present and commanding company.

*3d Cpl. Furlow, John P. (22)
$150, $25; detached as nurse at
Murfreesboro, TN, 1/2/63 (as private); not
returned, all rolls to October, 1863; POW
Murfreesboro-(d), USA General Hospital #4,
Murfreesboro, 2/2/63.

*4th Cpl. Beckton, James B. (19)
$130, $25; no later record.

Other:

*Ensign Gofourth, Reuben (21)
$135, $25; (w), Chickamauga, leg-severe;
4/5/64-present as teamster; POW,
Citronelle, AL, 5/4/65.

*Bugler Keel, Jacob (47)
$125, $25; (d), at Guntown, MS, 5/25/62
(as private).

*Bugler Wise, Charles W. (30)
appointed regimental carpenter; POW,
Citronelle, AL, 5/4/65.

*Farrier Miller, Mark M. (51)
$140, $20; discharged at Des Arc, AR.

Privates:

*Ames, Alford (31)
$135, $15; discharged, due to chronic
rheumatism, paralysis; 6'2", fair complexion, blue eyes, dark hair. A farmer.

280

*Anderson, James (30)
$225, $25; (w), Chickamauga, 9/19/63
arm amputated, 10/31/64, Morton, MS-
placed in Invalid Corps.

*Adgell, James R. (27)
at Yandell Hospital, Meridian, MS, for debili-
tas.

Arnold, George W.
(w), Murfreesboro, TN, 12/31/62-left side
slightly; (w) New Hope Church. (d),
7/10/64 at Flewellen Hospital, Cassville,
GA,

*Barber, P.B. (18)
$140, $20; POW, Citronelle, AL, 5/4/65.

Barham, S.H.
(w), Murfreesboro, TN, 12/31/62, leg
severe; placed in Invalid Corps.

Becton, Joseph S.
(w), Chickamauga, leg; (k), Spanish Fort.

*Bell, Lycurgus (18)
$140, $25; (d), Little Rock, 6/7/62.

*Birdwell, Benjamin F. (19)
$160, $30; discharged at Knoxville,
11/1/62, "on account, of wounds received
in battle, Richmond, KY." Gunshot wound
right front; reenlisted (w), Atlanta, 6'0" fair
complexion, blue eyes, dark hair. A farmer.

*Birdwell, George P. (23)
$-, $25; promoted to Chaplain, 8/7/63.

*Bobbett, S.H. (21)
no later record.

*Bothall, Edward (26)
$100, $25; (w) Chickamauga
slight; detailed in QM Dept. on 11/17/63,
by Gen. Ector.

*Britt, A.M. (25)
$125, $30; 4/5/64-present and reenlisted.

Brownlow, R.S.
POW, Allatoona, GA, 10/5/64; 6'1", light
complexion, dark hair, blue eyes.

*Butler, William (21)
$150, $25, POW, Chickamauga, 9/19/63-
received at Camp Douglas, IL.

*Carter, Andrew A. (20)
$150, $25; POW, Citronelle, AL, 5/4/65.

*Chambliss, Stephen M. (20)
AWOL in Rusk County.

Davis, B.G.
4/5/64-absent and reenlisted-Brigade
Butcher; POW, Citronelle, AL, 5/4/65.

*Day, Lawrence (17)
$130, $25; discharged.

*Dickson, David L. (22)
$140, $25; "In hospital 6 months, unfit for
any service;" 6', fair complexion, blue eyes,
sandy hair. A farmer.

Dixon, Robert
at St. Mary's Hospital, LaGrange, GA.

*Dunegan, A.J. (21)
$150, $30; (d).

*Durkee, A.G. (27)
$150, $25; "appointed QM, July 24, 1862."

*Furlow, Charles (24)
$160, $25; January-June, 1863; absent due
to (w), Murfreesboro, TN,

Furlow, J.T.
(w), Murfreesboro, TN, 12/31/62, right arm-
seriously, and POW; (d), 3/20/63 at USA
General Hospital.

Furlow, R.M.
4/5/64-present.

Furlow, T.A.
4/5/64-present and reenlisted; 5'11", light
complexion, blue eyes, fair hair.

Garner, William
POW near Tilton, GA, 10/13/64; 6'4", dark
complexion, hazel eyes, brown hair.

*Garrett, Mansfield (29)
$150, $25; (d), pthisis, 2/1/65.

Gaston, F.B.
attached temporarily by order of Gen. Polk.

Gatlin, J.H.
POW, Murfreesboro, TN, 12/31/62; (w),
Chickamauga, slight; POW, Citronelle, AL,
5/4/65.

*Gibson, Q.K. (22)
$125, $20; Captain of Company K, 5/8/62.-
see Company K records.

Gladney, J.M.
(d), 5/25/62.

*Gladney, Thomas L. (20)
$140, $25; (w), Richmond, KY, 8/30/62;
POW, Allatoona, GA, 10/5/64; age, 22, 5'7",
dark complexion, blue eyes, light hair.

*Hale, Howell P. (22)
$160, $25; (w) Atlanta.

Hale, J.C.
discharged at Tupelo, MS.

*Harnage, George H. (33)
$165, $25; (d) in MS.

*Heath, John N. (22)
$120, $25; (d), Little Rock, 4/6/62.

*Hicks, Isaac K. (26)
$125, $20; (d), Loudon, TN, 11/20/62.

*Hicks, John M. (27)
$140, $25; (d), at Little Rock, 3/24/62.

*Hicks, John W. (37)
$150, $25; POW, Chickamauga, 9/19/63; 5'8", fair complexion, brown hair, hazel eyes.

Holland, J.V.
name appears on roll at Texas Hospital, Auburn, AL, 6/30/64.

Hollingsworth, W.H.
(w), Spanish Fort, name appears on register of sick/wounded POW's City Hospital, Mobile, AL.

*Holt, John T. (17)
$150, $30; 5', fair complexion, blue eyes, light hair, a farmer. Reenlisted, 1/12/63; 4/5/64-present.

*Hopson, Briggs W. (29)
$140, $25; (w), Richmond, KY, 8/30/62; (w), Chickamauga, shoulder-severe; POW, Citronelle, AL, 5/4/65.

Hopson, E.H.
POW, Citronelle, AL, 5/4/65.

Hopson, J.M.
(w), Murfreesboro, TN, 12/31/62, leg-mortally; (d), 1/29/63.

*Hopson, W.A. (25)
$150, $30; 4/5/64-reenlisted and absent on duty with Pioneer Corps, by Gen. Ector.

*Hoyle, John A. (44)
$140, $20; discharged at Tupelo, MS.

*Hutchins, Stokely (31)
$130, $30; (w), Chickamauga, arm-slight; 4/5/64-present and reenlisted.

*Irvin, Robert V. (21)
$150, $25; (w), Chickamauga, knee slightly, returned to duty; surrendered at Columbia, Tn, 12/18/64; 5'11", fair complexion, gray eyes, dark hair.

*Irving, Asa G. (18)
$100, $25; (w), Murfreesboro, TN, 12/31/62.

*Jeffreys, N.B. (20)
$150, $25; (d), Knoxville, TN, 11/3/62.

*Johnson, Jasper T. (24)
$100, $25; discharged, 6/16/62.

*Johnson, John H. (20)
$140, $25; (w), Murfreesboro, TN, 12/31/62, shoulder-slight; (w), Atlanta.

*Johnson, Ranson B. (18)
$130, $20; (d), roll dated 3/1/62-8/31/62.

*Kannard, George T. (16)
$140, $20; discharged, 6/13/62.

*Kirkendall, George B. (21)
$140, $25; (d), Lauderdale Springs, MS, 4/24/62.

Langston, J.L.
4/5/64-absent, on detached service by order of Gen. French.

Lay, B.W.
(w), Murfreesboro, TN, 12/31/62, foot slightly; (k), Chickamauga, 9/19/63.

Leach, T.M.
"unfit for 50 days", due to pthis pulmonalis. 6'0 1/2", fair complexion, hazel eyes, dark hair. A blacksmith.

*Lee, John A. (22)
$140, $25; (w), Chickamauga, severe-hip; (d), Fair Ground Hospital #2, Atlanta, GA, 10/7/63.

*Linthacum, Thomas B.
$140, $25; appears on roll at Texas Hospital, Auburn, AL, 6/30/64; name appears on list of POW's captured by 1st Brigade, 2d Cavalry Division; 5'8", fair complexion, dark hair, blue eyes.

Littlejohn, E.G.
(w), Murfreesboro, TN, 12/31/62, head and hip; POW, Citronelle, AL, 5/4/65.

*Lloyd, William W. (17)
$140, $25; no later record.

Long, J.T.
transferred to Douglas' Texas Battery.

*Martin, Andrew J. (27)
$175, $25; left sick in KY, 9/15/62.

*Martin, Isaac (23)
$140, $25; apparantly (w) at Nashville and captured on trip to rejoin the 10th Texas. POW, Tuscaloosa, AL, 5/22/65.

Mayfield, W.M.
discharged at Des Arc, Arkansas.

*McCall, Lamar D. (20)
$150, $25; discharged for disability, 2/3/62.

McCallum, F.G.
(d), Lauderdale Springs, MS, 5/4/62.

McClure, T.L.
left sick at Memphis.

Mitchell, S.T.
4/5/64-present; died of wounds at Atlanta.

Monk, C. H.
(w), Chickamauga, slight; 4/5/64-present.

*Monk, John R. (22)
$135, $22; (w), Murfreesboro, TN, 12/31/62, POW, near Nashville, TN, 12/16/64.

*Moore, George W. (23)
$175, $25; (w),Murfreesboro, TN, 12/31/62,
head-severely; POW, Spanish Fort, AL,
4/8/65.

*Moore, James H. (27)
$125, $25; (w), Murfreesboro, TN,
12/31/62, foot-slightly; (d), 1/24/63.

Page, Halley
4/5/64-shown as present; to be found in
Monroe County, MS.

*Parker, Henry R.T. (23)
$140, $20; 4/5/64-present.

*Parker, William W.W. (21)
$140, $20; (w), Murfreesboro, TN,
12/31/62, foot mortally; (d), 2/3/63.

*Patrick, G.D. (29)
$125, $25; discharged, for pthis, pulmonalis; age, 30 5'9", fair complexion, gray
eyes, light hair. A farmer.

Patrick, R.D.
POW, Citronelle, AL, 5/4/65.

*Pertrum, W.M. (23)
$135, $20; no later record.

Phillips, E.H.
(w), Murfreesboro, TN, 12/31/62; POW,
Citronelle, AL, 5/4/65.

*Phillips, E.L. (27)
$140, $20; (w), Murfreesboro, TN,
12/31/62, right side; (w), Chickamauga,
slight, returned to duty; absent in Trans-MS-
shown as AWOL.

Phillips, E.M.
(w), Murfreesboro, TN, 12/31/62, right
breast; POW, Yazoo City, MS.

*Prather, John T. (16)
$140, $20; absent accounted for sick.

Renfro, J.L.
(k), Richmond, KY, 8/30/62.

*Rettig, Charles (18)
$140, $25; (d), 9/26/62, from wounds
received at battle of Richmond, KY,
8/30/62.

Richards, W.F.
4/5/64-present; POW, Henderson, Texas.

Robertson, W.A.(28)
(w), Murfreesboro, TN, 12/31/62, right
thigh-serious; 5'10", blue eyes, auburn hair,
fair complexion. A farmer.

Robinson, James T. (20)
$135, $30; (d), Clinton, TN, 11/6/62.

*Rosson, Thomas J. (19)
$100, $20; (w), Murfreesboro, TN,
12/31/62, right arm; (w), 6/18/64, at

Latimer House, right arm; (w), Atlanta,
right leg by a shell; POW, Citronelle, AL,
5/4/65.

*Russell, J.R. (29)
$140, $20; transferred to 14th Texas
Cavalry.

*Russell, Crue C. (24)
transferred to 14th Texas Cavalry.

*Smith, A.C. (23)
$150, $25; left at Holly Springs, MS.

Smith, William
(w), Chickamauga, slight.

*Spine, John W. (22)
$150, $25; no later record.

Spinks, J.M.
POW, Citronelle, AL, 5/4/65.

Spinks, Samuel
(w), Richmond, KY, 8/30/62-(d), of wound,
9/5/62.

*Starr, John W. (19)
(d), Enterprise, MS, 6/11/62.

Still, C.A.
POW, Citronelle, AL, 5/4/65.

*Still, John W. (18)
$115, $20; (d), Canton, MS, 6/6/62.

Still, T.H.
(w), Murfreesboro, TN, thigh, 12/31/62

*Stone, J.H. (35)
$60, $25; discharged.

*Stone, W.F. (44)
$150, $25; discharged.

*Stroud, Alpheus D. (22)
$125, $35; detailed as Asst. Surgeon.

Stroud, M.L.
discharged at Tupelo, MS. 5'11", fair complexion, blue eyes, sandy hair. A farmer.

*Sutherland, John J. (21)
$135, $25; (d), Macon, MS, 6/1/62.

Thompson, B.F.
discharged at Des Arc, AR, 4/17/62.

Thompson, T.M.
discharged.

Trammell, T.J.(21)
6'0", dark complexion, black hair, hazel
eyes. 4/5/64-present.

*Truitt, F.D. (16)
$140, $25; no later record.

Tubbs, J.S.
(w), Richmond, KY, right arm fractured by
rifled ball; discharged; 5'7", fair complexion,
blue eyes, dark hair. A farmer.

*Tupp, G.H. (32)
(d), Chammons Station, MS, 5/10/62.

*Turner, S.W. (25)
$150, $30; 4/5/64-present.

*Wade, James H. (20)
$125, $15; shown as missing at
Chickamauga; present 4/5/64, POW,
Atlanta, GA, 9/2/64.

*Waits, James (19)
$130, $15; POW, Citronelle, AL, 5/4/65.

Walling, J.R.
present, 4/5/64.

Watkins, J.A.
absent, west of MS River.

*Watkins, James H. (20)
$200, $25; (d), Jackson's Port, 3/24/62.

*Watson, A.B. (18)
$140, $30; (d), General Hospital, Okalona,
MS, 8/30/62.

*Watson, James M.
$130, $15; (w), Chickamauga, severe; POW,
Citronelle, AL.

*Weaver, John J. (33)
$150, $25; 4/5/64-present.

Welch, Alexander
detailed to Maj. W.B. Ector by Gen Ector's
order, 2/28/64.

*Whitfield, James (22)
$150, $25; (w), Murfreesboro, TN,
12/31/62, foot
seriously; (w) Atlanta, admitted to
Ocmulgee Hospital, Macon, GA, 7/11/64,
for gunshot wound to left hand, fracture of
metacarpal bone, ring finger, 60 days [fur-
lough].

*Wilkins, Mortimore (17)
$100, $25; no later record.

*Wilson, William O. (22)
$140, $25; shown on roster at Walker's
Division Hospital, Newton, MS, November-
December, 1863.

*Wright, James A. (23)
$125, $25; 4/5/64,present and reenlisted,
on extra duty, Gen. Ector's order.

*Wright, John H.R. (26)
$150, $25; (d), Aberdeen, MS, 7/1/62.

*Wyche, Drury (-)
$150, $25; absent on furlough.

*Wynne Richard W. (19)
(w), Murfreesboro, TN, 12/31/62, ankle-
slightly; (w), Nashville, 12/15/64-simple
flesh wound of neck; POW, Franklin, TN;
5'11", light complexion, gray eyes, dark hair.

COMPANY H,
10TH TEXAS CAVALRY REGIMENT
"Warriors"

Original Officers:

*Captain Whetstone, Anderson (42)
$200, $30; absent, "on account of sickness
in family.

*1st Lt. Henry, J.C. (23)
$160, $20; absent with leave to see his
father.

*2d Lt. Russell, David (39)
$150, $25; absent, due to sickness in family.

*Jr. 2d Lt. Moore, W.B. (30)
$200, $30; "detached after private who left
without leave from 2/8/62 up to
2/20/62."No later record.

Original Non-commissioned Officers:

*1st Sgt. Crockett, H.J. (25)
$160, $20; discharged, 4/18/62.

*2d Sgt. Price, J.W. (22)
$100, $20; shown as deserted.

*3d Sgt. Hampton, C.P. (18)
$125, $20; POW, Citronelle, AL, 5/4/65.

*4th Sgt. Wilson, W.J. (24)
(w), Murfreesboro, TN, 12/31/62, head
slight; (w) Nashville, hand. Admitted to hospital at Okalona, MS, 1/7/65.

*1st Cpl. Summers, T.W. (24)
$150, $20; (d), 9/25/63, Newman, GA.

*2d Cpl. Beelville (or Beelvill), A.W.
no later record.

*3d Cpl. James, W.P.
(d), Little Rock, 4/8/62.

*4th Cpl. Beaty, W.W. (33)
$100, $25; (k), Richmond, KY, 8/30/62.

Other:

*Ensign Dickerson, A.P. (37)
$100, $25; discharged.

*BugLer Rose, David (27)
$140, $20; discharged.

*Farrier Irwin, J.R. (37)
$150, $20; paroled at Meridian, MS, 5/9/65.

Privates:

*Allen, W.A. (32)
$100, $25; POW, Chickamauga, 9/19/63.

*Beetler, J.R. (31)
$100, $20; (d), Little Rock, 4/8/62.

Belvin, A.W.
enlisted 9/25/61 at Quitman, Texas; (k),
Richmond, KY, 8/30/62.

*Benton, P.S. (52)
$115, $20; discharged.

*Benton, T.H. (17)
$130, $20; (w), Chickamauga; 4/5/64-present.

*Boykin, J.F. (21)
$160, $25; (d), Jacksonport, Ark., 4/6/62.

Boykin, Robert S.
POW, 9/19/64 at St. Joseph, LA; 5'8 1/2", fair complexion, blue eyes, light hair.

*Cameron, Jerre (30)
$80, $15; issued Certificate for Disability discharge, due to pthisis pulmonalis.

*Cantrell, J.R. (19)
$125, $25; discharged, 5'8", dark hair, complexion, and eyes. A farmer.

Center, W.J.
(d), Enterprise, MS, 6/5/62.

*Christman, J.G. (23)
$80, $20; (w), Murfreesboro, TN, 12/31/62.

*Christman, J.M. (21)
$100, $25; 4/5/64-present.

Clarady, R.H.
(d), Jacksonport, 4/8/62.

*Clark, G.W. (18)
$100, $25; AWOL since 3/10/64.

*Clark, Leman (23)
$130, $10; (d), Guntown, MS, 5/13/62.

Cochran, Claiborne
absent "to arrest W.S. Cosby of this command"; (d), Little Rock.

*Coker, L.R. (21)
$150, $20; (d), Jacksonport, Ark., 3/22/62.

Collins, A.
(d), Tupelo, MS, 6/9/62.

Collins, Carrel
(d), Rockport, Ark., 2/20/62.

*Cox, Joseph A. (28)
$100, $25; discharged.

*Cox, J.P. (17)
$100, $20; discharged.

*Dickerson, A. (27)
$100, $10; sick, 2/15/63.

Edgar, J.M.
4/5/64-present.

*Edgar, Richard
discharged.

*Ellidge, S.W. (18)
$100, $25; (d), Enterprise, MS, 6/20/62.

*Ellis, J.A. (27)
$140, $25; (d), Little Rock, 4/22/62.

*Fanner, F.M. (23)
$150, $25; no later record.

*Fannin, William W. (25)
$130, $25; discharged, phthis pulmonalis; age, 26, 6', fair complexion, dark eyes, light hair. A farmer.

Fanning, J.J.
(d), Shelbyville, March 9 or 10, 1863.

*Farmer, Ewell O. (26)
$130, $25; POW at Jackson, MS; (d), of inflammation of the lungs, 6/22/64.

*Farmer, Frederick (27)
$140, $20; no later record.

Fleetcher, J.F.
left sick at Fairview, AR.

Flowers, J.L.
discharged, 1/30/62.

Flowers, M.F.
4/5/64-AWOL in Texas.

Gibson, H.P (23)
POW, 10/27/62 at Richmond, KY; 5'7 3/4", black eyes and hair, light complexion; 4/5/64-present.

Gibson, J.M. (23)
POW, Richmond, KY, 10/30/62; 5'10", gray eyes, black hair, light complexion; POW, Citronelle, AL, 5/4/65.

Gibson, T.J.
on extra duty as Division Ordnance Guard; POW, Citronelle, AL, 5/4/65.

Gilbreth, Alex. J.
POW, Chickamauga, 9/19/63.

*Hampton, L.P. (19)
$100, $15; (w), Murfreesboro, TN, 12/31/62, neck-slightly; (d), Shelbyville, TN, small pox hospital.

Hardee, B.S. (22)
(w), Richmond, KY, 8/30/62; 5'8", dark complexion and eyes. A farmer.

*Hardee, S.B.(22)
POW, Richmond, KY, 10/30/62, 5'8", light complexion, hazel eyes, dark hair; (w) Murfreesboro, TN, 12/31/62, breast-slightly; (d), Shelbyville, TN, 2/13/63.

*Harper, W.G. (21)
$130, $20; (w), Chickamauga, leg broke-shown as mortally wounded; POW, Citronelle, AL, 5/4/65.

*Hatton, H.M. (25)
$150, $25; (d), Smith County, Texas, on furlough.

Hatton, J.T.
(w), Chickamauga, heel, slight-9/19/63; POW, Citronelle, AL, 5/4/65.

*Hays, J.N. (22)
$140, $25; (w), Jackson, MS, 7/14/63; POW, Citronelle, AL, 5/4/65.

*Hazlewood, R.H. (18)
$100, $20; (w); Murfreesboro, TN, 12/31/62, leg-slightly; (d), 5/3/63.

Henry, W.D
discharged.

Ingram, William (21)
$130, $20; (d), Guntown, MS, 5/8/62.

Inman, J.A.
"absent to arrest W.S. Cosby of this command"; (d) 1/18/63.

Inman, L.R. (18)
$80, $20; (d), 1/31/63, near Shelbyville, TN.

*Jackson, W.M. (19)
$100, $20; (w), Murfreesboro; 12/31/62, leg; 4/5/64-present.

Kuykendall, P. (17)
$80, $15; 4/5/64-present.

*Lyles, R.S. (30)
$130, $20; (w), Chickamauga, 9/19/63, (w), at Allatoona.

*Manning, J.O. (20)
$75, $10; Manning appears on the Confederate Roll of Honor for Murfreesboro; (d) at Shelbyville, TN, 2/14/63.

*Marrs, A.J. (25)
(d), Jacksonport, 3/16/62.

*Martin, W.A. (21)
$130, $25; discharged at Shelbyville, TN, for pthis, pulmonalis; age, 22, 5'8", fair complexion, grey eyes, dark hair. A farmer.

McBride, D.M.
(w), Chickamauga, slight, 9/19/63,

*McEnturff, J.F. (22)
$50, $15; (w), Spanish Fort, at Ross Hospital, Mobile AL., admitted 4/1/65, for flesh wound, left shoulder and hip and back, shell wound; (d), no date given.

*McMillan, W.M. (26)
$140, $20; (d), Jacksonport, AR, 3/29/62.

*Miller, G.P. (22)
$130, $25; (w), Murfreesboro, TN, 12/31/62; POW, Citronelle, AL, 5/4/65.

Morris, E.N.
present, in arrest. No later record.

Morris, John P.
arrested at Lexington, KY, 10/30/62; (w), Murfreesboro, TN, 12/31/62; POW, Citronelle, AL, 5/4/65.

*Moseley, J.H. (43)
$125, $15; discharged.

*Nail, W.W. (24)
$125, $20; deserted on 7/21/63; POW at Jackson, MS; (d), 2/4/64 (of pneumonia).

*Neal, James H. (19)
$140, $20; (d), Enterprise, MS, 5/15/62.

*Neal, Joseph (18)
$125, $20; (d), Shelbyville, 3/23/63; dark complexion,
gray eyes.

*Neal, Joseph F. (23)
$75, $10; Citronelle, AL; 5/4/65.

*Odom, A.J. (32)
$100, $25; (w), Chickamauga, slight, returned to duty; POW, Citronelle, AL, 5/4/65.

Padget, C.P.
Shelbyville sick, 4/5/64-present; issued pants, 7/27/64, "destitute."

*Padget, J.M. (29)
$125, $15; (d), Tupelo, MS.

*Pickle, Isaac (22)
$100, $20; (d), Pittsburg, Texas, 12/31/61.

*Robnett, J.L. (29)
$100, $15; sick, 2/15/63; (d), 3/2/63.

*Robnett, Mike M. (18)
4/5/64-present.

*Rose, James (25)
(w) severely in skirmish, 5/29/62.

Smith, George
(d), Little Rock.

*Smith, Harvey V. (26)
$80, $15; POW, sent to Snyder's Bluff from Vicksburg, 7/30/63.

*Smith, Levi (21)
$100, $25; POW, 10/30/62, sent from Lexington to Louisville, KY; marked as dead, 11/25/62.

*Smith, Peyton (23)
$100, $20; missing, Chickamauga, 9/19/63.

*Smith, R.B. (26)
$80, $25; (w), Chickamauga, 9/19/63, slight; POW, Citronelle, AL, 5/4/65.

*Sosby, W.J. (18)
$80, $20; POW Chickamauga, 9/19/63.

Trammell, C.M.
(k), Richmond, KY, 8/30/62.

Whetstone, J.S.J.
resigned, due to "continued ill health."

*Stalcup, G.A. (18)
left sick at Little Rock.

*Stalcup, T.B. (19)
(d), at Shelbyville, 3/2/63.

*Tucker, Zill (33)
$150, $20; (d), at Clarksville, Texas.

*Wages, J.D. (19)
$125, $15; left sick at Readyville, TN, 12/27/62; (d), Readyville, 1/7/63.

*Williams, Leroy M. (22)
$150, $30; (d), Fulton, AR.

*Williams, Marion (20)
$100, $20; POW, Citronelle, AL, 5/4/65.

*Williams, W.G. (24)
$145, $30; (d), 2/22/63, at Shelbyville, TN.

Wilson, F.M.
discharged, 7/20/62.

*Wilson, J.N. (20)
$100, $10; discharged, 7/15/62.

*Wilson, W.H. (22)
$125, $20; name appears on list of deserters/absentees, reported to HQ at Bonham, Texas, 12/19/63, voluntarily under amnesty proclamation, assigned to duty in camp to Lt. Hart, Cavalry.

Wise, J.M.
(d), at Little Rock.

Wise, Joel
12/31/62, shown as POW; 4/5/64-present.

*Yerger, J.A. (35)
$65, $15; deserted, 7/17/62.

COMPANY I, 10TH TEXAS CAVALRY REGIMENT
"Cherokee Cavalry" Cherokee County

Original Officers:
*Captain Martin, Robert H. (34)
$150, $25; no later record.

*1st Lt. Roberts, William (38)
$175, $25; no later record.

*2nd Lt. McGinnis, Benjamin A. (26)
$150, $25; no later record.

*Jr. 2d Lt. Wiggins, John T. (27)
$150, $25; no later record.

Original Non-commissioned Officers:
*1st Sgt. Murry, J.T. (32)
$140, $25; resigned, 6/24/62, due to "chronic dysentery of 3 months standing, bronchial infection of the lungs."

*2nd Sgt. Park, William S. (38)
$75, $20; discharged on Surgeon's Certificate of Disability.

*3d Sgt. Gibson, George W. (29)
$175, $20; 4/5/64-present.

*4th Sgt. Farmer, M.W. (37)
$140, $20; detached by Gen. Smith "with-

out any notification to his command."

*1st Cpl. Evans, John D. (26)
$165, $25; discharged on Surgeon's Certificate of disability.

*2d Cpl. Shepherd, Thomas, A. (48)
$75, $20; (d) 5/20/62.

*3d Cpl. Miller, Jesse A. (34)
$140, $25; discharged for "extreme debility." 5'10", fair complexion, blue eyes, dark hair.

*4th Cpl. Coleman, James H. (34)
$125, $20; (d), 5/6/62.

Others:
*Ensign Thomason, Malcomb (60)
$125, $30, (d), 6/22/62.

*Bugler Holcomb, J.W. (22)
$125, $20; POW, Citronelle, AL, 5/4/65.

Privates:
*Armstrong, M.W. (19)
$130, $25; appears in Gen. French's official report of the battle of Allatoona, GA, "Lieut. M.W. Armstrong, Tenth Texas, seized the United States standard from the Federals, and, after a brief struggle, brought it and the bearer of it off in triumph."

*Aston, Hugh L. (22)
$140, $20; detailed as wagoner for ambulance and ordnance; POW, Citronelle, Al.

Ball, Rufus
(d), Duvall's Bluff.

Ball, Tandy
(w), Chickamauga foot; 4/5/64-present.

*Barrett, John G. (22)
$120, $20; (d), 5/10/62.

*Berry, Oscar (19)
$135, $25; (d), June 1 or 3, 1862.

Blakey, A.A.
detached to drive ambulance; 11/1/63; shown as (k), Spanish Fort, April 1865.

*Bowling, William (21)
$80, $20; (d) Jackson, MS, 6/7/62.

*Bradfrod, George (24)
$175, $25; POW, Jonesboro, GA, 9/1/64; (d), of "spiculation of the bone," 12/28/64.

*Broome, Milton E. (23)
$140, $20; (k), Franklin, TN, 11/30/64.

Burk, James P.
(d), 3/27/62.

*Burk, John H. (25)
$150, $25; POW, Chickamauga-at prison hospital, Nashville, 9/29/63.

*Burks, James L.
discharged on Surgeon's Certificate of Disability.

Cannon, J.H.
discharged on Surgeon's Certificate of Disability.

*Carlton, Bedford (20)
$135, $20; left in Tenn; disappeared, Hood's retreat from Tenn., 1864 "supposed dead."

*Carlton, C.B. (22)
$140, $15; POW, Spanish Fort, AL, 4/8/65.

Carlton, Orville
(d), 8/4/63.

*Cawthon, Benjamin (28)
$140, $20; (d), 6/9/62 at General Hospital, Macon, MS.

*Coleman, Edward H. (34)
$150, $25; detailed to guard division ordnance by Gen. Ector, 4/5/64.

Cornelison, Milton
shown as AWOL, May-October, 1863.

*Dalby, John W. (23)
detailed to provost guard by Gen. Ector.

*Dalby, Seth T.W. (20)
$140, $20; (d), roll dated January-February, 1863.

*Davis, Ben W. (18)
$125, $20; POW, Citronelle, AL, 5/4/65.

Dear, Owen
4/5/64-absent, "sent to Gen. Hosp", May 1, 1863.

*Demitt, Thomas H. (37)
$100, $20; sent to hospital; (d), 2/17/63.

*Dewitt, Charles B. (19)
$125, $25; (d), 5/26/62.

*Egbert, Daniel (23)
$165, $25; "unfit for duty, 30 days, due to chronic nephritis." Age 23, 5'10", fair complexion, gray eyes, light hair.

*Egbert, George T. (17)
$135, $25; POW, Chickamauga, 9/19/63; 5'9", dark complexion, brown hair, blue eyes.

*Faulkner, Frank B. (20)
$130, $20; POW, Citronelle, AL., 5/4/65.

*Francis, Joseph Mallory (18)
$125, $25; (w), Chickamauga,hip-severely; absent, due to (w).

*Frazier, James T. (18)
$150, $25; (d), 5/11/62.

*Glass, Alphonzo (30)
$130, $20; (w) Spanish Fort, AL, severe;
"fracture-right arm, shell."

*Glover, William P. (18)
$80, $25; 4/5/64-present.

*Goodson, John (21)
$140, $25; missing Murfreesboro; POW, 2/11/63-paroled; 4/5/64-present.

Goodson, J.P.
POW, near Chattahoochie, GA.

Hall, J.F.M.
(w), Chickamauga, slight; paroled on May 9, 1865.

Henderson, James
POW, Citronelle, AL, 5/4/65.

*Hendricks, Edward (17)
$90, $20, (d), 6/2/62.

Henson, W.C.
discharged, 11/1/61.

Hill, George B. (17)
$135, $25; detailed as wagoner; POW, Citronelle, AL, 5/4/65.

*Holcomb, Joel (20)
$80, $20; (d), 4/30/62.

*Holcomb, John L. (19)
$125, $20; 4/5/64-present.

*Holcomb, L.G. (26)
$130, $20; detached as wagoner; (d), Lee Hospital, of Phlg. Erysipelas, 5/28/64.

*Holcomb, S.A. (18)
$100, $25; (d), Little Rock, 4/25/62.

*Holmes, James A. (28)
$130, $20; (k), Chickamauga, 9/19/63.

*Holoway, Thomas (22)
$100, $20; (w), Murfreesboro, TN, 12/31/62.

*Jarrett, J.W. (29)
$200, $25; (d), MS, 1862.

*Jones, John R. (21)
$150, $25; mortally wounded, Allatoona, GA, 10/5/64.

*Jones, Lewis P. (20)
$60, $25; detailed as wagoner; POW, Citronelle, AL, 5/4/65.

Jones, Pinkney R.
(w), Allatoona, GA, 10/5/64.

*Keahey, Samuel (25)
$125, $25; discharged, 4/23/62.

Keahey, W.S.
transferred to Van Dorn's body guard, 4/17/62.

*Lloyd, James B. (24)
$100, $20; present, 4/5/64.

*Loden, James S. (20)
$140, $25; (w), Chickamauga leg, absent
due to wound.

Long, J.L.H.
discharged on Surgeon's Certificate of disability.

*Lowe, John (20)
$125, $25; (d), 6/3/63, at Bell Hospital,
Rome, GA.

*Lunsford, Jesse H. (26)
$100, $20; transferred to Douglas' Texas
Battery.

*Mankins, W.L. (18)
$110, $20; (d), 6/1/62.

Mann, C.T.
discharged under Conscript Act.

*Mansell, James (23)
$130, $25; (d), 4/28/62.

*Mansker, Samuel (17)
$150, $25; disability, 6/25/62, due to pthis,
pulmonalis; 5'10", fair complexion, blue
eyes, light hair, a farmer.

*McEachern, B.W. (25)
$165, $45; discharged for pthis, pulmonalis;
6'0", fair complexion, blue eyes, dark hair.

*McLeod, William
(d), 4/25/62.

*Meazell, William (41)
$135, $20; discharged, 4/23/62.

Monkers, James Henry (19)
$130, $25; POW, Murfreesboro, TN,
12/31/62; POW, Citronelle, AL, 5/4/65.

*Moore, James W. (26)
$150, $25; "feeble health unfit for duty 3
months," 5'10", fair complexion, blue eyes,
dark hair.

Newman, P.L.
discharged, 4/28/62.

Odom, A.E. "Archy"
POW, Citronelle, AL, 5/4/65.

*Odom, Calvin (26)
$75, $25; POW, Citronelle, AL.

*Odom, Cornelius G. (25)
$140, $25; POW, Chickamauga, 9/19/63;
(w), in Zollicoffer house disaster, Nashville.

*1st Lt. Oppenheimer, Daniel (24)
born: Burgkunstadt, Bavaria; POW, Franklin,
TN, 12/18/64.

*Parks, John (17)
$130, $20; (d), 4/1/62.

Payne, Robert C.
shown on list of shoemakers; thought to
have died in Tenn.

*Phillips, William (20)
$140, $20; "general debility, unfit 60 days-
emaciation of muscular tissues." 6', fair
complexion, blue eyes, sandy hair, a farmer.

*Quinlen, John (45)
$150, $25; (d), 5/30/62.

*Reynolds, Joel (19)
$125, $25; (k), Murfreesboro, TN,
12/31/62.

*Robnett, Isaac (18)
$75, $20; (d), 5/20/62.

*Scurlock, James W. (21)
$125, $20; (w), Murfreesboro, TN, 12/3/62,
leg severely; (w), Chickamauga, back severe;
POW, 5/26/65, roll of furloughed/ detached
men.

Shepperd, P.R.
discharged on Surgeon's Certificate of disability.

Simmons, R.F.
transferred to Van Dorn's body guard,
4/17/62.

Singletary, G.H.
POW, Citronelle, AL, 5/4/65.

Spaulding, J.A.
(w), Chickamauga, slight, returned to duty;
paroled at Meridian, MS, 5/9/65.

*Stafford, Harvey (17)
$130, $20; on detached duty in Johnston's
Dept., Madison, GA.

*Stafford, Samuel M. (25)
$150, $25; POW, Citronelle, AL, 5/4/65.

*Stafford, Thomas A. (21)
$140, $20, no later record.

*Stafford, Thomas J. (21)
$140, $20; (w), Atlanta, admitted to Floyd
Hospital, Macon, GA, for gunshot wound to
right hand, 7/1/64.

Stoner, A.B.
4/5/64-shown as absent sick.

Stubblefield, W.H.
left sick at Lauderdale Springs.

Templeton, John Allen (16)
POW, Chickamauga, 9/19/63.

Thomason, J.W.
discharged on Surgeon's Certificate,
11/2/61.

Thomason, T.C.
(d), 4/28/62.

*Thomason, C.A. (28)
$140, $20; no later record.

Thomason, C.H.
discharged, 8/26/62.

*Thomason, George W.
no later record.

*Thomason, Hilliard J. (24)
$135, $25; POW, Citronelle, AL, 5/4/65.

Thomason, James
(d), Pine Bluff, AR, 5/26/62.

*Thomason, K.B. (29)
$125, $35; (d), 4/28/62.

*Thomason, Wiley D. (32)
$135, $25; (d), 6/13/63 at Yazoo City, MS.

Thomason, W.J.
sick, 3/1/62-8/31/62. No later record.

Thomason, W.R. (29)
$110, $20; (w), in arm in skirmish with
enemy, 8/6/64; POW, Citronelle, AL,
5/4/65.

*Tilman, Henry M. (20)
$150, $25; (d), 5/30/62, Memphis.

*Timmons, Jordan (29)
$75, $25; (d) 5/20/62.

*Van Zandt, John R. (23)
$110, $25; detailed to guard division ordnance, by Gen. Ector's order.

*Wagoner, William A. (18)
$140, $20; (w), Murfreesboro, TN,
12/31/62; 4/5/64-present.

*Walker, Miller, B. (25)
$150, $20; (w), Richmond, KY, 8/30/62,
through the thigh and permanently disabled.

Wallace, F.C.
shown as absent-sick.

*Walters, Moses (20)
$135, $25; POW, Chickamauga.

Ware, Robert C.
(d), 4/9/62.

*Welsh, Thomas M. (23)
$100, $20; (w), Chickamauga, slight-
returned to duty; 4/5/64-present.

Whiting, C.H.
POW, Citronelle, AL, 5/4/65.

*William, John L. (40)
$140, $20; discharged on Surgeon's
Certificate, 12/2/61.

*Williams, Ferdinand L. (27)
$115, $20; POW, Chattahoochie, GA.

Yarett, J.W.
(d), 5/19/62.

COMPANY K,
10TH TEXAS CAVALRY REGIMENT

Original Officers:

*Captain Todd, L.M. (24)
$175, $30; (d), November 28, 1861.

*1st Lt. Wooten, J.W. (35)
$200, $35; relieved from duty at the reorganization, 5/16/62.

*2d Lt. Chandler, A.N. (30)
$300, $25; (d) on 5/26/62.

*Jr. 2d Lt. Todd, L.L. (26)
$175, $30; relieved from duty at the reorganization, 5/16/62.

Original Non-commissioned Officers:

*1st Sgt. Murry, C.G. (32)
$130, $25; resigned due to pthis, pulmonalis, 8/24/62,

*2d Sgt. Murry, J.M. (25)
$130, $20; (d), 2/8/62.

*3d Sgt. Allen, John W.
POW, near Chattahoochie, 7/5/64.

*4th Sgt. Wiley, T.R. (29)
$150, $30; discharged.

*1st Cpl. Smith, J.J. (50)
(d), 5/15/62.

*2d Cpl. Pool, James Flowers (20)
$120, $20; (w), Murfreesboro, TN,
12/31/62, pelvis-mortally, absent; POW,
Citronelle, AL, 5/4/65.

*3d Cpl. Chambless, B.A. (24)
$150, $20; POW, Murfreesboro, TN,
12/31/62; (d), 4/11/63.

*4th Cpl. Jarman, J.M. (17)
$125, $20; (w), battle of Murfreesboro, TN,
12/31/62; (k),(also shown as (d) from
wound), 1/2/63.

Others:

*Ensign McClung, L.M. (18)
shown as absent-sick.

*Bugler, Pool, Henry (18)
$130, $20; admitted to the Way Hospital,
Meridian, MS, 1/7/65, furloughed due to
wound Allatoona.

Privates:

*Adams, A.J. (18)
$135, $20; discharged under Conscript Act,
age, 17, 5'8", fair complexion, blue eyes,
light hair, a farmer.

*Adams, John Q. (19)
$120, $20; (d), 6/24/62.

Avants, James
discharged, 9/8/62.

***Birdwell, S.L. (18)**
$110, $25; listed on the Confederate Roll of Honor, at Murfreesboro, TN, (w), Allatoona.

Bryant, B.M.
POW, Citronelle, AL, 5/4/65.

Callahan, F.M.
4/5/64-absent, furloughed from hospital 2/15/64.

Chambliss, Edward (26)
$140, $30; 12/27/62-POW, "paroled prisoner," (d), Port Hudson, April 1863.

Chandler, R.J.D.
(d), 6/1/62.

***Clary, Martin V. (20)**
$130, $20; (w) Murfreesboro, TN, 12/31/62, breast-mortally; POW near Nashville, 12/15/64, 5'6", florid complexion, blue eyes, dark hair.

***Coker, R.S. (19)**
$130, $20; AWOL since 4/1/64, in Texas.

***Coker, Thomas**
no later record.

***Coker, W.T. (17)**
POW, Chickamauga, 9/19/63.

Dowis, Tyra J.
POW, Citronelle, AL, 5/4/65.

***Downey, Calvin (18)**
$140, $20; POW, Chickamauga, 9/19/63.

***Dunn, B.F. (23)**
$150, $25; sick, Barboursville, KY, paroled, 9/3/62; (w) Murfreesboro, TN, 12/31/62, (d), 1/2/63.

***Felton, Richard M. (24)**
$150, $25; admitted 4/2/64 to Ross Hospital, Mobile, for syphilis consecutiva, "discharged or assigned to duty."

Finley, W.H.
transferred to Douglas' Texas Battery, 8/1/62.

Gibson, Quinton K.
(w), Chickamauga, head-slight; (k), Allatoona, GA, 10/5/64.

Glenn, W. Riley
(w), Chickamauga, slight; POW, Allatoona, GA, 10/5/64.

***Gordon, Alfred (21)**
$125, $25; (d), 5/4/62.

***Gordon, David (17)**
$100, $20; (d), 5/14/62.

***Harrison, John A. (23)**
$110, $20; supposed to be in Texas-AWOL.

***Hazell, D.H. (20)**
$120, $20; (d), 6/14/62.

***Henderson, H.L. (21)**
$100, $20; POW, Citronelle, AL, 5/4/65.

***Henderson, P.B. (20)**
$140, $20; (d), 7/6/62.

***Hicks, J.T. (24)**
$200, $20; discharged 11/16/62, for pthis, pulmonalis; 6'2", dark complexion, hazel eyes, black hair, a farmer.

***Hicks, Houston (21)**
$100, $20; POW, Citronelle, AL, 5/4/65.

Hill, E.A.
transferred to Douglas' Battery, 8/1/62.

***Hitt, J. Wilson (19)**
$150, $25; POW, 1/10/63; 4/5/64-present.

Hyrmare, T.J.
(d), 1/17/62.

***Jarrett, John (17)**
$100, $25; (w), Richmond, KY, 8/30/62, fractured ulna; 5'8", fair complexion, blue eyes, dark hair, a farmer.

***Jarman, John J. (20)**
$100, $20; 4/5/64-present.

Johnson, J.H.
(w), at Richmond, KY; age 22, 5'10", hazel eyes, dark hair, light complexion.

Jordan, John R.
POW, Citronelle, AL, 5/4/65.

***Kelly, W.P. (27)**
$130, $15; (d), 3/25/62.

***Knight, W.R.C. (25)**
$140, $10; discharged.

***Lawrence, S.W. (22)**
$80, $20; detailed as teamster.

***Lee, Chesley (41)**
$135, $20; POW, Harrodsburg, KY; (d), 11/20/62.

***Lee, J.T. (18)**
$140, $20; (d), 5/5/62.

Lisle, A.J.
(d), 5/7/62.

***Matthews, Allen C. (23)**
$150, $30; (d), 5/17/62.

***May, J.C. (33)**
$140, $20; (d), 2/8/62.

***McAdams, F.R. (16)**
$110, $20; (d), 5/20/62.

***McDonald, Albert T. (17)**
$100, $25; POW, Atlanta, GA, 9/1/64; transferred for gunshot wound puncturing of lung. 9/13/64; 5'8", fair complexion, dark hair, gray eyes.

McDuffie, Eli
4/5/64-present.

McMurry, Joseph P.
POW, Citronelle, AL, 5/4/65.

*Miller, James C. (25)
POW, Citronelle, AL, 5/4/65.

Murray, T.J.
(k), Murfreesboro, TN, 12/31/62.

Muzzall, Wilson N.
resigned, due to chronic nephritis complicated by cystitis.

*Peck, D.W. (27)
$80, $25; 4/5/64-AWOL.

Pool, Joseph W.
POW, Barboursville, KY, 9/4/62; (w), Murfreesboro, TN, 12/31/62, left foot-mortally; May-October, 1863; POW, Cassville, GA, 5/19/64.

Powell, J.W.
(d), 5/25/62.

*Puckett, U.H. (30)
$100, $25; absent sick.

*Reeves, James E. (26)
$150, $25; shown at Lee Hospital, Lauderdale, MS, 11/14/63 as nurse, by order of Gen. Johnston.

*Reeves, Jerry (22)
$130, $20; discharged; 5'9", light complexion and hair, hazel eyes, a farmer.

*Simmons, R.H. (20)
$150, $25; "missing at Murfreesboro, TN, fight."

*Simmons, W.M. (23)
$130, $20; POW, Citronelle, AL.

*Slemmer, John N. (19)
$100, $20; POW, Chickamauga, 9/19/63; (d), 4/29/64 of small pox, Camp Douglas.

Smith, A.B.
absent, sick.

Smith, E.H.
4/5/64-present.

Smith, S.M.
(d), 6/9/62.

Smith, T.R.
(k), Richmond, KY, 8/30/62.

*Spear, J.D.W. (17)
$125, $25; (w), Chickamauga, slight, returned to duty; POW, Citronelle, AL, 5/4/65.

*Spear, John (45)
$150, $25; discharged.

Speer, L.L.
(w), Chickamauga, slight, returned to duty; 4/5/64-present.

*Splawn, B.A. (20)
$125, $20; issued Certificate of Discharge for Disability for "chronic diarrhea".

*Splawn, C.P. (22)
$135, $30; (d) Hospital #2, Atlanta, of chronic diarrhea, 6/20/63.

*Splawn, James (23)
$125, $25; (d), Pine Bluff.

*Splawn, John W. (24)
$130, $20; discharged, 11/16/62, due to ulcer of left leg; 6'0", fair complexion, blue eyes, light hair, a farmer.

Strickland, Peter
4/5/64-AWOL since 2/10/64.

*Stroud, J.C. (20)
$140, $25; (d), 12/29/61.

*Turner, J.D. (29)
$135, $20; discharged.

*Turner, Joshua C. (20)
$100, $15; POW, Citronelle, AL, 5/4/65.

*Wagoner, J.W. (21)
(d), 1/20/63.

*Watford, John A. (21)
$125, $25; POW with soldiers belonging to divers companies/ regiments.

*Watford, R.A. (23)
$135, $20; 4/5/64-absent sick since 9/30/63.

White, James S.
POW, Citronelle, AL, 5/4/65.

*Wooten, Edward
(w), Chickamauga-absent due to wound.

Wren, Tate
(d), 5/10/62.

Yarbrough, D.C.
(d), 4/7/62.

BIBLIOGRAPHY

The principal source of factual material for this book is to be found in the Official Records published by the War Department at Washington, D.C. Another main source was the Compiled Service Records in the National Archives, Washington, D.C. More valuable information came from the records at Hill Junior College, Harold B. Simpson History Complex, Hillsboro, Texas. I am indebted to the published sources as listed below:

Published Books

Barron, Samuel. *The Lone Star Defenders*. Washington, D.C.: Zenger Publishing Co., 1983.

Buell, Clarence, and Johnson, Robert. *Battles and Leaders of the Civil War* (4 Vols.). New York, 1887.

Cox, Jacob. *Sherman's Battle for Atlanta*. New York: Dacapo Press.

Fehrenbach, T. R. *Lone Star: A History of Texas and the Texans*. New York: The Macmillan Co., 1968.

French, Gen. S. G. *Two Wars — An Autobiography,* Nashville, 1901.

Hay, Thomas A. *Hoods Tennessee Campaign*. Morningside Bookshop, 1976.

Hood, J. B. *Advance and Retreat, New Orleans,* 1880.

Horn, Stanley, F. *The Army of Tennessee*. Norman, 1953.

Horn, Stanley, F. *Tennessee's War*. Nashville, 1965.

Hurst, Jack. *Nathan Bedford Forrest*. New York: Vintage Books, 1993.

Johnson, S. S. *Texans Who Wore the Gray*.

Jones, J. B. *A Rebel War Clerk's Diary*. Philadelphia: Lippincott, 1866.

Kennedy, Frances H. *The Civil War Battlefield Guide*. Houghton-Mifflin Co., 1990.

LaGrone, Leila. *This Very Unreasonable War,* 1972.

Lane, Mills. *War is Hell*. The Beehive Press, 1976.

Lewis, Lloyd. *J.M. Corse*. New York: Harcourt, 1947.

McClure, Judy Watson. *Confederate from East Texas*. Nortex Press, 1976.

McGlone, John. *Journal of Confederate History* (Vol 1, No. 1). Guild Bindery Press, 1988.

McMurray, W. J. *History of the Twentieth Tennessee Regiment,* Nashville, 1904.

Morton, John. *The Artillery of Nathan Bedford Forrest's Cavalry*, Cincinnati, 1895.

Nunn, W. C. *Ten More Texans in Gray*. Hillsboro, TX: Hill Jr. College Press, 1980.

Payne, Edwin W. *History of the Thirty-Fourth Regiment of Illinois Volunteers Infantry*, Clinton, Iowa, 1903.

Scaife, William. *Allatoona Pass*. Etowah Valley Historical Society.

Shanahan, Edward. *Atlanta Campaign Staff Ride Briefing Book*. Atlanta, 1995.

Simpson, Harold B. *Gaines Mill to Appomattox*. Waco, TX: Texian Press, 1963.

Simpson, Harold B. *Hood's Texas Brigade: Lee's Grenadier Guard*. Waco Texian Press, 1970.

———. *Douglas's Texas Battery*. CSA, Smith County Historical Society, 1966.

Tucker, Glenn. *Chickamauga*. Konecky & Konecky, 1961.

Watkins, Samuel R. *Co. "AYTCH," First Tennessee Regiment*, Nashville, 1882.

Wiley, Bill Irvin. *The Life of Johnny Reb*. Louisiana State Press, 1984.

Wyeth, John Allan. *Life of Gen. Nathan Bedford Forrest*. New York, Harper, 1899.

Yeary, Mamie. *REMINISCENCES of the Boys in Gray*. Smith and Line, 1912.

Periodicals

Confederate Veterans, 40 volumes, Nashville, 1893-1932.

East Texas Historical Journal, Stephen F. Austin State College.

Southern Bivouac, 6 volumes, Louisville, 1886-1887.

NOTES

CHAPTER 1

1. Vol. No. 9, East Texas Historical Journal, Stephen F. Austin State College.
2. T.R. Fehrenback, *Lone Star: A History of Texas and the Texans*, pp. 344, 345.
3. Nunn, W.C. *Ten More Texans in Gray*, preface.
4. 1861 Texas Adjutant Generals Correspondence, Texas State Archives, Austin, Texas.
5. Compiled Service Records National Archives, Washington, D.C.
6. 1861 Adjutant General's Correspondence.
7. LaGrone, Leila, *This Very Unreasonable War*, p. 4.
8. 1861 Adjutant General's Correspondence.
9. *Smith County Chronicles*, Spring 1967.
10. Watkins, Samuel R., *CO AYCHT*, p. 21.
11. Wood County Genealogical Society.
12. LaGrone, p. 50.
13. Center for American History, University of Texas at Austin, Templeton letters.
14. Templeton letters.
15. Templeton letters.
16. Templeton letters.
17. T. R. Fehrenbach, pp. 344, 345.
18. Wood County Democrat, reprint 8/1/1984.
19. Wiley, Bill Irvin, *Life of Johnny Reb*, p. 305.

CHAPTER 2

1. Wiley, Bill Irvin, p. 244.
2. Henry Watson letters (Harold B. Simpson History Complex, Hill County Junior College Hillsboro, Texas). Jacksonport, Arkansas is near the present-day Newport, Arkansas. On the trip to Mississippi, the 10th Texas made camp at Oil Trough Bottom in Arkansas. It derived its name from the early settlers who were forced to make troughs from logs because there were so many bears in the area that they did not have enough vessels to hold all the bear oil. This oil was used as a lubricant (Templeton letter).
3. Littlejohn letters, Harold B. Simpson History Complex and Smith County Chronicles, Winter 1978 and Summer 1979.
4. Confederate Veteran Magazine, Volume XIII, p. 494 (CV, XII, 494).
5. Center for American History, University of Texas at Austin, Jim Watson letters.
6. Jim Watson letters.
7. *Tri-Weekly Telegraph*, Houston, TX, July 16, 1962.
8. Official Records of the Union and Confederate Armies, Vol. 10, Part 1, pp. 793, 804 (OR 10, 1, 793-804).
9. Buell, Clarence, and Johnson, Robert, *Battles and Leaders of the Civil War*, Vol 111, p. 472.
10. Barron, Samuel, *The Lone Star Defenders*, p. 89.
11. Buell, Clarence, and Johnson, Robert, p. 604.
12. T. R. Fehrenbach, p. 362.
13. Watkins, Samuel, p. 46.
14. LaGrone, p. 26.
15. French, Gen. S. G., *Two Wars*, p. 304.

CHAPTER 3

1. CV, XXII, 404.
2. *The Fremantle Diary* by James L. Fremantle, Brown Co., 1954, p. 58.
3. Douglas' Texas Battery C.S.A., 1966, Smith County, p. 194.
4. CV, XXII, 20.

CHAPTER 4

1. CV, XXVII, 158.
2. Yeary, Mamie, *Reminiscences of the Boys in Gray*, p. 178.
3. CV, XXVII, 158-160.

4. Yeary, Mamie, p. 316.
5. CV XV 168.
6. Yeary, Mamie, p. 404.
7. Minick letter, Harold B. Simpson History Complex.
8. CV, XXXIV, 347.
9. CV, XXX, 298.
10. CV, XXVIII, 92.
11. Yeary, Mamie, pp. 618-619.
12. CV, XVIII, 559.
13. CV, VII, 19.
14. Buell, Clarence, and Johnson, Robert, pp. 5-7.

CHAPTER 5

1. Buell, Clarence, and Johnson, Robert, p. 5.
2. LaGrone, p. 10.
3. Douglas' Texas Battery CSA, 1966, Smith County, p. 194.
4. Compiled Service Records.

CHAPTER 6

1. Watkins, Samuel R., p. 76.
2. CV, XVI, 631.
3. CV, XXXI, 341.
4. McMurray, W.J., *History of Twentieth Tennessee,* Nashville, 1904, p. 228.
5. Yeary, Mamie, p. 188.
6. Yeary, Mamie, p. 144.
7. Payne Edwin W., *History of the Thirty-Fourth Regiment of Illinois Volunteers Infantry,* Clinton, Iowa, 1903, p. 44.
8. CV, XVI, 574.
9. J.B. Smyth letter, Harold B. Simpson History Complex.
10. CV, XII, 63.
11. CV, XII, 24.
12. CV, I, 264.
13. CV, VI, 309.
14. Horn, Stanley, *The Army of Tennessee,* Norman, 1953, p. 205.
15. CV, XXI, 588.

CHAPTER 7

1. CV, XXII, 404.
2. A.J. Fogle, letter Harold B. Simpson History Complex.
3. Center for American History, University of Texas at Austin, Kilgore letter in Templeton file.
4. CV, XXVI, 274.
5. CV, XXXI, 419.
6. LaGrone, p. 17.

CHAPTER 8

1. CV, XI, 113.
2. *East Texas Historical Journal,* Vol. 9, p. 98.
3. Watkins, Samuel, p. 55.
4. Wiley, Bill Irvin, p. 250.
5. Compiled Service Records.
6. Compiled Service Records.
7. CV, XII, 24.

CHAPTER 9

1. Buell, Clarence, and Johnson, Robert, p. 280.
2. CV, XXII, 404.
3. CV, IX, 113.
4. Nunn, W.C., preface.
5. Fehrenbach, T.R., p. 361.
6. CV, XXVII, 58.
7. CV, XXVIII, 448.
8. CV, XXII, 404.
9. *Rusk County News,* April 11, 1917.
10. LaGrone, p. 20.
11. 29th North Carolina Infantry Regiment Unit History, Harold B. Simpson History Complex.

CHAPTER 10

1. 29th North Carolina Infantry Regiment Unit History, Harold B. Simpson History Complex.
2. Wyeth, John, *Life of Gen. Nathan Bedford Forrest,* 1899, pp. 200-202.
3. CV, XXXV, 382.
4. CV, XIX, 329.
5. CV, XXIX, 231.
6. CV, XIII, 308.
7. Watkins, Samuel, p. 103.
8. CV, XXIII, 225.
9. Wyeth, John, p. 227.
10. OR, 30, 2, 523.
11. The Center for American History, University of Texas at Austin, Carlton letter in Templeton file..

12. OR, 30, 1, 428.
13. Yeary, Mamie, p. 178.
14. Morton, John, *The Artillery of Nathan Bedford Forrest Cavalry*, Cincinnati, 1895.
15. CV, III, 330.
16. Buell, Clarence, and Johnson, Robert, p. 654.
17. Horn, Stanley, p. 331.
18. McClure, Judy, *Confederate from East Texas*.
19. OR, 30, 2, 244; OR, 30, 2, 247.
20. CV, XXII, 404.
21. CV, IV, 18.
22. Horn, Stanley, p. 276.
23. CV, II, 337.
24. CV, II, 329.
25. CV, XXV, 74.
26. *Galveston Weekly News*, October 28, 1863.
27. A.J. Fogle letter, Harold B. Simpson History Complex.
28. *Odessa American* (newspaper, Ector County Texas, 7/4/76).
29. *Galveston Weekly News*, October 28, 1863.

CHAPTER 11

1. CV, XXXI, 238.
2. CV, X, 264.
3. CV, XXXII, 47.
4. CV, XI, 38.
5. CV, XV, 565.
6. CV, XVII, 613.
7. CV, XXI, 58.

CHAPTER 12

1. CV, I, 15.
2. LaGrone, p. 26.
3. OR 31, 3, 799.
4. Wiley, Bill Irvin, p. 55.
5. French, Gen. S. G., p. 188.
6. OR 39, 2, 569.

CHAPTER 13

1. CV, XVIII, 522.
2. McKnight letter, Harold B. Simpson History Complex.
3. CV, XVIII, 521.

4. French, Gen. S.G., p. 193.
5. Buell, Clarence, and Johnson, Robert, p. 281.
6. French, Gen. S.G., p. 199.
7. French, Gen. S.G., p. 201.
8. French, Gen. S.G., p. 201.
9. French, Gen. S.G., p. 201.
10. CV, XXVII, 477.
11. CV, XIV, 497.
12. CV, XV, 168.
13. French, Gen. S.G., p. 203.
14. CV, XXVII, 378, 380.
15. CV, VIV, 767.
16. Cox, Jacob, *Sherman's Battle for Atlanta*, p. 126.
17. CV, XV, 168.
18. OR 38, 3, 913.
19. McGlone, John, *Journal of Confederate History*, p. 74.
20. CV, XXX, 48-49.
21. CV, XV, 308.
22. CV, XI, 321.
23. CV, XXV, 166.
24. Watkins, Samuel, pp. 158-160.
25. McMurray, W.J., p. 317.
26. McMurray, W.J., p. 318.
27. CV, XII, 394.
28. CV, XII, 394.
29. CV, XI, 560.
30. French, Gen. S. G., p. 206.
31. CV, XXIX, 328.
32. Cox, Jacob D., p. 59.
33. CV, XXII, 404.
34. CV, VII, 221.
35. CV, XXII, 404.
36. CV, XVI, 332.

CHAPTER 14

1. Fehrenbach, T.R., p. 356.
2. CV, VIII, 69.
3. McMurray, W.J., p. 319.
4. Horn, Stanley, p. 346.
5. Horn, Stanley, p. 359.
6. Nashville Banner reprint, Feb. 22, 1964.
7. Yeary, Mamie, p. 316.
8. History of the 39th North Carolina Infantry Brigade, Harold B. Simpson History Complex.

9. Garrett letter, Harold B. Simpson History Complex.
10. Yeary, Mamie, p. 654.
11. French, Gen. S.G., p. 19.
12. A.J. Fogle letter, Harold B. Simpson History Complex.
13. CV, XXX, 287.
14. CV, XXII, 405.
15. Jessee P. Bates letters, Harold B. Simpson History Complex.
16. McMurray, W.J., p. 328.
17. CV, XXXVII, 419.
18. CV, XXVIII, 382.
19. Nashville Banner reprint, Feb. 22, 1964.
20. OR 45, 2, 639.

CHAPTER 15

1. Cox, Jacob D., *Sherman's Battle for Atlanta,* 1994, p. 231.
2. CV, IX, 507.
3. OR 39, 1, 815.
4. CV, XVIII, 372.
5. OR 39, I, 580.
6. Scaife, William, *Allatoona Pass,* Etowah Valley Historical Society, p. 121.
7. CV, XXV, 340-341.
8. Yeary, Mamie, p. 446.
9. French, Gen. S.G., p. 258.
10. French, Gen. S.G., p. 237.
11. Lewis, Lloyd, *J.M. Corse,* 1947, p. 132.
12. Lewis, Lloyd, p. 134.
13. CV, X, 31.
14. CV, I, 311.
15. Cox, Jacob D., p. 229.
16. CV, XXX, 287.
17. CV, XV, 168.
18. Yeary, Mamie, p. 617.
19. 10th Texas file, Harold B. Simpson History Complex.
20. OR 39, I 813, CV, III, 235.
21. OR 37, 3, 113.
22. Scaife, William, p. 39.
23. Somerville letter, Harold B. Simpson History Complex.

CHAPTER 16

1. CV, 1, 311.
2. CV, 1, 311.
3. Yeary, Mamie, p. 445.
4. Morton, John, p. 14.
5. Morton, John, p. 298.
6. CV, XV, 508.
7. Wiley, Bill Irvin, p. 1211.
8. CV, XXIV, 101.

CHAPTER 17

1. CV, XXIV, 102.
2. CV, XVII, 14.
3. CV, XIII, 563.
4. OR 45, 2, 44.
5. OR 45, 1, 716.
6. Wyeth, John, p. 485.
7. CV, XXXV, 179.

CHAPTER 18

1. OR 45, 1, 680.
2. Horn, Stanley, p. 417.
3. CV, XII, 269.
4. CV, XIII, 28.
5. Nashville Banner, reprint, Feb. 22, 1964.
6. Horn, Stanley, *Tennessee's War,* Nashville, 1965, p. 327.
7. CV, XII, 348.
8. OR 45, 1, 563.
9. CV, XII, 484.
10. CV, XII, 348.
11. CV, XI, 327.
12. CV, XXX, 88.
13. CV, XXVI, 251.
14. Hay, Thomas A., *Hood's Tennessee Campaign,* p. 136.
15. CV, XXVII, 58.
16. McGlone, John, p. 130.
17. Hay, Thomas A., p. 167.
18. Nashville Dispatch, December 18, 1864, reprinted *Nashville Banner,* Feb. 22, 1964.

CHAPTER 19

1. OR 45, 1, 577; 45,1, 591; 45, 1, 595
2. OR 45, 1, 578.
3. OR 45, 1, 765.
4. OR 45, 1, 749.

5. Hay, Thomas A., p. 163.
6. OR 45, I, 722.
7. CV, XII, 348.
8. CV, XV, 168.
9. CV, XXXV, 179.
10. CV, XII, 436.
11. OR 45, 2, 308.
12. CV, XV, 401-402.
13. McMurray, W. J., p. 351.
14. McGlone, John, p. 454.
15. Wyeth, John, p. 503.
16. Morton, John, p. 292.
17. CV, XV, 406.
18. CV, XXXV, 94-95.
19. Morton, John, p. 296.
20. Morton, John, p. 298.
21. CV, XV, 407.
22. OR 45, 2, 324.
23. CV, XV, 404.
24. CV, XII, 348.
25. CV, XVII, 20.
26. CV, XXVI, 442-443.
27. CV, XV, 404.
28. CV, XV, 402.
29. McMurray, W. J., p. 352.
30. Hay, Thomas A., p. 176.
31. OR 45, 2, 758.
32. OR 45, 2, 770.
33. OR 45, 2, 774.
34. OR 45, 2, 783.
35. OR 45, 1, 1255.
36. OR 45, 2, 786.
37. Barron, Samuel, p. 268.
38. OR 48, 1, 1113.
39. OR 45, 2, 804.

CHAPTER 20

1. CV, VII, 490.
2. Johnson, S. S., p. 244.
3. OR 49, 2, 1180.
4. OR 49, 1, 277.
5. CV, VIII, 23.
6. OR 49, 2, 1210.
7. CV, VIII, 53-55.
8. CV, VIII, 23-24.
9. CV, XIII, 226.
10. CV, XII, 591.
11. CV, VII, 490.
12. OR 49, 1, 278.

13. OR 49, 1, 278.
14. CV, XXII, 405.
15. CV, VII, 490.
16. CV, XIV, 264.

CHAPTER 21

1. CV, VII, 312.
2. Center for American History, University of Texas at Austin, William Stanton letters.
3. Yeary, Mamie, p. 740.

ABOUT THE AUTHORS

Native Texan Chuck Carlock lives in Fort Worth, where he is the director of taxes for a prominent Texas family. His position involves the structuring of some of the nation's largest business deals. Chuck is married to his high school sweetheart and has three daughters and four grandchildren.

Chuck served in the U.S. Army for four years, including one year as a combat helicopter pilot in Vietnam, fighting in all three Tet offensives. In 1994, he wrote the best-selling book, Fireirds, about his combat experiences. The proceeds from the sales of that book are donated to the Firebirds military association.

After leaving the military, he graduated from the University of Texas at Arlington and became a certified public accountant.

Chuck's mother was a Hamilton. Her grandfather was Alvin Finley Hamilton, who served in the Tenth Texas. A. F. Hamilton was raised and buried in the area close to Taylor, Texas, around Austin. He was living near Gilmer, Texas when the Tenth Texas was formed and he joined Company B, the "Wood County Rebels." He was one of the ones "spiling for a fight."

Author Carlock beside the tombstone of his great-grandfather, A. F. Hamilton. The tombstone reads: "A. F. Hamilton, CO B, 10 TEX CAV, CSA, BORN OCT 15, 1842, DIED MAY 21, 1932, GONE BUT NOT FORGOTTEN." The date of birth on the stone, however, is wrong. Hamilton was actually born in 1841. He died at the age of ninety after being thrown from a horse.

V. M. Owens is a writer and adult educator. She spends her time reading, writing, teaching, and enjoying her family. She resides in Arlington, Texas, with her husband.